Grammars in Contact

EXPLORATIONS IN LINGUISTIC TYPOLOGY

GENERAL EDITORS: Alexandra Y. Aikhenvald and R. M. W. Dixon
Research Centre for Linguistic Typology, La Trobe University

This series focuses on aspects of language that are of current theoretical interest and for which there has not previously or recently been any full-scale cross-linguistic study. Its books are for typologists, fieldworkers, and theory developers, and designed for use in advanced seminars and courses.

PUBLISHED

1 Adjective Classes
edited by
R. M. W. Dixon and Alexandra Y. Aikhenvald

2 Serial Verb Constructions
edited by
Alexandra Y. Aikhenvald and R. M. W. Dixon

3 Complementation
edited by
R. M. W. Dixon and Alexandra Y. Aikhenvald

4 Grammars in Contact
edited by
Alexandra Y. Aikhenvald and R. M. W. Dixon

PUBLISHED IN ASSOCIATION WITH THE SERIES

Areal Diffusion and Genetic Inheritance:
Problems in Comparative Linguistics
edited by
Alexandra Y. Aikhenvald and R. M. W. Dixon

Grammars in Contact

A Cross-Linguistic Typology

edited by
ALEXANDRA Y. AIKHENVALD and
R. M. W. DIXON

Research Centre for Linguistic Typology
La Trobe University

OXFORD
UNIVERSITY PRESS

OXFORD
UNIVERSITY PRESS

Great Clarendon Street, Oxford OX2 6DP

Oxford University Press is a department of the University of Oxford.

It furthers the University's objective of excellence in research, scholarship, and education by publishing worldwide in

Oxford New York

Auckland Cape Town Dar es Salaam Hong Kong Karachi
Kuala Lumpur Madrid Melbourne Mexico City Nairobi
New Delhi Shanghai Taipei Toronto

With offices in

Argentina Austria Brazil Chile Czech Republic France Greece
Guatemala Hungary Italy Japan Poland Portugal Singapore
South Korea Switzerland Thailand Turkey Ukraine Vietnam

Oxford is a registered trade mark of Oxford University Press
in the UK and in certain other countries

Published in the United States
by Oxford University Press Inc., New York

British Library Cataloguing in Publication Data

Data available

Library of Congress Cataloguing in Publication Data

Data available

Typeset by SPI Publisher Services, Pondicherry, India
Printed in Great Britain
on acid-free paper by
Biddles Ltd., King's Lynn, Norfolk

ISBN 0–19–920783–6   978–0–19–920783–1

1 3 5 7 9 10 8 6 4 2

Contents

Preface

Languages can be similar in many ways—they can resemble each other in categories, constructions, and meanings, and in the actual forms used to express these. A shared feature may be based on common genetic origin, or result from geographic proximity and borrowing. Some aspects of grammar are spread more readily than others. The question is—what are they? When languages are in contact with each other, what changes do we expect to occur in their grammatical structures? Only an inductively based cross-linguistic examination can provide an answer. This is what this volume is about.

The volume starts with a typological introduction outlining principles of contact-induced change and factors which facilitate diffusion of linguistic traits. It is followed by revised versions of twelve of the fifteen presentations from the International Workshop 'Grammars in contact', held at the Research Centre for Linguistic Typology, La Trobe University, 13–18 June 2005. An earlier version of Chapter 1 had been circulated to the contributors, to ensure that the detailed studies of contact-induced phenomena in individual languages were cast in terms of a common set of typological parameters. (This is the fourth monograph in the series *Explorations in linguistic typology*, devoted to volumes from the International Workshops sponsored by RCLT.)

The week of the workshop was an intellectually stimulating and exciting time, full of discussions and cross-fertilization of ideas. All of the authors have first-hand experience of intensive, fieldwork-based investigation of languages, as well as in dealing with linguistic typology, historical comparative issues, and problems of areal diffusion. The analysis is cast in terms of basic linguistic theory—the cumulative typological functional framework in terms of which almost all descriptive grammars are cast—and avoids formalisms (which provide reinterpretations rather than explanations, and come and go with such frequency that any statement made in terms of them is likely soon to become inaccessible).

The volume covers languages from a wide variety of areas where the impact of language contact has been particularly noticeable but relatively un-described—these include Amazonia, East and West Africa, Australia, East Timor, and the Sinitic domain. More familiar languages include those of the Balkans, Pennsylvania German influenced by English, and Basque in contact with Romance languages. In view of the considerable number of extensive studies of language contact in South and South-East Asia, and in North America, it seemed unnecessary to include a special chapter on each of these in this volume.

It is our hope that this volume will provide a consolidated conceptual and analytic framework covering the major parameters and preferences in contact-induced change and its effects on grammar. The chapters follow a unified typological approach. All this contributes to the reliability and comparability of the inductive generalizations suggested throughout the volume.

We thank all the authors for taking part in the Workshop, for getting their papers in on time, and for revising them according to recommendations of the editors.

We owe a special debt of gratitude to Siew-Peng Condon and May Tan, Executive Officers of RCLT, for organizing the Workshop in a most efficient and caring manner, and to Rosemary Purnell for editorial assistance.

Notes on the Contributors

Willem F. H. Adelaar is Professor of Amerindian Languages and Cultures at Leiden University. He has conducted extensive field research on different varieties of Quechua and on the minor languages of the Andes. He has also worked on the genealogical relations of South American languages and has been involved in international activities addressing the issue of language endangerment. He is an associate editor of *International Journal of American Linguistics*. His publications include *Tarma Quechua* (1977) and a comprehensive volume *The languages of the Andes* (2004) of which he is the main author.

Address: University of Leiden, Vakgroep VTW, Postbus 9515, 2300 RA Leiden, The Netherlands; *e-mail*: W.F.H.Adelaar@let.leidenuniv.nl

Alexandra Y. Aikhenvald is Professor and Associate Director of the Research Centre for Linguistic Typology at La Trobe University. She has worked on descriptive and historical aspects of Berber languages and has published, in Russian, a grammar of Modern Hebrew (1990). She is a major authority on languages of the Arawak family, from northern Amazonia, and has written grammars of Bare (1995, based on work with the last speaker who has since died) and Warekena (1998), plus *A grammar of Tariana, from northwest Amazonia* (Cambridge University Press, 2003), in addition to essays on various typological and areal features of South American languages. Her monographs *Classifiers: a typology of noun categorization devices* (2000, paperback reissue 2003), *Language contact in Amazonia* (2002), and *Evidentiality* (2004, paperback reissue 2006) were published by Oxford University Press. She is currently working on a reference grammar of Manambu, from the Sepik area of New Guinea.

Address: Research Centre for Linguistic Typology, La Trobe University, Victoria 3086, Australia; *e-mail*: a.aikhenvald@latrobe.edu.au

Felix K. Ameka teaches in the Department of African Languages and Cultures, Leiden University, and is a Research Associate in the Language and Cognition Group, Max Planck Institute for Psycholinguistics, Nijmegen, the Netherlands. His interests are in language description and documentation, typology, semantics, pragmatics, areal and anthropological linguistics and ethnography of communication with special reference to West African languages. He has also edited volumes on grammar writing, locative predication, tense, aspect and modality, Ghanaian linguistics, and interjections. Currently, he is working on the documentation of the language and culture of Likpe (Ghana) and preparing a pan-dialectal grammar of Ewe (with James Essegbey). He is Editor-in-Chief of the *Journal of African Languages and Linguistics*.

Address: Department of African Languages and Cultures, University of Leiden, Postbus 9515, NL-2300 Leiden, The Netherlands; *e-mail*: f.k.ameka@let.leidenuniv.nl

Kate Burridge studied linguistics and German at the University of Western Australia and then did her Ph.D. at the University of London, on syntactic change in medieval Dutch. She taught at La Trobe University before taking up the Chair of Linguistics at Monash University in 2003. Her main areas of research are grammatical changes in Germanic languages; the Pennsylvania German spoken by Anabaptist communities in Canada; euphemism and language taboos; and the structure and history of English. She is a regular contributor to ABC Radio on language issues and the author of two highly successful volumes: *Blooming English: observations on the roots, cultivation and hybrids of the English language* (2002), and *Weeds in the garden of words: further observations on the tangled history of the English language* (2004), both published by ABC books and Cambridge University Press. She is also the co-author of *Forbidden words* (Cambridge University Press, 2006).
Address: Department of Linguistics, Monash University, Victoria 3168, Australia; *e-mail*: kate.burridge@arts.monash.edu.au

Eithne B. Carlin holds a tenured position as a lecturer in the Department of Languages and Cultures of Native America at Leiden University. She has been working on the Cariban and Arawak languages of the Guianas since 1997. Besides authoring several articles, she has co-edited with Jacques Arends the *Atlas of the languages of Suriname* (2002) and in 2004 published *A grammar of Trio, a Cariban language of Suriname*. She is currently working on a comprehensive reference grammar of Mawayana, a moribund Arawak language, and on a grammar of Wapishana, also Arawak.
Address: University of Leiden, Vakgroep VTW, Postbus 9515, 2300 RA Leiden, The Netherlands; *e-mail*: E.B.Carlin@let.leidenuniv.nl

R. M. W. Dixon is Professor and Director of the Research Centre for Linguistic Typology. He has published grammars of a number of Australian languages (including Dyirbal and Yidiñ), in addition to *A grammar of Boumaa Fijian* (University of Chicago Press, 1988), *The Jarawara language of southern Amazonia* (Oxford University Press, 2004), and *A semantic approach to English grammar* (Oxford University Press, 2005). His works on typological theory include *Where have all the adjectives gone? and other essays in semantics and syntax* (1982) and *Ergativity* (1994). *The rise and fall of languages* (1997) expounded a punctuated equilibrium model for language development; this is the basis for his detailed case study *Australian languages: their nature and development* (2002).
Address: Research Centre for Linguistic Typology, La Trobe University, Victoria 3086, Australia; no e-mail.

Patience Epps currently holds an Assistant Professorship in linguistics at the University of Texas at Austin, with a focus on documentation and description of indigenous languages of Latin America. She recently completed her Ph.D., 'A grammar of Hup', at the University of Virginia and the Max Planck Institute for Evolutionary Anthropology, Leipzig, based on intensive fieldwork among the Hup speakers in north-west

Amazonia, Brazil. Her publications include 'Areal diffusion and the development of evidentiality: evidence from Hup' (*Studies in Language*), and 'Birth of a noun classification system: the case of Hup' (*Language Endangerment and Endangered Languages*).

Address: Department of Linguistics, University of Texas at Austin, University Station B5100, Austin TX 78712-0198, USA; *e-mail*: pepps@mail.utexas.edu

Victor A. Friedman is Andrew W. Mellon Professor in the Department of Slavic Languages and Literatures at the University of Chicago, where he also holds an appointment in the Department of Linguistics and an associate appointment in the Department of Anthropology. He is also Director of the University's Center for East European and Russian/Eurasian Studies. He is a member of the Macedonian Academy of Arts and Sciences, the Academy of Arts and Sciences of Kosova, Matica Srpska, and he holds the '1300 Years of Bulgaria' Jubilee Medal. During the Yugoslav Wars of Succession he worked for the United Nations as a senior policy analyst in Macedonia and consulted for other international organizations. Recent publications include *Macedonian* (Lincom Europa, 2002), *Turkish in Macedonia and beyond* (Harrassowitz, 2003), and *Studies on Albanian and other Balkan languages* (Dukagjin, 2004).

Address: Department of Slavic Languages and Literatures, University of Chicago, 1130 East 59th Street, Chicago, IL 60637, USA; *e-mail*: vfriedm@uchicago.edu, vfriedm@midway.uchicago.edu

John Hajek is an Associate Professor in the School of Languages at the University of Melbourne. His research interests include language typology, Romance linguistics, phonetics and phonology, and the languages of the Asia-Pacific region. He is currently working on the description of Austronesian and non-Austronesian languages spoken in East Timor, and is co-author of *Tetun Dili: a grammar of an East Timorese language*.

Address: French and Italian Studies, University of Melbourne, Victoria 3010, Australia; *e-mail*: j.hajek@unimelb.edu.au.

Gerd Jendraschek is a Research Fellow at the Research Centre for Linguistic Typology. He obtained an MA in linguistics from the University of Bielefeld (Germany, 2000) focusing on Turkish ideophones. His Ph.D. from the University of Toulouse-Le Mirail (France, 2004) centred on modality in Basque. His research interests also include language change (in general and in Basque in particular), and the language use and functions in multilingual societies. He is currently writing a comprehensive reference grammar of Iatmul (Ndu family, East Sepik Province, Papua New Guinea).

Address: Research Centre for Linguistic Typology, La Trobe University, Victoria 3086, Australia; *e-mail*: g.jendraschek@latrobe.edu.au

Stephen Matthews studied modern and medieval languages at Trinity Hall, Cambridge, and pursued doctoral studies in linguistics at the University of Southern California. He is currently Associate Professor in Linguistics at the University of Hong Kong. His research interests include the grammar of Sinitic languages, typology, and language contact. Since co-authoring *Cantonese: a comprehensive grammar* with

Virginia Yip, he has studied Cantonese grammar from various perspectives, including those of areal typology and sentence processing. His work with Virginia Yip on the bilingual acquisition of Cantonese and English is the subject of a forthcoming monograph, *The bilingual child: early grammatical development and language contact* (to be published by Cambridge University Press).

Address: Department of Linguistics, The University of Hong Kong, Pokfulam, Hong Kong; *e-mail*: matthews@hkucc.hku.hk

Anne Storch is Professor of African Languages and Linguistics at the University of Cologne. The major focus of her research involves the Jukun languages of Nigeria, the Atlantic language family, and Western Nilotic languages. Her publications include *Die Anlautpermutation in den westatlantischen Sprachen* (Frankfurt, 1995), *Das Hone und seine Stellung im Zentral-Jukunoid* (Cologne, 1999), *Magic and gender* (with Sabine Dinslage, Cologne, 2000), and several co-edited volumes. She has recently published a monograph, *The noun morphology of Western Nilotic* (Cologne, 2005). She is currently working on language contact and speech registers in Africa.

Address: Institut für Afrikanistik, Universität zu Köln, Meister Ekkehart-Strasse 7, D-50923, Cologne, Germany; *e-mail*: anne.storch@uni-koeln.de

Abbreviations

1	1st person
2	2nd person
3	3rd person
A	transitive subject
ABL	ablative
ABS	absolutive
ACC	accusative
ACT	active
ADJ	adjective
ADV	adverb
ADVZ	adverbalizer
AFF	affective
AG	agentive
AGR	agreement
ALL	allative
AN	Austronesian
ANA	anaphoric
ANAPH	anaphoric
ANIM	animate
AOR	aorist
APPLIC	applicative
APPR	apprehensive
ASP	aspect
ASS	assertive
ASSOC	associative
ATR	Advanced Tongue Root
AUG	augmentative
AUX	auxiliary
BCS	Bosnian/Croatian/Serbian

BEN	benefactive
CAUS	causative
CL	classifier
CM	class marker
CMPL	class marker plural
COLL	collective
COMIT	comitative
COMP	complement
COMPAR	comparative
COMPL	completive
COP	copula
COREF	coreferential
DAT	dative
DEF	definite
DEM	demonstrative
DESID	desiderative
DET	determiner
DIM	diminutive
DIR	directional
DISC	discourse marker
DIST	distal
DISTR	distributive
DS	different subject
DST	distributive
DST.CNTR	distant past contrast
DT	Duff-Tripp
du, DU	dual
DUR	durative
E	English
EMPH	emphasis
ERG	ergative
EVID	evidential
exc	exclusive
FACS	facsimile

FACT	factive, factitive
FEM, F, f	feminine
FLR	filler
FOC	focus
FRUST	frustrative
FUT	future
GEN	genitive
GENL	general
HAB	habitual
HG	High German
IDEO	ideophone
IMP	imperative
IMPER	imperfect
IMPERS	impersonal
IMPERV	imperfective
INAN	inanimate
inc	inclusive
INCH	inchoative
INDEF	indefinite
INFER	inferred
INFIN	infinitive
INST	instrumental
INT	intentional
INTENS	intensifier
INTER	interrogative
INTERJ	interjection
IO	indirect object
IT	itive
ITER	iterative
JUSS	jussive
L1	first language
L2	second language
LIG	ligature
LOC	locative
LOG	logophoric pronoun
MASC, M, m	masculine
MR	modifier

N	noun
NAN	non-Austronesian
NCL	noun class
NEG	negation
NEUT, N, n	neuter
nf	non-feminine
NFIN	non-finite
NFUT	non-future
NOM	nominative
NOMZ	nominalizer
NON.A/S	non-subject
NP	noun phrase
NPAST	non-past
nsg, NSG	non-singular
NUM.CL	numeral classifier
NVIS	non-visual
O	transitive object
OBJ	object
OBL	oblique
OOM	Old Order Mennonites
OPT	optative
PART	particle
PARTIC	participle
PASS	passive
PC	particle of concord
PERSIST	persistive
PERV	perfective
PG	Pennsylvania German
pl, PL	plural
PM	Progressive Mennonite
PN	pronoun
Port	Portuguese
POSS	possessive
POSSN	possession marking
POT	potential

PRES	present
PRIV	privative
PROG	progressive
PROHIB	prohibitive
PROX	proximal
PRTV	partitive
PURP	purposive
QUANT	quantifier
QUOT	quotative
REC	recent
RECIP	reciprocal
REDUP	reduplicated
REFL	reflexive
REL	relative
REM	remote
REP	reported
RES	resultative
S	intransitive subject
S_a	'active' S, marked like A
SCR	subject cross-reference marker
SEQ	sequential
SF	stem formative
sg, SG	singular
SGVE	singulative
SIMIL	similative
SING	singulative
S_o	'stative' S, marked like O
SP	subordinating particle
SR	subordinator
SS	same subject
STAT	stative
SUBJ	subjunctive
SUBORD	subordinate
SUPER	superlative
SVC	serial verb construction

TAM	tense-aspect-mood
TD	Tetun Dili
TF	Tetun Fehan
TM	Traditional Mennonite
TMP.NOMZ	time, manner, place nominalizer
TOP	topic
TP	today past tense
TR	transitive
TT	Tetun Terik
UFP	utterance final particle
UNP	uninvolved mode of non-past tense
UP	uninvolved mode of 'before today' past tense
V	verb
VBZR	verbalizer
VENT	ventive
VIS	visual
VP	verb phrase
WIT	witnessed
WRT	West Rumelian Turkish

1

Grammars in Contact
A Cross-Linguistic Perspective

ALEXANDRA Y. AIKHENVALD

1 Why can languages be similar?

Languages can resemble each other in categories, constructions, and meanings, and in the actual forms used to express them.[1] Categories can be similar because they are universal—for instance, every language has some way of asking a question or framing a command. Occasionally, two languages share a form by pure coincidence. In both Dyirbal, an Australian language from North Queensland, and Jarawara, an Arawá language from Southern Amazonia, *bari* means 'axe'. Both Goemai (Angas-Goemai subgroup of Chadic, Afroasiatic: Birgit Hellwig, p.c.) and Manambu (Ndu family, New Guinea) happen to use *a:s* for 'dog'. Similarities due to universal properties of a language are of interest for universal grammar, while chance coincidences are no more than curious facts. What these two kinds of similarities have in common is that they tell us nothing about the history of languages or their speakers. In this volume we focus on two other types of similarities: those due to genetic inheritance and those due to areal contact.

A shared feature may be based on common linguistic origin. Then, the languages can be shown to have descended from the same ancestor (this is achieved by using rigorous procedures of historical and comparative linguistics). Related languages 'will pass through the same or strikingly similar phases': this 'parallelism in drift' (Sapir 1921: 171–2; LaPolla 1994; Borg 1994)

[1] I am grateful to R. M. W. Dixon, Aet Lees, Peter Bakker, Eithne Carlin, Victor Friedman, John Hajek, Birgit Hellwig, Gerd Jendraschek, Randy LaPolla, Marianne Mithun, Stephen Morey, Anne Storch, and Ghil'ad Zuckermann, and to all the other participants and auditors of the International Workshop on Grammars in Contact, for their incisive comments, feedback, and criticisms.

accounts for additional similarities between related languages, even for those 'long disconnected'.

Alternatively, shared features may result from geographic proximity, contact, and borrowing. If two or more languages are in contact, with speakers of one language having some knowledge of the other, they come to borrow linguistic features—including phonetic traits and habits of pronunciation, distinctive sounds (phonemes), construction types, grammatical categories, and the organization of lexical and grammatical meanings. There can also be borrowing of lexical and of grammatical forms. The extent of this varies, depending on a number of cultural and social factors, including the degree of speakers' awareness and sense of purism, and also on the structure of the languages in contact.

Historically, every language must have undergone a certain amount of influence from its neighbours. The impact of contact is stronger and easier to discern in some languages, weaker and more diffuse in others. See §2 below.

No linguistic feature—be it a form, or a pattern—is entirely 'borrowing-proof'. Most statements about constraints and limits to diffusion warrant exceptions. Curnow's (2001) suggestion that 'the attempt to develop any universal hierarchy of borrowing should perhaps be abandoned' is correct in its essence. And yet some grammatical and other features are particularly open to—and others are more resistant to—diffusion. A form can be transferred from one language into the next, a language's own forms and constructions may be reanalyzed, or a pattern translated morpheme per morpheme into another language (creating a 'calque'). Even when the same form, or category, is borrowed between structurally different languages and in different circumstances, both the mechanisms and the outcomes are likely to be different. In Haase and Nau's (1996a: 7) words, 'anything can be borrowed, but not any way'. Kinds of contact-induced changes and their mechanisms are discussed in §3.

As Friedman puts it in §3.1 of Chapter 8, 'it is certainly the case that anything *can* be borrowed, but it is equally the case that not everything *is* borrowed in a contact situation in which languages maintain separate identities'. To come closer to identifying what is borrowed, we approach 'borrowability' of forms and patterns in terms of facilitating factors rather than hierarchies, restrictions, and constraints (let alone putative universals). Preferences at work in borrowing patterns and forms depend on the expression and function of a category, on its usage, and on the ways it correlates with cultural stereotypes. A plethora of social factors play a role—these include language attitudes and receptivity to 'foreign' forms. Pre-existing structural similarities between languages in contact also facilitate contact-induced change. However, the claim that only 'typologically compatible' systems can influence each other is erroneous. The more facilitating factors there are at work, the higher the chance of contact-induced change: we return to this Mutual Reinforcement Principle in §4.1.

Languages reflect the sociolinguistic history of their speakers. A plethora of sociolinguistic parameters have an impact on the outcomes of language contact, interacting with preferences in contact-induced change in grammar and affecting typological diversity. Languages become similar in different ways; and the net results of language contact differ. §5 below provides a summary and an overview of the volume.[2]

This introductory chapter is effectively two in one: setting the scene for the volume on the basis of an examination of the literature, and drawing together the conclusions resulting from the discussion and results in the individual chapters within this volume.

Only in-depth empirical studies of a variety of language contact situations and their impact on the overall structure of one or more languages, based on first-hand fieldwork, will enable us to work out inductive generalizations and preferences according to which some aspects of grammar spread more readily than others. This is what chapters in this volume aim at.[3]

---

[2] Curnow (2001) provides an overview of borrowed forms and patterns. The question of what can and what cannot be borrowed has been the focus of studies of language contact since at least Whitney (1881). Various hierarchies of, and constraints on, borrowability have been suggested and subsequently criticized in numerous publications, among them Weinreich (1953), Moravcsik (1978), Aikhenvald (2002), Matras (1998), Campbell (1993), Harris and Campbell (1995: 120–50), and Curnow (2001). Some scholars have even expressed doubt as to whether looking for such constraints and hierarchies is at all a sensible task (Thomason 2001*a*, 2001*b*; Thomason and Kaufman 1988: 14). However, the failure to establish an overarching hierarchy of borrowability does not imply the absence of valid tendencies in linguistic diffusion (cf., for instance, the incisive analysis by Heath 1978: 105–15).

Given the enormous amount of literature on language contact, I could not do justice to more than a fraction of it in this (necessarily programmatic) chapter which is not intended to be an exhaustive encyclopedia of language contact. Full or partial studies have been accomplished for some parts of the world. These include contacts between Iranian and Turkic languages thoroughly researched by Johanson (2002), Soper (1996), and others; Australia (especially Heath 1978, 1981; Dixon 2001; Dench 2001; and a comprehensive study in Dixon 2002); the Balkans (e.g. Joseph 1983; Friedman 1997 and references there); Europe (Haase 1992; Nau 1995; Stolz 1991), India and South Asia (e.g. Emeneau 1980; Masica 1976, 1991; Abbi 1991, 2002; Masica 2001; Hock 2001); Mesoamerica (Campbell et al. 1986; Stolz and Stolz 1996; Brody 1995); the Vaupés in north-west Amazonia (Aikhenvald 1996, 1999*c*, 2002), various areas of language contact in Africa (especially Nurse 2000; Nurse and Hinnebusch 1993; Dimmendaal 2001; Myers-Scotton and Okeju 1973; an overview in Heine and Kuteva 2002; and Heine and Kuteva 2005) and in the Sino-Tibetan domain (LaPolla 2001), as well as in the Pacific (Thurston 1987, 1989, 1994; Ross 2001); and North America (Sherzer 1973, 1976; Beck 2000; Newman 1974; Brown 1999; overview in Mithun 1999). Due to limitations of space, I could only provide a limited number of illustrative examples. At this stage, I have chosen to avoid any definite statements concerning frequency of different kinds of language contact. This is a task for the future, when further empirically based systematic studies of language contact situations throughout the world have become available.

[3] We thus keep in line with the Saussurian principle that every language is a balanced system rather than a random set of meanings and forms, captured in Antoine Meillet's (1948: 16) famous statement

A word on terminology. The term 'borrowing' is used here in its broad sense, as 'the transfer of linguistic features of any kind from one language to another as the result of contact' (Trask 2000: 44).[4] Linguistic diffusion is understood as the spread of a linguistic feature within a geographical area or as recurrent borrowing within a linguistic area. Diffusion within an area can be unilateral (when it proceeds from one source) or multilateral (when it involves several sources). See the glossary of terminological conventions at the end of the volume.

2 How languages affect each other: the effects of language contact

2.1 'Layered' languages

If one language is significantly different from its proven genetic relatives, language contact is the 'usual suspect'. Cantonese (Chapter 9) has features not found in most Sinitic languages—such dissimilarities warrant a non-genetic explanation. And if two languages are (or have been) in contact and share certain features, we immediately suspect that these features have been transferred from one to the other. Our suspicion will be strengthened if the two languages are genetically unrelated, and the features they share are typical of the family to which only one of them belongs. Tibeto-Burman languages spoken in the 'Sino-sphere' tend to be more isolating, while those spoken in the 'Indo-sphere' tend to be more morphologically complex (LaPolla 2001). Many features of the Austronesian languages of the Siasi subgroup (spoken in the interior of West New Britain: Thurston 1987) which differentiate them from other Siasi languages are shared with Anêm, a non-Austronesian language, and can thus be attributed to language contact.

In these and other instances discussed in the present volume, intensive language contact results in discernible diffusion of patterns—phonetic, phonological, morphological, syntactic, and especially pragmatic. This can be, but does not have to be, accompanied by some diffusion of forms. Contact-induced innovations are constantly being added to languages over the course

---

that a language is 'système où tout se tient' (a system where everything holds together'). We eschew metaphors like 'feature pool' (Mufwene 2001) which gloss over the fact that the interaction of features and their borrowability may well depend on typological correlations between them (for instance, if a language becomes verb initial through contact, it may be expected to also develop prepositions), and on typological naturalness of a phenomenon—for instance, if a language develops gender under contact influence, it is likely first to develop it in third person, rather than in first person.

[4] An alternative term for both borrowing and linguistic diffusion is 'interference', defined as a transfer of features from one's first language into one's second language (cf. Trask 2000: 169). Unlike diffusion, interference often applies to cases of individual bilingualism, and second language acquisition. A recently suggested alternative is 'code-copying' (see Johanson 2002).

of their development, as if piling tier upon tier of 'naturalized' foreign elements. The result is LAYERED languages: the inherited 'core' is discernible underneath the subsequent 'layers' of innovative influence from outside.

In most cases, contact-induced change affects only some aspects of the language. Take the Arabic of Nigeria. Its morphology, lexicon, and phonology show that it is undoubtedly Semitic. Many of its syntactic structures and the semantics of numerous idioms are strikingly similar to the neighbouring languages of Lake Chad. This does not make Nigerian Arabic 'unclassifiable'. Neither does it 'prove' that Nigerian Arabic is not a Semitic language any more. It is simply the case that, as far as genetic classification goes, sharing forms and reconstructing forms is more important than sharing structures (see Owens 1996).

Figure 1, inspired by Owens (1996), reflects the scale of potential layering: which parts of the language are more likely to be shared with genetic relatives, and which are easily attributable to language contact and diffusion. The scale reflects the 'state-of-the-art' of historical and comparative linguistics. As Nichols (1996: 64) put it, 'the diagnostic evidence [for genetic relationship] is grammatical, and it combines structural paradigmaticity... and syntagmaticity with concrete morphological forms', thus stressing the importance of shared inflectional paradigms in identifying genetic links between languages.

For example, Tariana is an Arawak language with a distinct and often easily recognizable 'layer' of Tucanoan influence (Chapter 10). Hup undoubtedly belongs to the Nadahup (Makú) family—but the comparison with related languages shows the layer of Tucanoan influence (Chapter 11). And we can detect a Romance 'layer' in Tetun Dili (Chapter 6); the Ubangi influence on Belanda Bor, a Western Nilotic language; the Eastern Nilotic 'coating' in the Western

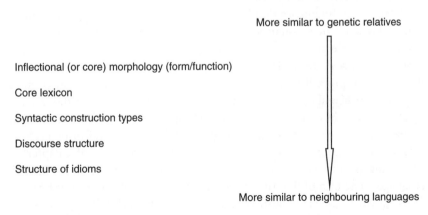

More similar to genetic relatives

Inflectional (or core) morphology (form/function)

Core lexicon

Syntactic construction types

Discourse structure

Structure of idioms

More similar to neighbouring languages

FIGURE 1 Genetic versus contact-induced elements in a language

Nilotic Labwor, coming from Karamojong (Chapter 3); the Ewe influence in Likpe (Chapter 4); the Carib elements in Mawayana, from the Arawak family (Chapter 13); the Quechua imprints in another Arawak language, Amuesha (Chapter 12); and the Romance component in Basque (Chapter 5).

Along similar lines, Romani remains recognizably Indic despite layers from Greek and other European contact languages (Chapter 8). Maltese remains Semitic, despite numerous forms and patterns of Italian descent (Tosco 1996; and see Borg 1994, on parallel development in Maltese, Cypriot Arabic, and other Arabic dialects). Despite the strong Indo-European influence in Modern Hebrew phonology and idioms, no reputable comparative linguist would suggest that this is no longer a Semitic language. In none of these cases has language contact affected the affiliation of languages.

Every language must have undergone some influence from its neighbours at a certain point in time. In Thurston's (1987: 93) words, 'all languages are mixed languages insofar as all have copied lexical forms and other linguistic resources from neighbouring languages'. So, isn't every language 'layered' in one way or another? The answer is 'yes'. But the significance of this varies.

The impact of contact—or, in Swadesh's words (1951), 'diffusional cumulation'—is stronger and more central in some languages than in others. These languages are 'atypical' for their families. Tariana, Mawayana, and Amuesha look strikingly un-Arawak in a number of ways. And a few structures in Modern Hebrew, Maltese, and Nigerian Arabic have a clear non-Semitic 'feel' to them. Many distinctive features of Cantonese (§4 of Chapter 9) are strikingly non-Sinitic—and they can be convincingly attributed to areal diffusion. Dawkins (1916: 198) expressed the same idea of different 'layers' in Cappadocian Greek in somewhat more imaginative terms—'the body has remained Greek, but the soul has become Turkish'.

Metaphors in linguistics should be used sparingly: we may never be able to define the 'soul' of a language, or reconstruct 'cognitive structures' which perhaps underlie contact-induced change reflected in calqued idioms and shared discourse patterns. The idea of 'layering' is much more 'down to earth': it reflects the procedure of teasing apart subsequent 'layers' of discernible impact from neighbouring language, on the way to identifying the 'genetic core'. 'Layering' has an additional flavour to it inasmuch as this term reflects chronologically organized stages of linguistic diffusion (see, for instance, §1 in Chapter 3 and Storch 2003: 177, Matras 2003/4, and §§4–5 of Chapter 12, examining distinct layers of Quechua borrowings in Amuesha, an Arawak language). The idea of 'layering' is also linked to the notion of 'stratification' (also known as 'ditaxia': Matthews and Yip 2001; Chappell 2001: 341), whereby different speech registers reflect different contact patterns. So, 'high-register'

Cantonese is much more like Mandarin Chinese than its lower register which shares features with Tai-Kadai and Miao-Yao languages (§4.1 of Chapter 9).

Detecting 'layers' in languages is a heuristic procedure. And in all the instances quoted in this section the procedure has been successful: we know how to separate the layers of diffusion from the 'core' of genetic affiliation. But in quite a few other cases the picture is blurred.

2.2 *How language contact can affect the language's affiliation*

Teasing apart similarities due to genetic inheritance and those due to borrowing of varied kinds is one of the hardest problems in comparative linguistics (cf. the classic controversy between Boas and Sapir: see Boas 1917, 1920; Sapir 1921: 205–20; Swadesh 1951). Ideally, if two languages descend from the same ancestor, the forms and their meanings must be easily relatable, via the application of established rules for phonological change and semantic change. In actual fact, the distinction between inherited and diffused similarities may be difficult to discern, especially in the situation of prolonged and uninterrupted diffusion of cultural and linguistic traits across an area.

If languages within an area are in a state of equilibrium, with no one language or group dominating others, languages converge towards a common prototype, with features and forms diffusing back and forth. A long-lasting diffusion area may result in layering of patterns and forms to such an extent that genetic relationships are undiscernible. This is the situation described for the Australian linguistic area (Dixon 1997, 2002), and for a number of sub-areas within it (see the excellent case study of the linguistic area of Arnhem land by Heath 1978, 1981, and also see Dench 2001; Dixon 2001).[5] As a result of an intensive long-term diffusion, 'no large genetic groups are recognizable

---

[5] Similar problems arise when a language is claimed to be difficult to classify as belonging to one family or to another. LaPolla (2001: 241) mentions the case of Raji (Jangali), in north-eastern Uttar Pradesh (India), which is 'so mixed with features that it is hard to determine if it is a Tibeto-Burman language heavily influenced by Indo-Aryan and Munda, or a Munda language heavily influenced by Tibeto-Burman and Indo-Aryan'. The question of contact-induced or genetic similarities is also relevant for proving the validity of large language groupings. The similarities among some Niger-Congo groupings and among Atlantic languages, and so-called 'Altaic' languages, may in fact be due to language contact, rather than any shared inheritance (Johanson 2002; Dixon 1997; and Aikhenvald and Dixon 2001*b*).

The effects of contact can obscure the relationships of languages to each other within an established family. Establishing subgroupings within a genetic family involves recognizing 'a set of changes common to a particular subgroup which has occurred between the period of divergences of the family as a whole and that of the subgroup in question' (Greenberg 1953: 49). Criterial features must be shared innovations. But innovations—crucial for establishing proper subgrouping within the family—may be due to contacts with neighbouring languages. And if we do not have enough information about the origin of a particular innovation, we will not be able to establish what the subgroups are. See further examples in Aikhenvald and Dixon (2001*b*).

within the Australian linguistic area' (Dixon 2002: p. xiv). Diffusion of this sort involves a high degree of multilingualism and more-or-less symmetrical diffusion of both form and pattern within each group without any strict hierarchy or dominance. If such large-scale diffusion within a linguistic area (see below) goes on for a considerable time, 'the convergence will obscure the original genetic relationships' (Dixon 1997: 96). Then linguists ought not to be afraid to honestly say 'we do not know, and are never likely to know', whether a certain similarity is due to genetic origin or to geographical diffusion.

Extreme 'layering' of languages, with features and forms diffusing back and forth over thousands of years, results in obscuring the erstwhile genetic relationships and making it impossible to 'peel off' the actual layers. In the Australian context, only a number of 'low-level genetic groups' can be safely identified, by carefully applying the established comparative method (Dixon 2002: p. xxiv). Saying that Australian languages form one genetic family effectively bypasses the established criteria for recognizing genetic relationships followed in most other parts of the world.[6] Yet, as the result of their long-standing interaction, 'Australian languages share a distinctive typological profile, characterized by a number of parameters of variation ... The two most important characteristics of the Australian linguistic area are (1) the areal distribution of most linguistic features, due to diffusion; and (2) cyclic change in terms of a number of area-defining typological properties' (Dixon 2002: 691). To illustrate this, Dixon (Chapter 2) discusses the contact-induced spread of bound pronominals as an areal feature throughout Australia, promoting 'mutual grammatical accommodation' over contiguous languages and across the dialects of two multidialectal languages.

Similarities between languages can be suggestive of a genetic relationship, but not sufficient to postulate it with full assurance. Murrinh-patha and Ngan.gi-tjemerri, two languages spoken in the Daly River region of Northern Australia, share only the cognate paradigms for portmanteau forms of inflecting simple verbs, but scarcely any other forms in grammar and almost none in the lexicon (Dixon 2002: 675). The paradigm of free pronouns is the only fully 'Chadic' feature in Tangale (Jungraithmayr 1995). Such examples are bound to remain 'fringe' puzzles to comparative linguists.

The origin of a non-inherited component may be obscure, even if the language's affiliation is clearly established. Palikur, a North Arawak language spoken in northern Brazil and French Guiana, displays an array of highly

---

[6] As demonstrated by Dixon (2001: 89–98; 2002: 44–54), hypotheses like that of a 'Pama-Nyungan phylic family' do not stand up to careful scrutiny.

unusual non-Arawak features, only some of which can be explained by diffusional influence from neighbouring Carib languages. Amuesha, another Arawak language, also has a number of non-Arawak structural features; only a minority of these can be explained by contact with its former neighbour, Quechua, while the origin of many of its unusual traits remains unknown (see Chapter 12). Since most indigenous languages in these areas are extinct, we are unlikely ever to know the exact source. In the absence of fully reliable data and historical records, we will never be able to go beyond mere hypotheses.

2.3 *Language contact: further alternatives and challenges*

We may assume, for a moment, that languages can change either because of internal processes, or as a result of 'external' influence—that is, language contact. But the very dichotomy 'language-internal change' versus 'language-external change' is not at all clear-cut (see Gerritsen and Stein 1992*b*). Several factors are usually at work in orchestrating a change. To put it simply: in each case, the possibility of multiple motivations muddies the waters. Here are some examples.

Similarities between Irish English and Celtic languages have often been interpreted as a result of direct contact influence. For example, the extensive use of *be*-perfect in Irish English, e.g. *they're gone mad* (Filppula 2003: 166–7), is strikingly parallel to the *be*-perfect in Irish. Irish has no equivalent to English *have* and has always used the verb 'be' to form the periphrastic perfect. The case for contact influence would have been very strong, if the Irish English *be*-perfect had had no equivalent in other dialects or in early stages of English. In actual fact, 'the rivalry between *be* vs. *have* in earlier English was not settled in favour of the latter until relatively late, namely, the early part of the nineteenth century' (Filppula 2003: 167). This means that the *be*-perfect in itself is better viewed as the result of language-internal development whose frequency in Irish English—and its retention there—was reinforced by close contact with Irish. We are faced with MULTIPLE CAUSATION—both external and internal factors have played a role. Similar examples abound—see Chapter 5, on Basque, and especially Chapter 7, on Pennsylvania German.

If languages are genetically related, we expect them to develop similar structures, no matter whether they are in contact or not. And if genetically related languages are in contact, trying to prove that a shared feature is contact induced and not a 'chance' result of Sapir's drift may be next to impossible. A prime example of this is Pennsylvania German in contact with English (see, for instance, §2.4 of Chapter 7). We can only say for sure that the intrinsic tendencies in Pennsylvania German to develop in a similar direction to English were reinforced by the current impact of English as—to a certain extent—a dominant 'intruder'.

The complex interaction between the 'internal' and the 'external' in language change, and the ways in which one may reinforce or help reactivate the other, are a further obstacle to devising a 'universal' hierarchy for borrowability of forms and patterns. What is simply difficult to decide for linguists working on Germanic languages may be an insurmountable problem for languages from other, less 'fortunate', families and areas. If a language has hardly any historical record—and no grammatical reconstruction of a proto-language is available—we may not even be aware of possible alternative analyses. What we take for purely contact-induced change may turn out to be another instance of multiple causation.

Identifying the details of multiple causation is often fraught with the unknown—like pieces of a puzzle irrevocably lost. Amuesha, an Arawak 'mystery' language, is a prime example (§9 of Chapter 12). But we do not even have to go as far as South America. Hebrew, throughout over 2,000 years of its documented history, has absorbed influences from Semitic and non-Semitic languages at every stage of its development. That is, an Indo-European-looking pattern in Modern Israeli Hebrew is subject to multiple interpretation in terms of its origin: it may be the result of an older layer of influence, reinforced by recent impact from Yiddish or Polish. We can recall that the major driving force in the 'revival' of Hebrew started in the 1880s was speakers of the Indo-European language Yiddish from Eastern Europe (that is, the Ashkenazi Jews) (Zuckermann 2003; Aikhenvald 1990).

As Bloomfield (1933: 481) put it, the historical 'processes themselves largely escape our observation; we have only the assurance that a simple statement of their results will bear some relation to the factors that created these results'.

A careful examination of all relevant facts may allow us to filter out independent innovations, parallel development, and accidental similarities from bona fide contact-induced changes—any of which can reinforce the other. And even then we may not be able to arrive at one, definitive, conclusion.

2.4 *Layered languages and 'mixed', or 'intertwined' languages*

Intensive language contact with heavy diffusion of patterns—phonetic, phonological, morphological, syntactic, and especially pragmatic—with or without any diffusion of forms results in a LAYERED, not a mixed language.

Languages known as 'MIXED' or 'INTERTWINED' arise as a result of a combination of special sociolinguistic circumstances with semi-conscious efforts to 'create a language', in which different parts of grammar and lexicon come from different languages. Media Lengua has a Spanish vocabulary and a

Quechua grammatical system; Romanichal Gypsies in Britain speak a language with a Romani lexicon and English grammar; while Michif spoken by the Métis (descendants of French fur traders and American Indian women) in Canada uses Cree (Algonquian) verbs and French nouns, and Copper Island Aleut, from the Bering Strait, has Aleut noun morphology and the Russian finite verb inflection, with vocabulary coming from both sources (Golovko 1994; Bakker 1996, 1997; further papers in Bakker and Mous 1994; Matras 2003, and in Matras and Bakker 2003). These languages—apparent exceptions to the assumption that each language has one genetic affiliation—are typically the result of an attempt to purposely create a special language, or a language register, by an ethnic group asserting its identity.

They come about as a result of semi-conscious language engineering, and reflect 'either (a) split allegiance to two parental communities, in cases where the parental generation's women and men have distinct origins, and the young generation forms a new ethnic group, or (b) maintenance of ethnic awareness in non-territorial minorities,' often nomadic cultures—such as Para-Romani speakers in Europe (Matras 2003: 151–3). As Bakker (1996, 1997, 2000, 2003) has convincingly shown, the documented intertwined languages do not result from code switching or code mixing; neither are they products of heavy borrowing. The ways in which they come about are closely linked to speakers' awareness of different components of a 'language' used for 'identity-flagging', and to the extent of conscious language engineering.[7] Conscious engineering has affected languages which are not traditionally considered 'mixed' or 'intertwined'—such as Estonian and Modern Hebrew. The impact of—and preferences in—language engineering shares similarities with contact-induced change (see §4.2.1–4.2.2).

2.5 *Linguistic areas*

The concept of linguistic area is central to the notion of diffusion. A linguistic area (or sprachbund) is generally taken to be a geographically delimited region including languages from at least two language families, or different subgroups of the same family, sharing traits, or combinations thereof, most of which are not found in languages from these families or subgroups spoken outside the area (see Emeneau 1956; Sherzer 1973: 760; and discussion in Tosco 2000).

---

[7] Another well-known instance of 'non-genetic' languages which did not arise as a result of a normal and spontaneous course of language evolution and have more than one source or parent are trade languages, pidgins, and creoles. Given the ongoing controversy concerning their validity as a special language type and the highly specific social circumstances which warrant their emergence, we chose not to expand the present volume into this field.

How to locate the diagnostic traits, especially when at least some similarities between contiguous languages can be explained by accident, universals, and parallel development? As shown in the study of Mesoamerica as a linguistic area, by Campbell, Kaufman, and Smith-Stark (1986: 535–6), not all shared features have the same 'weight': 'highly "marked", exotic, or unique shared traits weigh more than does material that is more easily developed independently, or found widely in other languages.' Since 'meaningful linguistic areas are the historical products of linguistic diffusion, the stronger linguistic areas are those whose shared traits can be shown to be diffused—and cannot be ascribed to a common ancestor, to chance, or to universals'. Thus, a highly frequent phenomenon—for instance, verb-final constituent order, the existence of nasalized vowels, or the presence of perfective-imperfective opposition in the aspectual system—would not be assigned so much weight as a more rare, unusual characteristic— such as evidentiality (obligatory marking of information source). A further example of a fairly unusual feature is suppletive formation of negative and positive paradigms found in Mande languages, as well as in the genetically unrelated but geographically contiguous Songhay and Hausa (Kastenholz 2002).

Drastic changes in the use of syntactic constructions (such as, for instance, the replacement of infinitives in the languages of the Balkans) or in morpheme shape in the languages within an area could be seen as a highly distinctive trait, indicative of areal diffusion. Such features may be unusual for a subgroup or a family, without being typologically 'exotic'. Chadic languages in contact with Benue-Congo languages have developed a mono-syllabic word structure (Jungraithmayr 2000: 94). Cross-linguistically, having monosyllabic lexemes is not unusual. But this feature is not found in Chadic languages outside the contact area. Since the source of diffusion (from Benue-Congo, Kwa, or Adamawa-Ubangi languages to Chadic) can easily be established, this feature should be assigned special weight in this situation.

Along similar lines, the reciprocal is marked with a suffix on a verb in Oceanic languages on the north-west coast of West New Britain, rather than with a prefix, as in Oceanic languages elsewhere. By itself, this is not an exotic feature. However, the languages of West New Britain share it just with their (unrelated) neighbour, a Papuan language Anêm. This makes it a distinctive characteristic of the area (Thurston 1987: 79–80).

A typologically well-attested property cannot by itself be considered area defining. But the way properties cluster may be area specific. Campbell, Kaufman, and Smith-Stark (1986) single out four morphosyntactic features characteristic of the Mesoamerican area:

(*a*) Nominal possession of the type *his-dog the man*;
(*b*) Relational nouns (that is, body part nouns used as markers of spatial relationships);
(*c*) Vigesimal numeral systems; and
(*d*) Non-verb-final basic order, which may correlate with the absence of switch reference.

There are, in addition, numerous 'pan-Mesoamerican' formations, e.g. 'knee' as 'head of the leg', or 'boa constrictor' as 'deer-snake'.

Along similar lines, a combination of properties defines the multilingual linguistic area of the Vaupés River Basin in Brazil and Colombia with languages belonging to the genetically unrelated Tucanoan and Arawak families (see Chapters 10 and 11). These include:

(i) nasalization as a prosodic feature; voiced alveolar stop and liquid as allophones;
(ii) four to five evidentials marking the way in which the speaker has acquired information (whether seen, heard, inferred, assumed, or learnt from someone else);
(iii) classifiers used with demonstratives, numerals, and in possessive constructions;
(iv) a nominative-accusative profile, which includes one case form marking topical non-subjects;
(v) one locative case covering all of direction ('to'), location ('in, at'), and source ('from');
(vi) verb compounding, or contiguous verb serialization, to express aspectual meanings and changing valency;
(vii) numerous identical formations, e.g. 'father of goods' = 'rich man'.

None of these properties is restricted to Mesoamerica or to the Vaupés area. The way in which they co-occur is area specific. Similarly, none of the properties given for mainland South-East Asia as a linguistic area (see Matisoff 2001; Enfield 2001, 2005) is unique. It is the way they go together— and correlate with areal patterns of grammaticalization—that accounts for the existence of a 'pan-South-East Asian' area (see §2.1.2 of Chapter 9). The same applies to numerous other areas, including the Balkans—the first linguistic area ever to be recognized by linguists. A list of most salient 'Balkanisms' is in §5 of Chapter 8. (Also see Sherzer 1976, Mithun 1999, and Beck 2000, for other areas.)

The more areally defining features a language has, the more central it is to the area. The fewer features it has, the more 'peripheral' it is. Hup is more central to the Vaupés diffusion area than Dâw, from the same Nadahup (Makú) family (Chapter 11). South Slavic is the central member of the Balkan linguistic area—as Victor Friedman put it, 'it is precisely on current South Slavic and adjacent territory that features spread and diminish' (§7 of Chapter 8).

A larger area may consist of micro-areas; and various layers of areal diffusion may superimpose onto one another. Micro-areas within the larger Volta Basin and the Sudanic Belt areas suggest that areas themselves may be diachronically layered, with traits differing in terms of their timing, speed of spread, and resistance to contact (see §2 of Chapter 3). To disentangle various types of similarities between related languages, a fine-grained reconstruction on the level of individual subgroupings is needed, as is the case with Indo-European languages in the Balkan linguistic area. And it may well turn out that each area consists of micro-areas (see discussion in Chapter 8). A proper typology of linguistic areas is still in its infancy, due to the lack of sufficient number of in-depth historical descriptions.

In most linguistic areas, speakers of all languages share cultural traits. However, shared culture does not imply the existence of a linguistic area. A necessary condition for a linguistic area is some degree of bi- and/or multilingualism. The Great Plains in North America has been recognized as a cultural area, but not as a linguistic area—the languages of the area did not have a long enough time to develop areal traits (Sherzer 1973; Bright and Sherzer 1976: 235). Bilingualism was almost non-existent there (Douglas Parks, p.c.) (see §4.2.1 below).

Linguistic areas involve two or more languages. Diffusion within an area can be unilateral and unidirectional (that is, from one language to the other), or multilateral and multidirectional (from multiple sources). Evenki has undergone unilateral influence from Russian (Grenoble 2000). In contrast, Basque has been influenced by a variety of surrounding Romance languages (Haase 1992; and Chapter 5). In each case, the source of diffusion can only be established if we have access to the relevant synchronic data and linguistic reconstructions.

Languages which have never been in contact or never formed a linguistic area can share properties if they have borrowed features independently from the same or similar sources. This was probably the case for numerous Ethio-Semitic languages which share similar features, each taken from different Cushitic languages (Tosco 2000).

A major problem with 'layered' languages spoken within the context of long-standing linguistic areas is disentangling the effects of recent contact from the impact of long-standing diffusion areas which themselves may have consisted of varied micro-areas. Diffusional impacts themselves are prone to be layered and intertwined. At least three overlapping 'layers' of diffusion can be identified within East Timor as a linguistic area: that between Tetun Dili and Mambae as part of a long-standing contact domain; that between Tetun Dili and Malay (and, more recently, Indonesian); and between Tetun Dili and Portuguese (Chapter 6). These account for multiple motivations for many grammatical changes. Further examples from this volume include: Tariana and Hup within the Vaupés area; the impact of the older 'Sudanic belt' area on Belanda Bor and Bviri, Luwo and Dinka, and Labwor and Karamojong interactions; the impact of the 'Volta Basin' as an old area on the effects of contact between Likpe and Ewe (and also Akan). Tai and Miao-Yao-like structures are recognizable in Cantonese as indicative of old diffusion; the story is complicated by the general impact of South-East Asian diffusional features. Languages of the Balkans present a most complex array of 'layering'. And the recent contact itself can be either ongoing, as in Tariana, or completed, as in the Nilotic languages discussed by Storch (Chapter 3).

3 Contact-induced change and its mechanisms

3.1 *Which grammatical features can be borrowed?*

Languages borrow forms and patterns. Borrowed forms may include a lexeme, a pronoun, an affix, a phoneme or intonation pattern, or a way of framing discourse (see Campbell 1997; Curnow 2001). Borrowing patterns does not presuppose borrowing forms. Languages in the Vaupés area share patterns, but have hardly any loan morphemes.

Chapters in the volume provide examples of diffusional impact in just about every area of the language.

PHONOLOGICAL FEATURES include nasalization as a word-level prosody, alternation between alveolar stop and flap intervocalically and change of a palatal approximant y into a palatalized stop ^{d}y in word-initial position, and restrictions on the word-initial position in Hup (§3 of Chapter 11), tone and pitch accent in Hup (§3 of Chapter 11), Cantonese (Chapter 9), and Tariana (Aikhenvald 2002); also see Nurse and Hinnebusch (1993), on the loss of vowel length in some North-East Coast Bantu languages in contact with Swahili. Diffusion of these features occurred independently from lexical loans.

New phonemes in Amuesha (§7 of Chapter 12) may have made their way into the language through reanalysis of lexical loans, as did the bilabial nasal in Basque (Trask 1998). Developing clitics and bound pronominal forms are an areally spread pattern within the Australian area (Dixon, Chapter 2). And partial decliticization of prepositional proclitics in Israeli Hebrew is a recent phenomenon associated with the influence of 'Standard Average European' prepositional structures (Ghil'ad Zuckermann, p.c.). Diffusion affects segmental units (e.g. allophones, and phonemes), phonological processes, and the structure of a higher phonological unit, word.

Diffused NOMINAL CATEGORIES include noun classification. Hup is developing a totally new system of classifiers in multiple environments under the influence of Tucano (§4.2 of Chapter 11), while Cantonese displays a system of classifiers in possessive constructions which shares striking similarities with Miao-Yao languages (§3.3 of Chapter 9). Number systems and number marking have been restructured under areal influence in Western Nilotic, Hup (§4.4 of Chapter 11), and Likpe. In Basque, contact with Spanish has enhanced the spread of a pronominal plural marker to most pronouns (§2.2 of Chapter 5). Both Hup and Tariana developed a typologically unusual system of core cases whereby a definite non-subject acquires a special marking; and one catch-all locative case (§4.8 of Chapter 11 and §5.2–5.3 of Chapter 10). The category of nominal past, prominent in Carib languages, made its way into Mawayana (§4.2 of Chapter 13).

VERBAL CATEGORIES include evidentials—as in Tariana (Chapter 10), and in Hup (§4.5–4.6 of Chapter 11)—modalities—such as frustrative in Mawayana (§4.4 of Chapter 13), optative and apprehensive in Hup, and apprehensive in Amuesha (§8.2.2 of Chapter 12)—tense and aspect (Hup (§4.6 of Chapter 11), Basque (§§2.4.2–3 of Chapter 5)), and verb compounding to express an array of aspectual, valency and other meanings, as in Hup (§4.7 of Chapter 11). Verbal negation in Hup also closely resembles the Tucano 'prototype' (§4.9 of Chapter 11), and negation in Amuesha is much more similar to that in Quechua than to other languages of the Arawak family (§8.2.1 of Chapter 12).

DIFFUSED SYNTACTIC FEATURES cover both phrase-level and clause- and sentence-level syntax. The argument structure and marking of some verbs in Basque bears the impact of Romance languages (§2.3.3 of Chapter 5; also see §4.1 of Chapter 13 on the verb 'say'). Along similar lines, the usage of locative cases and argument structure in Tigak (Jenkins 2000: 249–50) is changing to match the pattern of the dominant Tok Pisin. In traditional Evenki (Tungusic), the agent of the passive was marked with dative case; under Russian influence, it is now frequently marked with instrumental (Grenoble 2000: 109–10). In Karaim (Turkic), a construction employing the postposition 'with' is used to express the meaning of 'be in the function of', under the influence of the Russian instrumental case used with exactly the same meaning (Csató 2001: 274).

Clausal constituent order is highly susceptible to diffusion. Hup and Tariana are becoming verb final under Tucanoan influence (see §4.9 of

Chapter 11 and Aikhenvald 2002; further examples are provided by Dimmendaal 2001; Tosco 2000; and Heine and Kuteva 2003, 2005). The development of verb-initial structures in Tetun Dili is associated with Portuguese impact (Chapter 6). Borrowed clause types include postposed relative clauses in Basque (§2.3.2 of Chapter 5) and new 'modal' clause types and complementation in Likpe (§4.4 of Chapter 4). Hypotaxis in Tetun Dili is also 'foreign'—it is largely attributable to influence from Portuguese (§3.2.5 in Chapter 6).

DIFFUSION OF DISCOURSE STRUCTURES and their marking includes the head-tail structure of clause sequencing in discourse (as in Hup: §5 of Chapter 11), and spread of numerous discourse particles, as in Likpe (§6 of Chapter 4), in Pennsylvania German, and other German varieties in North America (§3 of Chapter 7; also see King 1999: 109–10; Matras 1998). Throughout the world, clefting as a focus-marking device is often diffused from one language to another (as in Baniwa, an Arawak language from north-western Brazil, where a cleft construction has developed under the influence of Portuguese).

Discourse formulae and the ways of telling stories are often shared if languages are in contact—striking examples come from Basque (§2.5 of Chapter 5), Likpe (§6 of Chapter 4), and Hup (§5 of Chapter 11); also see Haig (2001). This is directly linked to the DIFFUSION OF PRAGMATIC PATTERNS, AND TYPES OF CONTEXTS. Linguistic communities in contact come to share speech genres, narrative organization, means of marking speech reports, and other 'ways of saying things'.

The more culturally important the pattern is, the more it is diffusible. Triadic communication patterns throughout West Africa—whereby information is reported to a second person through a necessary intermediary—can be held responsible for shared patterns of speech report and for the emergence of logophoric pronouns (Ameka 2004). As a result of contact with Hopi, Arizona Tewa acquired a number of traditional speech genres and ways of marking them, such as the use of an evidential particle: these are absent from Tewa varieties outside the contact zone (Kroskrity 1998). Similar examples come from Jenkins (2000: 66, 255), Haig (2001), and Johanson (2002).

DIFFUSION OF SEMANTIC PATTERNS, LEXICAL CALQUES, AND IDENTICAL DERIVATIONS abounds in Hup (§5 of Chapter 11), Likpe (§6 of Chapter 4), and Basque (Chapter 5). In each case the absence of a particular pattern in a closely related language is an indicator of its areal origin. For a speaker of Nigerian Arabic 'head of house' means 'roof', as it would in many of the languages not related to Arabic but spoken in the same location, around Lake Chad. For a speaker of any other Arabic variety the same combination would mean 'head of the household'. This is because Nigerian Arabic borrowed patterns—but not so much forms—from its neighbours (Owens 1996: 82–3;

also see Dimmendaal 2001: 363 and Thurston 1987, for similar examples from other areas). An example of an identical pan-European derivation is the word for 'skyscraper' in French, Portuguese, and Russian.

All, or some, of these can take place simultaneously. The effect of each of them may be complicated by language engineering, and multiple causation—as in Irish English, where the influence of the 'source' language simply helped 'activate' what the language already had (see §2.3 above).

3.2 *What changes in language contact*

In terms of the overall impact on the language, diffusion may involve contact-induced gain, or loss, of a form, or of a pattern. The original and the diffused form, or pattern, can coexist in the language, with—or without—some functional differentiation. Or a hybrid form may be created.

We distinguish:

(I) Borrowing of a grammatical system. The Australian language Yanyuwa developed a system of noun-classes in imitation of its westerly neighbours, which had such a system, creating the actual forms from the borrowing language's own resources (Dixon 2002: 500–1). Similarly, Hup developed a system of evidentials matching the one in Tucano (§4.5 of Chapter 11).

Or a language can lose a grammatical system in language contact. Hõne has lost the Benue-Congo noun-class-cum-number marking system as a result of contact (Storch 2003: 183). Loss of patterns may imply loss of forms: some Oceanic languages in the New Guinea area lost their possessive classifiers under the influence of surrounding Papuan languages (Lynch, Ross, and Crowley 2003). Others 'generalized' one classifier at the expense of others which were lost. Tangale, a Chadic language, lost gender distinctions as a result of contact with Adamawa (Jungraithmayr 1995: 200–1), generalizing the 'feminine' form. Along similar lines, the loss of gender in Arawak languages Mawayana (§5 of Chapter 13), Amuesha, and perhaps Chamicuro (§8.2 of Chapter 12 and Aikhenvald 1999*b*) is, in all likelihood, due to impact from languages with no gender distinctions. The loss of a pattern thus involved the loss of some forms, and reinterpretation of others.

Alternatively, a grammatical system becomes severely eroded as a result of contact: the influx of conveniently compact monomorphemic verbs from Portuguese into Tetun Dili played some part in a reduction in productivity for serial verb constructions (§3.2.5 of Chapter 6).

Only occasionally can a whole subsystem of forms be borrowed. Ayacucho Quechua and Tagalog have adopted the subsystem of Spanish gender marking and agreement—but these borrowed systems are fairly marginal in that they involve a limited set of items. Instances of wholesale borrowing of Arabic numbers have been reported in some Berber languages (Aikhenvald and Militarev 1991). An influx of loan adjectives into Tetun Dili has resulted in developing a new word class. There are no instances of one language borrowing a complete paradigm, say, of pronominal forms,[8] or verbal inflection.

More frequently language contact results in:

(II) ADDING A TERM TO AN EXISTING SYSTEM. If one language has a number system consisting of just singular and non-singular while a neighbour has singular, dual, and plural, then the first language may innovate a dual (either by internal grammaticalization, or by borrowing a dual form from the second language, as in Resígaro, an Arawak language influenced by the unrelated Bora-Witoto: Aikhenvald 2001). We may also get loss of a term: if one language in a region has a dual category but this is lacking from all its neighbours, then there may be diffusional pressure to lose the dual. That is, the system gets reduced or expanded without being restructured. Mawayana has borrowed a first person exclusive pronoun from Waiwai, in an attempt to fill a perceived gap in the system (§4.1 of Chapter 13). Cantonese innovated a proximal demonstrative morpheme, possibly from a Tai-Kadai source (§1 of Chapter 1). And Yidiny has borrowed a first person pronoun ŋali 'any two people, one of them me' from Dyirbal (Dixon 2002: 286–7).

Contact-induced changes may involve significant restructuring of a grammatical system, changing the language's typological profile. As a result of such SYSTEM-ALTERING changes a head-marking language may develop dependent marking—as did Tariana and Hup, under the East Tucanoan influence. Sri Lankan Portuguese has undergone a similar change of its overall typological profile—it has acquired core case markers and become more synthetic under Tamil influence (Bakker 2000, 2005). In contrast, Basque and Israeli Hebrew are becoming more analytic under Indo-European influence: while it can be argued that a certain analytic tendency was already there, there is no doubt that this was speeded up and enhanced by the contact.

---

[8] In contrast, it is not uncommon to have paradigms restructured and new ones developed out of the language's own resources in a situation of language contact. Individual pronominal forms or parts of a paradigm can be borrowed (see further on, on Mawayana): for instance, the English *they, their, them* were borrowed from Scandinavian, replacing the Old English forms *hie, hiera, him*. Two independent singular personal pronouns in Miskito ('I' and 'you') were borrowed from Northern Sumu (with the third person singular pronoun originating from a demonstrative). Kambot, an isolate from the Sepik area of New Guinea, is said to have borrowed some pronominal forms from Iatmul, a neighbouring Ndu language (these forms are first singular, second singular feminine, first plural, and possibly also third singular feminine: Foley 1986: 210–11). Resígaro (Arawak: Aikhenvald 2001: 185) borrowed one bound and one free pronoun from Bora. Daiso, a Bantu language, borrowed a first person plural prefix from the neighbouring Shambala (Nurse 2000: 59). See Campbell (1997: 340), for other examples from North American Indian and South-East Asian languages.

Further system-altering changes involve case-marking patterns. The erstwhile split ergative case-marking system in Ardeşen Laz became nominative-accusative under the influence of Turkish (Haig 2001: 215). Estonian (Raag 1998: 57) is thought to have developed prepositions (which now coexist with postpositions) under the influence of Indo-European languages. Tariana (Chapter 10) developed an unusual system of marking topical objects and focused subjects under the impact of Tucanoan languages. Hup, spoken in the same area, developed similar object-marking devices (Chapter 11).

A spectacular example of system-altering contact-induced change comes from the morphology of Semelai, an Aslian language. The only indigenous morphological processes involve the 'non-concatenative' system: affixes are attached to the left edge of the word as prefixes or as infixes depending on the number of syllables in the word. So, the comparative marker *raʔ* is prefixed to a monosyllabic root, as in *sey* 'be thin' versus *raʔ-sey* 'be thinner'. If a root has two syllables it is infixed, as in *jləŋ* 'be long' versus *jə-raʔ-ləŋ* 'be longer'. Semelai borrowed a variety of suffixes, prefixes, and circumfixes from Malay, and thus acquired a whole new concatenative morphological system as a result of intensive contact. 'Light syllable' reduplication has also been borrowed from Malay; nowadays, all these processes apply to roots of Semelai and also of Malay origin (Kruspe 2004: 64–9, 81–5).[9]

In contrast, SYSTEM-PRESERVING changes do not involve creating any new categories. They may involve partly or fully replacing an already existing category or form: for instance, Ingrian Finnish borrowed a past tense marker from Estonian (Riionheimo 2002: 201–2). The borrowed marker tends to be in complementary distribution with the original one (depending on the phonology of the verb stem). Or a new term can be added to an already existing category—Semelai borrowed half a dozen numeral classifiers from Malay, complementing the indigenous classifier system (Kruspe 2004: 206–8); see further examples in Aikhenvald (2000: 386–8).

A language contact situation may simply not last long enough for a system to be restructured—as was the case in the Luwo and Dinka interaction (see §3 of Chapter 3). The impact of Karamojong 'gender' markers into Labwor (§4.2 of Chapter 3) did not introduce any new system-shattering gender distinctions—the borrowed morphemes were reinterpreted as number markers and thus integrated into the number system already in place.

---

[9] The very idea of such restructuring and concomitant system-altering changes goes against the oft-quoted 'structural compatibility requirement'. In its strong form, this states that borrowing can operate only between similar systems (see e.g. Moravcsik 1978 and Weinreich 1953: 25). This claim holds only as a tendency (see Harris and Campbell 1995; Haig 2001).

The distinction between system-altering and system-preserving changes is hardly watertight. Contact-induced changes may result in creating a new, somewhat marginal, subsystem within a language, without affecting the 'core'. This is often the effect of an influx of loans. Unassimilated loans are likely to produce 'loan phonology', much in the spirit of the 'coexistent phonemic systems' discussed by Fries and Pike (1949). Loans then stand out as phonologically different from the rest: the very sound *dž* in the Russian word *džúngli* 'jungle' (borrowed from English) betrays its foreign origin. Borrowed morphological markers or processes—such as Latinate plurals in English, Hebrew plurals in Yiddish, or Cushitic gender-marking derivational suffixes in the genetically unrelated Ongota (Savà 2002)—may also apply just to loans, thus creating a 'loan morphology', as in Tetun Dili.

A change may be system altering to varying extents, often depending on speakers' speech style. Some speakers of English make a point of pronouncing French-style nasalized vowels in words like *croissant*, to sound 'posh'. This choice involves adding a term to the phonological system, for stylistic reasons.

In the long run, a loan subsystem may get integrated into the language—the sound *f* in Russian used to be part of loan phonology, but since most loans containing it have now been assimilated, it is now part of the mainstream phonological system. Words with initial voiced fricatives in English, such as *very*, were borrowed from French; their adoption has contributed to the phonemicization of an already existing allophonic variation between voiced and voiceless fricatives—having thus set in motion a process of structural changes in English phonology. Tetun Dili has a loan subsystem of Portuguese adjectives which are very different from verbs—unlike the native system where there is no watertight distinction between the two. In the long run this may result in restructuring the word class system in Tetun Dili.

In terms of their time frame and in their stability, contact-induced changes can be COMPLETED or ON-GOING (or CONTINUOUS) (Tsitsipis 1998: 34). Completed changes cover those aspects of the grammatical system of a language which do not show any synchronic variation. Speakers are hardly aware of these as 'foreign'. Alternatively, speakers of one language may have moved into an area where another language was already spoken. This language had a 'detectable effect' upon the new arrival, but the contact is now in the past (this effect is also known as 'substratum' influence). At the time of study there is no more contact. Amuesha (Chapter 12) provides a prime example of such 'vestigious', or 'prehistoric', language contact with Quechua. A similar example is the impact of non-Austronesian Waskia on the Austronesian Takia (Ross 2001, 2003).

On-going or continuous changes are those in progress; here the degree of influence of the other language depends on the speaker's competence and possibly other, sociolinguistic, variables, such as speakers' proficiency in the language, as in Tariana.

3.3 *How foreign forms and patterns make their way into a language*

Once borrowed, a form or a pattern is likely to diverge from what it was in the source language, in terms of its formal adaptation, and also its semantics and function. A form may be simply transferred from one language into another—as the non-first-hand evidential marker -*miš* was borrowed from Uzbek into Tajik (Soper 1996: 59–61). Loan forms are thought to be introduced via code switching, or parallel use of more than one language. Loans vary in terms of their degree of phonological and morphological integration into the 'target' language (see Haugen 1950).

Further mechanisms are:

(I) ENHANCEMENT OF AN ALREADY EXISTING FEATURE. If languages in contact share a category or a construction, language contact may increase its frequency or its productivity. Pre-existing analytic tendencies in Basque and Israeli became more pronounced under the influence of Indo-European languages. (Analytic tendencies have been documented for modern Semitic languages—see, for instance, Diakonoff 1989.) The language-internal tendency towards word-medial constituent order in Israeli was enhanced by the Standard Average European pattern. Contact between English and Pennsylvania German often accelerated a change already in place—such as avoiding the 'verbal brace' whereby the non-finite part of a complex verb goes at the very end of a sentence. The same applies to the increased use of the progressive construction, 'be at doing something', in Pennsylvania German—English is simply 'helping along'. Similar examples abound: another example is the 'get'-passive in Pennsylvania German (§2.3.6 of Chapter 7). This is also known as 'activation' (see Clark 1994: 118, on how Outlier Polynesian languages in contact with non-Polynesian languages use possessive suffixes much more often than their Polynesian relatives).

Conversely, a structure which is atypical for those languages with which the target language is in contact becomes marginalized. As a result of contact with English, the requirement for verb-final order in subordinate clauses in Pennsylvania German became more relaxed (Kate Burridge, p.c.). The typical Semitic consonantal root is weakened in Israeli Hebrew, and the erstwhile proclitic prepositions lose some of their clitic properties—all this due to the influence of Yiddish and other Indo-European languages (Zuckermann 2003).

(II) EXTENSION BY ANALOGY. An existing structure can develop additional meanings, matching the ones in a contact language: this is why pronominal plural in Basque was extended to all pronouns, to match the Spanish pattern, and verb compounding in Hup came to be used in a variety of Tucano-like meanings. Serial verbs in Likpe expanded in their use due to a strong presence of serial verbs throughout the area (see §5 of Chapter 4).

Many speakers of Basque do not distinguish between direct and indirect object in verb morphology, matching Romance languages (§2.3.3 of Chapter 5). In Hup, a single form is used to mark a verbal reflexive and emphasis with nouns, matching the polysemous pattern in Tucano (§4.9 of Chapter 11).

(III) REINTERPRETATION AND REANALYSIS. These may involve borrowing words and reanalysing the morphemes. In the Frasheriote Aromanian dialect of Gorna Belica, the marker -*ka* of the Albanian third singular admirative has been reanalysed as an evidential particle -*ka* which is suffixed to indigenous participle forms (Friedman 2003: 190). This can be limited to loans only, as in Tetun Dili (Chapter 6). Or the reanalysed material can then be used with native as well as foreign forms, as in Israeli Hebrew. Other examples include the replacement of the fricative *f* by a labial stop and loss of vowel length in Tajik under Turkic influence, which must have started from loans and then expanded into native words (Windfuhr 1990: 543–4). Reduplication and prefixation in Semelai started from reanalysing Malay loans, and then spread to the native lexicon.

A borrowed bound morpheme, reanalysed and reinterpreted, may acquire a quite different meaning in the target language: gender markers were borrowed from Karamojong and Teso-Turkana into Labwor and became exponents of number, thus fitting into the pre-existing system (§4.2 of Chapter 3). Or a borrowed lexical item can be reanalysed so as to replace a grammatical morpheme. In Acadian French the English loan *back* 'takes on the role of the French prefix *re-* with verbs such as *revenir* "to come back", as in *revenir back* (or *back venir), arriver back, mettre back*' (King 1999: 116–25).

Reanalysis and reinterpretation of native material does not have to involve borrowed forms: passive and relative clauses in Basque were reinterpreted to fit in with a Romance prototype using the language's own devices. The Israeli intransitive possessive construction with the existential verb is developing into a transitive structure reminiscent of Germanic 'have' (Ghil'ad Zuckermann, p.c.).

(IV) AREALLY INDUCED GRAMMATICALIZATION. This is a process whereby a lexical item is grammaticalized to express a category or a meaning in a target language. The basic paths are: (*a*) The target language follows the same grammaticalization path as the influencing language (partly subsumed under 'replica grammaticalization' in Heine and Kuteva 2005). The verbs 'go' and 'carry' in Basque (§2.4.2–3 of Chapter 5) developed the same aspectual meanings as the corresponding verbs in Spanish. Some Likpe postpositions grammaticalized from the same source as those in Ewe, e.g. 'above' from 'SKY' or 'inside' from 'STOMACH' (Felix Ameka, p.c.).

(*b*) Alternatively, grammaticalizing a lexical item to create a new category matching the one in the influencing language, without following the exact same grammaticalization path. The verb 'hear' evolved into a non-visual evidential in Hup and in Tariana, to match a corresponding distinction in Tucano (whose non-visual evidential does not derive from such a verb). Classifiers in Hup are grammaticalized plant parts; the noun 'wood, stick' grammaticalized into a general nominalizer, and then into a future marker. In both cases, the resulting categories match the ones found in Tucano; but the grammaticalization paths are special to Hup (see §4.6 of Chapter 11).

(V) GRAMMATICAL ACCOMMODATION. This process involves a change in meaning of a morphological marker or a syntactic construction based on superficial segmental similarity with a marker or a construction in a different language. That is, a native morpheme can be reinterpreted on the model of the syntactic function of a phonetically similar morpheme in the source language. The marker of possession -*pal* in Pipil, a Uto-Aztecan language (Campbell 1987: 263–4), was originally a relational noun, as in *nu-pal* 'mine', *mu-pal* 'yours', and so on. On the basis of similarity with Spanish *para* 'for, in order to', this morpheme can now appear without any prefixes and have the meaning of 'in order to, so that' and is used to introduce a subordinate clause.

Present progressive aspect in Likpe is expressed with a periphrastic construction consisting of the verb *lé* 'hold' and a nominalized verb. This construction evolved under the influence of the Ewe present progressive marked with a lookalike form *lè* 'be at:PRESENT' in Likpe (pronounced as *lέ* in the Ewe dialects geographically close to Likpe). This is another example of grammatical accommodation (see §4.3 of Chapter 4).

A similar example comes from Hup (§4.5 and n. 9 of Chapter 11): here an inferred evidential construction developed to match a Tucano structure, and using a lookalike form *ni* (see Aikhenvald 2002: 128, on a strikingly similar phenomenon in Tariana).

(VI) LOAN TRANSLATIONS. These involve mostly adhoc word-for-word or morpheme-per-morpheme translations from one language into another—examples include Hup numerals, verb-noun combinations in Israeli Hebrew, motion-cum-purpose constructions in Likpe, and numerous pragmatic formulae including greetings in Basque— see Table 6 in Chapter 5. Another striking example comes from Mawayana (§4.2 of Chapter 13) where the nominal past *-ba* 'translates' morphemes meaning 'dead' and 'former' in two contact languages—Waiwai and Trio. Along similar lines, many of the preverb-verb combinations in Estonian arose as morpheme-per-morpheme translations from German (e.g. Estonian *läbi-hammustama*, German *durch-beissen* (through-bite) 'bite through', Estonian *välja-kannatama*, German *aus-halten* (out-hold) 'tolerate, bear': Nau 1995: 92–3). The calquing may start from 'nonce' calques (similar to one-off borrowings), which may at first be perceived as mistakes. For instance, speakers of Manambu (a Ndu language from New Guinea) occasionally, in their English, use the preposition *for* with the verb 'fear', calquing Manambu argument marking (the verb 'fear' in Manambu requires the dative case on a following noun). The more often it gets corrected, the less chance this calque has of becoming part of the New Guinea variety of English. As Bunte and Kendall (1981) have shown, an error is not an error any more, when it becomes part of an established variety.

Why do only some and not all structures get 'translated'? This is motivated by their correlation with salient cultural practices, perceived 'gaps', and sheer frequency. This is the topic of §4.1.

(VII) LEXICAL/GRAMMATICAL PARALLELISM. This involves native and borrowed grammatical forms appearing together, as illustrated by Hajek (example 2 in §3.2.3 of Chapter 6) for Tetun Dili. Portuguese forms are in italic:

(1)   *durante   Agustu*   nia   laran
      during   August   3sg   inside
      during August

This 'parallel use' is a means of allowing foreign constructions to make their way into the language, in a situation which appears to disfavour downright expansion of recognizably foreign, Portuguese-only, structures.

The relative 'age' of each grammatical change and their relative chronology is another issue to be investigated in depth for each contact situation. Areally induced grammaticalizations with clearly identifiable origins are assumed to be relatively recent: the older the change, the more opaque the boundaries, and the more difficult it is to establish the semantic links. Bviri, a Ubangian language, must have acquired prefixes through areal diffusion before its contact with Belanda Bor, a Western Nilotic; some such prefixes and marking singular-plural pairs were subsequently borrowed into Belanda Bor (see Chapter 3, and also Storch 2003, for a discussion of different chronological layers of areal diffusional phenomena recognizable in Hõne, a Jukunoid

Benue-Congo language). Pre-existence of prefixal slots facilitated further convergence in language structures. This brings us to the next section.

4 Making diffusion possible

We cannot predict with full assurance which way a language will change. Nor can we postulate universal 'constraints' on language change. We can, however, determine which changes are more likely—and which are less likely—to occur under particular circumstances. The same applies to 'borrowability' of linguistic features (cf. Thomason 2000). An exception can be found to just about any restriction or constraint on borrowing. But some kinds of morphemes are borrowed more often than others. For example, there are more instances of borrowing word-class-changing derivational morphemes than there are of bound pronouns and inflections. Yet, Meillet's (1948: 87) categorical statement that an inflection can never be borrowed is incorrect (see Gardani 2005, for a summary of exceptions).

We may admit that 'as far as strictly linguistic possibilities go, any linguistic features can be transferred from any language to any other language' (Thomason and Kaufman 1988: 14), and then 'content ourselves with sitting back and watching how languages change syntactically and semantically according to their own inner, inscrutable laws' (Matisoff 1991: 447). I propose a more positive route. Diffusion of grammatical forms and patterns will be viewed in terms of a variety of facilitating factors or preferences. We discuss these in §4.1. Then, in §4.2, we turn to sociolinguistic and cultural parameters relevant for diffusion of grammar.

4.1 *Linguistic factors facilitating diffusion*

Several linguistic factors facilitate diffusion of forms, and of patterns. Some of these here have been overtly identified by Heath (1978); and a few others correlate with tendencies in grammatical borrowing (e.g. Moravcsik 1978; Matras 1998, 2000; Dalton-Puffer 1996: 222–5).

1. Pragmatic salience of a construction: the more pragmatically motivated, the more diffusible. Constructions used for marking pragmatic functions of constituents—focus, topic, backgrounding, and foregrounding—are the easiest to diffuse. Examples include the spread of passive as a way of focusing on a participant (see Blake 2001; Enfield 2001; and Li and Thompson 1981: 496–7). Similar examples come from Hup (§4.9 of Chapter 11), and from Basque (§2.3.1 of Chapter 5). The order of clausal

constituents also typically correlates with discourse functions of arguments, and is highly diffusible.

Along similar lines, Yaron Matras (2002: 212) suggests that the categories which are least resistant to contact-induced change include discourse markers, fillers, and interjections. In contrast, stable categories resistant to borrowing are those that 'capture the internal structure of meaning' including deictics, case markers, and tenses. The semantic and pragmatic profile of borrowable categories provides evidence for cognitive motivation for contact-induced change, as an overall tendency for the languages in contact to have similar and compatible pragmatic organization.

Discourse organization patterns and various discourse formulae appear shared in most situations of ongoing contact described throughout the volume: Hup, Likpe, Mawayana, Pennsylvania German, and Basque. This is directly linked to Factors 2, 3, 4, 5, and 6.

2. MATCHING GENRES. This involves sharing pragmatic patterns and types of context and subsequent diffusion of organizing discourse structures, resulting in common genres, idiomatic expressions, and further ways of saying. Examples of calquing of greetings, and calquing or downright borrowing of discourse markers, abound throughout the volume (also see Matras 1998; Brody 1995). Kroskrity (1998) demonstrated striking parallelism in the surface structure of stories of similar genres in Tewa and Hopi, spoken in the same area in Arizona, and notably absent from Tewa spoken outside the area.

The spread of noun class prefixes throughout the Australian languages of Arnhem land is facilitated by their 'usefulness' in discourse (Heath 1978: 116): a referent can be mentioned just by using an appropriate noun class marker. That is, matching discourse structures and referent-tracking techniques necessarily involve diffusion of noun classes.

The outcome is convergence in organizing the text 'from top to bottom', covering larger discourse units, and clause and sentence structures (Stolz and Stolz 1996; Matras 1998; Haig 2001). This is corroborated by diffusibility of switch-reference systems, and marking of subordination and coordination (Stolz and Stolz 1996; Matras 1998; Mithun 1992a). Turkic-type clause-chaining structures have made their way into neighbouring Iranian languages (Soper 1996; Perry 1979; Johanson 2002).

The matching of discourse and pragmatic organization correlates with narrating events and communicating in compatible ways. This entails convergence in marking participants. Hence the diffusibility of patterns of marking grammatical relations, and argument structure (see Mithun 2000, Fortescue 1997, and Dixon 1994, on the diffusibility of ergative-absolutive and nominative-accusative, and also marked nominative patterns). Meanings of individual cases and adpositions are easily calqued from one language to another. Haase (1992: 67–70) provides numerous instances of how the instrumental case is being replaced by comitative in Basque, under Romance influence (also see Chapter 5); further examples can be found in Liivaku (1993), for Estonian; Nau (1995), for Finnish, and Grenoble (2000), for Evenki.

Similar situations are conceptualized in similar ways and warrant similar verbal description. If one language uses serial verbs for describing a complex of subevents as one event, the other language is likely to evolve a verb-sequencing construction to match this, as did Hup, to match the Tucano 'prototype' (§4.9 of Chapter 11). Semantically similar verbs are likely to follow similar grammaticalization paths in languages in contact, as shown by Matthews (§2.1.2 of Chapter 9) and Burridge (§2.3.3 of Chapter 7); also see Enfield (2001) on shared grammaticalization patterns of the verb 'acquire' throughout mainland South-East Asia.

Borrowing a genre may directly correlate with replicating the surface realization of a category. Multiple occurrences of the evidential particle as token of Arizona Tewa traditional stories are shared with the unrelated Hopi spoken in the same area; both the genre, and the multiple occurrence of the evidential, result from language contact (Kroskrity 1993: 144–63; 1998: 27–8). This takes us to Factor 3.

3. TENDENCY TO ACHIEVE WORD-FOR-WORD AND MORPHEME-PER-MORPHEME INTERTRANSLATABILITY. This is a corollary of Factor 2. Languages in contact, especially those with a high degree of bilingualism, will often come to have matching discourse patterns, and intonation unit contours. The structure of clauses, phrases, and, further on, phonological words is also expected to become similar.

If phonological word coincides with grammatical word, we expect converging languages to have the same word structure. Stress and tone are a salient property of phonological words, and—in some languages—syllables; hence their 'proneness' to diffusion. Hup and Tucano came to share restrictions on word-initial boundaries. One catch-all locative case in Tariana and Hup ensures morpheme-per-morpheme intratranslatability of nominal forms from these languages into Tucanoan. Within Australia, the development of bound pronouns out of free pronouns which become obligatory, then cliticize to the verb, and then even fuse with it, is determined by the principle: 'be as iconic with your neighbour as you can' (§7 of Chapter 2). The spread of analytic verbal forms in Basque (§2 of Chapter 5) allows Basque speakers to 'match' them with their Spanish equivalents (also see Factors 7 and 8 below).

4. FREQUENCY: THE MORE FREQUENT THE CATEGORY IN ONE LANGUAGE, THE LIKELIER IT IS TO DIFFUSE INTO ANOTHER. This is congruent with Du Bois's (1985: 363): 'Grammars code best what speakers do most.' The frequency of serial verb constructions accounts for their spread into Tariana and into Hup from Tucanoan languages (Aikhenvald 1999c and §4.7 of Chapter 11), as well as throughout the Volta Basin. Frequency played a role in the integration of borrowed French derivational morphology into Middle English (Dalton-Puffer 1996: 224–5), and of Italian derivations into Maltese (Tosco 1996). And it comes as no surprise that high-frequency verbs in Mawayana—especially the verb 'say'—bear more contact-induced impact than other verbs (§4.1 of Chapter 13). And see Trudgill (2004: 159), on the role of frequency in the spread of phonetic patterns in the formation of dialects of English. Frequency often correlates with obligatoriness of a category or a meaning, and this takes us to Factor 5.

5. THE MORE IMPACT A CATEGORY HAS ON CULTURAL CONVENTIONS, THE MORE DIFFUSIBLE IT IS EXPECTED TO BE. An obligatory category in a language which correlates with behavioural requirements is more susceptible to diffusion than one which does not. Such a category is also salient in terms of its frequency in texts of varied genres. The existence of obligatory evidentials presupposes explicit statement about how one knows things. Those who are not explicit run the danger of being treated as liars, or as incompetent. This cultural requirement may explain why evidentiality spreads so easily into contact languages, including some varieties of American Indian English (Bunte and Kendall 1981), Latin American Spanish (Laprade 1981), and Amazonian Portuguese (Aikhenvald 2002), and diffuses across linguistic areas. Evidentiality made its way from Carib languages into Mawayana (Eithne Carlin, p.c.), and from Tucanoan independently into Hup and Tariana (§4.5 of Chapter 11 and Aikhenvald 2002). And a reported evidential in Amuesha (§8.2 of Chapter 12) could also be due to areal diffusion.

Pennsylvania German abounds in 'English-inspired' expressions for future time, involving verbs like 'plan', 'suppose', and 'count' (§2.3.3 and examples (6)–(9) in Chapter 7). According to Burridge, 'these constructions are expressing a cultural value that is central to the Anabaptist belief system; namely, subordination of individual will to the will of God'. The English 'tentative' expressions of future time were 'made-to-measure for a group of speakers reluctant to talk about the future'—as a result, they increased in frequency and became parts of speakers' routine. A correlation with cultural conventions speeded up a contact-induced change.

Along similar lines, the cultural practice of triadic communication in West African languages (Ameka 2004) could have promoted diffusion of patterns of marking responsibility in discourse.

In small tribal societies, anchored on a classificatory kinship system, kinship terms are a communicatively salient category. The development of suffixal plural on kinship nouns in Likpe out of a third person marker replicating the pattern in Ewe could be conditioned by the special status of kinship terms. The relative diffusability of semantics of noun categorization devices, of types of commands, and of politeness could also be anchored to the spread of the associated cultural conventions.

6. BORROWING A PRACTICE MAY FACILITATE BORROWING A SET OF LINGUISTIC EXPRESSIONS WHICH CORRELATE WITH IT. Speakers of languages in contact may share cultural practices, as for instance, building houses and making artefacts. One expects a set of similarly structured expressions to arise for referring to these. The diffusion of the structure of numerals in eastern Anatolia (Haig 2001), and also in Hup and neighbouring languages (§4.3 of Chapter 11) is linked to shared trade and counting practices. Languages which develop trade under contact influence often either borrow or calque numbers.

7. THE EXISTENCE OF A PERCEIVABLE 'GAP' FACILITATES DIFFUSION. Australian languages had no 'conventionalised counting systems', that is, no numbers used for counting (Hale 1975: 295–6). As the Aborigines came in contact with European invaders and their counting practices, this gap was filled either through borrowed forms, or by exploiting native resources. A similar example comes from Likpe (§4.1 of Chapter 4): kinship terms lacked a plural and developed it following a Ewe mould (also see Factor 8 below). Borrowing of the exclusive 1+3 pronoun *amna* into Mawayana from Waiwai fills the existing 'gap' in the pronominal system (see §4.1 of Chapter 13). As Carlin (§5, Chapter 13) put it, 'it was for reasons of "feeling the need" to express the same obligatory categories' present in Cariban languages that Mawayana had to develop a nominal past. Iroquoian languages have developed coordinating conjunctions out of erstwhile adverbs (Mithun 1992*a*) to fill a structural gap.

This is linked to Factors 1–6. Borrowing a cultural practice creates a 'gap' in the linguistic expression and the necessity to fill it (Factor 6). This tends to be done by matching the expression in the source language. So, speakers of languages with evidentials often 'feel the need' to express how they know things in any language they speak; this is an additional factor in diffusibility of evidentials.

A combination of a tendency to fill a gap and to be able to say what your neighbours say similarly to the way they say it (Factors 1–3 above) accounts for the borrowability of conjunctions, and especially the disjunction 'or' (cf. e.g. Matras 1998).

8. TYPOLOGICAL NATURALNESS, OR AN ESTABLISHED TYPOLOGICAL PATTERN ANCHORED IN HUMAN COGNITION, facilitates diffusion of a morpheme or pattern, or development of a category. Many languages develop future out of a motion verb (see Heine and Kuteva 2002)—so no wonder this is happening in Pennsylvania German, with English 'helping along' and accelerating a development which may have eventuated anyway (§2.3.2 of Chapter 7). This is directly linked to the enhancement of pre-existing patterns. The development of an impersonal meaning in third person verb forms is a very common process; it was further enhanced in Pipil by contact with Spanish (Campbell 1987: 277). Plural is more likely to be marked on human nouns and on kinship terms than on nouns of other semantic classes (see Smith-Stark 1974). This typological naturalness was a facilitating factor in the development of number marking on kinship terms in Likpe (§4.1 of Chapter 4). Reduplication is highly likely to be employed as an expressive device, hence its diffusability (see §3.1.2 of Chapter 9). (And also see Dalton-Puffer 1996: 224, for further examples from Middle English.)

If a form or construction develops a new meaning or a new pattern of polysemy under the impact of language contact, the typological naturalness of the newly arising polysemy helps. Examples include the development of interrogative to relative pronoun in Basque; the polysemy of reflexive and 'emphatic' ('self'), and reflexive and emphatic in Hup (matching Tucano), the polysemy of comitative-instrumental and agentive subject marking in Tariana; and the development of reflexive/passive and inchoative polysemy in Israeli Hebrew.

9. COMPACTNESS OF EXPRESSION enhances diffusion, as in the cases of a ready spread of modal impersonal expressions and their syntax, and compact conjunctions such as 'so that' from Ewe to Likpe. One-word causative verbs of Portuguese origin are more compact and easier to handle than multiword causative verb constructions; this helps explain their influx into Tetun Dili. This, alongside other developments, has system-altering consequences: serial verbs in Tetun Dili show signs of gradually losing their productivity (§3.2.5 of Chapter 6). The successful incorporation of the French suffix *-able* into Middle English was 'primarily due' to the fact that Middle English lacked a compact expression for deriving ability adjectives (Dalton-Puffer 1996: 225). Bilingual Navajo easily borrows compact one-word English terms, like 'shelf',

rather than using a bulky Navajo-only expression 'the [thing] into which multiple objects are placed'.

A semantic pattern and a way of mapping it onto a syntactic construction are often borrowed together. Serial verb constructions are a syntactic resource which allows the speaker to express various aspects of a situation as one entity within one clause and with one predicate. Such a cognitive packaging strategy is highly diffusible—as a result, verb serialization is typically a property of a linguistic area, as demonstrated by Ameka (in §5 of Chapter 4).

10. PRE-EXISTING STRUCTURAL SIMILARITY is conducive to diffusion of both forms and patterns (also see footnote 9, on the 'structural compatibility requirement'). Cross-linguistically, borrowing is much more frequent between structurally similar systems than otherwise. If languages in contact have similar constructions and patterns, they reinforce each other. A prime example is borrowing prefixes from Karamojong into Labwor: a pre-existing prefixal slot helped make this possible (§4.2 of Chapter 3). Similarly, as serial verb constructions are an areal feature shared by Likpe, Ewe, and Akan, contact with Ewe and Akan reinforced the productivity of serial verbs in Likpe (see §5 of Chapter 4). This is linked to Factors 11 and 12.

11. A FORM OR A PATTERN IS LIKELIER TO SPREAD IF IT FITS IN WITH THE INNOVATIONAL PROCLIVITIES OF THE TARGET LANGUAGE. This tendency can be considered a variant of 10 (and has been alternatively described as system adequacy, whereby the diffused pattern follows the direction the system is going anyway: Dalton-Puffer 1996: 224). The spread of analytic verb forms in Basque reflects the language-internal tendency enhanced by contact with Spanish. An analytic tendency shared by all Modern Semitic languages was enhanced in Israeli Hebrew by its contact with Indo-European languages (Zuckermann 2003).

The lack of pre-existing structural similarities, or the failure of a pattern to follow the innovation possibilities of a language, does not preclude diffusion. Before the contact, neither Tetun Dili and Portuguese, nor Hup and Tucano, had much in common, typologically. Numerous examples of diffusion of categories which are at 'odds' with the existing system are given in Harris and Campbell (1995: 123–7); also see Bakker (2000, 2005) on dramatic changes in Sri Lankan Portuguese completely atypical of a Romance language. If the 'structural compatibility' requirement had been true, we would hardly be able to expect contact-induced system-altering changes to occur.

12. ANALOGY AND FUNCTIONAL PARALLELISM TO AN EXISTING FORM OR PAT-
TERN IN A LANGUAGE FACILITATES DIFFUSION. Once one construction has been
calqued, the calque is likely to extend to similar constructions. Developing
Slavic-like aspectual meanings in Yiddish may have started with one prefix, but
soon involved all the members of the paradigm (cf. Talmy 1982). The introduction of O-V-V nominalizations in Likpe may have been facilitated by an
already existing process of nominalizing a VO structure (§4.2 of Chapter 4).

13. THE EXISTENCE OF A LOOKALIKE IN A CONTACT LANGUAGE serves as a
trigger to developing a similar structure. The relational noun *-se:l* 'alone' in
Pipil traditionally required possessive prefixes, e.g. *nu-se:l* 'I alone, I by
myself'. It has also been remodelled after phonetically similar Spanish *sólo*
'alone', and has become an 'adverb'—no longer requiring a prefix. The form
has also shifted its meaning from 'alone' to 'only', to match the 'only' meaning
of Spanish *solo* (Campbell 1987: 263–4). We saw above (§3.3, under (V)) how
Likpe developed a present progressive construction under the influence of
surface similarity with a progressive in Ewe; also see n. 9 to Chapter 11, on the
development of a Tucano-inspired inferred evidential in Hup. Such 'grammatical accommodation' was supported by a previously existing structural
pattern similar in both languages. Further examples are in Zuckermann
(2003) and Aikhenvald (2002). The factors which we have considered so far
facilitate diffusion of both forms and patterns. The two are sometimes hard to
tease apart, as in the case of grammatical accommodation.

The following factors primarily facilitate the borrowing of forms.

14. MORPHOTACTIC TRANSPARENCY AND CLARITY OF MORPHEME BOUNDAR-
IES facilitate the diffusion of a morpheme (Heath 1978: 105; Aikhenvald 2002:
271; Gardani 2005). Easily separable forms with clear boundaries are more
prone to being borrowed than forms involving complex morphophonological
alternations. All examples involving borrowing markers of case, aspect, mood,
and tense identified by Dawkins (1916) and Heath (1978) involve easily
separable morphemes with no fusion on the boundaries (also see Gardani
2005: 67–101 and Matisoff 1991). And calquing transparent constructions is
also typical of Basque (§2 of Chapter 5).

The degree of 'acceptance' of foreign material has been frequently associated with language type. As Weinreich (1953: 61) put it, 'a language with many
restrictions on the form of words may be proportionately more resistant to
outright transfer and favour semantic extension and loan translation instead'
(also see Haugen 1956: 65).

The reason why Mohawk does not borrow verbs is 'due to the fact that the
obligatory affixes on verbs are especially complex'; then, 'the particular structure

of Mohawk... acts as a restriction impeding the borrowing of foreign words' (Bonvillain 1978: 32). Along similar lines, no verbs were borrowed from French into any Athabaskan language (Prunet 1990; Krauss MS). A recent study of 'Bilingual Navajo' (also known as 'Boarding School Navajo') characterized by a large number of English code switches showed a variety of techniques employed to 'smuggle in' an English verb: one can use a Navajo 'make' with an English 'main verb' root as a copula complement; or a Navajo auxiliary with a nominalized English verb as its complement (Schaengold 2004: 52–7).

The fact that, in many languages, verbs are less borrowable than nouns tends to be directly linked to their morphological complexity—see Mifsud (1995) and Field (2001) (and a summary in Curnow 2001). There are no such restrictions concerning borrowing verbs into an isolating language, say, Thai (Tony Diller, p.c.). Borrowed verbs have been documented in many languages—these include Hup, Tetun Dili, Maltese, and Tariana (see §4.2.2). In contrast, bound verb roots are as borrowable as nouns in Amuesha—showing that a facilitating factor creates a preference and not a 'law' (§6 of Chapter 12).

15. PROSODIC SALIENCY AND SYLLABICITY. Heath (1978: 105–6) demonstrated that, within the context of Australian languages of Arnhem land, independently pronounceable morphemes are more likely to be diffused than monoconsonantal ones. The same applies to the few instances of borrowed forms in Tariana (Aikhenvald 2002: 271).

16. UNIFUNCTIONALITY AND SEMANTIC TRANSPARENCY. Australian languages in Arnhem land show a propensity to borrow unifunctional affixes rather than 'portmanteau' ones. Ritharngu borrowed the suffix -*ka?* from Ngandi -*ko?* to mark the dyadic dual with kinterms (Heath 1978: 91–2, 116). This is not to say that a borrowed morpheme is never polysemous: a polysemous morpheme has a predominant function, and the polysemy is typologically natural, as with the ergative-instrumental case marker borrowed into Ngandi from Ritharngu (Heath 1978: 75–7). These facilitating factors have explanatory power. They help predict what is going to happen, but only up to a point— that is, inasmuch as they allow students of language contact to identify the target points where diffusion is likely to hit. For instance, a cross-linguistically common link between numeral systems and trade patterns, or between evidentials and cultural conventions, make them a likely domain to be first affected by diffusion. Same preferences appear to be at work in dialect contact and the formation of new dialects (see, for instance, Lipski 1994: 45, on the formation of colonial Spanish), helping disentangle the 'linguistic alchemy' behind the 'kaleidoscopic jumble' of contact-induced phenomena. This topic, fascinating as it is, lies outside the immediate scope of the present chapter.

Several factors are usually at work in each particular instance of identifiable contact-induced change. The post-contact development of a demonstrative into a definite article, and of the numeral 'one' into an indefinite article, in Pipil is a typologically natural path (Factor 8) enhanced by the Spanish influence, and by a tendency to match the information structure (Factor 2) and the linear structure of Pipil and Spanish noun phrases (Factor 3). In addition, lack of obligatory definiteness marking could have been perceived as a 'gap' (Factor 7). Borrowing the marker of dyadic dual with kinterms into Ritharngu from Ngandi was a 'useful' borrowing (Factors 5 and 7), since it correlated with a culturally salient pattern of dyadic kinship already present in the language (Heath 1978: 116).

The more preferences are at work, the likelier is the pattern to become well established in a language—following a Mutual Reinforcement Principle. Frequency enhances change of any sort: the combination of distant with reported evidential in Hup (highly frequent in traditional narrative) is developing into a fused structure, at odds with the agglutinating tendencies of Hup (and the almost isolating structures in some of its sister languages), but concordant with a fused expression of the same meanings under the same circumstances in Tucano (Epps 2005).

A combination of various facilitating factors is akin to multiple causation in language change. The emergence of the demonstrative ni^1 in Cantonese (§1 of Chapter 9) could have arisen (1) because of a tendency to disambiguate two demonstratives which came to be distinguished by tone only, and/ or (2) to fill a gap left by an erstwhile demonstrative becoming specialized as a third person pronoun (Randy LaPolla, p.c.) (Factor 7); its emergence was supported by the typological naturalness of having a proximate demonstrative with a high vowel (Factor 8). Along similar lines, those structures— such as hypotactic syntax—which were shared by Portuguese and written Indonesian to start with (presumably, due to previous contact of Indonesian with European languages) came easily to infiltrate Tetun Dili (see §3.2.5 and n. 3 to Chapter 6). And a number of functional and pragmatic features of Cariban languages made their way into Mawayana through Waiwai, only to be further reinforced by the same features in Trio (Chapter 13). The same principle lies behind what Ameka calls 'pressure to adopt areal patterns' in Likpe (§1 of Chapter 4)—a combination of factors which reinforce each other.

The 'reverse' of a facilitating factor creates an impediment to a contact-induced change, but does not rule it out. Bound verbal roots are less 'easy' to borrow than free forms; yet Amuesha went against this tendency.

Exactly what structure is affected depends on what is available in the languages in contact. In the situation of Estonian-Russian and Evenki-Russian contacts, the change affects some aspects of the usage of nominal cases. The semantics of cases in Basque was affected by Romance prepositions (the Romance contact languages, Spanish and French, do not have cases on nouns). The tendency to create equivalent noun phrases underlies these changes (Factor 2). Strong areal features—that is, the ones that are already found in other places in the area—are among the most resistant ones (Factor 10), e.g. grammaticalization of 'acquire' in Cantonese (§2.1.2 and examples 9–12 in Chapter 9) and *k*- plurals in the Sudanic belt area (§2 of Chapter 3).

Some of the factors identified are intertwined with each other and their effects can be hard to disentangle. Factors 1, 2, 4, 5, 6, and 7 are tightly knit together, and so are Factors 2 and 3; and 10, 11, 12, and 13. Factors 14–16 provide additional motivation for borrowing of forms; and are not immediately linked to any other factors. Factors 8 and 9 provide an overall motivation for linguistic change. There is no hierarchy involved—these factors operate simultaneously.

As a corollary of factors 14–16, isolating and agglutinating languages are expected to be more 'open' to borrowed forms than those with fusion. It is easier to borrow a free morpheme than a bound morpheme. However, this does not always hold, when 'anti-foreign' language attitudes come into play. This brings us to the next section.

4.2 *Sociolinguistic parameters in language contact*

No language contact situation is 'context free'. In each particular case, social and historical environment and culture history create a slightly different social ambience for a language contact situation. The process and the outcomes of language contact depend on a large number of parameters (see Ross 2001; Andersen 1988; Aikhenvald and Dixon 2001*b*). Those discussed here have been best described in the literature as having particular impact on diffusion.

4.2.1 *Degrees of knowledge of each other's languages ('lingualism') and kinds of contact* Crucial factors in understanding types of language contact are whether there is multilingualism or simply bilingualism, involving what proportion of the community, and which social groups. One expects more extensive grammatical borrowing in a situation of stable, well-established multilingualism—as in East Arnhem Land in Australia, or the Vaupés area of Amazonia. Different degrees of 'lingualism' can be connected to cultural practices, such as intermarriage, sporadic or seasonal trade, slavery

(as in Africa), or intertribal dance-and-fight gatherings (as in Australia).[10] Knowledge of each other's languages is a necessary condition for the creation of a linguistic area (§2.5). It is also necessary for the operation of Factors 1–7 above. The impact of a prestigious second language in a predominantly monolingual community typically results in an abundance of loanwords, but hardly any structural influence—English loans in Japanese are a prime example (Loveday 1996).

Relationships between languages and their spheres of use can involve diglossia (see Ferguson 1964; Schiffrin 1998; Fishman 1967; Hudson 2000; Dorian 2002). Diglossic language situations normally involve two (or more) varieties that coexist in a speech community, in complementary distribution between the domains of usage (for example, one used at home, and another in other environments). Long-term stable multilingual situations do not necessarily require diglossic relationships between languages (cf. Appel and Muysken 1987: 5; Smith 1986; Aikhenvald 1996, and many others). The degree of mutual intelligibility between languages within an area may influence the direction of contact-induced change. 'The odd one out' considered 'difficult to learn' may be in danger of undergoing more diffusional changes than other languages. Kuot, the only non-Austronesian language spoken in New Ireland, has undergone more obvious diffusional impact from the neighbouring Austronesian languages than the other way round (Jenkins 2000 and Lindström 2002).

The degree of 'lingualism' is directly linked to kinds of contact with other communities. This can be regular or sporadic. It can occur under a variety of circumstances (e.g. trade, sport, religion, marriage patterns), and at different social levels. Interaction is sometimes restricted to a ritual language, e.g. the influence of Classical Arabic on the vernacular languages of Muslim peoples, exclusively through the Koran. The contact can be stable and prolonged, or short-term and sporadic which may engender discontinuous, one-off changes.[11] Contact can be on-going, or completed (this correlates with the

---

[10] One form of a language may turn out to be better known and thus more influential than another: Lehiste (1979) showed how translations from Russian influenced the usage of cases, the patterns of negation, and word order within possessive noun phrases in the written form of Estonian during the occupation. Passive constructions in Mandarin Chinese used to convey negative, 'adverse' meaning; this construction largely lost this overtone as a result of pervasive translations from Indo-European languages (English and Russian) into Mandarin Chinese (Li and Thompson 1981: 496–7; Chao 1968: 703). Commercial adverts (often influenced by English) may bear more diffusional impact than other genres; this is the case in Spanish and Israeli Hebrew.

[11] Here we do not focus on short-term contact-induced changes in immigrant languages which, with almost no exception, result in rapid absorption by the majority language. For comprehensive investigation of these issues, see Clyne (2003).

classification of linguistic changes in §3.2). Completed, or pre-contemporary, contact can produce what is known as substratum influence—as for instance, non-Austronesian influence in the phonology of Madak, an Austronesian language from New Ireland (Ross 1994), or Chukchi influence in the stress system of Sireniki Eskimo (Fortescue 2004). Such contact effect can—but does not have to—be the product of language shift (and subsequent imperfect learning).

Language interaction correlates with the type of community. Communities can be EXTERNALLY OPEN (with plentiful social and economic interaction with their neighbours) as opposed to relatively closed (also see Milroy 1987, on the concept of 'social networks'). Heath (1981) describes a high degree of shared lexical and grammatical forms and patterns among the various groups of Arnhem land in Australia, resulting from extensive contact (including intermarriage) between small ethnolinguistic groups without hierarchical relations of dominance and in the absence of any strong tribal organization. A fascinating account of how a structural change in the community may entail linguistic change comes from Pennsylvania German (§2.5 of Chapter 7). Traditionally, these communities were small and tightly knit. Unlike the mainstream English-speaking world around, 'the kind of mandatory speech used to establish social rapport during an encounter is not needed in such an integrated community, where people are deeply involved with one another and where there is no social distance... However, increased dealings with the outside mean the English routines are being adopted,' especially in newly introduced routines such as phone converations. As a result, numerous English-style discourse markers have made their way into the language, both as loan forms and as calques.

A community may be 'externally open' as a result of traditional warfare. The Matses, a Panoan-speaking group in Peru (Fleck forthcoming), used to raid their neighbours' villages, killing men and capturing women who would then be incorporated into the Matses community as full-fledged members. These women were first-language speakers of languages other than Matses (some of the same family, some not). Their linguistic integration into the Matses life may have involved a certain amount of foreigner talk, and the variety of Matses they speak to their children may reflect their incomplete knowledge of Matses and the substrata from their own languages. These factors may account for significant grammatical differences between Matses and other Panoan languages.

Alternatively, a community can be INTERNALLY TIGHTLY KNIT AND CLOSED (bound together by linguistic solidarity) as opposed to loosely knit (involving a diversity of language groups) (Andersen 1988; Ross 1994, 1996). In some of the latter there may be an established lingua franca which can in time lead to the development of a more tightly knit profile. A tightly knit community is expected to be resistant to foreign influences and 'importations'. The Yaqui, a loosely knit community, are receptive to cultural, as well as lexical and grammatical influence from Spanish, while the more tightly knit Tewa are much less open to Spanish influence of any sort, and the amount of loans and calques is considerably less (Dozier 1956; Kroskrity 1993; also see Vočadlo 1938). This takes us to the next section.

4.2.2 *Language attitudes* Attitudes towards non-native forms vary, both between communities and within a given community. Some adopt loan forms on a large scale, while others consider using 'foreign' importations as tokens of unacceptable language mixing. Speakers of Athabaskan languages preferred not to accept loanwords from the languages with which they had contact but would instead create names for new objects and ideas from their own lexical and grammatical resources (see the insightful discussion of lexical acculturation in Brown 1999).

Different attitudes to external cultural influence among speakers of Iroquoian languages resulted in a different impact of English and French on one aspect of their grammar—namely, clause coordination (Mithun 1992a). The conservative Onondaga have not developed any coordinating conjunctions. The Mohawk—who have a 'long history of functioning enthusiastically and successfully in both their own culture and that of their non-Indian neighbours' (Mithun 1992a: 126)—have developed coordinating conjunctions, matching the English prototype. A community can be closed with respect to one kind of influence, and open to the input from another. The Arizona Tewa have resisted influence from Spanish invaders, but not from their traditional neighbour, the Hopi. Stable societal multilingualism in both Hopi and Tewa, enhanced by generations of intermarriage, is characterized by intense indirect diffusion (but very little borrowing of actual forms) and shared discourse patterns (Kroskrity 1998: 32). This also relates to questions of conscious language planning: as when Kemal Atatürk resolved to rid Turkish of its Arabic loans—some of fair antiquity—replacing them with native coinages; however, he did not object to loans from western Indo-European languages.

A cultural inhibition against recognizably foreign items and ensuing linguistic purism provides a mechanism for stopping an influx of borrowed forms. As noted by Herzog (1941: 66), their major property is that they can be 'traced most readily', by linguists and speakers alike. Once speakers are conscious of the foreign material in their lexicon—or grammar—they can try and get rid of it (as happened in the history of various literary languages: Fodor 1984; Tauli 1984; Hint 1996). This is the case in Basque (§3 of Chapter 5), Likpe (§6 of Chapter 4), Tetun Dili (Chapter 6), Tariana (Chapter 10), Hup (Chapter 11), and Mawayana (§5 of Chapter 13). Another, oft-quoted, example of a cultural inhibition against foreign forms is Arizona Tewa, a Kiowa-Tanoan language from North America (Kroskrity 1993; Dozier 1956). The diffusion of patterns is much less controllable.

This is intuitively plausible—as Thurston (1987: 93) put it, 'since people generally construe languages as being collections of words, it is primarily by lexical form that linguistic groups identify linguistic contrasts among themselves'. In contrast, only a linguist with a penchant for purism is likely to systematically detect unwanted contact-induced structural similarities, as does Mati Hint (1996: 802). He stresses that the major danger for Estonian lies not in the presence of occasional loanwords, which can easily be got rid of, and are therefore a minor 'trouble'. What 'distorts' the language is the rapid expansion of grammatical and lexical calques which are pervasive and, as he admits, more difficult to control than foreign forms.

It is not always an easy matter to draw a line between borrowing forms and borrowing patterns. Once reanalysed, borrowed forms may entail borrowed patterns (cf. Factor 12). The process of 'grammatical accommodation' (see §3.3) results in creating compromise forms of a sort—native forms are 'adapted' to those found in the source language. The form in the target language remains the same—but it acquires a further meaning.

Borrowed forms are easier to detect than borrowed patterns, and this is why many linguists think—in all likelihood, erroneously—that they are always more common. A careful inductively-based analysis of individual language contact situations suggests the opposite. Languages with few if any borrowed forms tend to show a variety of borrowed patterns. The fact that Hungarian or Finnish do not have an overwhelming number of Indo-European loans does not stop them from having markedly 'Standard Average Indo-European' structures (see Haspelmath 2002; Kuteva 2001a, 2001b). Borrowing forms is by no means a prerequisite to borrowing patterns, as demonstrated in several of the chapters below.

Unwanted loans as free forms are easier to detect and to 'ban' from the language than bound forms. This is the reason why the few forms borrowed from Tucano into Tariana, and into Hup, are bound (Aikhenvald 2002: 224, and §5 of Chapter 11). This goes against the general tendency to borrow free rather than bound roots and morphemes. Yet the sociolinguistic motivation behind this is clear.

Emblematicity of features is an additional factor in diffusion. A formal or, more rarely, a structural feature can be considered 'emblematic' of a language community (see Enfield 2001: 267–8). A prominent feature of the Yawalapiti language of the Xingu area is the unusual sound, *ř*, carefully nurtured by the speakers of this highly endangered language as an identity marker. Such emblematic features—for example, a non-Mandarin-like constituent order pattern in Cantonese whereby the adverb *sin¹* 'first' follows the verb (§3.2 of Chapter 9, example (18)), or noun classification devices in some Nilo-Saharan languages (see §6 of Chapter 3)—can be particularly resistant to change of any sort.

A contact-induced feature can become emblematic. The Taiwanese variety of Mandarin underwent massive calquing from Southern Min rather than from the officially dominant Mandarin, probably because Southern Min, and not Mandarin, is 'emblematic of current loyalties', serving as 'a badge of being Taiwanese' (Chappell 2001: 353). The definite article in Macedonian perceived as one of its most distinctive traits within Serbia is an example of an emblematic—or plainly stereotyped—areal feature in the Balkans (see §7 of Chapter 8).

An ethnic variety of the dominant language (L2 for the community) can also become emblematic, as a 'signal of ethnic group membership'. A stereotype of 'verhoodelt' (or mongrel) English of speakers of Pennsylvania German—with their *throw Father down the stairs his hat once* and the suchlike—has acquired a certain value of signalling the identity of the Traditional Mennonites, with their emblematic *Demut*, or 'humility' (see §§3 and 4.2 of Chapter 7).

And even 'hybrid' nature of a group's native language may grow into a mark of identity. As Burridge points out in §5 of Chapter 7, Pennsylvania German appears to be 'heading towards something akin to an English lexicon embedded within a structure still distinctively PG. Although there is no conscious language engineering involved here, speakers are definitely aware of the hybrid nature of their language. For the Old Order Mennonites 'its "bitser" quality has a positive, almost sacred, value:... the low status of the dialect variety is... an appropriate symbol of their humility.'

Speakers' attitudes to linguistic change are yet another factor. Innovations have a better chance in a situation where there is little, or no, resistance to them (Nadkarni 1975: 681). Take speakers of Pennsylvania German. They are quite tolerant to variation in their own language, but resist any change in the prescriptive English they acquire as second language. As a result, their first language bears a strong impact from English, while their English remains fairly intact (see §4.1 and Figure 2, Chapter 7).

Language engineering and planning offer a fertile ground as to how diffusion of forms can be controlled. When it comes to diffusion or borrowing of patterns, speakers and even language planners are often not conscious of their pervasive effects. Israeli Hebrew has kept the bulk of the morphological make-up of a Semitic language, but has incorporated numerous semantic, syntactic, and discourse patterns from Yiddish and other Indo-European languages, despite the efforts of its 're-creators' to retain its 'purely' Semitic profile (Zuckermann 2003; Aikhenvald 1990).

In the early twentieth century, Estonian underwent considerable restructuring in its grammar and in its lexicon as a result of a conscious effort (mostly by Johannes Aavik) to make its lexicon less 'German-like' and its grammar more 'elegant': for instance, a 'synthetic' comparative was conceived as 'better' than an analytic construction (see Raag 1998; Kurman 1968; Tauli 1984). Conscious language engineering was also oriented against spreading some structural patterns branded as 'foreign': this is how Johannes Aavik got rid of 'German-like' verb-final constituent order in written Estonian (Ehala 2000). At the opposite extreme, there has been forceful introduction of foreign elements from Chinese into the minority languages of China in order to 'improve' them (Matisoff 1991). And Pontius (1997) showed that social enmities (as in the case of Czech and German) can create an obstacle to formal and even to structural borrowings. Some categories are more prone to being manipulated by 'language engineers' than others. Gender, classifiers, and counting systems are among the former (Hagège 2004: 109–11; Aikhenvald 2000: 349–50), most probably because they are often perceived as relevant for cultural practices and the role of the sexes within a society (in agreement with Factor 5).

4.2.3 *Balanced and displacive language contact*   The impact of intensive multilingualism and of language contact on a language's profile depends on the relationships between languages. In a situation of a long-standing linguistic area and stable multilingualism without any dominance relationships, language contact is 'balanced'. It does not entail loss of languages, or of patterns. Quite the contrary: borrowing and reinterpreting patterns from one's neighbours results in enrichment, and in increasing linguistic complexity and typological diversity. A prime example of balanced contact was the traditional Vaupés area (Aikhenvald, Chapter 10; Epps, Chapter 11), and West New Britain (Thurston 1987). The linguistic outcome of this 'peaceful coexistence' promotes typological diversity.

Hierarchies of prestige groups (castes, etc.) and relations of dominance (social and/or political) between languages or dialects influence the direction of borrowing and diffusion. There is, typically, borrowing from a prestige into a non-prestige language, e.g. from Mandarin Chinese into other Chinese varieties. A politically dominant language usually influences a less dominant one. Estonian bears an impact from a variety of foreign 'invaders' in its lexicon and grammar, including Russian, English, Swedish, and German (Hint 1996: 802). In Papua New Guinea, Tok Pisin is succumbing to the influence of English, and so are numerous vernaculars (Jenkins 2000; Aikhenvald 2004*b*).

If one group aggressively imposes its language on another group, language contact results in language displacement, loss of the language's own features, and, ultimately, language shift. Instances of such displacive language contact abound—the oft-quoted examples include forceful Russification of minorities in the Soviet Union and Russia, forceful implementation of Mandarin Chinese destined to oust the minority languages, Hellenization of minorities in Greece, and laws against minority languages in France. Further examples include separating children from their parents and punishing them for using the traditional language, in Australia and also in the Americas. This is described as 'linguistic stress' by Silva-Corvalán (1995).

Table 1 summarizes the salient features which distinguish balanced language contact from displacive language contact, covering relationships between languages, linguistic effects, and the outcomes for the languages' survival (this is reminiscent of symmetrical versus asymmetrical bilingualism in language acquistion discussed in §4.2 of Chapter 9 and Table 2 there).

Balanced language contact promotes typological diversity and results in increased structural complexity. In contrast, displacive language contact produces the opposite: the dominant language imposes its patterns, resulting in simplification of the other language. Its ultimate result is loss of typological diversity accompanied by language loss.

TABLE 1. Balanced and displacive language contact: a comparison

Parameters	Balanced contact	Displacive contact
Relationships between languages	roughly equal, or involving a traditional hierarchy; stable	dominance; unstable
Linguistic effects	rise in complexity; gain of patterns	loss of patterns; potential simplification
Results	language maintenance	potential replacement of one language with another

The differentiation between displacive and balanced language contact may not always be clear-cut. A particular language contact situation may involve some displacive tendencies; and the relations between languages may abruptly change or even get reversed. The contact-induced influence of Russian on Estonian, or Latvian, was potentially displacive in the times of Soviet domination. Once this stopped, and Estonia and Latvia gained independence, the ethnic Russians there became a largely ignored minority, under pressure to abandon their own language in favour of the national languages. A less dominant language may occasionally 'fight back'—this is reflected in the well-described resistance in Czech against German influence (Pontius 1997; Vočadlo 1938).

4.2.4 *Further sociocultural parameters*   The parameters outlined in this section have proved useful in the existing investigation of various patterns of language contact. Other potentially important variables include size of community (see Nurse 2000: 260–2); interaction between rural and urban communities; marriage patterns; patterns of trade and warfare (§1 of Chapter 4, and Chapter 3); the lifestyle of speakers (e.g. whether nomadic hunters/gatherers, village-dwelling agriculturalists, nomadic cattle herders, or largely urbanized groups); division of labour between the sexes and between generations; social organization and the kinship system; and religion/mythology.

A variety of language-external circumstances—some of them outlined above—underlie the 'how' and the 'why' of language contact. Languages can change due to incomplete language acquisition, foreigner talk, koineization, situations of di- or polyglossia (with functional differentiation of languages), or stable multilingualism without such functional differentiation. A binary distinction between 'language shift' and 'language maintenance' (as in Thomason and Kaufman 1988) should be taken only as a metaphor: for languages which have or have not undergone massive structural convergence (see §5) and system-altering changes, one would be better off positing a continuum between these two extremes.

With loss of traditional culture over the past decades, the social factors which may have been instrumental in producing a language contact situation have to be reconstructed, or even conjectured. Kidnapping women among the Matses belongs to the very recent past—there are still kidnapped women among the Matses, and the traces of the traditional linguistic interaction can be observed. Not so among the Manambu of the Sepik area in New Guinea: raiding neighbouring tribes and subsequent integration of 'survivors' (speaking languages other than Manambu) into the Manambu communities is alive only in folk memory. The unusual complexity of Manambu grammar may well be due to incorporating various 'substrata' from conquered groups—but we will never know this for certain.

How long does it take for a language to acquire discernible 'layers' of contact-induced change? For now, we leave this question open. The contact between Ewe and Likpe is only about 300–400 years old (§2 of Chapter 4). None of the contact situations described in Chapter 3 is of deep antiquity. The contact situation between Basque and Romance 'has been in place for about two millennia' (§1 of Chapter 5). And for Amazonia—including the Vaupés area (Chapters 10 and 11), the Andes, and the Waiwai-Mawayana interaction—we simply cannot tell.

4.3 *The net result of language contact*

Languages in contact—where a significant proportion of the speakers of one also have some competence in the other—gradually become more like each other in certain features. This is known as convergence.[12] Languages become structurally isomorphic as a result of shared ways of saying things and similar underlying cognitive patterns, without necessarily sharing many forms. This goes with restructuring of semantics, discourse, and syntax involving a mutual adjustment of the languages and/or some patterns 'winning' over others. Semantic and pragmatic structures of one language become replicated in the other, following the tendency to achieve linear alignment.

A major factor behind the diffusion of patterns is the desire to be able to say what one's neighbour can say—making 'the categories existing in the languages that are in contact mutually compatible and more readily inter-translatable' (Heine and Kuteva 2003: 561). For the coexisting systems to converge, both (A) functional and semantic and (B) formal matching is desirable. This is facilitated by knowledge of each other's languages, language attitudes, and the linguistic factors outlined in §4.1.

As a result of language contact, grammatical structures may become almost fully isomorphic. Urdu, Marathi, and Kannada, the three languages spoken in the village of Kupwar (Gumperz and Wilson 1971), provide an oft-quoted example of how grammatical structures and their semantics can be identical without many borrowed forms. In Gumpertz and Wilson's (1971: 155) words, 'so great is the similarity among [Kupwar] grammatical structures that we were able to analyze an extensive corpus of bilingual texts involving all three

---

[12] An alternative term for convergence is metatypy (Ross 2001). This has gained a little currency recently. I avoid this term because (*a*) it is vague in its definition, and (*b*) it is easy to misuse, since it may be considered to be linked with system-altering changes involving 'change of type'.

local varieties without having to postulate syntactic categories or rules for one language which were not present in the other languages. We may say, therefore, that the codes used in code-switching situations in Kupwar have a single syntactic structure.' Rongpo, a Tibeto-Burman language from Uttar Pradesh, has been heavily influenced by two Indo-Aryan languages (Hindi and Garhwali); this influence resulted in an almost morpheme-per-morpheme equivalence between Rongpo and its neighbours (LaPolla 2001). This can only happen if speakers are proficient in each other's languages.

Contact-induced change in typologically different linguistic structures produces different results, even if they are influenced by language(s) of a similar type. In the Vaupés linguistic area, Tariana has become more poly-synthetic than related Arawak languages: it has developed additional slots for bound morphology, expanded the system of classifier and gender agreement under the influence of Tucanoan, and acquired Tucano-type clause-linking devices. Hup is on the way towards developing mildly synthetic structures. Portuguese spoken by north-west Amazonian Indians and the Portuguese in Sri Lanka developed very different contact-induced categories (Bakker 2005; Aikhenvald 2002).

When languages converge, they gain some features and lose others. We envisage at least three alternative scenarios:

1. ALL LANGUAGES IN THE AREA ADOPT NEW PATTERNS WITHOUT LOSING THE OLD ONES. In all languages in a diffusion area the erstwhile patterns come to coexist with new ones, and new rules develop governing the functional differentiation of new and old patterns. Konkani has adopted Indo-European type relative clauses, together with Dravidian-type relative clauses; both are now used under different circumstances (Nadkarni 1975). Likpe acquired features from Ewe, at the same time keeping its own properties (Chapter 3). The same applies to the three Arawak languages discussed in this volume: Mawayana, with its few Cariban features and a strikingly Arawak profile (Chapter 13), Amuesha with its highly unusual grammatical structure (Chapter 12), and Tariana, many of whose complexities are due to an intricate interplay of Tucanoan and Arawak linguistic traits (Chapter 10). This conver-gence implies mutual enrichment of languages in contact in a situation of prolonged multilateral contact without any relationship of dominance. This is indicative of balanced contact, with balanced multilingualism.

These languages in contact have become structurally similar without losing their differences; they tend to become more synthetic; and have gained in structural complexity, adopting patterns from multiple sources with subse-quent functional differentiation of each.

2. LANGUAGES IN CONTACT ACQUIRE NEW COMMON GRAMMAR. One-to-one language contact without dominance may result in creating new shared grammatical structures, combining features of both of the languages in contact and creating a compromise between the previously existing structures. Grammatical isomorphism and intertranslatability can be almost complete. An example comes from the contact between Retuarã (Tucanoan) and Yucuna (Arawak) in Colombia. Retuarã has gained an Arawak-type cross-referencing prefix and reanalysed its Tucanoan suffixes as gender-number agreement markers. Yucuna has become fully nominative-accusative having lost its split ergative patterns, and keeping suffixes just to mark gender-number agreement. In marking possession, Retuarã gained Arawak-type prefixes, and lost Tucanoan-type possessive classifiers (Aikhenvald 2003c).

These languages in contact have become structurally similar—but not identical. Structurally, their grammars are neither fully Arawak nor fully Tucanoan.

3. ONE LANGUAGE ADOPTS THE GRAMMAR OF ANOTHER. In the situation of one language dominating the others, convergence may involve gradual adoption of the other language's structures at the expense of its own. This kind of convergence—a typical result of displacive contact—is often the precursor of language attrition and obsolescence (whose linguistic consequences are discussed in Campbell and Muntzel 1989; Brenzinger 1998; and Aikhenvald 2002: 243–61).

The net result of contact-induced change is the addition of new features, and general enrichment. Dominance and 'displacive' impact of one language over the others results in overall simplification and regularization, carrying the seeds of impending loss of linguistic diversity.

5 What can we conclude?

Languages reflect the sociolinguistic history of their speakers; and language attitudes influence the outcome of language contact, as do relationships between languages within a contact situation. It is however hard to whole-heartedly agree with the basic starting point in Thomason and Kaufman (1988: 35), that 'it is the sociolinguistic history of the speakers, and not the structure of their language, that is the primary determinant of the linguistic outcome of language contact'. Typologically different linguistic structures tend to change in different ways. For each category, in order to answer the question of how diffusible it is, we need to know its function, expression, and status within the language.

Disentangling similarities due to language contact from those due to genetic inheritance, independent innovation, chance, and typologically natural tendencies is the major challenge for a comparative linguist. There is rarely one reason for any particular contact-induced change: numerous factors conspire in a multiple motivation.

As Burridge put it in §2.4 of Chapter 7, 'most of the changes [in Pennsylvania German] appear to have mongrel origins with a number of different internal and external factors playing a role'. There is no doubt that, because of their common origin, these two genetically related languages (Pennsylvania German and English) 'are "drifting" (à la Sapir) in similar directions; in other words, the seeds for these changes...would have been sown long ago in the proto language.... In some cases English contact would have induced certain of these seeds to sprout. In other cases, it would have stimulated the growth of seedlings that had already emerged.'

Diffusion of grammar in contact is not a unitary mechanism of language change. Foreign forms and patterns make their way into a language through a number of paths—enhancement of an already existing feature, or extension by analogy, or reinterpretation and reanalysis, or areally induced grammaticalization, or grammatical accommodation, or loan translation, or lexical and grammatical parallelism. The status and the expression of a category in interacting languages determines the path.

No linguistic feature is entirely 'borrowing proof'. Neither are linguistic features 'equal'—some are more prone to diffusion than others. We have identified a number of factors favouring the diffusion of features and of forms listed in §4.1. Following the Mutual Reinforcement Principle, the more facilitating factors are at work, the likelier is a form, or a pattern, to be established in a contact-affected language.

But what if the facilitating factors do not work? In other words, which features would we expect to resist contact? These appear to include genetically inherited properties, especially those to do with marking grammatical relations—such as ergative marking in Basque (§3 of Chapter 5), and prefixal marking of possession and subjects in Arawak languages (Chapters 10, 12, and 13). Having strong areal support helps a feature survive and revive—as is the case with number and noun categorization in Nilotic languages (Chapter 3), serial verbs in Likpe (Chapter 4), and the isolating profile of Tetun Dili (Chapter 6). We hypothesize that the kinds of most resistant feature depend on the proto-language, and also on the composition and characteristics of the area itself.

Diffusion is typically affected by attitude to language and by the emblematicity of certain features in a community. A negative attitude to recognizably foreign forms can drastically limit their influx into a language. The overall result of language contact also depends on degrees of knowledge of each other's language, on regularity of contact, and, most importantly, on relations of dominance or rough equality between languages. 'Balanced' language contact, without one language trying to oust the other, goes together with long-standing multilingualism and promotes contact-induced increase in language complexity. This is conducive to language maintenance. The opposite—that is, 'displacive' language contact—promotes language loss and tends to diminish linguistic diversity. However, since, in Stephen Matthews's words (§4.2 of Chapter 9), 'dominance is necessarily a matter of degree', in many language contact scenarios, these two 'ideal' types may be better viewed as extremes on a continuum.

Converging languages in an area are likely to adopt new patterns from multiple sources, or acquire new shared grammatical structures, creating a 'compromise' pattern. Alternatively, one language may adopt the grammar of another—this is a typical result of displacive contact.

The aim of this volume is to evaluate diffusion and linguistic convergence from multiple perspectives, and at various levels—in different language contact situations, by systematically concentrating on diffusion of patterns and concomitant diffusion of forms so as to understand how languages come to share aspects of their grammars.

6 How this volume is organized

The main focus of this volume is on 'layered' languages, with a discernible impact of contact-induced change. It starts with R. M. W. Dixon's analysis of diffusion in the Australian linguistic area (Chapter 2, 'Grammatical diffusion in Australia: free and bound pronouns'). As mentioned in §2.2, Australian languages form a long-standing linguistic area—rather than one genetic unit—characterized by multilateral and multidirectional diffusion, and multiple instances of cyclic development, almost always spread through language contact. This leads to establishing critical structural similarities between languages, and adjoining dialects belonging to different languages, thus adding further complexities to the intricate interweaving of genetic links with areal allegiances.

The next two chapters address different aspects of language contact within the African continent. In Chapter 3, 'How long do linguistic areas last? Western Nilotic grammars in contact', Anne Storch investigates different grammatical consequences of one-to-one language contact between genetically unrelated Belanda Bor (Lwoo of Western Nilotic) and Bviri (Ubangi), and between genetically related languages. Two of these, Luwo and Dinka, belong to one, Western Nilotic, subgroup. Another pair of languages in contact belong to different subgroups of Nilotic: Labwor, a Western Nilotic language, and Karamojong, from Eastern Nilotic. The contact-induced changes are looked at within a larger areal perspective. None of the contacts is particularly long—due to frequent migrations, slave trade, and warfare. In this situation, the features most prone to diffusion are the ones 'that do not violate emblematic patterns and that can be integrated into the system without altering its most basic structures'.

In Chapter 4, 'Grammars in contact in the Volta Basin (West Africa): on contact-induced grammatical change in Likpe', Felix Ameka provides an incisive analysis of the contact-induced changes in Likpe (Na-Togo subgroup of Kwa) which underwent massive impact of patterns (though not so much of forms) from Ewe, a Kwa language of the Gbe subgroup. The contact between Ewe and Likpe is about 300–400 years old, and Likpe shows marked resistance to borrowing forms. The constructions in Likpe which bear an impact from Ewe include marking plural number on kinship terms and proper nouns (developed from a third person pronominal clitic), a O-V-V nominalization strategy, and a number of complementation strategies (some of these involve a borrowed complementizer which coexists with its native synonym). The most spectacular contact-induced change concerns the development of a present progressive construction involving the verb 'hold' in Likpe, which happens to be a lookalike of a progressive marker 'be (at)' in Ewe. This is a prime example of grammatical accommodation. There is an additional factor at work: both languages are spoken in the Volta Basin area, and so the changes come from multiple sources, with areally established constructions overlaying the immediate impact of one language upon another.

The next four chapters focus on Indo-European languages in contact. In Chapter 5, 'Basque in contact with Romance languages', Gerd Jendraschek discusses the impact of Western Romance languages upon the grammar of Basque, focusing on the language actively spoken in the Basque country. Basque has been in contact with Romance languages for about 2,000 years, and the exact source and timing of each contact-induced change is not easy to trace. The major changes include a tendency towards developing analytic constructions, contact-induced enhancement of constructions already existing in Basque (such as number marking on pronouns), reinterpretation of existing structures to fit in with the Romance mould (developing a passive, and postposed relative clauses marked with interrogatives), contact-induced Spanish-style grammaticalizations of verbs 'go' and 'carry' into aspect markers, analogical development of a derivational prefix to match Spanish *re-*, and rampant diffusion of pragmatic patterns. Only some changes are well and truly system altering: despite a superficial Romance flavour to it, Basque remains ergative, and strongly resists borrowed forms.

Tetun Dili, the main lingua franca of East Timor, is an Austronesian language whose predominantly isolating profile has developed as a result of its long-standing interaction with other languages in the area, especially Mambae. An intensive but relatively recent contact with Portuguese has resulted in a number of changes, which include restructuring word classes, decreasing productivity of serial verb constructions, and introducing Portuguese-type clause types and clause-linking devices. This is the topic of Chapter 6, 'Language contact and convergence in East Timor: the case of Tetun Dili', by John Hajek. A further problem in the analysis of Tetun Dili (especially when compared with its archaic varieties) is multiple motivation for syntactic changes, whereby an erstwhile impact from Malay was later reinforced by Portuguese.

What happens if one Germanic language affects another? In Chapter 7, 'Language contact and convergence in Pennsylvania German', Kate Burridge provides a lively account of how Pennsylvania German has been influenced by English. But here is a catch: since the two languages are closely related, every English-looking feature in Pennsylvania German could well be attributed to parallel development, or simple chance. The patterns of constituent order, the progressive construction, the expression of future, the passives, and the case syncretism offer prime examples of multiple motivation where 'language-internal' and 'language-external' factors are hard to disentangle. In Kate Burridge's own words, English acts as a 'fertilizer', pushing ahead a change which was in place already. At the same time, the Pennsylvania German community is gradually becoming more open to the outside, that is to the English-speaking world. As a result, English discourse-pragmatic particles and politeness formula infiltrate the language more and more. But why is it that Pennsylvania German bears a strong impact of English, while the English spoken by the same community is relatively intact? The answer lies in the language attitudes: the Pennsylvania German speakers do not mind speaking a humble 'hybrid' variety of their own language; but are fairly prescriptive as far as their English—a second language—goes.

No volume on language contact is complete without an account of the Balkans—the first linguistic area to have been identified as such. In Chapter 8, 'Balkanizing the Balkan sprachbund: a closer look at grammatical permeability and feature distribution', Victor Friedman provides a list of most salient 'balkanisms', and then examines two groups of features—the marking of future, and markers of deixis and definiteness. He concludes that the 'will' future in the Balkans is 'an example of mutual reinforcement and feature selection that began to take shape in the late middle ages', with western Macedonia and adjacent parts of Albania as the 'epicentre' of the innovation. The features discussed in the chapter 'spread and diminish' around the current South Slavic and adjacent territories which makes these the most central parts of the whole area.

This takes us to other linguistic areas, involving genetically unrelated languages of varied typological profiles. In Chapter 9, 'Cantonese grammar in areal perspective', Stephen Matthews focuses on the role of language contact in the development of Cantonese as the prestige and de facto standard variety of the Yue dialect groups. Striking differences between Cantonese and other Sinitic languages—especially Mandarin Chinese—are indicative of its 'layered' status: Matthews examines the patterns shared with other languages in a broadly defined south-eastern Asian linguistic area, and features shared with non-Sinitic Tai-Kadai and Miao-Yao languages. These include classifiers in possessive constructions and 'bare' classifiers as indicators of definiteness.

The linguistic area of the Vaupés—characterized by obligatory multilingualism controlled by linguistic exogamy, rampant diffusion of patterns, and cultural inhibition against diffusion of actual forms—is perhaps the best researched in the Amazonian region. The area involves Tucanoan, Arawak, and Nadahup (Makú) languages. In Chapter 10, Alexandra Y. Aikhenvald addresses the issues of 'Semantics and pragmatics of grammatical relations in the Vaupés linguistic area'. She starts with recapitulating general properties of the area, and then shows how semantically and pragmatically motivated marking of non-subjects, a strong feature throughout the Vaupés area, originated in Tucanoan, and—permeating both Tariana and Nadahup (Makú) languages—made its way into Tariana, the only Arawak language in the area. The diffusion involved matching pragmatic motivation, semantic motivation, and also grammatical function. Pragmatically determined marking of contrastive subjects, recently developed by some Tucanoan languages, readily infiltrated Tariana. The erstwhile balanced contact within the area resulted in making Tariana more complex, unlike the recent displacive contact with Tucano.

In Chapter 11, 'The Vaupés melting pot: Tucanoan influence on Hup', Patience Epps offers a new perspective on the Vaupés area. She convincingly demonstrates that Hup, a member of the Nadahup (Makú) family, is a bona fide representative of the Vaupés area, despite the fact that the Hup people are outside the exogamous network. The language shares numerous features with the Tucano language (with which it is in constant interaction)—these cover phonology, morphology, and syntax. Hup has developed an extensive system of evidentials, verb compounding, modality, numerals, and even classifiers to match the Tucanoan patterns. None of these features is found in the only member of the Nadahup (Makú) family spoken outside the area. Hup 'embraces the regional equation of language and identity' whereby 'grammatical patterns diffuse easily but borrowing of forms is actively resisted'.

The Arawak language family is the largest and the most diverse in the Amazonian region. Some languages of this family are strikingly unlike their relatives. Amuesha, a 'mystery' language of Amazonia, is one such example. In Chapter 12, 'The Quechua impact in Amuesha, an Arawak language of the Peruvian Amazon', Willem F. H. Adelaar discusses the make-up of Amuesha, disentangling various layers of lexical influence of different Quechua varieties, and the ways in which Quechua could be held accountable for the unusual phonology and morphosyntax of Amuesha. Many non-Arawak—and non-Quechua—features of the language remain unexplained and unexplainable. Many languages which could have played a role in shaping Amuesha are now extinct. We can only speculate— perhaps Amuesha could have been an old trade language which incorporated numerous elements from the then important Quechua; or it is the product of language shift of an unidentified community.

Mawayana is another unusual Arawak language. Unlike Amuesha, it is now moribund—but the few elderly people who speak it speak it well. The language has been influenced by a variety of North Cariban languages, all from the Guiana branch—first the Waiwai complex, and then, quite recently, Trio. Taruma, an isolate whose representatives were part of the Waiwai group, could have also played a role in shaping up Mawayana as it is now. In Chapter 13, 'Feeling the need: the borrowing of Cariban functional categories into Mawayana (Arawak)', Eithne Carlin discusses the various features Mawayana developed as a result of a 'perceivable gap'. These include borrowing an exclusive pronoun, and developing such Cariban-flavoured categories as nominal past, affective marker, frustrative, and similative.

The volume ends with a short 'Glossary of terms' used throughout, within the context of problems linked to how languages affect each other. This is provided in order to avoid terminological confusion, and to make sure the readers understand what the authors have in mind.

In Ameka's words (§6 of Chapter 4), 'a holistic understanding of language change requires multiple perspectives'. Due to the limitations of space, quite a few issues remained untouched—speed of contact and language change, time depth of areal diffusion, people's perception of multilingual situations, to name but a few. To unravel further complexities in language contact, we need many more in-depth factual studies of the 'how' and 'why' of language change. The chapters in this volume provide a start.

References

Abbi, A. (ed.), 1991. *India as a linguistic area revisited.* Special issue of *Language Sciences* 13.2.

—— 2002. 'Restructuring grammars in contact situations: a case of causative constructions in endangered languages', *International Journal of Dravidian Linguistics* 32: 69–80.

Aikhenvald, A. Y. 1990. *Modern Hebrew* [Sovremennyj ivrit]. Moscow: Nauka.

—— 1996. 'Areal diffusion in north-west Amazonia: the case of Tariana', *Anthropological Linguistics* 38: 73–116.

—— 1999a. *Tariana texts and cultural context.* Munich: Lincom Europa.

—— 1999b. 'The Arawak language family', pp. 65–105 of Dixon and Aikhenvald 1999.

—— 1999c. 'Areal diffusion and language contact in the Içana-Vaupés basin, north west Amazonia', pp. 385–415 of Dixon and Aikhenvald 1999.

—— 2000. *Classifiers: a typology of noun categorization devices.* Oxford: Oxford University Press.

—— 2001. 'Areal diffusion, genetic inheritance and problems of subgrouping: a North Arawak case study', pp. 167–94 of Aikhenvald and Dixon 2001a.

—— 2002. *Language contact in Amazonia.* Oxford: Oxford University Press.

—— 2003a. *A grammar of Tariana, from northwest Amazonia.* Cambridge: Cambridge University Press.

—— 2003b. 'Mechanisms of change in areal diffusion: new morphology and language contact', *Journal of Linguistics* 39: 1–29.

—— 2003c. 'Language contact and language change in Amazonia', pp. 1–20 of *Historical linguistics 2001: selected papers from the 15th international conference of historical linguistics, Melbourne, 13–17 August 2001,* edited by B. J. Blake and K. Burridge. Amsterdam: John Benjamins.

—— 2004a. *Evidentiality.* Oxford: Oxford University Press.

—— 2004b. 'Language endangerment in the Sepik area of Papua New Guinea', pp. 97–142 of *Lectures on endangered languages, 5: From Tokyo and Kyoto Conferences 2002,* edited by O. Sakiyama and F. Endo. The project 'Endangered languages of the Pacific Rim'. Suita, Osaka.

—— and Dixon, R. M. W. (eds.). 2001a. *Areal diffusion and genetic inheritance: problems in comparative linguistics.* Oxford: Oxford University Press.

—— —— 2001b. 'Introduction', pp. 1–26 of Aikhenvald and Dixon 2001a.

—— and Militarev, A. Y. 1991. 'Lybic-Guanche languages', pp. 148–266 of *Languages of Asia and Africa,* Vol. 4. Moscow: Nauka.

Ameka, F. K. 2004. 'Grammar and cultural practices: the grammaticalization of triadic communication in West African languages', *Journal of West African Languages* 30: 5–28.

Andersen, H. 1988. 'Centre and periphery: adoption, diffusion and spread', pp. 39–85 of *Historical dialectology,* edited by J. Fisiak. Berlin: Mouton de Gruyter.

Appel, R. and Muysken, P. 1987. *Language contact and bilingualism.* London: Edward Arnold.

Bakker, P. 1996. 'Language intertwining and convergence: typological aspects of the genesis of mixed languages', pp. 9–20 of Haase and Nau 1996*b.*

—— 1997. *A language of our own: the genesis of Michif, the mixed Cree-French language of the Canadian Metis.* Oxford: Oxford University Press.

—— 2000. 'Rapid language change: creolization, intertwining, convergence', pp. 585–620 of *Time depth in historical linguistics,* Vol. 2, edited by C. Renfrew, A. McMahon, and Larry Trask. Cambridge: The McDonald Institute for Archaeological Research.

—— 2003. 'Mixed languages as autonomous systems', pp. 107–50 of Matras and Bakker 2003.

—— 2005. 'The Sri Lanka sprachbund: the newcomers Portuguese and Malay'. To appear in *Language areas,* edited by Y. Matras, A. McMahon, and N. Vincent. Basingstoke: Palgrave Macmillan.

—— and Mous, M. (eds.). 1994. *Mixed languages: 15 case studies in language inter-twining.* Amsterdam: International Journal of American Linguistics.

Beck, D. 2000. 'Grammatical convergence and the genesis of diversity in the North-west Coast *Sprachbund,' Anthropological Linguistics* 42: 147–213.

Bernsten, J. G. and Myers-Scotton, C. 1993. 'English loans in Shona: consequences for linguistic systems', *International Journal of the Sociology of Language* 100–1: 125–48.

Bisang, W. 1996. 'Areal typology and grammaticalization: processes of grammaticalization based on nouns and verbs in east and mainland South East Asian languages', *Studies in Language* 20: 519–98.

Blake, B. 2001. 'Global trends in language', *Linguistics* 39: 1009–28.

Bloomfield, L. 1927. 'Literate and illiterate speech', *American Speech* 2.10: 432–9.

—— 1933. *Language.* London: George Allen and Unwin.

Boas, F. 1917. 'Introductory', *International Journal of American Linguistics*: 1–8.

—— 1920. 'The classification of American languages', *American Anthropologist* 22: 367–76.

Bonvillain, N. 1978. 'Linguistic change in Akwesasne Mohawk: French and English influences', *International Journal of American Linguistics* 44: 31–9.

Borg, A. 1994. 'Some evolutionary parallels and divergencies in Cypriot Arabic and Maltese', *Mediterranean Language Review* 8: 41–67.

Brenzinger, M. 1998. 'Language contact and language displacement', pp. 273–84 of Coulmas 1998.

Bright, W. and Sherzer, J. 1976. 'Areal phenomena in North-American Indian languages', pp. 228–68 of *Variation and change in language: essays by W. Bright.* Stanford, Calif: Stanford University Press.

Brody, J. 1995. 'Lending the "unborrowable": Spanish discourse markers in Indigenous American languages', pp. 132–47 of *Spanish in four continents: studies in language contact and bilingualism*, edited by Carmen Silva-Corvalán. Washington: George-town University Press.

Brown, C. H. 1999. *Lexical acculturation in Native American Languages*. New York: Oxford University Press.

Bunte, P. A. and Kendall, M. B. 1981. 'When is an error not an error? Notes on language contact and the question of interference', *Anthropological Linguistics* 23: 1–7.

Campbell, L. 1987. 'Syntactic change in Pipil', *International Journal of American Linguistics* 53: 253–80.

—— 1993. 'On proposed universals of grammatical borrowing', pp. 91–109 of *Selected papers of the ninth international conference on historical linguistics*, edited by R. Jeffers. Amsterdam: John Benjamins.

—— 1997. 'Amerindian personal pronouns: a second opinion', *Language* 73: 339–51.

—— Kaufman, T. and Smith-Stark, T. 1986. 'Meso-America as a linguistic area', *Language* 62: 530–70.

—— and Muntzel. M. 1989. 'The structural consequences of language death', pp. 181–96 of *Investigating obsolescence: studies in language contraction and death*, edited by N. Dorian. Cambridge: Cambridge University Press.

Chao, Y. 1968. *A grammar of spoken Chinese*. Berkeley and Los Angeles: University of California Press.

Chappell, H. 2001. 'Language contact and areal diffusion in Sinitic languages', pp. 328–57 of Aikhenvald and Dixon 2001*a*.

Clark, R. 1982. ' "Necessary" and "unnecessary" borrowing', pp. 137–43 of *Papers from the third international conference on Austronesian linguistics*, Vol. 3: *Accent on variety*, edited by A. Halim, L. Carrington, and S. A. Wurm. Canberra: Pacific Linguistics.

—— 1994. 'The Polynesian outliers as a locus of language contact', pp. 109–40 of *Language contact and change in the Austronesian world*, edited by T. Dutton and D. T. Tryon. Berlin: Mouton de Gruyter.

Clyne, M. 1987. 'Constraints on code-switching—how universal are they?', *Linguistics* 25: 739–64.

—— 2003. *Dynamics of language contact*. Cambridge: Cambridge University Press.

Coulmas, F. (ed.). 1998. *The handbook of sociolinguistics*. Oxford: Blackwell.

Csató, É. A. 1999. 'Analyzing contact-induced phenomena in Karaim', *BLS* 25: 4–62.

—— 2001. 'Syntactic code-copying in Karaim', pp. 271–83 of *Circum-Baltic languages*, vol. 1: *Past and present*, edited by Ö. Dahl and M. Koptjevskaja-Tamm. Amsterdam: John Benjamins.

Curnow, T. J. 2001. 'What language features can be "borrowed"?', pp. 412–36 of Aikhenvald and Dixon 2001*a*.

Dalton-Puffer, C. 1996. *The French influence on Middle English morphology: a corpus-based study of derivation*. Berlin: Mouton de Gruyter.

Dawkins, R. M. 1916. *Modern Greek in Asia Minor: a study of the dialects of Sílli, Cappadocia and Phárasa with grammar, texts, translations and glossary*. Cambridge: Cambridge University Press.

Dehghani, Y. 2000. *A grammar of Iranian Azari including comparisons with Persian.* Munich: Lincom Europa.

Dench, A. 2001. 'Descent and diffusion: the complexity of the Pilbara situation,' pp. 105–33 of Aikhenvald and Dixon 2001a.

Deutscher, G. 2000. *Syntactic change in Akkadian: the evolution of sentential complementation.* Oxford: Oxford University Press.

Diakonoff, I. M. 1989. *Afrasian languages.* Moscow: Nauka.

Dimmendaal, G. 2001. 'Areal diffusion versus genetic inheritance: an African perspective', pp. 358–92 of Aikhenvald and Dixon 2001a.

Dixon, R. M. W. 1994. *Ergativity.* Cambridge: Cambridge University Press.

—— 1997. *The rise and fall of languages.* Cambridge: Cambridge University Press.

—— 2001. 'The Australian linguistic area', pp. 64–104 of Aikhenvald and Dixon 2001a.

—— 2002. *Australian languages: their origin and development.* Cambridge: Cambridge University Press.

—— and Aikhenvald, A. Y. (eds.). 1999. *The Amazonian languages.* Cambridge: Cambridge University Press.

Dorian, N. C. 2002. 'Diglossia and the simplification of linguistic space', *International Journal of the Sociology of Language* 9: 63–70.

Dozier, E. P. 1956. 'Two examples of linguistic acculturation: the Yaqui of Sonora and Arizona and the Tewa of New Mexico', *Language* 32: 146–57.

Du Bois, J. 1985. 'Competing motivations', pp. 343–66 of *Iconicity in syntax,* edited by John Haiman. Amsterdam: John Benjamins.

Ducos, G. 1979. 'Évolution d'une langue à classes nominales', *La Linguistique* 15.1: 43–54.

Ehala, M. 1994. 'Russian influence and the change in progress in the Estonian adpositional system', *Linguistica Uralica* 30: 177–93.

—— 2000. 'How a man changed a parameter value: the loss of SOV in Estonian subclauses', pp. 73–100 of *Historical linguistics 1995,* Vol. 2: *Germanic linguistics,* edited by R. Hogg and L. van Bergen. Berlin: Mouton de Gruyter.

Emeneau, M. B. 1956. 'India as a linguistic area', *Language* 32: 3–16.

—— 1980. *Language and linguistic area.* Essays by Murray B. Emeneau, selected and introduced by Anwar S. Dil. Stanford, Calif.: Stanford University Press.

Enfield, N. J. 2001. 'On genetic and areal linguistics in mainland South East Asia: parallel polyfunctionality of "acquire"', pp. 255–90 of Aikhenvald and Dixon 2001a.

—— 2005. 'Areal linguistics and mainland Southeast Asia', *Annual Review of Anthropology* 34: 181–206.

Epps, P. 2005. 'Areal diffusion and the development of evidentiality: evidence from Hup', *Studies in Language* 29: 617–50.

Ferguson, C. A. 1964. 'Diglossia', pp. 429–39 of *Language in culture and society,* edited by D. Hymes. New York: Harper International.

Field, F. W. 2001. *Linguistic borrowing in bilingual contexts.* Amsterdam: John Benjamins.

Filppula, M. 2003. 'The quest for the most "parsimonious" explanations: endogeny vs. contact revisited', pp. 161–73 of *Motives for language change*, edited by R. Hickey. Cambridge: Cambridge University Press.

Fishman, J. 1967. 'Bilingualism with and without diglossia; diglossia with and without bilingualism', *Journal of Social Issues* 3: 29–38.

Fleck, D. Forthcoming. *A grammar of Matses*. Berlin: Mouton de Gruyter.

Fodor, I. 1984. 'Language reforms of the past and in the developing countries', pp. 441–54 of *Language reform: history and future*, Vol. 3, edited by I. Fodor and C. Hagège. Hamburg: Buske Verlag.

Foley, W. A. 1986. *The Papuan languages of New Guinea*. Cambridge: Cambridge University Press.

Fortescue, M. 1997. 'Eskimo influence on the formation of the Chukotkan ergative clause', *Studies in Language* 21: 369–409.

—— 2004. 'The westernmost extent of Eskimo languages and their influence in Asia'. Paper delivered at RCLT, La Trobe University.

Friedman, V. A. 1997. 'One grammar, three lexicons: ideological overtones and underpinnings in the Balkan *Sprachbund*', *CLS* 33: 23–44.

—— 2000. 'After 170 years of Balkan linguistics: whither the millennium?', *Mediterranean Language Review* 12: 1–15.

—— 2003. 'Evidentiality in the Balkans with special attention to Macedonian and Albanian', pp. 189–218 of *Studies in evidentiality*, edited by A. Y. Aikhenvald and R. M. W. Dixon. Amsterdam: John Benjamins.

Fries, C. C. and Pike, K. L. 1949. 'Coexistent phonemic systems', *Language* 25: 29–50.

Gardani, F. 2005. *Borrowing of inflectional morphemes in language contact*. MA thesis, University of Vienna.

Gerritsen, M. and Stein, D. (eds.). 1992a. *Internal and external factors in syntactic change*. Berlin: Mouton de Gruyter.

—— —— 1992b. 'On "internal" and "external" in syntactic change', pp. 11–15 of Gerritsen and Stein 1992a.

Golovko, E. 1994. 'Mednyj Aleut or Copper Island Aleut: an Aleut-Russian mixed language', pp. 113–21 of Bakker and Mous 1994.

Greenberg, J. H. 1953. *Essays in linguistics*. Chicago: University of Chicago Press.

Grenoble, L. 2000. 'Morphosyntactic change: the impact of Russian on Evenki', pp. 105–20 of *Languages in contact*, edited by D. G. Gilbers, J. Nerbonne, and J. Schaeken. Amsterdam: Rodopi.

—— and L. J. Whaley. 1998. 'Towards a typology of language endangerment', pp. 22–54 of *Endangered languages*, edited by L. Grenoble and L. J. Whaley. Cambridge: Cambridge University Press.

Gumperz, J. J. and Wilson, R. 1971. 'Convergence and creolization: a case from the Indo-Aryan/Dravidian border in India', pp. 151–68 of *Pidginization and creolization of languages*, edited by D. Hymes. Cambridge: Cambridge University Press.

Haarmann, H. 1970. *Die indirekte Erlebnisform als grammatische Kategorie. Eine Eurasische Isoglosse*. Wiesbaden: Harrassowitz.

Haase, M. 1992. *Sprachkontakt und Sprachwandel im Baskenland. Die Einflüsse des Gaskognischen und Französischen auf das Baskische.* Hamburg: Buske Verlag.

—— and Nau, N. 1996a. 'Einleitung: Sprachkontakt und Grammatikalisierung', pp. 3–8 of Haase and Nau 1996b.

—— —— (eds.). 1996b. *Sprachkontakt und Grammatikalisierung.* Special issue of *Sprachtypologie und Universalienforschung* 49.1.

Hagège, C. 2004. 'On the part played by human conscious choice in language structure and language evolution', pp. 105–17 of *Linguistic diversity and language theories*, edited by Z. Frajzyngier, A. Hodges, and D. Rood. Amsterdam: John Benjamins.

Haig, G. 2001. 'Linguistic diffusion in present-day Anatolia: from top to bottom', pp. 195–224 of Aikhenvald and Dixon 2001a.

Hale, K. 1975. 'Gaps in grammar and culture', pp. 295–315 of *Linguistics and anthropology: in honour of C. F. Voegelin*, edited by M. D. Kinkade et al. Lisse: Peter de Ridder Press.

Harris, A. and Campbell, L. 1995. *Historical syntax in cross-linguistic perspective.* Cambridge: Cambridge University Press.

Hashimoto, M. 1986. 'The Altaicization of Northern Chinese', pp. 76–97 of *Contributions to Sino-Tibetan studies*, edited by J. McCoy and T. Light. Leiden: E. J. Brill.

Haspelmath, M. 2002. 'The European linguistic area: Standard Average European', pp. 1492–510 of *Language typology and language universals: an international handbook*, edited by M. Haspelmath, E. König, W. Oesterreicher, and W. Raible. Berlin: Mouton de Gruyter.

Hasselblatt, C. 1990. *Das estnische Partikelverb als Lehnübersetzung aus dem Deutschen.* Wiesbaden: Otto Harrassowitz.

Haugen, E. 1950. 'The analysis of linguistic borrowing', *Language* 26: 210–31.

—— 1956. *Bilingualism in the Americas: a bibliography and a research guide.* University, Ala.: American Dialect Society.

—— 1969. *The Norwegian language in America: a study in bilingual behavior.* Bloomington: Indiana University Press.

Heath, Jeffrey. 1978. *Linguistic diffusion in Arnhem land.* Australian Aboriginal Studies: Research and Regional Studies 13. Canberra: AIAS.

—— 1981. 'A case of intensive lexical diffusion', *Language* 57: 335–67.

—— 1984. 'Language contact and language change', *Annual Review of Anthropology* 13: 367–84.

—— 1989. *From code-switching to borrowing: a case study of Moroccan Arabic.* London: Kegan Paul International.

—— 1997. 'Lost wax: abrupt replacement of key morphemes in Australian agreement complexes', *Diachronica* 14: 197–232.

—— 1998. 'Hermit crabs: formal renewal of morphology by phonologically mediated affix substitution', *Language* 74: 728–59.

Heine, B., Claudi, U. and Hünnemeyer, F. 1991. *Grammaticalization: a conceptual framework.* Chicago: University of Chicago Press.

—— and Kuteva, T. 2002. *World lexicon of grammaticalization*. Cambridge: Cambridge University Press.

—— —— 2003. 'On contact-induced grammaticalization', *Studies in Language* 27: 529–72.

—— —— 2005. *Language contact and grammatical change*. Cambridge: Cambridge University Press.

Herzog, G. 1941. 'Culture change and language: shifts in the Pima vocabulary', pp. 66–74 of *Language, culture and personality: essays in memory of Edward Sapir*, edited by L. Spier, A. I. Hallowell, and S. S. Newmann. Menasha, Wis.: Sapir Memorial Publication Fund.

Hill, J. and Hill, K. C. 1986. *Speaking Mexicano: dynamics of syncretic language in central Mexico*. Tucson: University of Arizona Press.

Hint, M. 1996. 'Eesti keel okupastiooni järel', *Keel ja kirjandus* 39: 802–8.

Hock, H. H. 2001. 'Typology vs convergence: the issue of Dravidian/Indo-Aryan syntactic similarities revisited', pp. 63–100 of *The yearbook of South Asian languages and linguistics: Tokyo symposium on South Asian languages contact, convergence and typology*, edited by P. Bhaskararao, K. V. Subbarao, and R. Singh. New Delhi: Sage Publications.

Hudson, A. 2000. 'Outline of a theory of diglossia', *International Journal of the Sociology of Language* 9: 1–48.

Jacobsen, W. 1980. 'Inclusive/exclusive: a diffused pronominal category in Native western North America', *Papers from the parasession on pronouns and anaphora*. *BLS*: 204–30.

Jakobson, R. O. 1938. 'Sur la théorie des affinités phonologiques des langues', pp. 48–59 of *Actes du quatrième congrès international de linguistes*. Copenhagen: Einar Munksgaard.

—— 1962*a*. 'Kharakteristike evrazijskogo jazykovogo sojuza' [Towards a characterization of Eurasian Language Union], pp. 144–201 of his *Selected writings*, Vol. 1: *Phonological studies*. The Hague: Mouton.

—— 1962*b*. 'Über die phonologischen Sprachbünde', pp. 137–43 of his *Selected writings*, Vol. 1: *Phonological studies*. The Hague: Mouton.

Jenkins, R. S. 2000. *Language contact and composite structures in New Ireland, Papua New Guinea*. Ph.D. dissertation, University of South Carolina.

Johanson, L. 2002. *Structural factors in Turkic language contacts*. London: Curzon Press.

Joseph, B. 1983. *The synchrony and diachrony of the Balkan infinitive: a study in areal, general, and historical linguistics*. Cambridge: Cambridge University Press.

Jungraithmayr, H. 1995. 'Was ist am Tangale noch tschadisch/hamitosemitisch?', pp. 197–205 of *Sprachkulturelle und historische Forschungen in Afrika*, edited by A. Fleisch and D. Otten. Cologne: Köppe.

—— 2000. 'Chadic—a network of genetic and areal relationships', pp. 90–8 of Zima 2000.

Kastenholz, R. 2002. '"Samogo" language islands, and Mande-Senufo (Gur) interference phenomena', pp. 91–110 of Nicolaï and Zima 2002.

King, R. 1999. *The lexical basis of grammatical borrowing: a Prince Edward Island French case study.* Amsterdam: John Benjamins.

Krauss, M. 1983. 'Slavey Jargon: diffusion of French in Northern Athabaskan'. MS.

Kroskrity, P. V. 1993. *Language, history and identity: ethnolinguistic studies of the Arizona Tewa.* Tucson: University of Arizona Press.

—— 1998. 'Discursive convergence with a Tewa evidential', pp. 25–34 of *The life of language: papers in linguistics in honor of William Bright,* edited by J. H. Hill, P. J. Mistry, and L. Campbell. Berlin: Mouton de Gruyter.

Kruspe, N. 2004. *A grammar of Semelai.* Cambridge: Cambridge University Press.

Kurman, G. 1968. *The development of written Estonian.* Bloomington: Indiana University Press.

Kuteva, T. 2000. 'Areal grammaticalisation: the case of the Bantu-Nilotic borderland', *Folia Linguistica* 34: 267–83.

—— 2001a. 'Large linguistic areas in grammaticalization: auxiliation in Europe', *Language Sciences* 20: 289–311.

—— 2001b. *Auxiliation: an enquiry into the nature of grammaticalization.* Oxford: Oxford University Press.

LaPolla, R. J. 1994. 'Parallel grammaticalizations in Tibeto-Burman languages: evidence of Sapir's "drift"', *Linguistics of the Tibeto-Burman Area* 17: 61–80.

—— 2001. 'The role of migration and language contact in the development of the Sino-Tibetan language family', pp. 225–54 of Aikhenvald and Dixon 2001a.

Laprade, R. A. 1981. 'Some cases of Aymara influence on La Paz Spanish', pp. 207–27 of *The Aymara language in its social and cultural context: a collection of essays on aspects of Aymara language and culture,* edited by M. J. Hardman. Gainesville: University Presses of Florida.

Lass, R. 1997. *Historical linguistics and language change.* Cambridge: Cambridge University Press.

Lehiste, I. 1979. 'Translation from Russian as a source of syntactic change in contemporary Estonian', *CLS: the elements: a parasession on linguistic units and levels:* 413–19.

Li, C. 1986. 'The rise and fall of tones through diffusion', *Proceedings of the Twelfth Annual Meeting of the Berkeley Linguistics Society:* 173–85.

—— and Thompson, S. 1981. *Mandarin Chinese: a functional reference grammar.* Berkeley and Los Angeles: University of California Press.

Liivaku, U. 1993. 'Venepärane rajav kääne' [Russian-like terminative case], *Keel ja Kirjandus* 36: 491–2.

Lindström, E. 2002. *Topics in the grammar of Kuot, a non-Austronesian language of New Ireland, Papua New Guinea.* Ph.D. dissertation, University of Stockholm.

Lipski, J. 1994. *Latin American Spanish.* London: Longman.

Lithgow, D. 1989. 'Influence of English grammar on Dobu and Bunama', pp. 335–48 of *VICAL 1. Oceanic languages: papers from the fifth international conference on Austronesian linguistics.* Auckland: Linguistic Society of New Zealand.

Loveday, L. J. 1996. *Language contact in Japan: a socio-linguistic history.* Oxford: Clarendon Press.

Lynch, J., Ross, M. and Crowley, T. 2003. 'The Oceanic languages', pp. 1–22 of *The Oceanic languages,* edited by J. Lynch, M. Ross, and T. Crowley. London: Curzon.

Masica, C. 1976. *Defining a linguistic area: South Asia.* Chicago: University of Chicago Press.

—— 1991. *Indo-Aryan languages.* Cambridge: Cambridge University Press.

—— 2001. 'The definition and significance of linguistic areas: methods, pitfalls, and possibilities (with special reference to the validity of South Asia as a linguistic area', pp. 205–68 of *The yearbook of South Asian languages and linguistics: Tokyo symposium on South Asian languages contact, convergence and typology,* edited by P. Bhaskararao, K. V. Subbarao, and R. Singh. New Delhi: Sage Publications.

Matisoff, J. A. 1991. 'Areal and universal dimensions of grammatization in Lahu', pp. 383–453 of *Approaches to grammaticalization,* Vol. 2, edited by E. C. Traugott and B. Heine. Amsterdam: John Benjamins.

—— 2001. 'Genetic versus contact relationship: prosodic diffusibility in South-East Asian languages', pp. 291–327 of Aikhenvald and Dixon 2001*a.*

Matras, Y. 1996. 'Prozedurale Fusion: Grammatische Interferenzschichten im Romanes', pp. 60–78 of Haase and Nau 1996*b.*

—— 1998. 'Utterance modifiers and universals of grammatical borrowing', *Linguistics* 36: 281–331.

—— 2000. 'How predictable is contact-induced change in grammar?', pp. 585–620 of *Time depth in historical linguistics,* Vol. 2, edited by C. Renfrew, A. McMahon, and Larry Trask. Cambridge: The McDonald Institute for Archaeological Research.

—— 2002. *Romani: a linguistic introduction.* Cambridge: Cambridge University Press.

—— 2003. 'Mixed languages: re-examining the structural prototype', pp. 151–76 of Matras and Bakker 2003.

—— 2003/4. 'Layers of convergent syntax in Macedonian Turkish', *Mediterranean Language Review* 15: 63–86.

—— and Bakker P. (eds.). 2003. *The mixed language debate.* Berlin: Mouton de Gruyter.

Matthews, S. and Yip, V. 2001. 'Aspects of contemporary Cantonese grammar: the structure and stratification of relative clauses', pp. 266–82 of *Sinitic grammar: synchronic and diachronic perspectives,* edited by H. Chappell. Oxford: Oxford University Press.

Meillet, A. 1948. *Linguistique historique et linguistique générale.* Paris: Librairie Ancienne Honoré Champion.

Mifsud, M. 1995. *Loan verbs in Maltese: a descriptive and comparative study.* Leiden: Brill.

Milroy, J. 1982. 'Probing under the tip of the iceberg: phonological normalisation and the shape of speech communities', pp. 32–48 of *Sociolinguistic variation in speech communities,* edited by S. Romaine. London: Arnold.

Milroy, L. 1987. *Language and social networks*, 2nd edn. Oxford: Blackwell.

Mithun, M. 1992*a*. 'External triggers and internal guidance in syntactic development: coordinating conjunction', pp. 89–129 of Gerritsen and Stein 1992.

—— 1992*b*. 'The substratum in grammar and discourse', pp. 103–15 of *Language contact: theoretical and empirical studies*, edited by E. H. Jahr. Berlin: Mouton de Gruyter.

—— 1999. *The languages of native North America*. Cambridge: Cambridge University Press.

—— 2000. 'Ergativity and language contact on the Oregon Coast: Alsea, Siuslaw and Coos', *BLS* 26: 77–95.

Moravcsik, E. 1978. 'Language contact', pp. 93–123 of *Universals of human languages*, Vol. 1, edited by Joseph H. Greenberg, Charles A. Ferguson, and Edith A. Moravcsik. Stanford, Calif.: Stanford University Press.

Mufwene, S. 2001. *The ecology of language evolution*. Cambridge: Cambridge University Press.

Myers-Scotton, C. 1993. *Social motivations for codeswitching: evidence from Africa*. Oxford: Oxford University Press.

—— 2003. *Contact linguistics*. Oxford: Oxford University Press.

—— and Okeju, J. 1973. 'Neighbours and lexical borrowings', *Language* 49: 871–89.

Nadkarni, M. V. 1975. 'Bilingualism and syntactic change in Konkani', *Language* 51: 672–83.

Nau, N. 1995. *Möglichkeiten und Mechanismen kontaktbewegten Sprachwandels unter besonderer Berücksichtigung des Finnischen*. Munich: Lincom Europa.

Newman, S. 1974. 'Linguistics retention and diffusion in Bella Coola', *Language in Society* 2: 201–14.

Nichols, J. 1986. 'Head-marking and dependent-marking grammars', *Language* 62: 56–119.

—— 1996. 'The comparative method as heuristic', pp. 39–71 of *The comparative method reviewed: regularity and irregularity in language change*. Oxford: Oxford University Press.

Nicolaï, R. and Zima, P. (eds.). 2002. *Lexical and structural diffusion: interplay of internal and external factors of language development in the West African Sahel*. Publications de la Faculté des Lettres, Arts et Sciences humaines de Nice et de la Faculté des Études Humaines, Université Charles de Prague.

Nurse, D. 2000. *Inheritance, contact, and change in two East African languages*. Cologne: Rudiger Köppe Verlag.

—— and Hinnebusch, T. J. 1993. *Swahili and Sabaki: a linguistic history*. University of California publications in linguistics 121. Behelay and Los Angeles: University of California Press.

Owens, J. 1996. 'Grammatisierung, Semantisierung und Sprachkontakt: Arabisch im Tschad-See-Gebiet', pp. 79–85 of Haase and Nau 1996*b*.

Perry, J. R. 1979. 'Uzbek influence on Tajik syntax: the converb constructions', *CLS: The Elements: a parasession on linguistic units and levels: papers from the conference on Non-Slavic languages of the USSR*: 448–61.

Pontius, J. 1997. 'Language codification and the perception of otherness: the case of Czech and German', *CLS* 33: 23–44.

Prunet, J.-F. 1990. 'The origin and interpretation of French loans in Carrier', *International Journal of American Linguistics* 56: 484–503.

Raag, V. 1998. *The effects of planned change on Estonian morphology.* Acta Universitatis Upsaliensis, Studia Uralica Upsaliensia 29. Uppsala: Uppsala University Press.

Rayfield, J. R. 1970. *The languages of a bilingual community.* The Hague: Mouton.

Riionheimo, H. 1998. 'Morphological attrition and interference in language contact: sketching the framework', pp. 246–68 of *Language contact, variation and change,* edited by J. Niemi, T. Odlin, and J. Heikkinen. Joensuu: University of Joensuu.

—— 2002. 'How to borrow a bound morpheme? Evaluating the status of structural interference in a contact between closely related languages', *SKY Journal of Linguistics* 15: 187–218.

Rivierre, J.-C. 1994. 'Contact-induced phonological complexification in New Caledonia', pp. 497–522 of *Language contact and change in the Austronesian world,* edited by T. Dutton and D. T. Tryon. Berlin: Mouton de Gruyter.

Roberts, J. R. 1997. 'Switch-reference in Papua New Guinea: a preliminary survey', pp. 101–241 of *Papers in Papuan linguistics* 3. Canberra: Pacific Linguistics.

Ross, M. D. 1988. *Proto-Oceanic and the Austronesian languages of Western Melanesia.* Pacific Linguistics C-98. Canberra: ANU.

—— 1994. 'Areal phonological features in north central New Ireland', pp. 523–72 of *Language contact and change in the Austronesian world,* edited by T. Dutton and D. T. Tryon. Berlin: Mouton de Gruyter.

—— 1996. 'Contact-induced change and the comparative method: cases from Papua New Guinea', pp. 180–217 of *The comparative method reviewed: irregularity and regularity in language change,* edited by M. Durie and M. D. Ross. New York: Oxford University Press.

—— 2001. 'Contact-induced change in Oceanic languages in northwest Melanesia', pp. 134–66 of Aikhenvald and Dixon 2001a.

—— 2003. 'Diagnosing prehistoric language contact', pp. 174–98 of *Motives for language change,* edited by R. Hickey. Cambridge: Cambridge University Press.

Sapir, E. 1921. *Language.* New York: Harcourt, Brace & World.

Savà, G. 2002. 'Ts'amakko morphological borrowings in Ongota (or Birale)', *Afrikanistische Arbeitspapiere* 71: 75–94.

Schaengold, C. C. 2004. *Bilingual Navajo: mixed codes, bilingualism, and language maintenance.* Ph.D. dissertation, Ohio State University.

Schiffrin, H. 1998. 'Diglossia as a sociolinguistic situation', pp. 205–16 of Coulmas 1998.

Schmidt, A. 1985. *Young people's Dyirbal: an example of language death from Australia.* Cambridge: Cambridge University Press.

Seki, L. 1999. 'The Upper Xingu as an incipient linguistic area', pp. 417–30 of Dixon and Aikhenvald 1999.

Sherzer, J. 1973. 'Areal linguistics in North America', pp 749–95 of *Current trends in linguistics*, 10, edited by T. Sebeok. The Hague: Mouton.

—— 1976. *An areal-typological study of American Indian languages north of Mexico.* North-Holland Linguistic Series 20. Amsterdam: North Holland.

Silva-Corvalán, C. 1995. 'The study of language contact: an overview of the issues', pp. 1–13 of *Spanish in four continents: studies in language contact and bilingualism*, edited by Carmen Silva-Corvalán. Washington: Georgetown University Press.

Slater, K. W. 2002. *A grammar of Mangghuer: a Mongolic language of China's Qinghai-Gansu Sprachbund.* London: Routledge Curzon.

Smith, I. 1986. 'Language contact and the life or death of Kugu Muminh', pp. 513–32 of *The Fergusonian impact: in honor of Charles A. Ferguson on the occasion of his 65th birthday*, Vol. 2: *Sociolinguistics and the sociology of language*, edited by J. A. Fishman, A. Tabouret-Keller, M. Clyne, Bh. Krishnamurti, and M. Abdulaziz. Berlin: Mouton de Gruyter.

Smith-Stark, S. 1974. 'The plurality split', *Papers from the annual regional meeting of the Chicago Linguistic Society* 10: 657–71.

Soper, J. 1996. *Loan syntax in Turkic and Iranian.* Bloomington, Ind.: Eurolingua.

Stolz, C. and Stolz, T. 1996. 'Funktionswortenentlehnung in Mesoamerika. Spanisch-amerindischer Sprachkontakt (Hispanoindiana II)', *STUF* 49: 86–123.

Stolz, T. 1991. *Sprachbund im Baltikum? Estnisch und Lettisch im Zentrum einer sprachlichen Konvergenzlandschaft.* Bochum: Universitätsverlag Cr. N. Brockmeyer.

Storch, A. 2003. 'Layers of language contact in Jukun', pp. 176–95 of *Dynamics of systems: lexical diffusion, language contacts and creolisation in West Africa*, edited by P. Zima, J. Jeník, and V. Tax. Prague: Pastelka.

Swadesh, M. 1951. 'Diffusional cumulation and archaic residue as historical explanations', *Southwestern Journal of Anthropology* 7: 1–21.

Talmy, L. 1982. 'Borrowing semantic space: Yiddish verb prefixes between Germanic and Slavic', *Proceedings of the Berkeley Linguistics Society* 8: 231–50.

Tauli, V. 1984. 'The Estonian language reform', pp. 309–30 of *Language reform: history and future*, vol. 3, edited by I. Fodor and C. Hagège. Hamburg: Buske Verlag.

Thomason, S. G. 1997. 'On mechanisms of interference', pp. 181–208 of *Language and its ecology: essays in Memory of Einar Haugen*, edited by S. Eliasson and E. H. Jahr. Berlin: Mouton de Gruyter.

—— 2000. 'On the unpredictability of contact effects', *Estudios de sociolinguistica* 1: 173–82.

—— 2001a. *Language contact: an introduction.* Edinburgh: Edinburgh University Press.

—— 2001b. 'Contact-induced typological change', pp. 1640–8 of *Language typology and language universals: an international handbook*, edited by M. Haspelmath, E. König, W. Oesterreicher, and W. Raible. Berlin: Walter de Gruyter.

—— 2003. 'Contact as a source of language change', pp. 687–712 of *The handbook of historical linguistics*, edited by B. D. Joseph and R. D. Janda. Oxford: Blackwell.

—— and Kaufman, T. 1988. *Language contact, creolization and genetic linguistics.* Berkeley and Los Angeles: University of California Press.

Thurston, W. R. 1987. *Processes of change in the languages of northwestern Britain*. Canberra: Pacific Linguistics.

—— 1989. 'How esoteric languages build a lexicon: esoterogyny in West New Britain', pp. 555–80 of *VICAL 1: Oceanic languages: papers from the fifth international conference on Austronesian linguistics*. Auckland: Linguistic Society of New Zealand.

—— 1994. 'Renovation and innovation in the languages of northwestern New Britain', pp. 573–610 of *Language contact and change in the Austronesian world*, edited by T. Dutton and D. T. Tryon. Berlin: Mouton de Gruyter.

Tosco, M. 1996. 'Morfologia italiana in Maltese', pp. 319–32 of *Semitica: seria philologica Constantino Tsereteli dedicata*, edited by R. Contini, F. A. Pennacchietti, and M. Tosco. Turin: Silvio Zamorani editore.

—— 2000. 'Is there an "Ethiopian linguistic area"?', *Anthropological Linguistics* 42: 329–65.

Trask, L. 1998. 'The typological position of Basque: then and now', *Language Sciences* 20: 313–24.

—— 2000. *The dictionary of historical and comparative linguistics*. Edinburgh: Edinburgh University Press.

Trubetzkoy, N. S. 1939. 'Gedanken über das Indogermanenproblem', *Acta Linguistica* (*Hafniensa*) 1: 81–9.

Trudgill, P. 1995. 'Grammaticalisation and social structure: non-standard conjunction-formation in East Anglian English', pp. 136–47 of *Grammar and meaning: essays in honour of Sir John Lyons*, edited by F. R. Palmer. Cambridge: Cambridge University Press.

—— 2004. *New dialect formation: the inevitability of colonial Englishes*. Oxford: Oxford University Press.

Tsitsipis, L. D. 1998. *A linguistic anthropology of praxis and language shift: Arvanítika (Albanian) and Greek in contact*. Oxford: Clarendon Press.

Vočadlo, O. 1938. 'Some observations on mixed languages', pp. 169–76 of *4th International Congress of Linguists*. Copenhagen: Actes.

Weinreich, U. 1953. *Languages in contact*. New York: Linguistic Circle of New York.

Whitney, W. D. 1881. 'On mixture in language', *Transactions of the American Philosophical Association* 12: 1–26.

Windfuhr, G. L. 1990. 'Persian', pp. 523–46 of *The world's major languages*, edited by B. Comrie. New York: Oxford University Press.

Wolff, E. 1983. 'Tonogenese in tschadischen Sprachen', *Afrika und Übersee* 66: 203–20.

Zima, P. (ed.). 2000. *Areal and genetic factors in language classification and description: Africa south of the Sahara*. Munich: Lincom Europa.

Zuckermann, G. 2003. *Language contact and lexical enrichment in Israeli Hebrew*. Basingstoke: Palgrave Macmillan.

2

Grammatical Diffusion in Australia
Free and Bound Pronouns[1]

R. M. W. DIXON

1 Introduction

Aboriginal people and their languages have been in Australia for at least 40,000 years. The first settlers, speaking one or more languages, would within a few thousand years have spread out over the whole continent; at that time, a 'family tree' model of relationships would probably have been retrievable. This initial phase was then followed by tens of millennia of an 'equilibrium situation' (see Dixon 1997: 67–96), during which the overall number of languages would have remained roughly constant; the number might from time to time have doubled or halved, as water resources waxed and waned, but would not have changed in any more extreme fashion. The people were typically multilingual and there was constant social interaction, so that grammatical and phonological features— and lexemes—underwent steady geographical diffusion.

At the time of European invasion (a couple of centuries ago) there were around 250 distinct languages in Australia. By application of the standard methodology of comparative linguistics, about forty low-level genetic groups can be recognized (most with just two or three members, none with more than fifteen), plus scores of isolates. It is not feasible to set up an all-encompassing 'family tree' of Australian languages. (The much-vaunted 'Pama-Nyungan' idea—founded on lexicostatistics, and later reinterpreted in other terms—is not defensible scientifically. A lengthy discussion of the history of the idea, and its insufficiency, is in Dixon 2001: 89–98; 2002: 44–54.)

The languages of Australia share a broad typological profile, but differ in terms of a number of phonological and grammatical parameters, all with an

[1] Thanks are due to Alexandra Aikhenvald, Alan Dench, Amee Glass, Cliff Goddard, Ken Hansen, and Stephen Morey for perceptive and constructive comments on a draft of this chapter.

areal basis. This is exemplified through the thirty or so maps of feature distribution in my recent book *Australian languages: their nature and development* (Dixon 2002), dealing with such things as laminal and apical contrasts for consonants, number of rhotic phonemes, dropping of initial consonants and syllables, vowel systems and vowel length, types of verbal organization, noun incorporation, noun classes and gender, and switch-reference marking.[2] The present chapter will focus on bound and free personal pronouns, with two specific case studies.

2 Syntactic orientation

The ancestral situation in Australia was for syntactic relations to be marked in different ways on pronouns and on nominals—a mixed accusative/ergative system. In a number of languages one finds (using the standard abbreviations: A, transitive subject; S, intransitive subject; and O, transitive object):

- Singular free pronouns: A/S/O, i.e. all of A, S, and O marked differently, a tripartite system.
- Non-singular free pronouns: AS/O, with A and S marked in the same way (nominative) and O marked differently (accusative).
- Nouns and adjectives: A/SO, with S and O marked in the same way (absolutive) and A marked differently (ergative).

There are then the recurrent developments:

(i) A and S come to be marked in the same way for singular pronouns, bringing them into line with the non-singulars. We then have all pronouns on an AS/O—accusative (ACC)—system and all nominals on an A/SO—ergative (ERG)—system.

(ii) Bound pronouns develop out of the free ones, and show the same ACC system. Bound pronouns are at first optional. The system then becomes obligatory with the result that free pronouns are used only sparingly, mostly for emphasis or as a one-word response to a question.

(iii) Free pronouns, which are then used selectively, come to function like nominals, with an ERG pattern.

---

[2] If the 'Pama-Nyungan'/'non-Pama-Nyungan' distinction were a viable one, it would surely be expected that a good few of the distributions of linguistic features would relate to this distinction. In fact they do not.

In summary:

	NOUNS AND ADJECTIVES	FREE PRONOUNS SINGULAR	FREE PRONOUNS NON-SINGULAR	BOUND PRONOUNS
original	ERG (A/SO)	A/S/O	ACC (AS/O)	—
(i)	ERG (A/SO)		ACC (AS/O)	—
(ii)	ERG (A/SO)		ACC (AS/O)	ACC (AS/O)
(iii)	ERG (A/SO)		ERG (A/SO)	ACC (AS/O)

Languages are attested at every stage of this development.

3 Free and bound pronouns

Some languages have a single set of personal pronouns, whereas others have two sets, typically called 'free' and 'bound' pronouns. For example, Heffernan (1984: 25) provides alternative versions of a sentence in the Luritja dialect, (g), of the Western Desert language (WD):

(1) (a) ŋayulu   njuntu-nja   pu-ŋu
          1sg:NOMINATIVE   2sg-ACCUSATIVE   hit-PAST
          I hit you

     (b) pu-ŋu-rna-nta
          hit-PAST-1sg:NOMINATIVE-2sg:ACCUSATIVE
          I hit you

Sentence (1a), with free pronouns (which are separate words) preceding the verb, has essentially the same meaning as (1b), with bound pronouns encliticized to the verb.

There is no constant set of criteria for deciding whether a given pronominal is free or bound. We can, however, contrast the properties of free and bound pronouns in Australian languages, in Table 1. Taking these properties together, it is always possible to decide what is a bound pronoun.

Slightly more than half of Australian languages have bound pronouns, as shown in Map 1. Note that, for ease of reference the c.250 languages are organized into fifty groups, labelled A-Y, WA-WM (where W stands for west), and NA-NL (where N stands for north).[3] Some groups have a genetic

---

[3] Groups NA–NL are those considered to be 'non-Pama-Nyungan' in the current version of the 'Pama-Nyungan hypothesis'; this convention has been chosen so that the reader may readily perceive that the boundary between NA–NL and other groups only corresponds to one of the feature distribution boundaries shown in the maps of Dixon (2002).

TABLE 1. Contrastive properties of free and bound pronouns

	Free pronoun	Bound pronoun
FUNCTION	Functions as head of an NP, and may be substitutable by a noun. Can generally take modifiers within its NP.	Is not head of an NP. Is not substitutable by a noun. Takes no modifiers.
POSITION	Has the freedom of positioning of words within an NP, and of NPs within a clause (and thus of words within a clause).	If prefix or suffix to verb, has fixed position within the verb. If enclitic, may only occur at one (or perhaps one or two) positions in the clause; see (VII) in §4.
FORM	Is one phonological word and one grammatical word. In most (but not quite all) languages, must be of at least two syllables. Can never be zero form.	Almost always has status of clitic (separate grammatical word but not a distinct phonological word) or affix. Often constitutes a single syllable. One or more terms in system may have zero realization (these generally include third person singular).
DISCOURSE PROPERTIES	Typically used for first mention of a participant, for special emphasis, and/or in verbless clauses.	Obligatory in some languages. Optional in others; then, typically used to mark inter-clausal cohesion.
PERSONS	Sometimes free pronouns for all three persons; other times only for first and second persons (with the function of third person covered in part by demonstratives).	There are generally bound pronouns for all three persons.

basis, others being simply geographical. There are sometimes subdivisions, shown by a, b, …; individual languages are indicated by a final number. For example, the Western Victoria geographical group, T, involves the Kulin genetic group, Ta, with three languages (Ta1, Wemba-Wemba; Ta2, Watha-wurrung; and Ta3, Wuy-wurrung), the Tb genetic group (Tb1, Bungandik; and Tb2, Kuurn-kopan-noot), and the single language Tc, Kolakngat (there is insufficient information available to decide whether this extinct language had a close genetic link with Ta or with Tb). A full list of languages is in Dixon (2002: pp. xxx–xlii).

Bound pronouns originated as clitics and in some languages retain this status. In others they have developed into suffixes or prefixes; if they became affixes to the verb, then bound pronouns have often fused with adjacent tense or other affixes; full details are in chapters 8 and 9 of Dixon (2002). A major division is between languages with prefixes (which always include pronominal prefixes) as well as suffixes, and those which only employ suffixes. Prefixing languages are shown by vertical shading in Map 1. (Note that the prefixing/non-prefixing distinction is the only parameter which coincides roughly—although not precisely—with the putative classes of 'non-Pama-Nyungan' and 'Pama-Nyungan' languages.)

It will be seen that bound pronouns are found in three main geographical areas:

- A very large continuous region in the north, centre, and west (including all the prefixing languages).
- A fairly large region in the south-east (excluding four of the five languages in areal group U, and one dialect of language Ta1, Wemba-Wemba; see §5).
- An area in the north-east, including a number of languages from genetic group B, geographical group D, and group C (which comprises a single language).

There are, in addition, small pockets of bound pronouns in Eb, Ee, Ja, and W.

The fascinating thing is that the bound pronoun isogloss often runs through one genetic group. This applies for genetic groups B in the north-east, Ja in the central east, WM in the north centre, Na in the south-east, and Y in the central north. Indeed, this isogloss can also divide dialects within one language. The occurrence of types of free and bound pronouns in two such languages—Ta1, Wemba-Wemba, and WD, the Western Desert language—are discussed in some detail in §§5–6. Before getting into that, we need to summarize some of the parameters of variation for bound pronouns.

4 Parameters of variation for bound pronouns

(I)   Types of grammatical relations involved. A bound pronoun can relate to:

(*a*) An argument of a clause—a core argument in A, S or O function, or a peripheral argument (such as might be marked by dative or locative case on an NP).

(*b*) The possessive relation within an NP.

About seventy languages show both (*a*) and (*b*), and about fifty have just (*a*). For there to be bound possessive pronouns, (*b*)—covering more than kinship

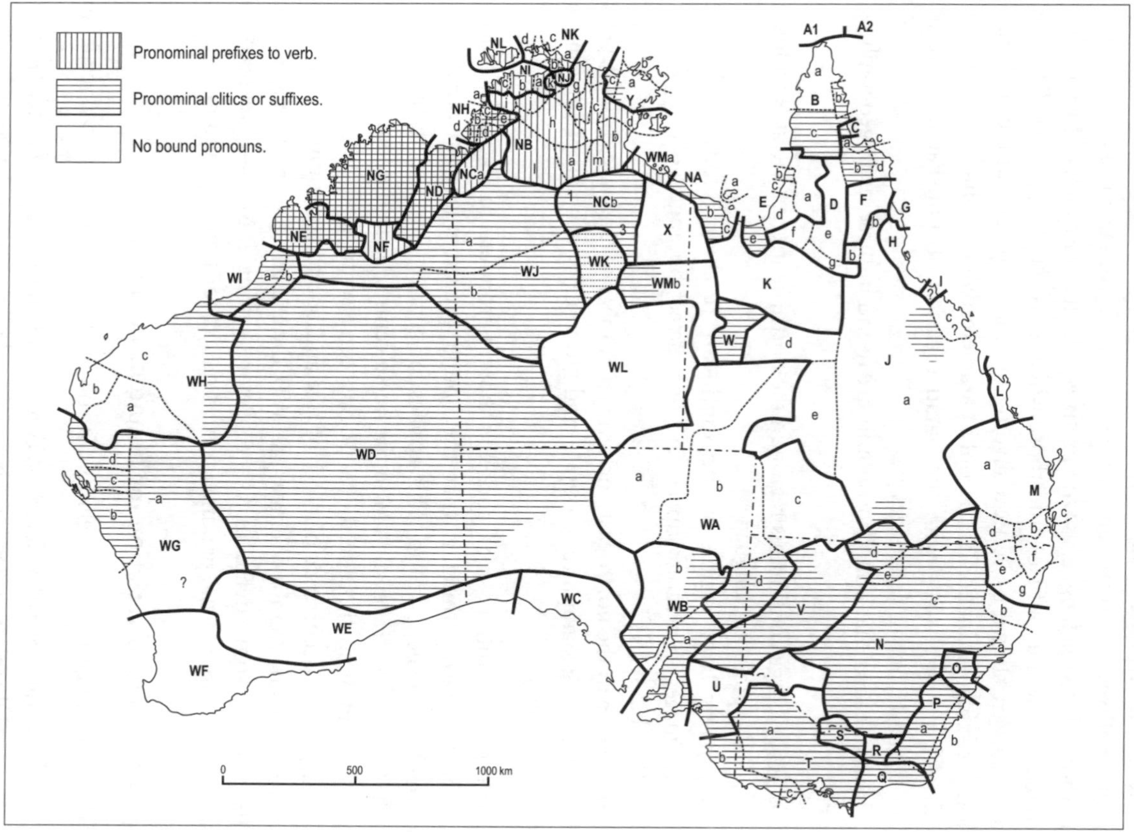

MAP 1 Distribution of bound pronouns

relations—without bound pronouns for clausal arguments, (*a*), is rare, being known only for the Mathi-Mathi dialect of Ta1, Wemba-Wemba, and the Gurnu dialect of V, Baagandji (see §5).

In most languages, bound pronouns marking possession have different forms from those marking clausal arguments (examples are in §5). However, in some languages, just as a free pronoun may combine dative function as a clausal argument and genitive function as a modifier to the head of an NP, so a bound pronoun may also combine these properties. For example, the Ngaanjatjarra dialect, (*i*), of WD has 1sg bound pronoun -*tju* both as marker of indirect object (here, beneficiary) within a clause, as in (2a), and of possessor within an NP, as in (2b) (Glass and Hackett 1970: 42–3):

(2) (a) ninti-la-tju   (b) kuka-tju
          give-IMPERATIVE-1sg:DATIVE   meat-1sg:GENITIVE
          Give (it) to me!   my meat

In a handful of languages, one set of bound pronouns functions both as direct object and as possessive marker. For example, in Tb2, Kuurn-kopan-noot (Blake 2003*a*: 40–3), 1sg -*ŋan*, may mark the object argument of a clause, as in (3a), or the possessor of a noun, as in (3b):

(3) (a) pund-an-ŋan   kuramuk-a
          bite-PAST-1sg:ACCUSATIVE   possum-ERGATIVE
          The possum bit me

     (b) tjerapin   kulaŋ-ŋan
          hurt   head-1sg:GENITIVE
          My head hurts

(II) Which arguments are encoded.

Only a few Australian languages have bound pronouns for a single core argument; this is always S in an intransitive and A in a transitive clause. The great majority of languages may include two bound pronouns in each clause. For some languages, the arguments coded are always A and O in a transitive clause; for other languages, one argument is A and the other can either be indirect object (or some peripheral argument) or O, usually with different bound pronominal forms for the different arguments.

(III) Syntactic orientation.

As mentioned in §2, bound pronouns are prototypically on an accusative (ACC) basis, with one form for A and S and another for O function. Just a few languages display an ergative (ERG) system for free pronouns, and also for bound pronouns, which have recently developed from their free congeners—on the evidence of similarity of forms—effectively reversing steps (ii) and (iii) from §2. That is, free pronouns would have taken on an ERG system, like nouns, and bound pronouns then developed from free, also with an ERG system. All pronouns and nominals now inflect in the same way, with one marking for S and O and another for A.

(IV) Choice between free and bound pronouns.

For a language with both free and bound pronouns, when should one employ each of these? Varying principles apply in different languages. The main possibilities are:

(*a*) *Bound pronouns obligatory for core functions* (in some or all clause types). Free pronouns are essentially an optional extra, for emphasis or contrast. In some languages, where bound pronouns are attached to the verb, free pronouns occur in verbless clauses (such as a one-word reply to a question, which can be a free pronoun).

(*b*) *Bound pronouns not obligatory.* There are then two types of language:
   Bound and free pronouns (referring to the same argument) may co-occur.
   A given argument may be expressed by a bound or a free pronoun, not by both.

In languages of type (*b*) a free pronoun may be used for first mention of a discourse participant, with a bound pronoun being preferred thereafter.

(V) Forms.

Some bound pronouns are identical in form to the corresponding free pronouns, or are a transparent reduction from them (for example, just omitting the initial consonant). This indicates that the system of bound pronouns has developed rather recently from the system of free forms. Alternatively, bound pronouns may have a quite different form from the corresponding free pronouns, indicating that they developed at a fair time in the past. In a number of languages, just some bound pronouns are transparently related to free forms.

(VI) Person and number.

All languages have free form pronouns for first and second person, almost always in three numbers—singular, dual, and plural. Many also show a distinction between inclusive and exclusive for first person non-singulars. Some include third person in the paradigm, with similar categories and inflections to first and second persons. In other languages, there are no third person free pronouns per se, some of the functional load normally assumed by them being taken up by demonstratives.

As indicated in Table 1, languages with a full set of bound pronouns almost always include third person in the system. Quite often, third singular (in some of its functions) is realized by zero. In just a few languages there can be a degree of neutralization for bound pronouns—between second and third person in non-singular number, or between dual and plural number. There are also languages with a partial set of bound pronouns, for just some person/number combinations; this is illustrated for WD dialects in §6.

(VII) Position.

Most often, all bound pronouns relating to core arguments occur together, on the same participant. Sometimes their ordering is decided by person (most often first person before second before third) and sometimes by function (either A before O, or O before A). In a number of languages there are more complex principles of ordering.

Bound pronominal prefixes and suffixes are always attached to the verb, as are proclitics in the only language in which they occur. Bound pronouns with the status of enclitics have varying attachment:

(*a*) After the verb.

(*b*) After the first constituent of the clause.

(*c*) After the word immediately preceding the verb.

Most languages restrict their pronominal enclitics to just one of these positions; a few allow either (*a*) or (*b*), some either (*a*) or (*c*). In a number of languages, bound pronouns attach to a special auxiliary constituent, which may itself be in position (*a*) or (*b*); it is not reported in the rather uncommon position (*c*).

Bound pronouns in possessive function always attach to the noun referring to the thing (or person) possessed.

Note that only a brief summary of parameters (I)–(VII) has been possible here; an exhaustive account will be found in Dixon (2002: 344–76).

We can now proceed to case studies of two multidialectal languages for which the free and bound pronouns show variations. Note that, within the limits of this chapter, I have not been able to provide an absolutely exhaustive account of the pronouns in either language. (For example, there is no mention here of the special marking for imperatives.)

The information in §§5–6 is based on hundreds of sources. It would not be practical to list them all here, and it would break up the text to provide the source for every fact mentioned. I have included the most important sources in the list of references, with an indication of which language and dialect(s) each relates to.

5 The Wemba-Wemba language (Ta1)

This language was spoken over a considerable area of western Victoria north of the Great Dividing Range, involving about a dozen distinct tribes. Recognizing 'a language' on the basis of mutual intelligibility of adjacent dialects, there seems little doubt that a single language was shared by these tribes. On the information available, the tribal dialects had very similar grammars (the major differences relating to free and bound pronouns, discussed here) and also vocabularies. Each dialect had about 80 per cent vocabulary in common with its neighbours, and the furthest dialects (Latji-Latji and Jaja-wurrong) share 63 per cent, even though 300 kilometres apart and separated by several other tribes. However, words turn up in a slightly different form in different areas—one dialect may omit a medial vowel, or a final vowel, or a final consonant, or even a final syllable. For example, Hercus (1986: 291) gives 'woman' as *laiurg* or *leurg* in Tjatjala (dialect set J), as *lerg* in Wemba-Wemba (set W), and as *laiur* in Mathi-Mathi (set M).

The last of these dialects ceased to be used many generations ago. In a superb piece of salvage linguistics, Luise Hercus recorded all she could from the last rememberers of the Mathi-Mathi, Tjatjala, and Wemba-Wemba dialects during the 1960s. All other information comes from amateur sources, and was gathered between 1841 and 1911. For the surrounding languages, information is similarly limited and often patchy.

Ta1, Wemba-Wemba, appears to make up a small genetic group (Ta) with its neighbours to the south-east: Ta2, Watha-wurrung, and Ta3, Wuy-wurrung; it shares about 45 per cent vocabulary with each and also many similarities of grammatical form. To the south are Tb1, Bungandik; and Tb2, Kuurn-kopan-noot, which probably also make up a small genetic group. Although Wemba-Wemba shares about 45 per cent vocabulary with each of these languages, grammatical forms are markedly different, making unlikely a close genetic connection between Ta and Tb.

Ta1's other neighbours are vastly different both in vocabulary (all score less than 15 per cent with Ta1) and in grammar; these are the five tribes in the Lower Murray areal group, U, to the west and north; and Nc2, Wiradhurri, and the two languages in areal group S (S1, Yota-Yota, and S2, Yabala-Yabala), to the east.

The northerly dialects of Ta1 were named by a reduplication of the word for 'no' (as also their northerly neighbour, U5, Yitha-Yitha). Southerly dialects were named by a descriptive label plus -*wurrong* 'lip, speech'. For example, Dawson (1881: 1) states that the language of the Kolor (Mount Rouse) tribe 'is called "Chaap wuurong," meaning "soft" or "broad lip," in contradistinction to other dialects of harder pronunciation'. The same method of naming was used for Ta2, Ta3, and some dialects of Tb2, to the east and south. As elsewhere in Australia, there was no overall term for the set of mutually intelligible dialects making up the one language, Ta1; I have chosen the name of the central dialect about which we have the fullest information as label for the entire language, Wemba-Wemba.

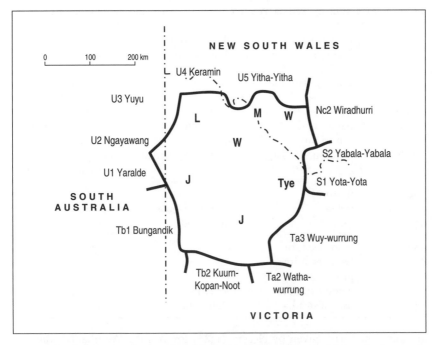

MAP 2 The Wemba-Wemba language (Ta1), with dialect sets and neighbouring languages

For present purposes—the description of pronouns—the dialects of Ta1 can be placed in five sets (see Map 2):

- Set L, including Ladji-Ladji and Wadi-Wadi, in the north-west. There are vocabularies for these dialects but negligible grammatical information; as a consequence, they cannot be included in this study.
- Set M, consisting of one dialect, Mathi-Mathi, in the north; surrounded on three sides by U5, Yitha-Yitha.
- Set W, in the north centre, including Wemba-Wemba, Baraba, and Baraba-Baraba.
- Set Tye, consisting of one dialect 'Tyeddyuwurru', its grammar known only from a six-page account, in German, by Mathews (1904a).[4]
- Set J, a fair number of dialects in the southern part of the language area, including Tjatjala, and Jaap-wurrong (Dawson's Chaap Wuurong).

The forms of the main free and bound pronouns in AS function, and the possessive bound pronouns, for dialect set W are shown in Table 2; these

---

[4] There are other sources which just provide word lists in the dialect, spelling the name as 'Jaja-wrong' and 'Ja-jow-er-ong'.

TABLE 2. Pronouns in Wemba-Wemba, Baraba-Baraba, and Baraba dialects (set W)

	Free pronouns A and S functions	Bound pronouns A and S functions	Bound pronouns possessive function
1 sg	yandaŋ, ŋatj, yedi	-an(da)	-eg (-andag after a case suffix), -ag
1 du inc	ŋal(ein)	-a-ŋal	-a-(ŋa)l(-ag)
1 du exc	ŋal-aŋ	-a-ŋal-aŋ	-a-(ŋa)l(-ag)-aŋ
1 pl inc	yaŋur(ein)	-a-ŋur	-a-ŋur-a(g)
1 pl exc	yaŋuraŋ, yandaŋ	-a-ŋur-aŋ, -andaŋ	-a-ŋur-ag-aŋ, -a-ŋandaŋ, -andag
2 sg	ŋin(din)	-ar	-in
2 du	ŋulen	-a-wal, -a-ŋula	-al-ag
2 pl	ŋud(ein)	-adj, -ŋuda	-ad-ag
3 sg	<no free form 3rd person free pronouns;	ø	-ug
3 du	demonstratives	-bula(ŋ)	-bul-ag
3 pl	used instead>	-(dh)an(a)	-djan-ag

combine the forms given by Hercus (1986) for Wemba-Wemba, by Mathews (1902a) for Baraba, and by Mathews (1904b) for Baraba-Baraba. (It is likely that the bound forms were all enclitics.) There were further sets of free pronouns, for O function, for possessive function, and in allative, locative, and ablative cases. And there were bound pronouns in O function (see Hercus 1986: 34–43). For the Wemba-Wemba dialect, Hercus also reports a trial number in free pronouns (the forms end in -guli, added to 1sg O and 2pl AS forms).

All nouns and adjectives inflect on an ERG and all free and bound pronouns on an ACC basis. Bound pronouns in clausal function appear to be added to the first word of a clause, which is typically the verb but can be, for example, the negator or an interrogative verb. It appears that bound pronouns were optional; a core argument could be expressed by a free pronoun or by a bound pronoun or (probably) by both.

The free pronoun paradigm is, by and large, similar in organization and forms to the paradigms found in other Australian languages. It will be seen, in Table 2, that most of the non-singular bound pronouns are fairly clearly based on the corresponding free form. But a number of forms—notably 2sg—differ between the columns.

Of the languages surrounding Ta1, there appear to have been no bound pronouns at all in U2, U3, U4, or U5. There were bound pronouns in U1, Yaralde—to the south-east—but these are transparently related to the free pronouns and have undoubtedly developed recently, probably under diffu-sional pressure from its neighbours Tb1 and Ta1 (and also neighbours to the west). In the slim materials on S1 and S2, a set of free pronouns is reported; often, these immediately follow the first word of the clause and may have been cliticized to it. To the east, Nc2, Wiradhurri, has a full set of bound pronouns; they are transparently related to the free forms and are likely to have been a recent innovation. To the south-east, south, and south-west, a full system of bound pronouns is found in the other two languages of group Ta, and in those of Tb.

Dialect sets M, Tye, and J differ from set W in their pronouns, but in diverse ways, as set out in Table 3. First, Mathi-Mathi (set M) has no bound pronouns for clausal functions (A, S, and O). Note that M is bordered on three sides by U1, Yitha-Yitha, which lacks bound pronouns, making it likely that M lost the core bound forms under diffusional influence from U1. A significant factor is that M does retain bound pronouns in possessive function, which appears to be an archaic feature. As mentioned under (I) in §4, this is one of only two instances known in Australia of there being a set of bound pronouns in possessive function (covering more than kinship relations) but none in core clausal functions. The other example is Gurnu, the north-eastern dialect of language V, Baagandji—see Map 1. It is likely that Gurnu has, like Mathi-Mathi, lost bound pronouns in subject and object functions under areal pressure from its northerly neighbours in group WAc (WAc1, Wangkumara, and WAc3, Badjiri) which lack all bound pronouns (see the discussion in Dixon 2002: 391–5; 2001: 77–9).

Whereas set M differs from set W in having no bound pronouns in core functions, sets Tye and J differ in lacking a normal set of free pronouns. In place of this, they create free pronouns by adding bound forms to an

TABLE 3. Pronouns in dialects of Ta1, Wemba-Wemba

Dialect group	Free pronouns	Bound pronouns		
		For A and S functions	For O function	Possessive
M	normal set	—	—	yes
W	normal set	optional	optional	yes
Tye	root plus AS bound forms	obligatory	obligatory	yes
J	root plus possessive bound forms	obligatory	obligatory	yes

invariable root. Each dialect appears to have used a different root; those attested in the literature include: *beŋ-* ('human being, body'), *win-*, *baŋ-*, *waŋ-*, *waluŋ-*, *nhuŋ-*, and *djurm-* (meanings not identified).

We can illustrate with the 1sg and 2sg subject free pronouns in set Tye and in one dialect from set J (from Mathews 1904*a*, 1902*b*); other pronouns follow the same pattern.

(4)   Tyeddyuwurru (set Tye)   Tjatjala (set J)
  1sg   waŋ-an   yurw-eg
  2sg   waŋ-ar   yurw-in

The point to note here is that, by comparison with the bound pronouns shown in Table 2 (which are found with minimal variation across sets W, Tye, and J), in Tye the AS bound form is used to create free pronouns, whereas in all the J dialects the possessive form is used.

As with M, there is similarity between the pronoun systems in dialects of Ta1 and those in neighbouring languages. The genetically related languages to the south-east (Ta2 and Ta3) are very similar to dialect set J, in the forms of bound pronouns, and in creating free pronouns by adding possessive bound forms to an invariable root; this is *beŋ-* for Ta2, Watha-wurrung, and *waŋ-* for Ta3, Wuy-wurrung (Blake 1998: 75; 1991: 70).

The two languages in genetic group Tb, to the south, have one paradigm of bound pronouns for A and S functions, and—as illustrated in (3a/b) of §4— another which can mark O function in a clause and possessive function within an NP (in contrast to the three Ta languages, which have different forms for the two functions). The Tb languages have recurrent Australian forms for the singular free pronouns, but create non-singulars by adding the appropriate bound subject suffix to the singular form. For example, in Tb2, Kuurn-kopan-noot, the free subject pronouns include 1sg *ŋathug* (corresponding bound form *-u*), 1du inc *ŋathu-ŋal* (involving bound form *-ŋal*), and 1du exc *ŋathu-ŋalin* (involving bound form *-ŋalin*) (Blake 2003*a*: 37).

In summary, within a single multidialectal language, Ta, there is considerable variation for both free and bound pronouns. It is likely that the central dialects, W, more or less preserve the original system of free and optional bound forms. In the north, dialect M has lost bound subject pronouns, probably under diffusional pressure from neighbouring U5, Yitha-Yitha. Bound pronouns became obligatory in the southern dialects Tye and J. Free pronouns would have become less used and the original forms were lost, being replaced by bound pronouns added to a dialect-specific invariable root; the subject bound pronouns were used for this purpose in Tye and the possessive bound forms in set J (as in the neighbouring—and related—languages Ta2 and Ta3).

6 The Western Desert language

Group WD consists of a single language, spoken over a huge and inhospitable region (about 1,250,000 square kilometres, or one-sixth of the area of Australia) in Western Australia, South Australia, and the Northern Territory; see Map 1. The people live in small groups, constantly travelling, continually forming and re-forming, adjusting in size and composition in response to climatic conditions and the availability of food (as well as in response to social factors). The name 'Western Desert language', suggested by the late Wilfrid H. Douglas, missionary linguist, has received general acceptance to describe this extensive chain of interactive dialects. We are fortunate to have Hansen's thorough study (1984) of what he calls 'Communicability of some Western Desert Communilects', showing that the levels of intelligibility between people in geographically dispersed centres is high, and that it justifies the recognition of a single language.

There are strong lexical and grammatical similarities across the language; a major parameter of variation concerns free and bound pronouns, which are examined here. It is useful to recognize fifteen dialect groups, labelled (*a*)-(*o*); see Map 3 for locations and the left-hand column of Table 4 for names. Many dialect names end with the suffix -*tjara* 'having'; e.g. Pitjantja-tjara means 'having the word *pitjantja-* "come"', and Ngaanya-tjara is 'having the word *ngaanya* "this"'.

Because of their isolation, speakers of WD were contacted by researchers relatively late. Whereas the last information on Ta1, in Victoria—before Hercus' salvage work in the 1960s—comes from 1911, the first word list on WD was not until 1891. Most dialects are still actively spoken, and reliable grammatical information is available for most of them.

Surrounding WD are eighteen languages—numbered and named on Maps 3 and 4—with varying degrees of lexical and grammatical similarity. Shared vocabulary scores vary: 50–55 per cent with neighbours 1, 2, 6, and 14; 40–49 per cent with 8, 9, 11, and 12; 30–39 per cent with 3, 10, and 13; and 20–29 per cent with 5, 7, and 15–18. There is no firm evidence for a close genetic link with any particular neighbour(s). Interestingly, the biologist Joseph Birdsell (1993: 452–3), in his study of human genetic clines in Aboriginal Australia, pointed out a major discontinuity between WD and neighbour 18 (Arrernte, WL1), suggesting that these groups have come into contact relatively recently; WD and WL1 are very different, lexically, grammatically, and phonologically.

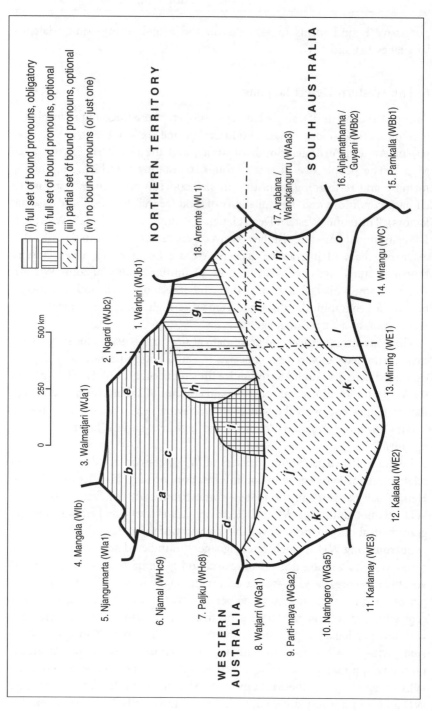

MAP 3 The Western Desert language (WD), its dialects and neighbours (showing types of bound pronouns)

TABLE 4. Pronouns in dialects of WD, the Western Desert language

	Free pronouns (with changes)	Bound pronouns		
		AS and O functions (all ACC)		Possessive
(a) Warnman	(i) ERG (v) new, based on innovated 1sg	obligatory	(i) full set	—
(b) Yulparitja	(i) ERG (iii) du/pl by number suffixes to sg	obligatory	(i) full set	—
(c) Manjtjiltjara	(i) ERG (iii) du/pl by number suffixes to sg	obligatory	(i) full set	—
(d) Kartutjarra	(i) ERG (iii) du/pl by number suffixes to sg	obligatory	(i) full set	—
(e) Kukatja	(i) ERG (iii) du/pl by number suffixes to sg	obligatory	(i) full set	—
(f) Pintupi	(i) ERG (ii) 2pl→2sg, (iv) du/pl by bound pronouns to sg free forms	obligatory	(i) full set	yes
(g) Luritja	ACC Canonical system	optional	(ii) full set	yes
(h) Ngaatjatjarra	ACC reported to be like (i)	optional	(ii) full set	?
(i) Ngaanjatjarra	ACC (iv) du/pl by bound pronouns to sg free forms	AS: obligatory O: optional	(ii) full set	yes
(j) Wangkatha	ACC (iii) du/pl by number suffixes to sg (?)	optional	(iii) partial set	?
(k) Wangatja	ACC (ii) 2pl→2sg, 2pl by number suffix to 2sg	optional	(iii) partial set	—
(l) Ngaliya	ACC (ii) 2pl→2sg, 2pl by number suffix to 2sg	optional	(iv) only 1sg AS	—
(m) Pitjantjatjarra	ACC Canonical system	optional	(iii) partial set	yes
(n) Yankuntjatjarra	ACC Canonical system	optional	(iii) partial set	yes
(o) Kukarta	ACC (ii) 2pl→2sg, (iii) 2du/pl by number suffix to 2sg	optional	(iv) none	—

As in many other Australian languages, nouns and adjectives inflect on an ERG basis. Free pronouns are ACC in most dialects but ERG in others (see Table 4), while bound pronouns, where they occur, are always ACC.

The canonical system of free pronouns can be illustrated for dialects (*m*), Pitjantjatjarra, and (*n*), Yankuntjatjarra:

(5)		singular	dual	plural
	1st person	ŋayu(lu)	ŋali	ŋana(rna)
	2nd person	njuntu	njupali	njurra
	3rd person	—	pula	tjana

There is no 3sg pronoun per se (see Goddard 1983: 116–19). Case forms on pronouns are: nominative ø (AS functions), accusative -*nja* (O function), locative/ablative -*la*, and purposive/genitive -*ku* (on 1sg), -*mpa* (elsewhere). (These are similar to corresponding case forms used on proper nouns.)

Bound pronominal enclitics show irregularity in singular forms. The paradigm for (*b*), Yulparitja, is:

(6)	(a)		AS	O	locative	dative
		1sg	-rna	-tja	-tja-ra	-tju
		2sg	-n	-nta	-nta-ra	-ŋku
		3sg	ø	ø	-lu/-li	-ra

For non-singulars, the AS forms of the enclitics are:

(6)	(b)		dual	plural
		1	-li	-la
		2		-njurra
		3	-pula	-ya for AS, -tjana for non-AS forms

To these are added -*nja* for O function, -*nja-ra* for locative, and -*mpa* for dative. For 2du the 3du suffix -*pula* is added after the appropriate 2sg form; for example, -*n-pula* for 2du AS, -*nta-ra-pula* for 2du locative.

An inclusive/exclusive distinction is made for bound pronouns, in dialects which show a full set of these (but not, generally, for free pronouns); suffix -*tju*—or -*tja* in dialect (*a*)—is added to 1du and 1pl to indicate exclusive, with its absence showing inclusive; for example, -*li-mpa-tju* (1du-DATIVE-EXCLUSIVE), dative of 1du exclusive.

The 2pl, 3du, and 3pl non-AS forms are identical to free pronouns and are likely to be recent innovations as bound forms; as may also be exclusive -*tju/a*, since it is almost always added after case endings. The singular forms and 1du -*li*, 1pl -*la*, and 3pl AS -*ya* are different from free pronouns and appear to be of greater antiquity.

Whereas northern dialects such as (*b*) have a full set of bound pronouns, other dialects include only a partial set. In (*n*), Yankuntjatjarra, there are just the AS and O 1sg and 2sg forms, just the 1sg dative/genitive form -*tju* (not 2sg dative -*ŋku*), and 1du -*li*, 1pl -*la*, 3pl AS -*ya*. That is, it shows almost exactly the forms which were suggested—in the last paragraph—to have historical depth.

It is likely that Proto-WD had a full paradigm of free pronouns, as illustrated in (5), and just a partial set of bound pronouns, similar to those in (*n*), both on an ACC basis. Some northern dialects developed a full set of bound pronouns and reanalysed the free forms; others lost bound pronouns. In each case, the developments were in keeping with the profiles of neighbouring languages. The changes will be discussed first for bound and then for free pronouns.

6.1 *Bound pronouns (all retain an ACC system)*

(i) Dialects (*a–f*)—which are one geographical block—have a full set of bound pronouns, as illustrated in (6a–b), with only minor differences between dialects. They have filled in the gaps from the free pronoun paradigm and added a final -*tju* for exclusive. These bound pronouns are used obligatorily in each clause; free pronouns may be used as well, sparingly, for particular emphasis.

(ii) Dialects (*g–h*) have a full set of bound pronouns, like (*a–f*), but use of them is optional. That is, a clausal argument may be expressed by a bound pronoun, or by a free pronoun—as in (1a–b) of §3—or by both. Dialect (*i*) is similar but here an AS bound pronoun is obligatory and an O form optional.

(iii) Dialects (*j–k*) and (*m–n*)—which also make up a geographical block— have a partial set, similar to those described above for (*n*), there being only minor differences between dialects. Bound pronominal enclitics are optional; an argument can be expressed by a free pronoun, or by a bound pronoun (if there is one), or by both.

(iv) The most south-easterly dialect, (*o*), has lost all bound pronouns. It is reported that its neighbour, dialect (*l*), has a single bound pronoun, 1sg AS -*rna*, which 'appears redundantly very occasionally', attached to the 1sg AS free form (O'Grady, Voegelin, and Voegelin 1966: 141).

The four sets are shown in Table 4 and on Map 3. As mentioned before, there is in many cases a similarity with contiguous languages. Adjoining dialects (*a–f*), neighbours 1–5 and 7 have a full set of bound pronouns for core functions (being obligatory in at least 1–3) and there are partial sets in 6 and 8. In contrast, there are no bound pronouns in core functions in neighbours 9–14 and 18. Neighbours 15–17 have recently developed bound forms, these being transparently reduced from free pronouns.

In all the WD dialects, bound pronouns—most appropriately regarded as enclitics—attach to the end of the first constituent of the clause (which may be a single word). This also applies for neighbours 1–4 and 8, whereas for 5–6 (and 15–17) they are enclitic to the verb. In many WD dialects the order of bound pronouns is determined by person: first before second before third (independently of syntactic function). However, in (*n*) the critical factor is function: O before A (independently of person). Dialect (*e*) has first followed by second/third in A function, and then second/third in O function; in (*f*) the last two are reversed: first, then second/third in O function, then second/third in A function. Most of neighbours 1–5 have first before second before third person (as do 15–17).

What of bound pronouns in possessive function, a characteristic of all dialects of Ta1, in Victoria? These are fairly rare in WD, but do occur in, at least, dialects (*f*), (*g*), (*i*), (*m*), and (*n*), which make up one geographical block; here, one set of bound pronouns has dative function within a clause and genitive function with an NP, as illustrated for dialect (*i*) in (2a–b) of §4. In (*n*) there are dative/genitive clitics just for first person, and in (*m*) just for first person and 3sg, which can be used for possession.

Possessive bound pronouns are almost absent from the eighteen languages surrounding WD; (just a 1sg possessor is reported for neighbour 8). And language 18 (Arrernte, WL1)—which adjoins WD dialects with possessive bound markers—has developed 1sg, 2sg, and 3sg bound pronouns just to mark possession with kinterms.

6.2 *Free pronouns*

Only dialects (*m*), (*n*), and (*g*)—which are contiguous—retain the original system of ACC free pronouns, as set out in (5) (with forms that have cognates in many other Australian languages). The other dialects have undergone one or more of a number of recurrent changes; see Table 4 and Map 4.

(i) The ACC syntactic profile is retained for free pronouns in dialects (*g–o*) but replaced by an ERG system in (*a–f*).[5] This is in accord with the scheme of development set out in §2; those dialects for which bound pronouns are obligatory have realigned free pronouns (now used sparingly, mostly for emphasis or contrast) to inflect like nominals. Neighbouring languages 1–5, to the north, have adopted the same change.

---

[5] Amee Glass reports (p.c.) that the same change is taking place in the language used by young speakers of dialect (*i*). That is, this change is continuing to diffuse.

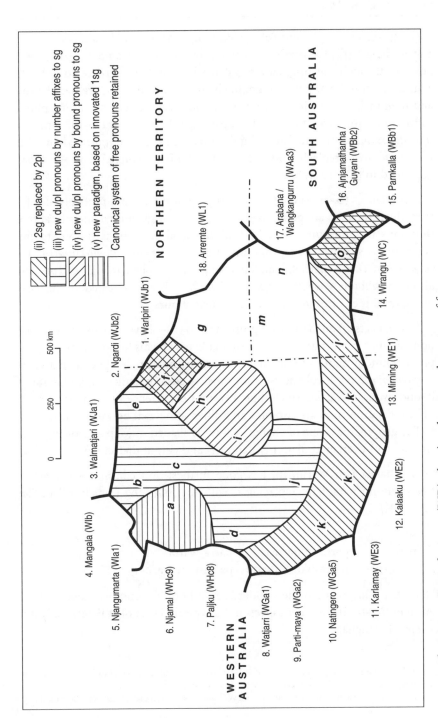

0   250   500 km

NORTHERN TERRITORY

SOUTH AUSTRALIA

WESTERN
AUSTRALIA

1. Warlpiri (WJb1)
2. Ngardi (WJb2)
3. Walmatjari (WJa1)
4. Mangala (WIb)
5. Njangumarta (WIa1)
6. Njamal (WHc9)
7. Paljku (WHc8)
8. Watjarri (WGa1)
9. Parti-maya (WGa2)
10. Natingero (WGa5)
11. Karlamay (WE3)
12. Kalaaku (WE2)
13. Mirning (WE1)
14. Wirangu (WC)
15. Parnkalla (WBb1)
16. Ajnjamathanha / Guyani (WBb2)
17. Arabana / Wangkangurru (WAa3)
18. Arrernte (WL1)

MAP 4 The Western Desert language (WD), showing changes to the system of free pronouns

(ii) In dialects (*k–l*) and (*o*)—making up one geographical region—and also in dialect (*f*), the original 2pl free pronoun *njurra* is now used for 2sg; possibly through 2pl originally being used for polite reference to a single addressee, with the original 2sg gradually dropping out of use (rather like *you* and *thou* in English).[6] In (*k–l*) a new 2pl has been derived by adding plural suffix -*muka* to *njurra*, the rest of the paradigm being as for (*m–n*), with 2du *njupali*. In dialect (*o*), dual and plural suffixes are added to *njurra*, giving 2du *njurra-kutjarra* (replacing *njupali*) and 2pl *njurra-murga*.[7] For what has happened in (*f*), see (iv) below.

(iii) Dialects (*b–e*)—a continuous geographical set—and probably also (*j*) (for which the data are poor) have replaced the original dual and plural free pronouns by pronouns created by adding dual and plural suffixes to the appropriate singular free pronouns; for example 1du *ŋayu-kutjarra*, 1pl *ŋayu-rti* in (*b*). A partially similar change has applied in dialect (*o*), and also in neighbour 3, where just 2du and 2pl have been re-created on the basis of 2sg (and there are similar changes in neighbours 12–13).

(iv) Dialects (*i*) and (*f*)—and probably also (*h*)—have also lost the original non-singular free pronouns, and have made new forms by adding the appropriate bound pronouns to singular free forms; for example, 1pl O in dialect (*i*) is *ŋayu-nja-lanja*, involving 1sg root *ŋayu*, accusative suffix -*nja*, plus 1pl O bound pronoun -*la-nja* (including a second occurrence of accusative -*nja*). (The formation rules are complex and differ somewhat between dialects.)

The geographic scope of changes (ii–iv) is shaded in Map 4, showing how (ii) and (iv) overlap at dialect (*f*) and (ii) and (iii) at dialect (*o*).

(v) Dialect (*a*), Warnman, has gone furthest and eliminated the entire free pronoun paradigm, replacing it with the following (which inflect like nominals):

	sg	du	pl
1	parra	parra-kutjarra	parra-warta
2	parra-ŋku	parra-ŋku-kutjarra	parra-ŋku-warta

Note that Warnman has the standard set of bound pronouns, close to those given in (6a–b). In all other aspects it is a typical dialect of WD (certainly not a separate language).

---

[6] This change is not reported for any of WD's neighbours, but a similar shift has taken place in Djabugay, spoken in north-east Queensland; see Dixon (2002: 287).

[7] Note that the lexeme 'two' is *kutjarra* across WD, and in southern dialects *murka* is 'lots of, many'.

A distinction between inclusive and exclusive for non-singular first person is pervasive in Australia. For Ta1, we saw that the distinction is made in both free and bound pronouns. In most or all of dialects (*a–i*) of WD, -*tju*—or -*tja* in dialect (*a*)—is added to appropriate bound pronouns to indicate 'exclusive'. The distinction is not made for free pronouns, except in dialects (*f*) and (*i*) where non-singular free forms involve the addition of the appropriate bound pronouns (including the exclusive suffix) to a singular free form.

Interestingly, neighbouring language 8, to the west, adds the same exclusive suffix, -*tju/a*, to free form first person non-singular pronouns. Neighbours 1–5 have an inclusive/exclusive distinction in free and bound forms but involving different forms, without use of a suffix -*tju/a*; the same applies for free forms in 17–18. Neighbours 6–7 have separate forms for 1pl.inc and 1pl.exc but create 1du.exc by adding suffix -*ya* (which may be cognate with WD -*tju/a*) to 1du.inc *ŋali*.

It is interesting to follow through some of the changes to free and bound pronouns. In dialect (*c*), Manjtjiltjara, for instance, we reconstruct the following historical stages:

- First, there was 2pl free pronoun *njurra*, and no 2pl entry in the partial paradigm for bound pronouns.
- The system of bound pronouns was extended; this included the adoption of -*njurra* as 2pl bound enclitic.
- Bound pronouns became obligatory with the original non-singular free pronouns being recast. 2pl *njurra* was replaced by *njuntu-rti* (2sg-PLURAL) (Burridge 1996: 29). Thus, *njurra*, originally the 2pl free pronoun, now survives just as the 2pl bound pronoun.

In dialect (*f*), there have been two changes. First, the 2sg free pronoun *njuntu* has been replaced by what was the 2pl form *njurra*; however -*njurra* was retained as 2pl bound pronoun. Secondly, new non-singular free pronouns have been formed by adding non-singular bound forms to singular free pronouns. Here we get the original 2pl free pronoun *njurra* replaced by (for S function) *njurra-n-pa-njurra*; this involves new 2sg free form *njurra*, followed by plural marker -*n*, then linker syllable -*pa*, and finally the 2pl bound pronoun -*njurra* (Hansen and Hansen 1978: 107).

In summary, northern dialects of WD have developed a full set of bound pronouns, which are now obligatory in each clause. As a consequence, free pronouns are little used; they now take ERG inflection, like nominals, and their forms have been reanalysed, making person and number components more transparent. These dialects have adopted a profile similar to those of neighbouring languages to the north. Central eastern dialects also have a full system of bound pronouns, but these are optional and free pronouns retain their ACC profile, as do southern dialects which retain a partial paradigm of bound forms. Two south-eastern dialects have lost, or almost lost, bound pronouns, adopting a profile similar to that of their neighbours to the south.

Free pronouns have been restructured in all but three dialects, involving one or more of a medley of changes: replacing the 2sg pronoun by 2pl; re-forming non-singulars on singulars, by adding either number suffixes or the appropriate bound pronouns. Or, in dialect (*a*), creating a new system of free pronouns based on 1sg *parra*, with -*ŋku* added for 2sg and then dual and plural number affixes.

New changes are taking place in the present-day situation of language contact. Ken and Lesley Hansen, who have worked for more than forty years with speakers of WD, have noted (in a personal communication) that nowadays there is a tendency to use free pronouns rather than bound forms, leading to a morphologically simpler structure. This is undoubtedly a consequence of prolonged contact with English, and a situation of encroaching language attrition.

7 Discussion

There are notable similarities and differences between the development of free and bound pronouns in our two case studies—Taı in Victoria, and WD in Western Australia and adjacent states. What is of particular interest is how a certain feature spreads over contiguous languages and across the dialects of one multidialectal language. A given group is likely to change its linguistic profile so that it more nearly matches that of one or more neighbouring groups, in terms of grammatical organization, prosodic template, etc. It can be seen that the diffusion of a certain value of a parameter of variation is a gradual affair (rather than a sudden shift, applying to a language all at once). This is symptomatic of a steady equilibrium situation, as put forward in Dixon (1997) and exemplified in considerable detail for Australia in Dixon (2002).[8]

There is in Australia a recurrent tendency for bound pronominal clitics to develop out of free pronouns, for these clitics to then take on the status of affixes, for them to then fuse with the verb root or with tense or other affixes, and so on. Such changes are in large part motivated by the principle 'be as

---

[8] See also Dench's (2001) seminal study of diffusion in the Pilbara region of Western Australia, just to the north-west of the Western Desert language.

iconic with your neighbour as you can'. Phonological change may then lead to loss of semantic information in a bound pronoun/tense portmanteau suffix. And this can motivate the creation of new bound pronominal clitics, imitating a grammatical structure which occurs in a neighbouring language (this is illustrated in Dixon 2001: 71–83; 2002: 379–93). Multiple instances of such cyclic patterns of development, almost always spread through areal contact, are documented throughout Dixon (2002).

We have examined two languages each of which has an unusually large number of dialects. Dialects in the centre of the language area—those which have little or no contact with other languages—are likely to be the most conservative. Dialects on the periphery of a language area tend to change so that their grammatical profile becomes more similar to that of a neighbour language. Note that there is unlikely to be any unidirectionality of influence. I am not suggesting, for example, simply that a peripheral dialect of WD changed in the way described here in order to be more like a neighbouring language. Rather, both would have changed, the WD dialect and the dialect of a neighbouring language, in order that each should become more like the other. Mutual grammatical accommodation would have led to neighbouring dialects (although belonging to different languages) establishing critical structural similarities and this will, of course, facilitate communication.

References (with indication of language and dialect each refers to)

Aikhenvald, A. Y. and Dixon, R. M. W. (eds.). 2001. *Areal diffusion and genetic inheritance: problems in comparative linguistics.* Oxford: Oxford University Press.

Birdsell, J. B. 1993. *Microevolutionary patterns in Aboriginal Australia: a gradient analysis of clines.* New York: Oxford University Press.

Blake, B. J. 1991. 'Woiwurrung, the Melbourne language', pp. 31–122 of *The handbook of Australian languages,* Vol. 4, edited by R. M. W. Dixon and B. J. Blake. Melbourne: Oxford University Press. [Ta3]

—— 1998. *Wathawurrong and the Colac language of southern Victoria.* Canberra: Pacific Linguistics. [Ta2]

—— 2003a. *The Warrnambool language: a consolidated account of the Aboriginal language of the Warrnambool area of the Western District of Victoria based on nineteenth-century sources.* Canberra: Pacific Linguistics. [Tb2]

—— 2003b. *The Bunganditj (Buwandik) language of the Mount Gambier region.* Canberra: Pacific Linguistics. [Tb1]

Bowe, H. 1990. *Categories, constituents and constituent order in Pitjantjatjara, an Aboriginal language of Australia.* London: Routledge. [WD (*m*)]

Burridge, K. 1996. 'Yulparitja sketch grammar', pp. 15–69 of *Studies in Kimberley languages in honour of Howard Coate*, edited by W. McGregor. Munich: Lincom Europa. [WD (*b*)]

Dawson, J. 1881. *Australian Aborigines: the languages and customs of several small tribes in the Western District of Victoria, Australia*. Melbourne: George Robertson. [Ta1 (J), Tb2]

Dench, A. 2001. 'Descent and diffusion: the complexity of the Pilbara situation', pp. 105–33 of Aikhenvald and Dixon 2001.

Dixon, R. M. W. 1997. *The rise and fall of languages*. Cambridge: Cambridge University Press.

—— 2001. 'The Australian linguistic area', pp. 64–104 of Aikhenvald and Dixon 2001.

—— 2002. *Australian languages: their nature and development*. Cambridge: Cambridge University Press.

Douglas, W. H. 1964. *An introduction to the Western Desert language*, rev. edn. Sydney: Oceania Linguistic Monographs. [WD (*i*; plus *c, j, k, l, o*)].

Eckert, P. and Hudson, J. 1988. *Wangka Wiru: a handbook for the Pitjantjatjara language learner*. Underdale: University of South Australia. [WD (*m*)]

Glass, A. 1997. *Cohesion in Ngaanyatjarra discourse*. Darwin: Summer Institute of Linguistics. [WD (*i*)]

—— and Hackett, D. 1970. *Pitjantjatjara grammar: a tagmemic view of the Ngaanyatjarra (Warburton Ranges) dialect*. Canberra: Australian Institute of Aboriginal Studies. [WD (*i*)]

Goddard, C. 1985. *A grammar of Yankunytjatjara*. Alice Springs: Institute for Aboriginal Development. [Publication of 1983 ANU Ph.D. thesis, *A semantically-based grammar of the Yankunytjatjara dialect of the Western Desert language*] [WD (*n*)].

Hansen, K. C. 1984. 'Communicability of some Western Desert communilects', pp. 1–112, *Work Papers of SIL-AAB*, Series B, no. 11. Darwin: Summer Institute of Linguistics. [WD]

—— and Hansen, L. E. 1978. *The core of Pintupi grammar*. Darwin: Summer Institute of Linguistics. SIL-AAB. [WD (*f*, plus *m, i*)]

Heffernan, J. A. 1984. *Papunya Luritja language notes*. Papunya: Literature Production Centre. [WD (*g*)]

Hercus, L. A. 1986. *Victorian languages: a late survey*. Canberra: Pacific Linguistics. [Revised and enlarged version of *The languages of Victoria: a late survey*. Canberra: Australian Institute of Aboriginal Studies, 1969.] [Ta1 (M, W, J)]

Marsh, J. 1976. *The grammar of Mantjiltjara*. MA thesis, Arizona State University. [WD (*c*)]

Mathews, R. H. 1902a. 'Languages of some native tribes of Queensland, New South Wales and Victoria', *Journal and Proceedings of the Royal Society of New South Wales* 36: 135–90. ['9—The Bureba language' is on pp. 172–5; Ta1 (W).]

—— 1902b. 'The Aboriginal languages of Victoria', *Journal and Proceedings of the Royal Society of New South Wales* 36: 71–106. ['The Tyattyala language' is on pp. 77–84; Ta1 (J).]

—— 1904a. 'Die Sprache des Tyeddyuwūrru-Stammes der Eingebornen von Victoria', *Mitteilungen des Anthropologischen Gesellschaft in Wien* 34: 71–6. [Tai (Tye)]

—— 1904b. 'The Wiradyuri and other languages of New South Wales', *Journal of the Anthropological Institute* 34: 284–305 ['The Bureba-Bureba language' is on pp. 291–4; Tai (W)]

O'Grady, G. N., Voegelin, C. F. and Voegelin, F. M. 1966. 'Languages of the world: Indo-Pacific Fascicle 6', *Anthropological Linguistics* 8.2. [WD (*a, b, i, l*)]

Platt, J. 1972. *An outline grammar of the Gugada dialect: South Australia.* Canberra: Australian Institute of Aboriginal Studies. [WD (*o*)]

Trudinger, R. 1943. 'Grammar of the Pitjantjatjara dialect, Central Australia', *Oceania* 13: 205–33. [WD (*m*)]

Valiquette, H. 1993. *A basic Kukatja and English dictionary.* Balgo: Luurupa Catholic School. [WD (*e*)]

Vaszolyi, E. G. 1979. *Teach yourself Wangkatja.* Mt Lawley: Mount Lawley College. [WD (*k*)]

3

How Long do Linguistic Areas Last? Western Nilotic Grammars in Contact[1]

ANNE STORCH

1 Introduction

Investigations into the realms and limitations of linguistic areas may take on different forms. The most obvious one, perhaps, would be to define a geographic area or region which is characterized by the occurrence of similar grammatical techniques and common typological patterns in a number of otherwise probably unrelated languages. A second approach would deal with the time depth of a Sprachbund or language contact area. Here, geographical boundaries may vary during the course of time, as the grammatical features that help to identify the contact zone could tend to diffuse into other languages or contact areas, while they may become unproductive in parts of their former zone of origin. In the East African set-up that will be discussed here—focusing on Western Nilotic languages of the Nilo-Saharan phylum— the emergence of intensive and extremely productive contact situations appears to depend on several sociolinguistic as well as geographic parameters that are not continuously present in the entire area. It seems that the introduction of new economic techniques and a different lifestyle can be correlated with the spreading of particular aspects of the grammar, and subsequently the creation of a linguistic area, which remained productive over a very long period of time. In later contact situations the grammatical properties that characterized the linguistic area spread again, but for

[1] This contribution is based on research that has been generously funded by the German Research Society (DFG) to whom I want to express my gratitude. I am deeply indebted to Sasha Aikhenvald and Bob Dixon for their many thorough comments on this chapter as well as for their hospitality. I am truly grateful to Gerrit Dimmendaal, Roger Blench, Ulrike Claudi, Birgit Hellwig, and to three anonymous referees for their many helpful suggestions, and to all those who assisted me in studying their languages in Sudan and Uganda.

completely different reasons. As a result, various strata of contact and diffusion can be identified in these 'layered languages' (Chapter 1, §2.1).

2 Early areal adaptations

The area that is studied here roughly ranges from the Fung region of the Blue Nile province of south-eastern Sudan through Bahr el-Ghazal in south-western Sudan to the Southern Lwoo-speaking parts of northern and eastern Uganda and adjacent regions of Kenya. Western Nilotic exhibits numerous structural and lexical similarities to other language families of the Sudanic belt and has consequently been assumed either to belong to old pan-African zones of common retentions (cf. Westermann 1911, 1927; Gregersen 1972; Blench 1995) or to have once been part of a common area of contact, an approach which is used in this chapter. The observation that certain morphological elements occur as nominal affixes in a fairly large number of distantly related or genetically unrelated languages of eastern and central Africa has led Margaret Bryan (1959) to the conclusion that these languages are part of a linguistic area and not necessarily part of a larger genetic entity. This has been reconsidered as a working hypothesis again by the same author in 1968, but was never again in any depth followed up by other scholars. But Bryan's hypothesis actually goes beyond just assuming an obscure substrate of unclear origin, as areal features are rather interpreted as a Sprachbund zone.

According to Bryan, there is an area of 'T/K languages', which are found in Eastern and Southern Nilotic, Didinga-Murle, Tama, Daju, Temein, and Kadugli-Krongo, while a second area called '*N/*K' is made up of language groups of a zone of much wider distribution (Bryan 1968: 169). Western Nilotic, besides a large number of Central and Eastern Sudanic groups, has been specifically identified as being part of an '*N/*K area'. Both groups are differentiated according to the elements shown in Table 1 (Bryan 1968: 170).

Examples from Western Nilotic languages may help to illustrate the significance of Bryan's observations. The Southern Burun language Mabaan categorizes its nouns with suffixed classifiers, which are marked for number and also express an object's size, shape, and motion. There are, however, semantically empty number markers in Mabaan, which tend to marginalize some of the classifiers. In example (1), the singular classifier -$\grave{a}$ marks nouns that denote round, smallish objects; the plural of this class is exclusively constructed with -$\grave{a}\eta$. Plurals of almost all other singular classifiers can be constructed with a suffix -$k(\Lambda) \sim$ -$g(\Lambda)$, which is an areal feature that has spread into Mabaan. As a consequence, the spread of this areally diffused

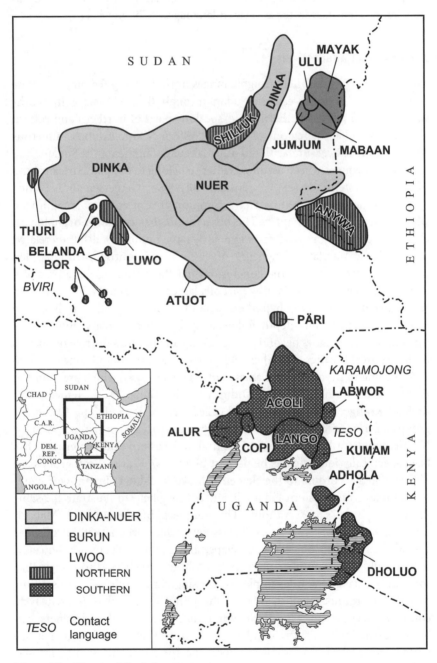

MAP 1 The Western Nilotic languages

TABLE 1. Features of T/K and *N/*K linguistic areas

	T/K	*N/*K
Function	indicate number in nominals	indicate number in pronominals and verbs
	T has a singulative, particularizing connotation	
Occurrence	affixes (prefixes, suffixes)	affixes, also inseparable parts of the stem
Frequency	T occurs more frequently than K	*K occurs more frequently than *N
Description	T is an alveolar, usually unvoiced plosive (/t/), K is a velar, usually unvoiced plosive (/k/)	*N is usually (/n/), but also occurs as /ndr, d, r, ɽ, ṇ, ŋ, ɲ, yy, y, j/, *K is usually a velar plosive or nasal /k, g, ŋ/, but also occurs as /x, w, c, s, q, h, kw, ŋkw, ŋw, ɲw, cw, gw, sc, nc, ŋg/

plural marker has resulted in neutralization of classificatory meanings of plural inflection in Mabaan.

(1) Mabaan classifiers

	SINGULAR	PLURAL	
'worm'	ʔúʌt-à	ʔúʌt-àṇ	retention of SG and PL
	worm-round.SG	worm-round.PL	classifier
'monkey'	jwɔ́m-ø	jɔɔm-gʌ	areal pluralizer substitutes
	monkey-ø	monkey-GENL.PL	original PL classifier

In Dinka the plural marker K occurs as well, both as a genitive linker morpheme and a nominal suffix (2a). Almost all other nominals are constructed by means of non-linear noun morphology (2b):

(2) Dinka number inflection

(2) (a) ɣɔ́ɔt kè̠ dít 'nests' ('houses of bird')
          house of.PL bird

          'jɔ̠ɔ̠-k   'dogs'   < jɔ̠-ŋ 'dog'
          dog-PL   dog-SG

     (b) SG   PL
          páál   'páàl   'knife'
          tím   tíím   'tree, wood'
          ŋaap   'ŋéép   'fig-tree'

As is shown below, the *k*-marker is also salient in the Lwoo languages, which besides Burun and Dinka-Nuer form the third coordinate branch of Western Nilotic. A brief example to cite at this instance would be the following:

(3)   SG   PL
    Shilluk méí   mɛɛk   'mother'
    Anywa   lèèò   làk   'honeycomb'
    Päri   ùdóò kíc   ùdóó-ki kíyò   'beeswax' ('glue of bee')
    Luwo   ŋṵ́ṵ́   ŋṵ́gʌ̀   'lion'
    Thuri   ʈíí   ʈìgì   'door'

From a contemporary perspective, a much wider region seems to be part of the T/K and *N/*K areas. Singulatives with *-*tV* have been found in Meroitic, which is at present assumed to have existed some 4,000 years ago (Rilly 2004), and a singular or singulative marker -*t/t*- is found as well in Cushitic and Afroasiatic, where it may have developed out of a feminine gender morpheme. The plural marker -*k/k*- is much more common and occurs in Niger-Congo, e.g. Ubangi—Bviri *ka*- (Storch 2003), Atlantic—Manjaku *ba-k*- (Doneux 1975), Benue-Congo—Jukun/Jibə *bə-k* (Storch and Dinslage 2000), Bantu—Zezuru *vadzi-/*ba-ki*- (Maho 1999), as well as in Meroitic (*-*gu*; Rilly 2004).

The features that go together with T, N, and K and which seem to characterize the entire Sprachbund area are a nominalizer *a*- (Westermann 1911, 1927), alternating number morphemes *A* (singular) and *I* (plural) (Bender 1991), a single gender for mass nouns *ma*- (Blench 1995), emergence of noun classification systems by means of massive grammaticalization (Westermann 1927; Greenberg 1963, 1981), case (ergative case systems; Dimmendaal p.c.), phonological properties (ATR-based vowel harmony systems, secondary features such as CREAKY:BREATHY oppositions not motivated by consonantal environment, retroflex consonants; Dimmendaal p.c.), and semantic properties (olfactory categorization; Storch and Vossen in press; Storch 2005).

If these properties can be interpreted as evidence for the early existence of vast contact areas in the Sudan, then they could be ruled out as immediate convergence phenomena of younger and better understood contact situations. Obviously, so many of these areal adaptations are universally present in the languages of Sudanic Africa—south of the Sahel and north of the rain forest—that the more recent migrations within the last five to eight centuries would not have been significant enough to account for their massive diffusion.

But which other contact situations have played a role within this already existing sprachbund area? And did features of the old linguistic area remain productive, have they even been borrowed more easily into the grammatical systems of neighbouring languages than other material? Could a linguistic area survive within newly formed contact zones—and do its characteristic properties have any secondary semantic function? Do people see themselves as speakers of languages that share common patterns and structures, and do people perceive their languages as being typologically diverse from others? And would this have any effect on what part of their grammars is retained and what is borrowed from a contact language? Answers to these questions will come from a comparative analysis of system-preserving changes (cf. Chapter 1, §3.2) in Lwoo noun morphology, focusing on Luwo, Belanda Bor—both spoken in Bahr el-Ghazal of Sudan—and Labwor, spoken in the hills of north-eastern Uganda.

3 Luwo suffixes

The noun morphology of Luwo employs class- and number-marking suffixes, derivational prefixes, and some rare non-segmental formatives. A singular noun may be morphologically opaque or have a suffix (-ɔ̰, -ɔ̰, -a, -ɥ, -k).

Number is inflected within the frame of a tripartite system, which exhibits three principles of number inflection, namely singulativization, pluralization, and substitution of number morphemes. The following examples illustrate the different patterns of number marking in Luwo:

(4–6) Luwo number inflection

(4) COLL   SGVE

    rìŋ   rìŋ-ɔ̰   'meat'

(5) SG   PL

    ŋṵ́ṵ́   ŋṵ́-gʌ̀   'lion'

(6) SG   PL

    àmán-á àmán-ɛ́ 'camel'

The morphologically formally unmarked form of 'meat' is a plural or collective form. The singulative form is derived from the opaque form by adding a singulative suffix -ɔ̰ and typically denotes an item that is singled out from a mass or group of similar items. Nouns which are semantically singular are opaque in the singular and derive a plural by adding the respective number morpheme (here the areal -k which is realized as -gʌ̀ in Luwo). A third pattern is characterized by the use of number-inflectional morphemes in both number categories.

In Luwo, almost every noun that fits semantically is put into the singulative category. The remaining nouns almost exclusively construct their plurals with either -ɛ́ or -nɛ́. Most of these suffixes derive from old noun classifiers and formerly expressed the tactile perceptional or cognitive characterization of an object. Such classifiers are much more productive in closely related Burun and in Northern Lwoo varieties such as Shilluk. Common semantic traits of noun classifiers in Western Nilotic are length, roundness, motion, inalienability, and animacy. In Luwo, most of the noun suffixes are now semantically empty, apart from their number-inflectional functions. In contrast to Northern Lwoo varieties Anywa or Shilluk, Luwo has few suffixes, which can be seen in the comparison in Table 2.

The reduced inventory of nominal suffixes in Luwo asks for an explanation, given the fact that these languages are so similar in many other respects. Exploring the sociolinguistic situation of Luwo may help to shed some light on this problem.

In contrast to the exclusive attitude towards strangers that is observed among Western Nilotic pastoralists such as Dinka, Nuer, and Shilluk, speakers of Luwo claim to have a strong interest in foreign peoples and new cultural and economic concepts. This may have originated in times of famine in the middle ages (Atkinson 1999; Herring 1979; Ehret et al. 1974) and the later era of slave-raiding attacks of the Turko-Egyptian rule, when entire villages were erased and the group had significant problems in keeping up a stable size of population (Pierli, Ratti, and Wheeler 1998; Werner, Anderson, and Wheeler 2000). The threat of genocide must have forced the Luwo to split off into smaller groups and to encourage outsiders to become part of the society. Moreover, ethnohistorical sources emphasize that the ancestors of the Luwo

TABLE 2. The singular suffixes of Mabaan, Anywa, and Luwo

	length, cultural dominance	derogative	SGVE.	GENL. SG.	abstract, cultural	abstract	round, small, mass, specialists	fast	locative, domestic	body, space	soft, circle	part of	mass
Mabaan	-(C)à	-gɔn	-tà	-n	-à	-gà	-à	-i	-ɔ	-ù/ -Nù	-Nà	- àŋ/ -ɲàŋ	-(C)iŋ
Anywa			-o	-VNò	-ò, -i	-k	-ò, -Vnò, -u, -á		-ò, -Vnò, -u-	-á, -V:-, -VN+			-i
Luwo			-ɔ̰, -ɔ̰̀	-a, -ɔ̰		-k	-ɔ̰		-a	-ʊ̰	-a		

underwent several migrations, which in the open and wide savannah meant covering large distances (Crazzolara 1950–4; Tucker 1931). The language contact situations Luwo has been in over hundreds of years must consequently have been highly diverse, not long lasting and not intensive enough to lead to the diffusion of salient grammatical morphemes. But the Luwo at some stage of their history began to share an almost symbiotic relationship with the Dinka, which lasted until very recently (Tucker 1931). While the Luwo had lost most of their livestock in previous times of migration, war, and hunger, the Dinka did not only maintain their cattle-breeding economy by all possible means, but also defined status and prestige according to the number of cattle owned by a group. They did not produce iron. The Luwo with their advanced metallurgy were able to provide the Dinka with iron weapons and tools and in turn were to a certain degree left undisturbed by their mighty neighbours. Intermarriages of Luwo women and Dinka men occurred, even though the Luwo were considered inferior by the Dinka (Tucker 1931).

Because of its speakers' general attitude, Luwo was always prone to intensive language contact situations. But while speakers of Central Sudanic, Ubangi, and Kordofanian languages never became numerous within the Luwo-speaking communities, Dinka was tremendously influential because of its enormous prestige in the Luwo area. One consequence of the close contact between the two languages is the significant reduction of suffixes, which is more developed in Luwo than in its close relatives. Instead of using any kind of affixation, many nouns in Luwo construct their plurals by means of vowel lengthening and tone alternation, which are all techniques that dominate in the nominal morphology of Dinka.

(7) (a) tone alternation

Luwo		Dinka		Päri		gloss
SG	PL	SG	PL	SG	PL	
tʊ̀ŋ	tʊ́ŋ	tùŋ	túŋ	tùŋó	tùŋi	'horn'
t̪ɔ́ɔl	t̪ɔ̀ɔl	wién	wìịn	t̪ɔ́ɔl	t̪ɔ̀ɔlì	'rope'

(b) vowel lengthening

Luwo		Dinka		Päri		gloss
SG	PL	SG	PL	SG	PL	
bat	baat	kóók	kòk	bàd	bʌ̀ʌdì	'arm'
láy	lááy	lá̤í	lá̤á̤í	lʌ́y	lʌ́yì	'animal'

The example shows that the rather archaic and geographically isolated Lwoo language Päri preserves suffixes, where Dinka hardly exhibits any productive nominal suffixes, but uses vowel gradation to indicate unmarked and marked forms, and Luwo has incipiently developed similar patterns. Because all share common areal adaptations and pre-existing structural similarities (Chapter 1, §4.1), prototypical features remain unchanged. Both Dinka and Luwo preserve remnants of nominal classifiers, use tripartite number marking, and share areally distributed number inflectional affixes such as the pluralizer.

The changes that can be observed in the nominal system of Luwo may not yet seem significant. But these structures provide a groundwork that is responsible for a number of dramatic changes which occurred in later contact scenarios. This will be exemplified by discussing the contact of Labwor and Karamojong and the case of Belanda Bor.

4 Grammar and meaning in Labwor

Grammatical categories of a language encode meaning. Certain concepts may be of such importance to the speakers of a language that they are not just expressed lexically, but are grammaticalized and thus form part of the language's morphology and syntax. The example of Labwor shows that reanalysis and reinterpretation of grammatical morphemes (Chapter 1, §3.3) are used to preserve patterns which are considered more characteristic or prototypical by the speakers. Again, pre-existing structural similarities in the morphology may encourage diffusion (as in Likpe and Ewe serial verb constructrions, cf. Ameka, Chapter 4).

4.1 *Prototypical patterns*

Labwor is a minority language of eastern Uganda, which, like all other Southern Lwoo languages, has originated from Luwo of Bahr el-Ghazal (Storch 2005). It borders on Eastern Nilotic gender-marking languages Teso and Karamojong. Culturally the Labwor are almost fully assimilated by the Karamojong. The time depth of contact is unknown, bilingualism absolutely common.

While in the more southern Lwoo languages the original suffixes have been reduced to such an extent that the tripartite number marking system has collapsed, Labwor has retained as many suffixes as Northern Luwo, as well as the tripartite number-inflectional patterns of Western Nilotic. The following examples help to illustrate this phenomenon:

(8) Labwor number inflection

		SINGULAR	PLURAL	plural formation
(a)				
	'mosquito'	òbɛ́r	òbɛ́r-ɛ́	

		COLLECTIVE	SINGULATIVE	singulative formation
(b)				
	'meat'	rîŋ	rîŋ-ɔ́	
	'bush, forest'	bùŋ	bùŋ-á	

(c)　　　　　　　　SINGULAR　PLURAL　　replacement pattern
　　'knife'　　　　pàl-à　　　pàl-é
　　'lame person'　á-ŋwÂl-ò　è-ŋwÂl-έ

Opaque singulars consist of the bare root (8a). These singulars very often express naturally singular phenomena, and occur in a large number of semantic fields. Opaque pluralic nouns tend to be collectives rather than plurals, and usually occur in Labwor with the same nouns as in Northern Lwoo, while their occurrence in the other Southern Lwoo languages is restricted to nouns denoting grains. Both opaque singulars and collectives can be inflected for number by the use of suffixes. A third category of nouns is marked in both singular and plural form, and it is in this morphological group that we get most of the borrowed Eastern Nilotic (Karamojong) morphemes. An example would be the plurals with -*á*. The suffix is not a Western Nilotic one, but is present in Karamojong (Novelli 1985: 46) and Teso (Hilders and Lawrance 1956: 3), and has also been reconstructed as one of the plural suffixes of Proto-Eastern Nilotic (Vossen 1982: 306). Examples from Karamojong are:

(9)　Karamojong
　　SG　　　　PL
　　ákì-myέt　ŋá-myέt-à　'fat, butter, oil'
　　a-bɔkɛt　ŋá-bɔkèt-á　'shovel'

In closely related Turkana (Dimmendaal 1983: 224–53) -*a* suffixes are found in concrete entity nouns—in opposition to abstract nouns—and usually characterize plurals. They do not occur in the replacement pattern and seem to be restricted to plurals of opaque singular nouns. The Labwor forms in (10) use Eastern Nilotic number inflectional morphology. The reason for borrowing the -*a* plural suffix is a process of rebalancing the number system, once a gap in the system had emerged (cf. Chapter 1, §4.1). In Labwor, singulatives occur very often, whereby the semantic aspect of number marking has become salient. The -*a* plurals in the replacement pattern typically express artificial or secondary plurals of not necessarily pluralic objects. Hence, number marking acquires a semantic dimension, which was not originally present in the Western Nilotic classifier system. This parallels the situation in Mawayana and Waiwai (Carlin, Chapter 13).

(10)　Labwor
　　SG　　　　PL
　　àɲîr　　àɲír-á　　'kidney'
　　myέl-í　myὲl-lá　'dance'　　<myέl 'to dance'

4.2 *Intragenetic borrowing*

Besides the number-inflectional and noun-categorizing suffixes, Western Nilotic languages also exhibit a number of nominal prefixes. Sex is always indicated by such prefixes, but Lwoo languages additionally developed many derivational prefixes. As Dimmendaal (2001) was able to show, most if not all of these prefixes are grammaticalized heads of endocentric compounds. Thus, there are two categories of prefixes; the first consisting of nominal prefixes that express sex or have once been used to do so—namely the Lwoo gender prefixes ò- (MASC, 11a) and à- (FEM, 11b). The second category is the derivative prefixes, which are more productive, being continuously derived from generic nouns by means of grammaticalization. In Labwor, as in other Lwoo languages, the original meaning of the gender prefixes has been gradually lost, so that sex is expressed by means of other formatives, e.g. separate nouns or kinship terms. The following examples include productive gender marking, in personal names as well as nouns, which no longer semantically refers to a certain gender:

(11)   Labwor
          SG   PL
   (a) ò-márá   'child with big stomach'   MASCULINE
        ò-bér   ò-bér̥-ɛ́   'mosquito'

   (b) à-jôk   'child with six fingers/toes'   FEMININE
        à-cút̥   à-cú-ɗí   'vulture'

The contact languages of Labwor—Karamojong and Teso—are entirely gender-marking languages. Labwor has borrowed prefixes from Teso-Turkana which originally indicated feminine gender. In Labwor, a semantic extension of the feminine gender marker leads to a diminutive and subsequently a singular meaning as an enhancement of the number-marking system. The plural is formed with è-, which in Karamojong serves as a masculine prefix and in Labwor has acquired its plural semantics via an augmentative meaning. In Karamojong, from which the prefix è- has been borrowed, the prefixed nominal morphemes exclusively denote gender.

(12) (a) Labwor
           SG   PL
           à-t̪ín   è-t̪ín-ò   'child'
           à-t̪ín ɗyáŋ   è-t̪ín ɗók   'calf'
           à-kwɔ́   è-kúw-é   'thief'

(b) Karamojong (Novelli 1985: 41)
     SG   PL
     é-kìl-é   ŋí-kíl-yók   'man'   MASC.
     á-béérʊ́   ŋá-berʊ̀   'woman' FEM.
     í-kɔ̀kʊ   ŋí-dwé   'child'   NEUTER

Contact between the noun classifier language Labwor and the gender-marking language Karamojong has been close and steady for a long time. This has led to the borrowing of an Eastern Nilotic vowel system, elements of the verbal system, and of nominal affixes. Gender as a grammatical category, however, has not diffused into Labwor. Apart from the indication of sex there is no evidence for the productive construction of masculine and feminine noun forms, even though the most salient gender-inflectional morphemes of Karamojong have been borrowed. The meaning encoded by these morphemes, however, was not considered salient. Instead, a semantic shift from masculine to augmentative and from feminine to diminutive is observed, which in a semantic and functional extension leads to the emergence of singular and plural pairings. In other words, the morphemes may be borrowed, but not the meaning, if it does not conform to the original semantics of the system. Or, more generally speaking, gender and noun classes did not jump over genetic boundaries. Apparently, from an ethnogrammatical point of view, both gender of Eastern Nilotic languages and noun classes of Niger-Congo are so different from what Western Nilotes seem to consider prototypical in their languages that neither grammatical principle has diffused into the Lwoian languages. In an attempt to summarize these considerations, we arrive at the following points:

- singulatives and tripartite number marking patterns are kept stable as long as there is grammatical material to do so;
- the indication of sex by means of prefixes is retained;
- semantic or functional categories, which are typologically diverse, do not diffuse into the nominal system: gender is not borrowed, but gender-inflectional morphemes are and acquire a new meaning (FEM → SG, MASC → PL).

Up to this stage, the analysis has mainly dealt with intragenetic contact, such as Dinka and Luwo or Karamojong and Labwor. Perhaps areal features such as T, N, and K number markers, and Nilotic features such as tripartite number marking, were retained just because there was no motivation in the composition of the contact situation to diverge from common features and structures. But what would this look like in an intergenetic contact situation that is as tightly knit as the Luwo–Dinka or Labwor–Karamojong one?

5 Cultural change, but no language shift: rebuilding archetypical features in Bor

Belanda Bor has lost the rich number-marking system of Western Nilotic altogether and does not retain any productive nominal suffixes. A few of the derivative prefixes remain, but are used for number-inflectional purposes. Most of the nouns are morphologically opaque in the singular and carry a prefix in the plural. The typological changes that have occurred in Bor— transforming a suffixing noun classifier language into a weakly prefixing language without any noticeable noun categorization devices—are the result of a massive process of cultural and ethnic amalgamation with an Ubangi-speaking group. The extremely tight relationship between both groups has led to an exceptionally close contact of both languages, which resulted in significant grammatical changes in Bor.

Contact between Western Nilotic Belanda Bor and the Ubangi (Niger-Congo) language Bviri is a recent phenomenon. It was only in the early nineteenth century that the Bor split off from the main Luwo body and migrated into the western hills of Bahr el-Ghazal. A major reason for these migrations was internal conflicts between subgroups of the Luwo, but also— and perhaps more than this—the frequent slave raids by Turko-Arab traders. As we know from early reports on the situation in the mid-nineteenth century Bahr el-Ghazal (Ali 1972; Santandrea 1964), the slave trade exercised such a pressure on the population that often only those remained in the villages and camps who were not fit for the slave market. The Bor must have reached the hills in a desperate state, and finally sought refuge there. Both lifestock and agricultural technology were lost, and the entire group began to live in caves. These former farmers and pastoralists had become foragers, who would live on what they gathered in the bush. Since constructing houses, hunting, and keeping livestock are all pastimes of the men in Lwoo societies, it is very likely that the Bor lost so many of their former cultural techniques because they had lost most of their men. The oral history of neighbouring groups emphasizes that the Bor had also forgotten about their former religion. Furthermore, a source of the early twentieth century tells us that the Bor held the lowest prestige and were marginalized by all other groups of south-western Bahr el-Ghazal ('The Jur despised by the Dinka and despising the Bor', Tucker 1931: 59).

This group, however, owned the land in which the Bviri, refugees themselves, decided to settle. During the Zande invasions, which meant a rapid expansion of this large Ubangi-speaking group of Central Africa, the Bviri were driven eastwards. In order to flee from enslavement by the Zande, they hid in the mountainous parts of Bahr el-Ghazal, where they encountered the Bor in their cave dwellings. A desperate deal between the two groups was made whereby the Bviri were allowed to settle down in the land owned by the Bor, who in turn were assisted in house building and clearing the bush for their farms, and also were allowed to participate in the religious life of the Bviri (Mur'ba Wau 2002). Thus, severe political, social, and economic circumstances led to the cultural amalgamation of both groups, which resulted in fascinating linguistic changes.

But which language type was it that came with the Bviri to Bahr el-Ghazal's hills? Ubangi languages tend to be suffixing noun class languages with class concord and a highly agglutinative morphology. The languages of the Sere-Ndogo Tagbu group, to which Bviri belongs, have, however, lost their noun classes—obviously before contact with Western Nilotic—and simply mark the plural forms by means of a classificatory prefix with a bleached meaning, e.g.:

(13) Ndogo—Bai plurals (Santandrea 1961)

SG	PL	
ɗako	ndá-ɗako	'man'
ni	ndá-ni	'woman'

Belanda Bor has largely borrowed this grammatical pattern. In the following examples the plurals exhibit a prefix *ká-*—which is of course one of the old areal features that are so omnipresent in Western Nilotic (see §2). The classificatory pluralizer has thus replaced the original plural classifiers and derivational morphemes:

(14) Belanda Bor

SG	PL	
kwʊ́ì	ká-kwʊ́ì	'eagle'
kà	ká-kà	'wound'
ríŋɔ́	ká-ríŋɔ́	'meat'
fíɲ	ká-fíɲ	'place'

The examples demonstrate that not only the original singular forms are pluralized, but also old singulatives, e.g. 'meat'. Here, the original singulative suffix -ɔ́ has been retained, but is fully lexicalized and remains in the prefixed plural form. The collective form *ríŋ* does not exist any more in Belanda Bor.

The Belanda Bor data also include nouns that employ the replacement pattern for number marking. These are mostly nouns that denote human beings, and—again—the formatives are exclusively prefixes and thus differ typologically from the formatives of the other Lwoo languages. In example (15), the singular forms are constructed with a prefix *ji-* that occurs in other Lwoo languages as well. According to Reh (1985: 56, cit. Dimmendaal 2000: 247) this prefix is derived from a common Western Nilotic root **jal-* 'traveller'. In the plural the *ji-* prefix is replaced by *jò-*. The former compound noun has thus been reanalysed as a prefixed replacive morpheme 'person' plus a noun stem functioning as specifier:

(15) Belanda Bor

SG	PL	
jì-tòt	jò-tòt	'liar'
jì-ɲâw	jò-ɲâw	'merchant'
jì-ɲὲrὲ	jò-ɲὲrὲ	'chief'

Furthermore, Belanda Bor uses a prefix *ɲí-* in order to construct singulatives. This marker has been grammaticalized from the root 'daughter of', which is not used as a full noun any more in Belanda Bor. Again, as in Labwor, a semantic extension of 'feminine' towards 'small' and 'single' has taken place here. Compare the following forms with an underlying morphologically opaque collective form:

(16) Belanda Bor

COLL	SGVE	
fìì	ɲí-fìì	'water/drop of water'
kúyɔ́	ɲí-kúyɔ́	'sand/sand corn'
bέl	ɲí-bέl	'sorghum/grain'

Interestingly, both the underlying collective as well as the singulative noun have plurals. In both cases the additive general plural prefix *ká-* is employed:

(17) Belanda Bor

ká-fìì	'quantities of water'	ká-ɲí-fìì	'drops of water'
ká-làk	'sets of teeth'	ká-ɲí-làk	'teeth'
ká-ŋɔ̀r	'quantities of beans'	ká-ɲí-ŋɔ̀r	'several beans'

The fact that the three categories of the tripartite number-marking system in Belanda Bor have been retained, even by using innovative strategies, shows that language contact does not necessarily include typological changes of the number system itself. Two salient features of Western Nilotic have been retained in Belanda Bor, namely the tripartite number-marking patterns of East Sudanic and number-inflectional morphemes stemming from the ancient linguistic area of which Western Nilotic has been a part. Contact with Ubangi led to significant structural changes in the fields of phonology, syllable structure, and affixation techniques in the noun morphology, but the semantic dimension of the number-inflectional system has been kept up without any other salient contact-induced changes. This is even more surprising, as Bor was certainly the less prestigious language of the contact scenario. With perhaps few people surviving, most of them elders, women, and children, the Bor were basically ill-equipped for the preservation of their language, let alone its typologically peculiar features. In contrast to its essentially converging with Ubangi, morphological material from Bor seems to have diffused into Bviri, as the following example suggests:

(18)   Bviri plurals (Behagel 1988)

SG	PL	
ni	ka-ni	'woman'
mvàa	ka-mvàa	'knife'
lè	ka-lè	'name'
ju	ka-ju	'rat'

These examples show exactly the opposite of the usual case: in accordance with numerous examples discussed in Chapter 1, where 'a politically dominant language usually influences a less dominant one' (§4.2.3), the borrowing process should have taken the opposite direction. But instead of the common Ndogo-Sere-Tagbu morpheme *ndá-*, the Belanda Bor plural prefix *ká-* is found here, and this morpheme clearly spread into Bviri as an areally distributed morpheme. It is intriguing to think that perhaps more than 2,000 years after its occurrence in Meroitic, this plural marker has been introduced into Ubangian Bviri as a prefix. If the historical hypothesis about the origin and time scale of T, N and K could ever be proven to hold true, then this linguistic area would have survived for perhaps two millennia.

6 Does contact really make grammars more similar?

After examining three representative, sociolinguistically different cases of grammars in contact in the Western Nilotic area, the answer to this question should be: no, not really. During its long history of steady migrations, Western Nilotic underwent no major changes in its nominal system, at least as far as categories like tripartite number inflection, noun categorization, and the areal nominal affixes are concerned. Moreover, areal adaptations appear to have remained productive over hundreds or even thousands of years, as long as later contact situations did not involve the creation of new

Sprachbund situations. Two important principles seem to be involved here: first, prototypical features are always retained or revitalized. They are never replaced by foreign grammatical material, but may rather aggressively spread into typologically different contact languages. Secondly, a closed set of grammatical properties serves as an identity marker, contrasting to the features of neighboured, typologically different contact languages. Speakers obviously consider such properties as a salient part of their identity. Given reasonably short contact between languages, these properties tend to keep productive morphosyntactic patterns.

As a result of this chapter, we see that in a number of sociolinguistically diverse contact situations certain parts of the grammar were replaced by borrowed grammatical material, while other parts of the grammar remained stable or even diffused into the contact languages. A brief summary of contact phenomena would look as in Table 3.

The social history and geographical situation of Western Nilotic has created an attitude where grammatical elements of a language encode local and ethnic identity and a case of balanced contact that persisted in asymmetrical sociolinguistic situations. Language must have for a very long time been perceived as being typologically special, and speakers of Western Nilotic would then have compared their own with languages of the foreign peoples west and south of them. There must also have been ethnolinguistic techniques of defining typologically salient parts of the grammar, which were not present in the foreign neighbouring languages. Frequency of grammatical categories might have been a first stimulus for the creation of prototypical patterns (Chapter 1, §4.1), but later these categories became rare in some of the languages and were merely kept up for emblematicity. Cultural impact would then play a role in the sense of ethnogrammatical techniques.

It seems likely that such techniques were created during a phase of lengthy migration and economic threat as an expression of the speakers' 'sense of purism' (Chapter 1). As we know from the ethnohistorical studies on the early migrations and the timescale set by the Egyptian Rhoda archives (Atkinson 1999; Herring 1979), there were several decades of drought in the twelfth and thirteenth centuries, when the Nile floods in Egypt failed and some two-thirds of the population died of starvation. The time frame given by Rhoda fits very well into what Lwoo oral history says about the era of their southward migrations, so that there might be a connection (Atkinson 1999). If we want to explain why in some cases of language contact originally typologically diverse grammars do become similar and why in other cases they would not converge, we may have to take ethnolinguistic and of course ethnohistorical data into account more than before. Apparently, the genesis of a communal identity

TABLE 3. Contact phenomena in the grammars of three Lwoo languages

	Luwo	Labwor	Belanda Bor
Vowel system	convergence towards Dinka (creaky/breathy)	convergence towards Karamojong (reduction of ATR vowel harmony)	convergence towards Bviri (reduction of phonemes)
Consonant system	stable	convergence towards Eastern Nilotic (plosives)	convergence towards Bviri (plosives, labiovelars)
Inflectional patterns	stable + convergence to Dinka (non-linear morphology)	stable	convergence to Bviri (prefixation)
Noun categorization	stable, slight reduction	stable, slight reduction	largely lost, incipient regrammaticalizations
Innovative gender/noun class patterns	none	none	none
Number marking	stable	stable (reanalysis of loans)	stable (restructured)

on the grounds of linguistic features has its roots in such ethnohistorical phenomena, where a group of peoples practically lost its entire material basis. In the case studied here, phonological properties are always borrowed easily, but morphological properties are not, more especially if they are connected to a salient typological pattern. A hierarchy of diffusion emerges, whereby part of the grammar converges to neighbouring systems, but never noun categorization and number-marking patterns. These were emblematic features which played a salient role in the speakers' language attitudes. Perhaps, language contact that affects the grammatical system first of all provides a motivation for defining the specific grammatical features for developing strategies of 'othering', so as to define those elements that tend to become part of the speakers' identity and those elements that do not. An answer to the question asked in Chapter 1—'Which linguistic features are prone to diffusion?'—should be simply: all those features that do not violate emblematic patterns and that can be integrated into the system without altering its most basic structures.

References

Ali, A. I. M. 1972. *The British, the slave trade and slavery in the Sudan (1820–1881)*. Khartoum: Khartoum University Press.

Atkinson, R. R. 1999. *The origins of the Acholi of Uganda*. Kampala: Fountain.

Behagel, A. 1988. 'Lexique', pp. 98–146 of *Lexique comparatif des langues ouban-guiennes*, edited by Y. Monino. Paris: Geuthner.

Bender, L. M. 1991. 'Sub-classification of Nilo-Saharan', pp. 1–35 of *Proceedings of the fourth Nilo-Saharan conference*, edited by L. M. Bender. Hamburg: Buske.

Blench, R. 1995. 'Is Niger-Congo simply a branch of Nilo-Saharan?', pp. 83–130 of *Actes du cinquième colloque de linguistique nilo-saharienne*, edited by R. Nicolai and F. Rottland. Cologne: Köppe.

Bryan, M. 1959. 'The T/K languages: a new substratum', *Africa* 29: 1–21.

—— 1968. 'The *N/*K languages of Africa', *Journal of African Languages* 7: 169–217.

Crazzolara, J. P. 1950–4. *The Lwoo*, vols. 1–3. Verona: Museum Combonianum.

Dimmendaal, G. 1983. *The Turkana language*. Dordrecht: Foris.

—— 2000. 'Number marking and noun categorization in Nilo-Saharan languages', *Anthropological Linguistics* 42: 214–61.

—— 2001. 'Areal diffusion versus genetic inheritance: an African perspective', pp. 358–92 of *Areal diffusion and genetic inheritance*, edited by A. Y. Aikhenvald and R. M. W. Dixon. Oxford: Oxford University Press.

Doneux, J. L. 1975. 'Hypothèses pour la comparative des langues atlantiques', *Africana Linguistica* 6: 41–129.

Ehret, C. et al. 1974. 'Some thoughts on the early history of the Nile-Congo Water-shed', *Ufahamu* 5: 85–112.

Greenberg, J. H. 1963. *The languages of Africa*. The Hague: Mouton.

—— 1981. 'Nilo-Saharan moveable-k as a stage III article (with a Penutian typological parallel)', *Journal of African Languages and Linguistics* 3: 105–12.

Gregersen, E. A. 1972. 'Kongo-Saharan', *Journal of African Languages* 11: 69–89.

Herring, R. S. 1979. 'Hydrology and chronology: the Rodah Nilometer as an aid in dating interlacustrine history', pp. 39–86 in *Chronology, migration and drought in interlacustrine Africa*, edited by J. B. Webster. New York: Africana.

Hilders, J. H. and Lawrance, J. C. D. 1956. *An introduction to the Ateso language*. Kampala: Eagle.

Maho, J. 1999. *A comparative study of Bantu noun classes*. Gothenburg: Acta Universi-tatis.

Mur'ba Wau, C. 2002. *The structure of the noun phrase in Viri*. MA thesis, University of Khartoum.

Novelli, B. 1985. *A grammar of the Karimojong language.* Berlin: Reimer.

Pierli, F., Ratti, M. T. and Wheeler, A. (eds.), 1998. *Gateway to the heart of Africa.* Nairobi: Paulines.

Reh, M. 1985. 'Reconstructing Proto-Western Nilotic and Proto-Nilotic lexicon'. MS.

—— 1996. *Anywa language.* Cologne: Köppe.

Rilly, C. 2004. 'Recent evidence for Meroitic as an Eastern Sudanic language'. Paper presented at 9th NSLC, Khartoum.

Rottland, F. 1982. *Die südnilotischen Sprachen: Beschreibung, Vergleichung und Rekonstruktion.* Berlin: Reimer.

Santandrea, F. S. 1931. 'The Belanda, Ndogo, Bai and Sere in the Bahr-el-Ghazal', *Sudanese Notes and Records* 14: 161–79.

—— 1961. *Comparative outline-grammar of Ndogo—Sere—Tagbu—Bai—Bviri.* Bologna: Nigrizia.

—— 1964. *A tribal history of the Western Bahr el Ghazal.* Bologna: Nigrizia.

Storch, A. 2003. 'Dynamics of interacting populations: language contact in Bahr el-Ghazal', *Studies in African Linguistics* 32: 1–29.

—— 2005. *The noun morphology of Western Nilotic.* Cologne: Rudiger Köppe Verlag.

—— and Dinslage, S. 2000. *Magic and gender.* Cologne: Köppe.

—— and Vossen, R. In press. 'Odours and colours in Nilotic: comparative case studies', in *Proceedings of the 8th Nilo-Saharan linguistic colloquium,* edited by D. Payne and M. Reh. Cologne: Köppe.

Tucker, A. N. 1931. 'The tribal confusion around Wau', *Sudanese Notes and Records* 14: 49–60.

Vossen, R. 1982. *The Eastern Nilotes: linguistic and historical reconstructions.* Berlin: Reimer.

Werner, R., Anderson, W. and Wheeler, A. 2000. *Day of devastation day of contentment.* Nairobi: Paulines.

Westermann, D. 1911. *Die Sudansprachen.* Hamburg: Augustin.

—— 1927. *Die westlichen Sudansprachen und ihre Beziehungen zum Bantu.* Berlin: Mouton de Gruyter.

4

Grammars in Contact in the Volta Basin (West Africa)

On Contact-Induced Grammatical Change in Likpe

FELIX K. AMEKA

1 The setting

The 'Volta Basin' corresponds to the core area of the (New) Kwa and Gur language groups within Niger-Congo. Geographically, it extends from the Nigeria-Benin border until Côte d'Ivoire to the west and northwards into Burkina Faso. This area is known for its high multilingualism with large repertoires of languages for individuals and different histories of contact among the people who today inhabit the region (Dimmendaal 2001). We focus in this chapter on the Likpe community living in the hills along the Ghana–Togo border surrounded by different groups speaking languages distinct from theirs including Ewe, the dominant lingua franca, Akan, a majority language in the Lower Volta Basin, and smaller languages like Siwu (Lolobi) and Lɛlɛmi (Buem), their genetic relatives, on the left bank of the Volta River (see Map 1).

Different factors have promoted contact among the peoples of the Volta Basin over the centuries including migration, trade, and warfare. The oral traditions of many of the peoples in the region, the interpretation of some older written records, and the lower-level relationships among the languages suggest that there have been different waves of migration: from the east to the west, and later some other expansions from the west towards the east. As population movements continued, different processes of linguistic assimilation took place. For instance, Agotime, a town in Ghana's Volta region, used to be Dangme-speaking but has now completely shifted to Ewe.

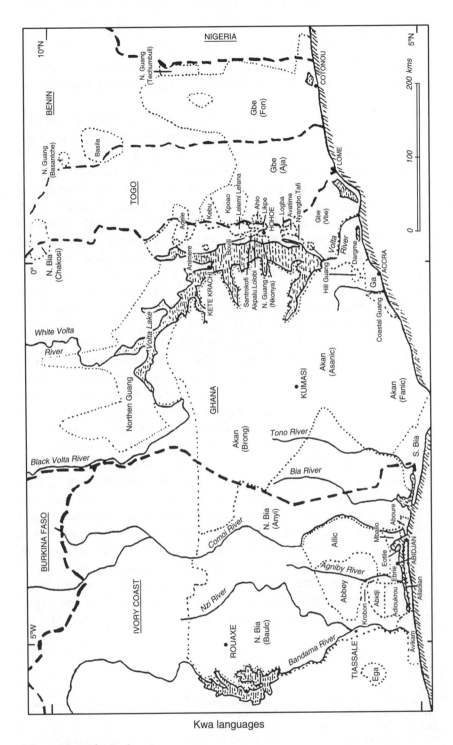

Kwa languages

MAP 1 The Volta Basin

Source: Bendor Samuel (1989: 216).

Another driving force is trade. There were trade routes from the north and west and from the east and also from the sea, introducing the European element.

A further motive for contact and language shift, and even language death, is the wars for hegemony among various groups. In fact the Ghana-Togo-Mountain borderland seems to have been a melting pot for language shifts by whole groups as it ultimately served as refuge for populations fleeing from Asante invasions from the west in the nineteenth century and from Daho-mean military operations from the later eighteenth century onwards (Nugent 1997, 2005). As Akyeampong (2002: 39) put it: 'Wars of state formation amongst the Akan west of the Volta between 1670s and 1730s inundated the Ewe of south-eastern Ghana with refugees.' As such movements and turbu-lence continued languages disappeared, or are—or were—only vaguely remembered. Debrunner (1962) found traces of languages once spoken in this hill area that by the mid-twentieth century were remembered by only a few people. The communities speaking these languages were apparently destroyed by local wars that scattered their populations (Dakubu 2006).

The aim of this chapter is to discuss the grammatical changes that have taken place in the Likpe, or, as they call themselves, the Bakpɛlé, cultural linguistic group. I argue that two external factors are responsible for the changes: first the intense contact with Ewe, and, second, 'pressure' to adopt areal patterns. The rest of the chapter is structured as follows. §2 sketches the geographical and sociohistorical context of the contact between Ewe and Sɛkpɛlé, the auto-denomination for the Likpe language. §3 compares Ewe and Likpe typologically. §4 discusses grammatical constructions that Likpe may have borrowed from Ewe. The constructions discussed are the extension of a 3pl pronoun to mark plural on genderless nouns (§4.1); the innovation of a gerund formation strategy involving permutation of noun complement order and the reduplication of the verb (§4.2) and of a periphrastic present progressive construction (§4.3); and complement constructions (§4.4). §5 surveys discourse patterns that have spread into Likpe from Ewe and other languages, such as verbal expressions for the notions of 'believe' and 'hope'. §6 summarizes the outcomes, preferences, and attitudes towards the changes.[1]

[1] A draft of this paper was written while I was a Visiting Fellow at the Research Centre for Linguistic Typology, La Trobe University, Australia (March–August 2005). I am very grateful to Sasha Aikhen-vald, Bob Dixon, Birgit Hellwig, and Melanie Wilkinson for their comments and support. Fieldwork on Likpe has been supported by the MPI for Psycholinguistics, Nijmegen. I am greatly indebted to my

2 The sociolinguistic and historical context of Likpe

Sɛkpɛlé is one of the fourteen 'Central Togo' (Dakubu and Ford 1988) or Ghana-Togo-Mountain (GTM) languages (Ring 1995). They were first recognized as a group and labelled *Togorestsprachen* 'Togo remnant languages' by Struck (1912). Westermann and Bryan (1952: 96) note that they have 'some vocabulary resemblance to the KWA (*sic*) languages, but the Class system is reminiscent of BANTU (*sic*)'. Nevertheless, they are classified as Kwa and are divided into Na-Togo, to which Likpe belongs, and Ka-Togo subgroups (Heine 1968). The two groups are presumed to branch out from Proto-Kwa as in Figure 1 (Williamson and Blench 2000; Blench 2001).

Sɛkpɛlé has two major dialects, Sekwa and Sɛkpɛlé, and is spoken in twelve villages in the area east and north-east of Hohoe (the Ewe-speaking district capital) up to the Togo border in the northern part of the Volta region of Ghana (Map 2). The area has about 23,000 residents who speak the language (1998 figures) including a small percentage of second language speakers. If other native speakers in the diaspora are added, there may well be over 30,000 speakers of the language today. Table 1 shows the distribution of sub-dialects across the villages.

This dialect division concurs with the Likpe oral settlement history. The Bakwa and Todome, i.e. Sekwa speakers, are said to have been in the area before the rest came. It is likely that Sekwa was shifted to or learnt by the other people when they came. What language the newcomers spoke is not entirely clear. Some may have spoken some other Tano languages since they trace themselves to Atebubu in Brong Ahafo. The Likpe and the Nkonya, a Northern Guang group, also purportedly used to share a common border. Others may have spoken some Gbe variety given that the Bakwa have cultural ties with a group across the border in Yikpa who today speak only Ewe (Nugent 1997). The implication for the language, even before Ewe contact, is that it may have some Guang or more generally Tano substrate elements.

The current dialect distribution also reflects the splits and migrations that have occurred since the first settlements. For instance, the people of Abrani used to live in Mate and a chieftaincy dispute led to their migration.

It is estimated that the Ewes settled in their present homeland in the late sixteenth and early seventeenth century (Amenumey 1986). Since the Ewes

Likpe language consultants especially the late Mr A. K. Avadu, Mr. E. K. Okyerefo, Madam Stella Atsyor Ekudi, Madam Georgina Dzata, Ms Justina Owusu, Mr Tevor, and his daughter Betty for helping me to understand their language. The Ewe examples are drawn from my observations of Ewe language use and from drama and narrative creative writings of native speakers.

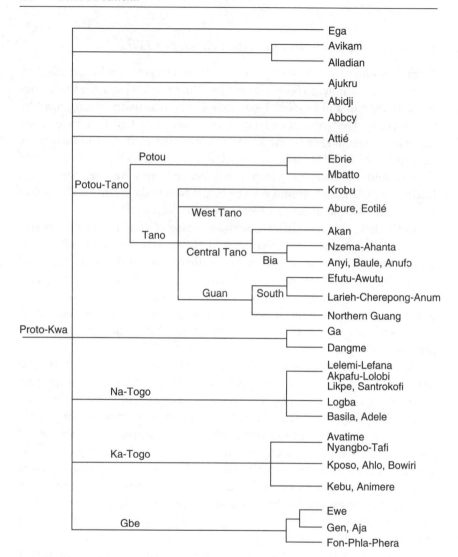

FIGURE 1 Classification of Kwa languages
Source: Williamson and Blench (2000: 29).

supposedly arrived later than the GTM groups, the contact between Likpe and the Ewes, especially the Gbis (the people of Hohoe, the district capital), must have started around this time. The name Likpe is derived from Ewe and literally means 'rub/file stone', and the Likpe oral tradition claims that they gave land to the Gbis.

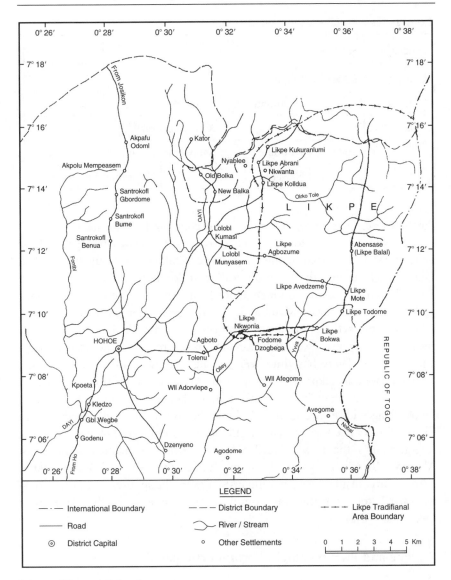

MAP 2 Likpe traditional area

The contact between the Likpe and Ewes has been on-going for centuries, and since Ewe is the dominant lingua franca in the Likpe area, almost all Likpe are bilingual in Likpe and Ewe. Additionally, several Likpe also speak Akan.

TABLE 1. Sɛkpɛlé dialects and their distribution

Language	Sɛkpɛlé				
Dialects	Sekwa	Sɛkpɛlé			
Subdialects		L2 communities	Situnkpa	Semate	Sela
Villages	Bakwa	Alavanyo	Avedzime	Mate	Bala
	Todome	Wudome	Agbozume	Abrani	
		Nkwanta		Koforidua	Kukurantumi

Furthermore, a good proportion has some command of (Ghanaian) English. It is, however, unusual for a speaker of one of the GTM languages to have another GTM language in their repertoire. Children grow up bilingual in Likpe and Ewe such that communication in kindergarten is sometimes in Ewe. Church services are conducted mostly in Ewe including announcements, and Ewe hymn books and Bible are used.[2] Ewe is taught as a subject in schools. Transactions at district offices and the district hospital for most people involve Ewe. Such domains of use reinforce the need to learn and use Ewe. There has thus been a long, intense, and ongoing contact between Ewe and Likpe with many more bilinguals in the two languages in the community than in any other pair of languages. Some of the older Likpe villages have Ewe names: Todome 'bottom of the hill'; Avedzime 'in the red forest'. The Ewe presence in Likpe is also reinforced by Ewe-speaking migrants into the area as settler farmers with Ewe-named settlements: Alavanyo 'It will be good'; Wudome 'under the Wu tree'. While Likpes marry from outside their ethnolinguistic group, the spouses do not necessarily learn Likpe since they can communicate in one of the 'big' languages: Ewe, Akan, or English.

3 Likpe and Ewe: typological profiles compared

Table 2 presents various typological features and their realization in Ewe and Likpe. Some of the more typical Likpe features are exemplified in the rest of this section.

Likpe has a root-controlled Advanced Tongue Root (ATR) vowel harmony system where the first syllable of the stem determines the ATR value of the

---

[2] Currently, there is a Bible translation project under way. The Epistles of Paul have been translated and these texts are used side by side the Ewe ones in church.

TABLE 2. Ewe and Likpe typological features compared

Feature	Ewe	Likpe
Vowel system	7 with oral and nasal counterparts (e and schwa are allophones)	8 with oral and nasal counterparts[a] (e and schwa are distinct phonemes)
Vowel harmony	No ATR but height assimilation	Root-controlled ATR and height assimilation, *i* and *u* are opaque vowels
Consonants	Contrast between labiodental and bilabial fricatives; voicing contrast in all places of articulation	[-anterior] consonants do not have voicing contrast; they are dialect variants
Tone	Two level tonemes High and Non-High plus Rising and Falling; lexical contrast plus derivational function	At least three level tonemes plus Rising and Falling; lexical contrast plus inflectional function
Syllable types	V, CV, CGV, CLV, CVV plus nasal coda syllables (but not VN)	All of these plus VN
Morphological type	Isolating with agglutinative features (and limited fusion)	Agglutinative with some fusion
Marking	Neither head nor dependent marking	Dependent marking in the NP, head marking at the clause level
Noun classes	Inherited nominal prefixes that have no classificatory function	Active noun classes marked by prefixes with concord markers for noun modifiers and for subject cross-reference
Constituent order	SV/AVO	SV/AVO
Grammatical relations	Defined by constituent order, Subject and non-subject distinguished by distinct forms of pronoun plus behaviour in syntactic constructions, e.g focus	Defined by constituent order, and subject is cross-referenced on the verb. Subject and non-subject distinguished by distinct forms of pronoun plus behaviour in syntactic constructions, e.g focus

(Continued)

Table 2. (*Continued*)

Feature	Ewe	Likpe
NP	Head can be preceded by an identifier, other modifiers follow	Head initial, modifiers follow and are marked for agreement with the head (except the qualifiers)
Adjectives	Small closed class of 5 underived adjectives	No underived adjectives
Nominal possession	Possessor precedes possessum and are juxtaposed in the inalienable construction (The order is reversed for 1SG and 2SG.) Alienable construction involves the linker *ƒé* 'POSS'	Possessor precedes possessum; Pronominal possessors juxtaposed Nominal possessors linked to the possessum by *(e)to* 'POSS'
Verb complex structure	Preverb markers (6 slots)-Verb-Habitual suffix	Prefixes/Proclitics (3 slots)-Verb-Suffixes (2 slots)
TAM expression	Preverb markers and dedicated grammatical constructions	Prefixes and dedicated **grammatical constructions for present progressive** (§4.3)
Negation	Marked by a bipartite structure, first part immediately before the verb complex and the other part at the end of the clause before any utterance final particles	Marked by a nasal prefix just before the verb root
Adpositions (Both prepositions and postpositions)	A class of about 10 prepositions grammaticalized from verbs, and over two dozen postpositions, grammaticalized from body part and environment nouns	A class of two prepositions: a locative and a comitative–grammaticalized from the associative verb suffix; and **a class of about a dozen postpositions grammaticalized from body parts and environment terms**
Locative predication	A single locative verb language; no preposition in the Basic Locative Construction (BLC)	A multiverb positional language with 15 verbs used in the BLC and the reference object obligatorily marked by the locative preposition

Argument structure constructions. In both languages, transitivity is not an inherent feature of verbs	• Unmarked one-place construction -*nyá* Undergoer voice construction	• Unmarked one-place -*nɔ* Undergoer voice construction (**Actor realization**)
	• Two place constructions • Theme-locative (e.g. BLC, Possessive) • Causal • Aspectual constructions of various kinds	• Two place constructions • Theme-Locative (e.g. BLC, Possessive) • 'Active'
	• Three place constructions • THEME-GOAL construction • GOAL-THEME construction	• Three place constructions • GOAL-THEME construction • Modal-aspectual constructions of various kinds with nominalized verb as OBJ2
Serial verb constructions	Subject marked only once, Negation marked only once, VPs can be marked for compatible aspect values, Predicate focus possible	Subject marked on each verb, Negation marked once on the first verb, Verbs can be marked for compatible aspect values
Complementation strategies	Nominalization, Overlapping clause; Complement clauses introduced by *bé* also a quotative marker, requires logophoric pronoun for non-1st person coreference *né* an irrealis complement introducer	Nominalization Complement clauses introduced by *ŋkə* a **complementizer, *bɔ́*, a borrowing from Ewe with functional differentiation** (§4.4), and reduced form of person marked *ŋkə* for equi complementation
Connectors NP Addition Contrast (Clauses)	*kplé*—(also comitative preposition) 'and; with' *gaké*—'but'	*kú*—(also comitative preposition) 'and; with' **kaké*—'but' adapted from Ewe**

(Continued)

Table 2. (*Continued*)

Feature	Ewe	Likpe
Disjunction phrases and clauses	*lóó*—'X or Y, I don't know which' *aló*—'X or Y, It doesn't matter which' *lóó aló*—'It could be X, It could be Y, I don't know which, It doesn't matter which	**lee—'X or Y, I don't know which'** *nye*—'X or Y, It doesn't matter which'
Adverbial clauses Temporal	*ési* 'when'	*lɔ́* 'when' < 'LOC' preposition grammaticalized
Conditional Manner	*né* 'if' *álési* 'how' < *álé* 'thus, like this', *si* 'REL'	*lɔ́* 'if' < 'LOC' preposition grammaticalized
Purpose	*álé bé* 'so that' < *álé* 'thus' be 'COMP'	*kase* 'how' (also functions as the question word)
Reason	*elabéná* 'because' postposition *ta* 'since' < HEAD	**alɔ́ bɔ́ 'so that' (borrowed from Ewe) (§4.4)** *nya-so* 'therefore', *e-so* 'because'
Information packaging scene setting	Terminal particles *lá*; *ɖé*	Phrase final vowel lengthening; **particle *lá* (borrowed from Ewe) (§5)**
Focus constructions	Term constituent preposed and marked by a focus particle *(y)é*	Term constituent preposed, no focus marking, subject cross-referenced by dependent markers.
Utterance final particles	Yes (some of which have diffused in the area)	**Yes** (some of which have diffused in the area)

[a] Likpe structures suspected to have been influenced by Ewe are in boldface.

prefixes. It does not affect suffixes. For instance, the ATR value of the first syllable in *-kpɛlé* 'Likpe' determines the ATR value of prefixes of its derivatives: *ɔ-kpɛlé* 'a Likpe person'; *ba-kpɛlé* 'Likpe people'; *sɛ-kpɛlé* 'Likpe language'.

Subjects (A/S), but not Objects, are cross-referenced on the verb. The subject cross-reference prefixes are neutralized for number and are distinct from pronominals. Two sets of subject cross-reference markers are distinguished: the non-dependent and the dependent sets. The former is used in pragmatically unmarked main clauses while the latter is used in dependent and pragmatically marked clause types like relative, focus, and content question constructions. The non-dependent cross-reference is unmarked in stative constructions (example 3) and is realized as a vowel whose form depends on the features of the vowel of the verb root (1a, b).

(1) (a) Pius   ə-bə́   mfo
          NAME   SCR-come   here
          Pius came here

     (b) be-síó   bá-mə́   á-nɔ   li-kpéfí   nə́-mə́
          CMPL-woman   AGR-DET   SCR-hear   CM-child   AGR-DET
          The women heard the child

The dependent cross-reference markers are *n-* and *IV-* where the V harmonizes with the vowel in the verb stem. The former is used with general present time; the latter for non-present situations. The focus counterpart of (1a) with a dependent cross-reference marker on the verb is (2).

(2) Pius   li-bə́   mfo
     NAME   SCR-come   here
     Pius came here

In predicative possessive structures, the possessor and the possessed can be linked to either the subject or object function as in (3).

(3) (a) Saka   kpé   a-taabí
          NAME   be.in   CM-money
          Saka has money

     (b) a-taabi   kpé   Saka
          CM-money   be.in   NAME
          Money is possessed by Saka

The reversed Possessed—Verb—Possessor order could have been influenced by Ewe where that order prevails in predicative possessive constructions (Ameka 1996).

Likpe, unlike Ewe, is an active noun class language with classes indicated by nominal prefixes. Modifiers follow the head in a noun phrase and, except for the qualifiers, agree with the noun head in number and class, marked by prefixes on the terms.

4 Constructions borrowed from Ewe

4.1 Plural number-marking strategy

A clear instance of the influence of Ewe on Likpe grammar is in suffixal plural number marking on a subset of kinship terms and proper nouns (for signalling associative plural). These nouns fall outside the singular/plural gender system. Throughout Niger-Congo gender systems, such nouns tend to be genderless and have other strategies for plural marking. In Bantu linguistics, they are assigned to class 1a (Katamba 2003). Arguably, genderless kinship terms and proper nouns are a retained feature in Likpe. How the plural is marked on these nouns has, however, been borrowed from Ewe. In Ewe plural is marked by a clitic =wó 'PL' which is attached to the last element in the NP before the intensifier. For example:

(4)   ame   (eve   má=)wó   ko
Ewe   person two   DEM=PL   only
       only (those two) people

The Ewe nominal plural marker =wó is in a heterosemic relation to the '3PL' pronominal wó, as used in utterances of the kind in (5).[3] That is to say, they are identical in form and are semantically related but belong to different grammatical categories. Some might use the term polysemy for this relation, but polysemy for me is a relation between semantically related forms where the senses belong to the same grammatical category.

(5)   (a)   wó-dzo   (wó)
Ewe   3pl-fly   3pl
             They flew jumped (them)

       (b)   wó-ƒé   afé   bi
             3pl-POSS   house   burn
             Their house burnt

One of the uses of the Ewe plural marker is as an associative plural, especially in collocation with proper nouns, i.e. N-wó means 'N and co', and not two or more instances of the same N. The two readings of the form are illustrated in (6).

---

[3] In some dialects, the heterosemic network extends to the possessive linker in the alienable construction (Ameka 1996).

(6)   Kofi=wó   *fé*   sukuu

Ewe   NAME=PL   POSS   school

> the school of several Kofi's/
> the school of Kofi and his associates
> (none of the associates need be called Kofi)

In Likpe, some kinterms, including borrowed ones, are gendered as shown in (7).

(7) ɔ-nyimi 'sibling'   ba-nyimi 'siblings'
      u-titábo 'nephew/niece' be-titábo 'nephews/nieces'
      o-tási   'paternal aunt'   ba-tási   'paternal aunts' (from Ewe tási)
      o-fa   'maternal uncle' ba-fa   'maternal uncles' (from Akan
                                            via Ewe)

Kinterms belonging to ego's parents' generation and above are genderless and are suffixed with *mɔ́* 'PL' to signal plurality, as in (8).

(8) anto   'father'   anto-mɔ́   'father-PL'
      ambe   'mother'   ambe-mɔ́ 'mother-PL'
      éwú   'grandmother' éwu-mɔ́   'grandmother-PL'
      nna   'grandfather'   nna-mɔ́   'grandfather-PL'

Furthermore, the term for 'great-grandparents', borrowed from Ewe, also forms its plural by *-mɔ́* suffixation, as in (9).

(9) así-ma-ká-tó-é-mɔ́
     hand-PRIV-touch-ear-DIM-PL
     great-grandparents

The form *-mɔ́* 'PL' is identical in form and is semantically related to the 3PL pronoun form *mɔ́*, a pattern that is parallel to the situation in Ewe noted earlier. While one cannot completely rule out internal developments in Likpe grammar in accounting for this situation, it seems more plausible that the pattern of the relationship between a 3PL and a PL marker came into Likpe via the copying of a similar Ewe heterosemic pattern. The use of the Ewe PL marker with proper nouns with an associative reading provides a good motivation for the copying. Heine and Kuteva (2005: 92) might prefer to call it 'replica grammaticalization', since it involves the transfer of a grammaticalization process rather than a grammatical concept.

4.2 *The so-called O-V-V nominalization strategy*

Ewe abounds in nominalized structures of the form N(P)-REDUP-V, also described as O-V-V structures (Aboh 2004). The structure involves preposing the internal argument of a verb to its reduplicated form. Gerunds are formed this way, as illustrated in (10).

(10)   (a)   *f*a   te   >   te-*f*a-*f*a[4]
Ewe   plant   yam   yam-REDUP-plant
               plant   yams   yam planting

        (b)   fiá   nú   >   nú-fiá-fiá
               teach   thing   thing-REDUP-teach
               teach   teaching

Likpe, by contrast, being an active noun class language, predominantly uses noun class markers as nominalizers. Thus an agentive nominal can be derived from the verb *yu* 'steal' by prefixing it with the class marker for animates, namely, *u-yu* 'thief', and a gerund by prefixing *bu-* to it, i.e. *bu-yu* 'stealing'. Actually, a gerund can be formed from any verb by affixing the prefix *bV-* to it. (The noun class marked by this prefix is equivalent to the class called infinitive in Bantu languages.) We see in §4.3 that the nominalized event complement in the present progressive is formed in this way.

Likpe uses other strategies for deverbal nominalization which do not seem to be due to influence from Ewe. These are:

   (i)   reduplication of the verb to form a nominal stem and assigning the derived stem to an appropriate noun class. For instance, the verb *sa* 'jump' is reduplicated and then assigned to the *le-a* gender to form *le-sa-sa* 'frog'.
   (ii)   conjoining a verb to its noun complement and then assigning it to a class. There are two subtypes: (*a*) the complement is a direct argument of the verb, functioning either as its object (12a), or as its subject (12b); (*b*) the nominal is a peripheral constituent of the verb as in (11).

(11)   yɛ   tsyúɔ́   >   sɛ-yɛ-tsyúɔ́
Likpe   walk   some(one)   CM-walk-some(one)
                                       companion

(12)   (a)   di   sá   >   di-di-sá
Likpe   eat   thing   CM-thing-eat
                 eat something   food

        (b)   tí   sá   >   e-ti-n-sá
               be.covered   thing   CM-covered-LIG-thing
               cover thing   lid

---

[4] Ewe has both bilabial and labiodental fricatives. They are written as '*f*' and 'f' for the voiceless and '*v*' and 'v' for the voiced respectively.

(iii) compounding of a noun stem plus a verb stem in reversed N-V order and then adding the appropriate class prefix.

(13)   kɛ   a-taabi   >   se-tabi-kɛ
Likpe   acquire   CM-money   CM-money-acquire
        to get money   richness

(iv) Gerund formation of the OV type by preposing the O to a nominalized verb using the *bV-* prefix, as in the saying in (14).

(14)   di-ku-bi   bu-lə́kə   lə́   di-nəmí
Likpe   CM-tree-DIM   CM-remove   LOC   CM-eye

        e-so   be-tídi   i-nuə́   laa-yɛ
        IMPERS-because   CMPL-person   AGR-two   SCR:HAB-walk
        Removing mote from the eye, that is why two people walk together

However, another gerund formation is modelled on the Ewe pattern in (10), involving verb reduplication with the nominal complement preposed. The same meaning, such as 'yam planting' (15), can be expressed using the two different strategies.

(15)   (a)   bi-sí   bu-tə́kə   [NP bV-Verb]
Likpe   CMPL-yam   CM-be.on
                yam planting

        (b)   bi-sí   tə́kə́-tə́kə́   [NP REDUP-VERB]
                CMPL-yam   REDUP-be.on
                yam planting

One source of the [NP REDUP-VERB] strategy for gerund formation in Likpe might be translation of Ewe texts into Likpe. For instance, the Likpe word for lesson is probably a calque modelled on the Ewe term. Compare (16a) and (16b).

(16)   (a)   nú-sɔ́-srɔ̃
Ewe   thing-REDUP-learn

        (b)   a-sa-kasé-kasé
Likpe   CMPL-thing-REDUP-learn
                lesson, learning

Similarly, in the song in (17), translated from the Ewe liturgy, the expression for prayer/praying uses the [NP REDUP-VERB] strategy derived from the VP *tó a-la* 'throw CM-want'.

(17)   o   bo-antó   nɔ   bo   lá-tó-to
Likpe   INTERJ   1pl-father hear:IMP   1pl   want-REDUP-throw
        O Our Father hear our praying

In addition to the affirmative pattern, Ewe has a privative nominalization which involves the prefixation of the privative marker *ma-* to a verb root and then reduplicating the resulting stem. If the verb has an internal argument, it is preposed to this form. Likpe seems to have adopted this structure as well, as in (18b), which is calqued on the Ewe form in (18a). This is added to an existing strategy for privative nominalization which uses the negative verb prefix, as illustrated in (18c).

(18)   (a)   nú-gɔme-ma-se-ma-se
Ewe   thing-under-PRIV-hear-PRIV-hear
             misunderstanding

        (b)   kasɔ́-ma-nɔ-ma-nɔ   ə-bɔ́-lu-fɔ́   mə lɔ́   ntí
Likpe   under-PRIV-hear-PRIV-hear SCR-VENT-leave-DIR 3pl LOC midst
              Misunderstanding emerged among them

        (c)   u-tídi-mɔ́n-bú
Likpe   CM-person-NEG-respect
              disrespect

The use of O-V-V structures in nominalization, both gerund and privative, in Likpe is due to Ewe influence. Their spread into Likpe may have been facilitated by the existence of a permutation strategy for nominalizing V-O sequences in Likpe. The translation of Christian and educational texts from Ewe into Likpe appear to be the channel for the transfer of the pattern. Moreover, reduplication in Likpe in nominalizations appears to have been adapted to Ewe modes.

4.3 *Present progressive aspect construction*

Likpe typically marks tense-aspect by verb prefixes. Sometimes they are fused with pronominal or subject cross-reference forms, as illustrated for the habitual in (19) and (20).

(19)   Atta   əə-siə   kò-lá
Likpe   NAME   AGR:HAB-dream   CM-dream
        Atta dreams (habitually)

(20) ɔ-la   ŋkəə woa-té   bo bakpɛlé   eto   ke-tsyí-kɔ
      3sg-like QUOT 3sg:HAB-know 1pl CMPL-Likpe POSS CM-origin-place
      He wants to learn about the history of we the Likpe people

There are paradigms for future, present and past perfects, past habitual, and the past. However, the present progressive is expressed periphrastically. The operator verb in this construction is lɛ́ 'hold' which takes a single or double complement. One of its complements is a nominalized verb formed by *bV-* prefixation representing the event whose temporal development is being characterized (Ameka 2002). For example,

(21) li-kpefí   nɔ́-mɔ́   lɛ́   wó   ambe   bɔ-kpɔ́-n-kó
Likpe CM-child CM-DET hold 3sg mother CM-fight-LIG-ASSOC
      The child is fighting with his/her mother

Two features suggest that this construction is borrowed from Ewe. First, the operator verb looks like the operator verb in the analogous Ewe construction. The Ewe form is *lè* 'be.at:PRES'. In the inland dialects surrounding Likpe, the form is pronounced *lè* (Capo 1991). Second, the order of the elements, especially of the nominalized verb and its internal argument, is parallel to the Ewe one. Heine (1976) characterized this 'quirky' constituent order (Gensler 1997) as Type B–S–Aux–O–V. I would argue that the operators in these constructions are not auxiliaries, nor is the nominalized verb a Verb in clause structure. Likpe provides good evidence for this position, since the nominalization of the verb is achieved through the prefixation of a noun class marker, and the derived form has distributional properties of nominals (see Ameka and Dakubu in press for further arguments). Compare an instantiation of the Ewe construction in (22).

(22) Kofí   le   mɔ́lǐ   ɖǔ
Ewe   NAME   be.at:PRES rice   eat:PROG
      Kofi is eating rice

There is an overt marker of the progressive in Ewe, a floating high tone in (22) (and in some dialects a high toned *m̀*). In Likpe, however, it is the whole construction that generates the present progressive interpretation. The entrenchment of this construction in Likpe could have been aided by similar double complement structures that are employed for other 'secondary concept' predicates (e.g. Dixon 2005) that translate as 'can' (23a), 'begin' (23b), or 'start'.

(23) (a) m-oo-fo   fə   bɔ́-sɔ   nɛ́   ló
Likpe   1sg-POT-can 2sg   CM-hit   INFER UFP
          I could spank you, you know
      (b) u-tsyiko   nwə   kasɔ-kasɔ   bɔ-lɛ́
          3sg-begin   ones down-down   CM-hold
          He started picking those (pears) at the lowest end.

The effect of this Ewe influence on Likpe grammar is that the present progressive is the only situational aspect expressed periphrastically; all others, including the past progressive, are marked by verbal prefixes. This construction appears to be innovated following the similarity in form of the operator verbs in Ewe and Likpe. As the verb 'hold' provides an event schema related to the Location schema underlying the Ewe progressive construction, there could have been analogical mapping as well (cf. Heine 1997). Above all, two internal factors may have promoted the development: the fact that the verb *lɛ* 'hold' in Likpe can occur in three-place constructions independent of the progressive construction, and the availability of double complement constructions.

4.4 *Complementation strategies*

Likpe has borrowed the quotative/complementizer *bé* from Ewe and added it to an indigenous quotative/complementizer *ŋkɔ*, which probably evolved from a verb of saying. This form *ŋkɔ* can be followed by direct, as in (25), or indirect speech, as in (24). It can be the only predicator in the report frame construction, just like the Ewe *bé*. In both languages, there is almost always a prosodic break after the quotative/complementizer. Such a prosodic break is signalled in Likpe by final vowel lengthening, hence in the examples the forms are written with double vowels whenever there is such a break.

(24)	Betty	ŋkəə	ń-tɛyí	fə	ŋkəə	ú-su	school
Likpe	NAME	QUOT	1sg-tell	2sg	QUOT	3sg-go	school

   Betty says I should tell you that she was going to school

(25)	u-sío	ɔ́-mɔ́	ŋkəə	oo	lɔ́	ŋkəə	e-kpé	wə
Likpe	CM-woman	AGR-DET	QUOT	INTERJ	LOC	QUOT	3sg-be.in	3sg
	ɔ́-kwɛ-ɛ	alee	fáã	ku-su	kpé			
	CM-neck-TOP	then	freely	CM-way	be.in			

   The woman said oh if he says that it interests him then freely there
   is permission

The form *ŋkɔ* 'QUOT' is used to introduce complements of speech (24), cognition (26), and perception verbs as well.

(26)	sé	ɔfu	kɔdzó	ɔ́-mɔ́	le-te	ŋkəə	məə-tsyá
Likpe	when	NAME	NAME	AGR-DET	SCR-know	QUOT	3pl-too
	a-sɔlé	eto	bé-tídi	be-ni	ko	ŋkəə	oo	atúu
	CM-church	POSS	CMPL-person	3pl-COP	INTENS	QUOT	INTERJ	welcome

   When Ofu Kwadzo got to know that they too were church people, he
   said oh welcome (he and they will work together)

The Likpe quotative-complementizer is also used to introduce an adjunct purpose clause, especially after a matrix clause headed by a motion predicate, as in (27).

(27) ú-su   totoninto ŋkəə wəə-sú   u-tsyi   n-tu
Likpe 3SG-go   NAME   QUOT 3sg:HAB-go 3sg-carry CM-water
      She went to the Tontoninto Mountain (saying she wanted) to go and
      fetch water

The form *ŋkə* 'QUOT' still functions as a verb in many contexts where it gets
marked for person and TAM features. This happens especially when it follows
a desiderative complement-taking predicate. For example,

(28) n-la   **mí-ŋkə**   maa-te
Likpe 1sg-want 1sg-QUOT   1sg:POT-know
      I want to know

(29) sé   be-kpí   bá-mə́   lέ-nɔ   bə́ə́ bo-la   **buə**
Likpe when   CMPL-Gbi   AGR-DET   SCR-hear QUOT 1pl-want   1pl:QUOT
      boa-taka   mə́   le-ma-a   ba-tɛyí mə́ bə́-tsyuə́ bə́-ŋkə
      1pl:HAB-raise 3pl   CM-war-TOP 3pl-tell 3pl   CMPL-part 3pl-QUOT
      bɔ-lέ   a-ba   bú-luə
      1pl-hold   CMPL-stone CM-sharpen
      When the Gbis heard that we wanted to wage war against them, they
      told their neighbours that we were sharpening stones [Hence the name
      Likpe which is Ewe for sharpening stones]

The person-marked 'QUOT' forms have apparently given rise to a reduced version
such as *buə* '1pl:QUOT' in (29) which is used as a complementizer after any
complement-taking predicate and even on its own as a reporting form (30b).
These reduced 'QUOT' forms developed in equi-type constructions signalling coreference between the matrix and complement clause subject, as illustrated in (30).

(30) (a) n-te   **míə**   kə-tə́   mfô
Likpe   1sg-know 1sg:QUOT ANAPH-be.at there
          I knew that it was there

      (b) nyã   **míə**   oo e-ní   kú   le-sa   en-sí-bə́
          and   1sg:QUOT no IMPERS-COP COMIT CM-thing SCR:NEG-ITER-come
          and I said no, nothing else came up again

The Ewe form *bé* 'QUOT' is assumed to have developed from a 'say' verb
into a quotative/complementizer (Westermann 1907, 1930; Heine and Reh 1984;
Lord 1993; but see Güldemann 2001 for an alternative suggestion). The Ewe
bé 'QUOT' form like the Likpe form *ŋkə* 'QUOT' introduces direct quotes (31a),
indirect speech (31b), and complement clauses of verbs of saying, thinking,
wanting, etc. (32) It can also be the only predicator in the quote frame (31a, b).

(31) (a) é-bé   vǎ
Ewe   3sg-QUOT   2sgIMP:come
           He said: 'come!'

      (b) é-bé   né   na-vá
           3sg-QUOT   COMP   2sg:SUBJ-come
           He said that you should come

A logophoric pronoun is used in a *bé* clause to signal coreference between participants in the domain of *bé* and those in the matrix clause other than the first person (Clements 1979; Ameka 2004). Consider the contrast between (32a) and (32b).

(32) (a) Kofi$_i$ gblɔ ná-m   bé   é$_{*i/j}$-gbɔ-na
Ewe   NAME say   DAT-1sg QUOT 3SG-come.back-HAB
           Kofi told me that he (not Kofi) was coming

      (b) Kofi$_i$ yɔ   Ami$_j$ bé   ye$_{i/*j}$-gbɔ-na
           NAME call NAME   QUOT LOG-come.back-HAB
           Kofi called Ami to say that he was coming

Ewe *bé* also introduces the complement clauses of impersonal subject verbs like psychological and 'secondary concept' predicates, and like Likpe *ŋkə* 'QUOT' also introduces adjunct clauses of purpose/result. In (33), the first *bé* clause is an emotive predicate complement and the second is an adjunct /purpose clause.

(33) É-vé-m   [bé   me-ɖe   así   le   vi-nye   ŋú]$_{COMP}$
Ewe   3sg-pain-1sg QUOT   1sg-remove hand   LOC   child-1sg   surface
      [bé   wò-wɔ   funyáfunyá-e]$_{PURP}$
      QUOT   3sg-do   torture-3sg
      It pains me that I released my child for him to torture as a criminal

The Ewe *bé* 'QUOT' is lexicalized with some adverbial clause introducers namely:

(34) (a) álé-bé
Ewe   thus-QUOT
           so that

Ewe   (b) tó-gbɔ́   bé
           pass-place   QUOT
           even though

I suggest that Ewe *bé* 'QUOT' has been borrowed into Likpe and used in similar contexts to the Likpe form *ŋkə* 'QUOT'. The adopted Ewe complementizer into Likpe is used to introduce direct speech (35b) and complement clauses of verbs of saying, cognition, and perception etc. (35a) and also complements of clefts (35c).

(35) (a) bɔ́-nyə **bɔ́ɔ́** be-tídi   bə-tsyúɔ́ sí lɔ́ kɔ-tíní
Likpe   3pl-see QUOT CMPL-person AGR-some sit LOC CM-mountain
           kálɔ
           under
           They saw that some people were at the bottom of the mountain

      (b) nyā **bɔ́ɔ́** oo   ka-sɔ   kpé
           and QUOT INTERJ CM-land be.in
           And they said oh there is land

      (c) kasé mi-nɔ   nyā ní **bɔ́ɔ́** bó ba-kpɛle   lá ...
           how 1sg-hear 3sg COP QUOT 1pl CMPL-Likpe TOP
           How I heard it is that we the Likpe people, ... (our last place of
           settlement where we stayed was Atebubu)

The Ewe complementizer *bé* probably entered Likpe through the borrowing of the connector *alébé* 'so that' (36b) and the obligation-expressing phrase *éle bé* 'IMPERS-be.at:PRES QUOT', i.e. it must be that (36a) as well as the necessity expression *hiɛ̃ bɔ́* 'need QUOT' (36c) from Ewe.

(36) (a) ãã   ... nya-so   **é-le-bɔ́**   ó-te
Likpe   INTERJ   3sg-because 3sg-be.at-QUOT   3sg-know
           Ah, ... therefore he must know

      (b) **álé-bé**   ŋko ni   kasé min-yi   ba-kpɛlé   eto
           thus-QUOT this COP how   1sg-know CMPL-Likpe POSS
           akokosa   nɛ
           history   INFER
           So this is how I know the history of Likpe

      (c) **é-hiɛ̃**   **bɔ́** u-tsyi   wə   ú-su   u-bíkə
           IMPERS-need QUOT 3sg-carry 3sg 3sg-go 3sg-bury
           It was necessary that he (skunk) should take her (his mother)
           to go and bury

The use of the Ewe borrowed form in such modal contexts has been extended to other impersonal-subject contexts leading to impersonal framing constructions such as *í-tə bɔ́* 'IMPERS-give QUOT', i.e. 'it caused it that' or *í-bə bɔ́* 'IMPERS-come QUOT', i.e. 'it happened that', as in (37).

(37) i-bə   **bɔ́ɔ́** ke-ni   e-yifo ataabi-nyə wə di-siə
Likpe IMPERS-come QUOT CM-skunk SCR-do money-one 3sg SCR-sit
      It happened that the skunk was a rich man who lived

The form *bɔ́* 'QUOT' in Likpe is a direct borrowing from Ewe. Its introduction has led to two complementizers in Likpe with overlapping functions. Both forms are used to introduce direct and indirect speech as well as complement clauses, but the borrowed term is specialized for 'secondary concept' predicates that take sentential complements. The Ewe complementizer may have entered Likpe through the borrowing of constructions in which it is a filler.

4.5 *Summary*

There is unilateral influence of Ewe on Likpe grammar through direct borrowing or the diffusion of patterns. There are different motivations for these effects. Some are due to gaps in Likpe grammar such as the plural for kinship terms. Others reinforce existing Likpe structures. The consequences of the Ewe contact-induced changes in Likpe grammar discussed in §§4.1–4.5 are summarized in Table 3.

TABLE 3. Summary of constructions borrowed from Ewe

Grammatical construction	Structuration process	Effect on the system
Plural marking on kinterms (§4.1)	Heterosemy copying	Fills a gap for genderless kin nouns. Introduces a suffixation process for the marking of nominal number
Gerund formation (§4.2)	Pattern borrowing, exploiting the existing verb-noun reversal strategy	Adding a pattern to existing means of nominalization; expansion of the function of reduplication; might lead to less use of the nominal prefixing strategy
Present progressive (§4.3)	Innovated on the basis of existing structures and of phonological matching of operator verbs	Introduces a periphrastic structure for the marking of situational aspect (instead of a prefixal system)
Complementation strategies (§4.4)	Form borrowing	Borrowed form overlaps with indigenous term but has additional functions, seems to fill the gap for modal sentential complementation

5 Areal patterns

In this section, I examine some Likpe structures that articulate underlying semantic and cultural scripts common to the languages in the Lower Volta Basin. Likpe expressions of several meanings align more closely with the Ewe one, indicating that Ewe served as the conduit for the spread of such meanings into Likpe. Hence we focus more on Ewe–Likpe parallels.

The concept of 'believe' construed as 'receiving something and imbibing it' is lexicalized in the area in two-verb component SVCs. The specific verbs used for the 'imbibe' part vary across the languages; see Table 4. Except for Tuwuli, V2 is invariably 'eat' or 'hear'. Akan uses both while Ewe and Likpe use 'hear'.

Ewe and Likpe SVCs differ in one respect: the shared subject is expressed in Ewe only with the first VP. In Likpe by contrast, it is expressed on subsequent VPs by a concordial marker as in (38). Akan and Ga have both single expression, like Ewe, and agreeing subject expression SVCs, like Likpe (Ameka 2005).

(38) **n-fo**   **n-nɔ**   míə   yɔɔ-lɛ́kɛ
Likpe   1sg-receive   1sg-hear   1sg:QUOT   3sg:FUT-be.good
        I believe it will be good

Significantly, the concept for 'expect' interpreted as 'see/look (on the) way' can be matched in the four languages, as in (39).

(39)   (a)   é-kpɔ́   mɔ́   bé...
Ewe   3sg-see   way   QUOT

Likpe   (b)   ó-be   ku-sú   ŋkə...
          3sg-look   CM-way   QUOT

TABLE 4. Lexicalization of 'believe'

Language	Subgroup	V1	V2
Ga	Ga-Dangme	he 'receive'	ye 'eat'
Nawuri	Northern Guang	kɔɔlu 'receive'	dʒi 'eat'
Tuwuli	GTM-Ka	tɛ 'receive'	do 'put in'
Ewe	Gbe	xɔ 'receive'	se 'hear'
Likpe	GTM-Na	fo 'receive'	nɔ 'hear'
Akan	Tano	gye 'receive'	tie 'hear'
		gye 'receive'	di 'eat'

Akan   (c)   ɔ-hwɛ   ɔ-kwaŋ   sɛ...
             3sg-look   CM-way   QUOT
             She/he hoped that...

Ga   (d)   mii-kwɛ   gbɛ   akɛ...
             1sg-look   way   QUOT
             I am expecting/hoping that...

Emotional experiences also tend to be expressed with similar body-image collocations. Consider (40) and (41).

(40)   Ewe   (a)   é-kpɔ́   dzikú
       Likpe   (b)   ə-nyə   ɔ́-blɔ
                     3sg-see   anger
                     She/he is angry

(41)   (a)   é-vé   dɔme   ná   likpe-á-wó
Ewe   3sg-pain   stomach   DAT   Likpe-DET-PL

Likpe   (b)   í-fi   ba-kpɛlé   ka-fó   tintí
                     3sg-pain   CM-Likpe   CM-stomach INTENS
                     It angered the Likpes

The difference between Ewe and Likpe in (41) is in the coding of the experiencer: Ewe codes it as a dative prepositional object while Likpe codes it as the Goal Object in a double object construction.

Euphemisms for bodily actions are also parallel in the two languages. For example:

(42)   (a)   má-dé   así   gǒ-me
Ewe   1sg:POT-put   hand   pants-containing.region

Likpe (b)   ma-kpé   kɔ-ni
             1sg:POT-be.in   CM-hand
             I want to urinate

Furthermore, interactional routines including proverbs have spread in the area. Some have similar underlying scripts, others appear to be direct translations of one another. Leave-taking expressions are an example (Ameka 1999).

(43)   Pre-closing request
Likpe (a)   ń-tɔ   ku-sú   ló
             1sg-ask   CM-way   UFP

Akan   (b)   yɛ-srɛ   kwan
             1pl-beg   road

Ewe (c) ma-biá   mɔ́
           1sg:POT-ask   way
           I ask permission to leave

(44)   (a) labe   kpóó
Likpe   lie:IMP   quietly

Akan (b) da   yie
           lie:IMP   well

Ewe (c) mlɔ́   anyí   nyuie
          lie:IMP   ground   well
          Sleep well

One goodnight expression, which reflects the belief that things that happen to people are due to God, is calqued in Likpe from Ewe as in (45).

(45)   (a) Máwú   né-fɔ́   mí
Ewe   God   JUSS-rise   1pl

Likpe (b) bo   anto   taka-sɔ́   bo
            1pl   father   raise-CAUS   1pl
            May God wake us up

6 Conclusion

In this concluding section, I draw attention to attitudes of the Likpes towards the areal and Ewe influences on their language, both grammatical and semantic, described in this chapter. Likpe speakers are acutely aware of the various languages on offer in their community. They are, however, not always conscious of the loans that have been integrated into the language. When some feature is identified as foreign, there are two stances that are taken. One is to accept it and nativize it by adapting it to Likpe norms. The other is to 'purify' the language by keeping foreign elements out.

One strategy of nativization is to reanalyse and reinterpret forms in Likpe grammatical ways. For instance, an areal attention-getting routine *agoo*, which is used to gain access to a place or to a group of people, has been reanalysed as consisting of a 2sg pronominal prefix *a-* and a stem *-goo* so that it is used for singular addressees. For plural addressees, the form *be-goo* '2pl-root' is used. This reinterpretation makes *agoo*, which has spread across languages along the West African littoral, look more Likpe-like, hence it is not seen as foreign (Ameka 1994).

The recognizable foreign elements are 'banned', at least in public. For example, the Ewe particle *lá* 'TOP' is frequently used in spontaneous discourse to mark background information instead of lengthening the vowel at the end of phrases, which is the Likpe way of marking such units.

Compare (46a) [=35c] containing the Ewe particle and (46b) with vowel lengthening.

(46) (a) kasé mi-nɔ   nyã ní   bɔ́ɔ́   bó ba-kpɛle   lá...
          how   1sg-hear   3sg COP   QUOT   1pl CMPL-Likpe TOP
          How I heard it is that we the Likpe people...

     (b) sé   ke-kú   eto dí-yi nɔ́-mɔ́   le-yo-o...
          when CM-funeral POSS CM-day AGR-DET SCR-reach-TOP
          When the day of the funeral arrived...

When speakers are reflective, for instance during transcription sessions of recorded texts, they ask for *lá* to be replaced by vowel length.

Similarly, an areal routine for gratitude *adase* 'thanks' which spread from Akan via Ewe and was adapted into Likpe as *lasio* specialized for expressing thanks at the end of social gatherings involving alcohol, has been officially 'banned' because it is identified as being Akan. Paradoxically, in another domain, an authentic Likpe title for chief *o-te* has been replaced by the Akan title *nana* 'grandfather, chief'. This was done in a sociopolitical climate of asserting a more Guang or Akan affiliation.

The contact-induced changes surveyed in this chapter come from multiple sources and have varied motivations (see Chapter 1). A holistic understanding of grammatical change requires multiple perspectives.

References

Aboh, E. O. 2004. *The morphosyntax of complement-head sequences: clause structure and word order patterns in Kwa*. Oxford: Oxford University Press.

Akyeampong, E. K. 2002. *Between the sea and the lagoon: an eco-social history of the Anlo of southeastern Ghana*. Oxford: James Curry.

Ameka, F. K. 1994. 'Areal conversational routines and cross-cultural communication in a multilingual society', pp. 441–69 of *Intercultural communication*, edited by H. Pürschel. Bern: Peter Lang.

—— 1996. 'Body parts in Ewe grammar', pp. 783–840 of *The grammar of inalienability: a typological perspective on body part terms and the part–whole relation*, edited by H. Chappell and W. McGregor. Berlin: Mouton.

—— 1999. '"Partir c'est mourir un peu": universal and culture specific features of leave taking', *RASK* 9/10: 257–83.

—— 2002. 'The progressive aspect in Likpe: its implications for aspect and word order in Kwa', pp. 85–111 of *New directions in Ghanaian linguistics*, edited by F. K. Ameka and E. K. Osam. Accra: Black Mask.

—— 2004. 'Grammar and cultural practices: the grammaticalisation of triadic communication in West African languages', *Journal of West African Languages* 30.2: 5–28.

—— 2005 'Multiverb constructions on the West African littoral: micro-variation and areal typology', pp. 15–42 of *Grammar and beyond*, edited by M. Vulchanova and T. A. Åfarli. Oslo: Novus Press.

—— and Dakubu, M. E. K. In press. 'The progressive and prospective in Dangme and Ewe', in *Aspect and modality in Kwa languages*, edited by F. K. Ameka and M. E. Kropp Dakubu. Amsterdam: John Benjamins.

Amenumey, D. E. K. 1986. *The Ewe in pre-colonial times*. Accra: Sedco.

Bendor-Samuel, J. (ed.). 1989. *The Niger-Congo Languages*. Lanham, Md.: University Press of America.

Blench, R. 2001. 'Comparative Central Togo: what have we learnt since Heine?' Paper given at the 32nd annual conference on African linguistics, University of California, Berkeley. Available at www.cispal.fsnet.co.uk.

Capo, H. B. C. (1991). *A comparative phonology of Gbe*. Berlin: de Gruyter.

Clements, G. N. 1979 [1975]. 'The logophoric pronoun in Ewe: its role in discourse', *Journal of West African Languages* 10.2: 141–72.

Dakubu, M. E. K. 2006. 'Linguistics and history in West Africa', pp. 52–72 of *Themes in West Africa's history*, edited by E. K. Akyeampong. Athens: Ohio University Press.

—— and Ford, K. C. 1988. 'The Central-Togo languages', pp. 119–54 of *The languages of Ghana*, edited by M. E. K. Dakubu. London: Kegan Paul International.

Debrunner, H. W. 1962. 'Vergessene Sprachen und Trick-Sprachen bei den Togorestvölkern', *Afrika und Übersee* 16/17: 273–91.

Dimmendaal, G. J. 2001. 'Areal diffusion and genetic inheritance: an African perspective', pp. 358–92 of *Areal diffusion and genetic inheritance*, edited by A. Y. Aikhenvald and R. M. W. Dixon. Oxford: Oxford University Press.

Dixon, R. M. W. 2005. *A semantic approach to English grammar*. Oxford: Oxford University Press.

Gensler, O. 1997. 'Grammaticalization, typology and Niger-Congo word order: progress on a still unsolved problem', *Journal of African Languages and Linguistics* 18.1: 57–93.

Güldemann, T. 2001. *Quotative constructions in African languages: a synchronic and diachronic survey*. Habilitation thesis, Leipzig University.

Heine, B. 1968. *Die Verbreitung und Gliederung der Togorestsprachen*. Berlin: Dietrich Reimer.

—— 1976. *A typology of African languages based on the order of meaningful elements*. Hamburg: Helmut Buske.

—— 1997. *Cognitive foundations of grammar*. New York: Oxford University Press.

—— and Kuteva, T. 2005. *Language contact and grammatical change*. Cambridge: Cambridge University Press.

Heine, B. and Reh, M. 1984. *Grammaticalisation and reanalysis in African languages.* Hamburg: Helmut Buske.

Katamba, F. 2003. 'Bantu nominal morphology', pp. 103–20 of *The Bantu languages,* edited by D. Nurse and G. Philipson. London: Routledge.

Lord, C. 1993. *Historical change in serial verb constructions.* Amsterdam: John Benjamins.

Nugent, P. 1997. *Myths of origin and origins of myth: politics and the uses of history in Ghana's Volta Region.* Berlin: Das Arabisch Buch.

—— 2005. 'A regional melting pot: the Ewe and their neighbours in the Ghana–Togo borderlands', pp. 29–43 of *The Ewe of Togo and Benin,* edited by B. N. Lawrence. Accra: Woeli.

Ring, A. J. 1995. 'Revisiting the Central Volta Region: Avatime/Santrokofi/Bowiri', pp. 169–78 of *Papers from GILLBT's seminar week January 30–February 3 1995,* edited by Terry Cline. Tamale: GILLBT Press.

Stewart, J. M. 1989. 'Kwa', pp. 217–46 of *The Niger-Congo languages,* edited by J. Bendor-Samuel. Lanham, Md.: University Press of America.

Struck, R. 1912. 'Einige Sudan-Wortstämme', *Zeitschrift für Kolonialsprachen* 2: 233–53, 309–23.

Westermann, D. H. 1907. *Grammatik der Ewe-Sprache.* Berlin: Diedrich Reimer.

—— 1930. *A study of the Ewe language.* Oxford: Oxford University Press.

—— and Bryan, M. A. 1952. *Languages of West Africa.* London: Oxford University Press.

Williamson, K. and Blench, R. 2000. 'Niger-Congo languages', pp. 11–42 of *African languages: an introduction,* edited by B. Heine and D. Nurse. Cambridge: Cambridge University Press.

5

Basque in Contact with Romance Languages

GERD JENDRASCHEK

1 Sociolinguistic description of the contact situation

Basque is a language isolate spoken by approximately 600,000 people, 80 per cent of whom live in the Basque Autonomous Community (in Basque 'Euskadi'), one of the seventeen Autonomous Communities of Spain. Euskadi is located on the Atlantic coast and composed of the territories of Bizkaia, Gipuzkoa, and Araba. Approximately 10 per cent of Basque speakers live in 'Iparralde' (literally 'northern side'), composed of the territories of Lapurdi, Low Navarre (*Nafarroa Beherea*), and Zuberoa, on the French side of the border. The remaining speakers live in (High) Navarre (*Nafarroa*). The Basque Country is not only divided by a national, but also by a linguistic border, which runs through the north of Araba and splits Bizkaia and High Navarre into a Basque-speaking and a Spanish-speaking area. Map 1 shows the geographic divisions in the Basque Country.

Approximately half of the population in the Basque-speaking area is bilingual, while the other half is monolingual in a Romance language, or has only limited knowledge of Basque. The percentage of monolingual Basque speakers is negligible.

It is in the south-western provinces of Araba, Bizkaia, and Gipuzkoa (i.e. Euskadi) where the Basque language has the highest status, as it is co-official with Spanish, obligatorily taught in schools, and widely used in public. The following description therefore focuses on the situation in the Basque-speaking area of Euskadi, which corresponds to Gipuzkoa and eastern Bizkaia, and only occasionally refers to the contact situation of northern Basque. It should be

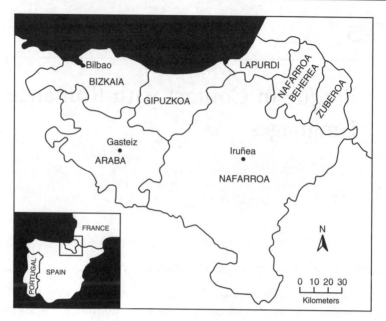

MAP 1 Geographic and administrative divisions in the Basque Country

borne in mind that the relationship between northern and southern varieties is a contact situation in itself.[1]

In Euskadi, there had been diglossia between Basque and Spanish until the linguistic legislation of 1979.[2] The distribution of Basque and Spanish is now one of coexistence in almost all domains. More precisely, the domains where Basque is well represented are of two kinds: the traditional domains inside the local speech community (cf. Haase 2001: 104) on the one hand, and formal domains where bilingualism can be required by law, such as administration, education, and written use in public, on the other. In the traditional domains, dialects are dominant; in the second, standardized varieties are used. One consequence of the educational policy is the incorporation of new speakers, i.e. second language learners and their children.

The contact situation has been in place for about two millennia, but reliable documentation started much later; the first texts (rather than single words or

[1] For a detailed description of language contact in the Northern Basque Country, see Haase (1992).

[2] 'El euskera, lengua propia del Pueblo Vasco, tendrá como el castellano, carácter de lengua oficial en Euskadi, y todos sus habitantes tienen el derecho a conocer y usar ambas lenguas' (Basque, the proper language of the Basque People, will have, like Spanish, the status of an official language in Euskadi, and all its inhabitants have the right to know and use both languages) (www.euskadi.net/europa_hizk/cas922.htm).

sentences) are from the sixteenth century. Because of the significant time depth of the contact, it is often difficult to determine whether a change is recent or old. Some of the changes affecting Basque grammar are clearly recent, e.g. the obsolescence of some of the remaining synthetic verbs or of allocutive agreement,[3] but these changes are only indirectly related to language contact. The contact-induced structural changes discussed here, however, seem to be quite old. Romance-style passive or relative constructions can be found in the classical texts from the sixteenth or seventeenth century (which were either translated from or inspired by Latin/Romance literature). The confusion between direct and indirect object agreement is mentioned in Lafitte's grammar (1944/2001), which deals with nineteenth-century-style Basque. Therefore, determining first appearances or periods when innovative patterns became conventionalized is beyond the scope of this chapter. And while some borrowed or enhanced patterns have entered all genres (including formal standard language), others remained stigmatized—or came to be avoided in the emerging standard: certain Romance-type constructions that were frequent in older literary Basque are avoided in modern Basque texts, because they *look* too obviously Romance (Haase 2001: 106–7).

The fact that Basque has a longer presence in the region than Castilian Spanish may lead to the question of a Basque substrate in Ibero-Romance; although toponymy and loans from Basque to Romance—the best-known example being Basque *esker(ra)* 'left' which led to Castilian *izquierda* and Catalan *esquerra*—indicate some overlapping between Basque and Romance-speaking areas, the issue remains controversial; see Trask (1997: 422–3) and Echenique (1997: 130). Similarly obscure is the contact situation between Basque and Celtic languages.

2 Borrowing of forms and borrowing of patterns

The general tendency is towards more analytic constructions, i.e. away from the agglutinative-fusional morphology that seemed to be typical for Basque, contact-induced enhancement of constructions already existing in Basque, and calquing of transparent (i.e. easily translatable) constructions, by reinterpreting, extending, and/or grammaticalizing native material.

Table 1 gives an overview of the grammatical phenomena described in this chapter and the mechanisms involved in their development in Modern Basque.

---

[3] This is agreement in sex with the addressee although the latter is not part of the argument structure.

TABLE 1. Overview of convergence phenomena in Basque

Enhancement	Reinterpretation	Extension	Grammaticalization
§2.1: from synthetic to more analytic inflection	§2.3.1: passive	§2.3.3: argument marking	§2.4.2 and 2.4.3: aspectual markers
§2.2: plural on pronouns	§2.3.2: relatives §2.4.1: 'be'/'have'		
		§2.4.4: derivational prefix *re-* §2.5: pragmatic patterns	

2.1 *Borrowing of a grammatical technique*

Basque has two classes of verbs, based on the way they inflect: verbs having both synthetic and periphrastic inflection forms ('synthetic verbs'); and verbs having only periphrastic forms ('periphrastic verbs'). Synthetic verbs are the only ones where tense can be fused with the stem, as in *dator* 'he's coming' vs. *zetorren* 'he came'. In the earliest texts from the sixteenth century, there occur about sixty verbs with at least some synthetic forms (Trask 1998: 319). Today, only ten to twenty verbs, depending on the speaker's age and native dialect, conserve synthetic forms. Synthetic tense can only be present, past, or hypothetical, whereas periphrastic tense allows the distinction of recent vs. remote past, as in (1) vs. (2).[4]

(1) etorr-i   da
     come-PARTIC   PRES.3sg
     he came (and is now here)

(2) etorr-i   zen
     come-PARTIC   PAST.3sg
     he came (before today)

This corresponds to the distinction in Spanish between *ha venido* and *vino*. That we are facing convergence is supported by the observation that the

---

[4] Data are from different sources. Short examples illustrating common constructions or derived from other examples in the chapter are artificial and therefore have no source indication ((1–6), (8–9), (12), (14–16), (18), (25–6), (28–9), (31), (37)). Examples (19–20), (27), (33), and (35) are from linguistic publications. Authentic examples are either from the daily newspaper *Euskaldunon Egunkaria* (now replaced by *Berria*) ((7), (21–24)), or from sources on the Internet and books ((10–11), (13), (17), (36)). Spanish examples ((4), (17), (30), (32), (34)) are provided only for comparative purposes.

distinction between recent and remote past is being neutralized by younger speakers from the north who are exposed to French where the remote past (*il/elle vint*) is archaic (Haase 1992: 93). More generally, periphrastic inflection parallels the tense-aspect categories of Spanish (and older stages of other Romance varieties in the region). It is therefore plausible to suppose that Basque has used the transition from synthetic to periphrastic inflection to reorganize its tense-aspect system to express the distinctions typical of Spanish verbs (cf. Haase 1992: 92).

Moreover, synthetic inflection could express modality on the lexical verb. The verb *egon* 'be, exist, stay' has the present tense 'real' (=non-potential) form *dago* 'he is' and the corresponding potential form seen in (3), where the modal suffix -*ke* is directly attached to the inflected verb.

(3)   dago-ke
      be:PRES.3sg-POT
      he can/may be

This last form is archaic today, and the reason for this might be, once again, the Spanish model, where *dago* has the counterpart *está*, whereas *dagoke* corresponds to Spanish (4), which is structurally more similar to (5), the modern periphrastic equivalent of *dagoke*.

(4)   puede   estar
      can:PRES.3sg   be:INFIN
      he can/may be

(5)   egon   daiteke
      be   PRES.3sg:POT
      he can/may be

In (5), the modal suffix (as well as tense and person marking) appears on an auxiliary that combines with an invariable verb stem. Note however that parallelism is not complete, since Basque conserves the basic rule that auxiliaries come after the lexical verb.

2.2 *Adding a term to an existing system*

Basque has a singular/plural distinction on some pronouns. These are listed in Table 2 together with their Spanish counterparts.

Consider (6), translating Spanish *quiénes somos*, 'who we are', which is typically found in self-presentations of business companies or institutions.[5]

---

[5] This is a good example of how Basque took over domains of use that were reserved to Spanish before the co-officialization of Basque in 1979. This takeover implied finding translations for Spanish expressions.

TABLE 2. Singular/plural distinction on pronouns

Basque		Spanish		English
Singular	Plural	Singular	Plural	
bat	*batzuk*	*uno*	*unos*	'one' vs. 'some'
nor	*nortzuk*	*quién*	*quiénes*	'who'
zein	*zeintzuk*	*cuál*	*cuáles*	'which'

(6) nor-**tzuk**   gara
    who-PL   PRES.1pl
    who we are

Note that the suffix *-tzuk* is only found on pronouns, the general plural marker for nouns being *-k*. This is unlike the Spanish forms which have ordinary plural marking. According to Trask (1997: 201), the Basque plural forms in *-tzuk* are originally Bizkaian; eastern varieties only have the plural form *batzu(k)* 'some', but not the other two. We may therefore assume that the suffix *-tzuk* was available in Basque, and has spread to other pronouns to express in a more systematic way the distinctions found in Spanish.

2.3 *Borrowing of syntactic constructions*

2.3.1 *Passive*   Basque has constructions that have some similarities to passive and antipassive (see Zabala 2003: 431), but voice alternation is restricted. Instead, several alternatives can be used as functional equivalents to passive clauses.

- third person plural;
- constituent order OAV or OVA;
- mediopassive.

One may use the third person plural when the actor is unknown, as in (7).

(7) emakume   bat   hil-da   ager-tu   da   Gasteiz-ko
    woman   one   die-RES   appear-PARTIC   PRES.3sg   Vitoria-MR
    taberna
    bar
    bat-ean,   uste-z   **bortxa-tu**   **egin**   **zuten**
    one-LOC   belief-INST   violate-PARTIC   do   PAST.3plERG.3sgABS
    A woman was found dead in a bar in Vitoria, supposedly **she had been raped** (lit.: ... they raped her)

                      (*Euskaldunon Egunkaria*, 15. Dec. 2000)

Another reason for using a passive (in languages that have a passive) is to put the undergoer in a thematic position. This can be achieved in Basque by putting the actor either in the preverbal focus position (8) or in the postverbal afterthought/antitopic position (9).

(8) liburu-a   Jon-ek   idatz-i   zuen
     book-DET   Jon-ERG   write-PARTIC   PAST.3sgERG.3sgABS
     It was Jon who wrote the book.
     The book, Jon wrote it

(9) liburu-a   idatz-i   zuen   Jon-ek
     book-DET   write-PARTIC   PAST.3sgERG.3sgABS   Jon-ERG
     It was the book that Jon wrote.
     He wrote the book, Jon

We can obtain a 'mediopassive' by promoting the direct object to subject position and inflecting the verb intransitively, as in (10). The fact that this construction is possible with almost all transitive verbs (cf. Trask 1997: 111–12) indicates that we have to do with voice alternation rather than with 'ambitransitivity', which would be a property of specific verbs.

(10) Azeriera   eta   Moldaviera   alfabeto   latino-z   **idaz-ten**
      Azeri   and   Moldavian   alphabet   Latin-INST   write-IMPERV
      dira
      PRES.3pl
      Azeri and Moldavian **are written** in the Latin alphabet
                                         (www.eibar.org/blogak/maite/34)

The Basque mediopassive basically corresponds to certain reflexive constructions in Spanish, where *idazten dira* would translate as *se escriben* 'REFL write:PRES.3pl'; see also (37). Mediopassives omit the agent completely; they are thus an example of deagentivization. Passives, in contrast, only demote the agent NP to a less prominent (and therefore optional) syntactic position.

Despite all the alternatives above, Basque has an additional construction that fulfils at least some of the requirements for a passive construction.

- the undergoer is in the subject position (but, as expected in an ergative language, remains absolutive),
- the actor is marked (by the ergative, as in subject position),
- and, most importantly, the verb phrase has intransitive morphology and agrees in person and number with the undergoer NP (which, in the absence of case change, is a criterion for considering the undergoer NP as the subject).

The lexical verb appears as a participle that agrees in number with the undergoer (like any adjective used as a copula complement). Let us first see an authentic example (11), and then analyse the emergence of the construction step by step (12–16).

In (11), we see the suffixal sequence -*takoak* on the verb *idatzi* 'to write'.[6] This 'passive' participle is followed by an auxiliary that shows number agreement with the subject.

(11) 'Euskara-ri   bai'   Sabin   Muniategi   eta
      Basque-DAT   yes   Sabin   Muniategi   and
      'Maitasun   gau-etan   laztan-a-k   bezala'   Jose Luis
      love   night-LOC.PL   caress-DET-PL   like   Jose Luis
      Otamendi-k
      Otamendi-ERG
      idatz-i-ta-ko-a-k   **dira**
      write-PARTIC-RES-MR-DET-PL   PRES.3pl
      'Yes to Basque' **was written** by Sabin Muniategi and 'Like caresses in love nights' by Jose Luis Otamendi
                       (www.oihuka.com/taldea.cfm?taldea=LABRIT&hizkuntza=o)

One thing that we can see is that the auxiliary is in the present tense although it translates as past tense. This is due to the fact that the Basque passive participle is derived from a resultative participle, indicated by the suffix -*ta*. The resultative alone is used as exemplified by (12).

(12) liburu-a   ingeles-ez   **idatz-i-ta**   **dago**
      book-DET   English-INST   write-PARTIC-RES   be:PRES.3sg
      The book is written in English

The suffix -*ko* makes it possible to use the participle form as a modifier, as in (13), where *idatzitako* modifies *liburuak*.

(13) emakume-ek   **idatz-i-ta-ko**   liburu-a-k   salgai
      woman-ERG.PL   write-PARTIC-RES-MR   book-DET-PL   for.sale
      egon-go   dira
      be-FUT   PRES.3pl
      Books written by women will be for sale...
                       (www.uztarria.com/agendie/1110209646)

---

[6] Particularly in northern Basque, the verb form would be *idatziak*, i.e. lacking -*tako*. The analysis would then have to be different; see Heine and Kuteva (2003: 551) and Haase (1992: 102).

Note that the case marking of actor (*emakumeek* 'the women') and undergoer (*liburuak* 'the books') NPs is the same as in the corresponding active construction. This can be seen in the functionally equivalent relative construction in (14), where *idatzi zituzten* '(which) they wrote' occupies the position of *idatzitako*.[7]

(14) emakume-ek   idatz-i   zituzten
      woman-ERG.PL   write-PARTIC   PAST.3plERG.3plABS(REL)
      liburu-a-k
      book-DET-PL
      Books the women wrote...

This parallelism between (13) and (14) indicates that the participle construction should perhaps be analysed as a reduced relative construction. The next step towards a passive construction is the deletion of the undergoer NP whereby the determiner (and a plural marker where required) is attached directly to the participle.

(15) emakume-ek   idatz-i-ta-ko-a-k   salgai   egon-go
      woman-ERG.PL   write-PARTIC-RES-MR-DET-PL   for.sale   be-FUT
      dira
      PRES.3pl
      The ones written by women will be for sale...
      The ones the women wrote will be for sale...

The final step consists of the reintroduction of the undergoer as the head noun of the relative/passive construction. The latter functions as a copula complement, as in (16).

(16) liburu-a-k   emakume-ek   idatz-i-ta-ko-a-k   **dira**
      book-ABS-PL   woman-ERG.PL   write-PARTIC-RES-MR-DET-PL   PRES.3pl
      The books are the ones the women wrote [= the books were written by women]

We can sum up the reinterpretation from resultative to passive as follows:

1. The books are written.   (12)
2. The books the women wrote...   (13)=(14)
3. The ones the women wrote...   (15)
4. The books are [the ones the women wrote].   (16)
5. The books were written by women.   (Reinterpretation of (16))

---

[7] This parallelism also holds for monovalent predicates, as in *kanpo-tik etorr-i-ta-ko jende-a* (outside-ABL come-PARTIC-RES-MR people-DET) 'people that have come from abroad'.

As can be concluded from the analysis above, the comparability to passive constructions in other languages is only partial. The closest equivalent in other European languages is a stative or adjectival passive; unlike dynamic passives, stative passives cannot express progressive or perfective aspect. This is because they inherently express resultative aspect. Dynamic passives have the same tense as the corresponding active clause; stative passives with present tense in contrast imply that the situation expressed in the predicate has taken place in the past, which explains different tenses in examples like (11) and (16) and their translations. Note also that *emakumeek* in (16) is an argument only of the participle; *emakumeek idatzitakoak* forms a constituent and cannot be broken up; and the verb is *dira* alone (cf. Trask 1997: 113). Hence, the 'Basque passive' cannot be used to translate Spanish (17), because it is (*a*) progressive, and (*b*) omits the agent. Therefore, one of the other strategies, e.g. first or third person plural, would have to be used, as in (18).

(17) otro-s   modulo-s   están   siendo   escrito-s
      other-PL   module-PL   be:PRES.3pl   be:GERUND   write:PARTIC-PL
      other modules are being written

                                        (www.usenet.cl/Misc/todo.2CFV.txt)

(18) beste   modulu-a-k   idaz-ten   ari   dira /   gara
      other   module-DET-PL   write-IMPERV   PROG   PRES.3pl PRES.1pl
      they/we are writing other modules

For differences between passive constructions in Basque and other languages, see also Ortiz de Urbina (2003: 298–9) and Zabala (2003: 431).

2.3.2 *Relative constructions*   The genuinely Basque way of modifying a noun by a clause is to use a finite relative clause which precedes its head, using a subordinating suffix -*n*. (19) and (20) and their description are from Trask (1998: 320).

(19) lore-a-k   eman   **dizki-o-da-n**   neska
      flower-DET-PL   give   PRES.3plABS-3sgIO-1sgERG-REL   girl
      hor   dago
      there   be:PRES.3sg
      The girl I gave the flowers to is right here

In (20), however, the syntactic position of the head *neska* 'the girl' in the relative clause is indicated by the pronoun *zein-i* 'to which'. The fact that the verb still bears the subordinating suffix -*n* indicates that the construction

corresponds to a transition stage between the genuine Basque construction
in (19) and the pronoun-only relativization strategy of surrounding Indo-
European languages.

(20) neska **zein-i**   lore-a-k   eman
      girl   which-DAT   flower-DET-PL give
      dizki-o-da-n   [...]
      PRES.3plABS-3sgIO-1sgERG-REL
      The girl to which I gave the flowers...

Example (21) illustrates an utterance with two relative clauses. The first precedes
the head noun *pertsona* 'person', the other comes after it and is introduced by the
pronoun *zein-ek* 'which-ERG'. Here, the combination of the two strategies is an
elegant alternative to the coordination of the two relatives.

(21) esperientza handi-ko   politikari-a   da,
      experience   big-MR   politician-DET   PRES.3sg
      botere-ra   bidera-tu-rik   **dago-en**   pertsona,
      power-ALL   lead-PARTIC-PRTV be:PRES.3sg-REL person
      zein-ek   jeneral pentsaera **du-en**
      which-ERG   general   thought   have:PRES.3sgABS(3sgERG)-REL
      He's a politician with much experience, a person heading towards
      power, who has a general's way of thinking

                                          (*Euskaldunon Egunkaria*, 25 Apr. 2002)

The fact that the suffix -*n* is also used for embedded questions (as in (22))
certainly contributed to its preservation after the interrogative/relative pronoun (cf. Haase 1992: 149–51). The functional expansion of embedded questions to relatives seems a plausible diachronic development, the more so as it is
paralleled by the Romance source languages (see Heine and Kuteva 2005: 130).

(22) [...] galdegin di-e-la-rik [...]   **zein-ek**
      ask   PRES.3sgABS-3plIO(3sgERG)-SR-PRTV which-ERG
      ditu-en   irten-bide hobe-ren-a-k
      PRES.3plABS(3sgERG)-SR.INTER   exit-way   better-SUPER-DET-PL
      aurkez-ten   herri-arentzat
      present-IMPERV   country-BEN
      when he asked them which one offered the best solutions for the
      country

                                        (*Euskaldunon Egunkaria*, 23 Feb. 2002)

The interrogative pronoun *zein* 'which' is not the only one to be used as a relative pronoun. A similar innovation can be found with *non* 'where', as exemplified by (23).

(23) herrialde bat-ean **non**   nortasun agiri   nazional-ik
      country   one-LOC where   identity certificate national-PRTV
      ere   ez   dago-en
      too   NEG   be:PRES.3sg-REL
      in a country where there are not even identity cards

                                        (*Euskaldunon Egunkaria*, 13 Sept. 2001)

Another compromise structure between the genuine preposed relative (cf. (19)) and the postposed relative of Romance is to create an appositive headless relative that comes after the clause containing the NP to be modified. This strategy can be seen in (24) (and has also been described by Haase 1992: 149).

(24) Danimarka-n   ba-dago   lege ez   idatz-i   bat,
      Denmark-LOC   AFF-be:PRES.3sg law   NEG   write-PARTIC   one
      Janteloven,
      Janteloven,
      gizabanako-a-ren   apaltasun-a   aldarrika-tzen
      individual-DET-GEN   modesty-DET   promulgate-IMPERV
      du-en-a
      PRES.3sgABS(3sgERG)-REL-DET
      In Denmark, there is an unwritten law, Janteloven, which promulgates an individual's modesty

                                        (*Euskaldunon Egunkaria*, 22 Nov. 2001)

The modified noun is *lege* 'law'. The determiner suffix -*a* represents this modified noun in the relative. Literally, (24) translates thus as '...a law,..., the one that promulgates...'.

In conclusion, Basque has created several compromise structures to imitate the relatives of Romance by using traditional constructions in new ways. All the examples show preservation of the original subordinating suffix -*n* which in the genuine preposed relative is all that is needed. To allow postposition, interrogative pronouns have been used as relative pronouns, or relatives appear with a dummy head when following the NP they modify; the discourse organization of the source language can thus be preserved without violating too much the patterns of the target language. This may explain why these innovations are not restricted to colloquial language, but have also made their way into formal genres (examples 21 to 24 are from newspaper articles).

2.3.3 *Argument marking* In Basque, the verb agrees with the three central arguments, i.e.

- the subject in a transitive construction marked with ergative case (short: 'ergative argument');
- (*a*) the subject in an intransitive construction or (*b*) the direct object, both marked with absolutive case ('absolutive argument');
- the indirect object.

With respect to verb-argument relations, Basque is both head-and dependent-marking. This normally guarantees clear distinctions between syntactic functions. However, many speakers do not always distinguish in verb morphology between direct and indirect object. In (25), the auxiliary *dit* expresses that the speaker is the recipient and encodes him as an indirect object. This is therefore the expected form of the auxiliary in this construction.

(25) ogi-a   ekarr-i   **di-t**
      bread-DET   bring-PARTIC   PRES.3SGABS-1SGIO(3SGERG)
      He brought me the bread

However, we can find in colloquial Basque the auxiliary *nau* which encodes the speaker as the direct object. The correct use is illustrated by (26), the 'extended' use for indirect objects by (27).

(26) kotxe-an   ekarr-i   **nau**
      car-LOC   bring-PARTIC   PRES.1SGABS(3SGERG)
      He brought me (here) by car

(27) ogi-a   ekarr-i   **nau**
      bread-DET   bring-PARTIC   PRES.1SGABS(3SGERG)
      He brought me the bread
      (Lafitte 1944/2001: 296)

It is not difficult to find the origin of this confusion. Spanish and French translate (25)/(27) and (26) with the same pronominal clitic *me* (*me ha traído…/il m'a apporté…*). The neutralization between the two syntactic functions in colloquial Basque under the influence of Romance has to do with translational equivalents, rather than with genuine syntactic changes. This means that a sequence like *me ha…* is equated with *nau*, without analysing the syntactic behaviour of those sequences. That the two contexts are syntactically different is shown by the fact that the different bound morphemes on the auxiliary correspond to different cases of the optional emphatic pronouns, here *niri* in (28) vs. *ni* in (29).

(28) ogi-a   **ni-ri**   ekarr-i   **di-t**
      bread-DET   1SG-DAT   bring-PARTIC   PRES.3SGABS-1SGIO(3SGERG)
      He brought me the bread
(29) kotxe-an   **ni**   ekarr-i   **nau**
      car-LOC   1SG(ABS)   bring-PARTIC   PRES.1SGABS(3SGERG)
      He brought me (here) by car

2.4 *Diffusion of semantic patterns and identical derivations*

2.4.1 *Distinctions in verb semantics*   Some semantic oppositions in Basque are shared with Spanish, but not French. It is not surprising then that these distinctions are more strictly observed in the southern varieties of Basque (cf. Haase 1992: 86).[8] While the Basque verbs *egon, izan,* and *eduki* are clearly old (they have synthetic inflections, cf. §2.1) and cannot be borrowings, their use in southern Basque parallels that of the Spanish verbs. We can therefore assume that the Basque verbs have been 'pressed into service' to reproduce the distinctions of the superstrate language Spanish.

The verb *egon* historically means 'wait' or 'remain'. In modern southern Basque, this verb is used in all circumstances in which Spanish uses its verb *estar* (Trask 1997: 292), while *izan* corresponds with *ser*. French has only one verb *être* and northern Basque similarly has the tendency to use *izan* for both meanings.

The verb *eduki* originally meant something like 'hold (on to)', 'contain' (Trask 1997: 293). In southern Basque, it is now used like Spanish *tener*. The infinitive *izan* is shared by two paradigms, the intransitive with third singular *da* 'is', and the transitive with *du* 'has'. In its transitive use, it corresponds to Spanish *haber*. Northern Basque has a separate infinitive form for transitive *izan*, which is *ukan*, though the inflected forms are the same. This verb unifies the meanings of the two verbs of southern Basque.

TABLE 3. egon vs. izan

Variety of Romance	Spanish		French
Romance verbs	*estar*	*ser*	*être*
Verbs in contact variety of Basque	*egon*	*izan*	*izan*
English	'to be (localized in space or time)'	'to be (inherently)'	'to be' (both meanings)

---

[8] Some distinctions borrowed from Spanish into southern Basque make their way into northern Basque, e.g. some northern speakers now imitate the distinction *egon* vs. *izan*.

TABLE 4. eduki vs. izan/ukan

Variety of Romance	Spanish		French
Romance verbs	*tener*	*haber*	*avoir*
Verbs in contact variety of Basque	*eduki*	*izan*	*ukan*
English	'to have' (possess)	transitive auxiliary	'to have' (both meanings)

2.4.2 eraman *'carry' as an aspectual marker*   Basque has not only borrowed semantic distinctions from Spanish, but also specific uses of some verbs. In Spanish, the verb *llevar* 'carry' has been grammaticalized to an aspectual marker which combines with the gerund of a lexical verb to express some kind of perfect progressive aspect (30). The corresponding construction in Basque is shown in (31). Again, this construction is not used in the northern varieties.

(30) cuántos   año-s   **llev-as**   estudia-ndo   euskera
      how.many   year-PL   carry:PRES.2sg   study-GERUND   Basque
      How many years have you been learning Basque?

(31) zenbat   urte **daramatza-zu**   euskara   ikas-ten
      how.many   year carry:PRES.3plABS-2sgERG   Basque   learn-IMPERV
      How many years have you been learning Basque?

2.4.3 joan *'go' as an aspectual marker*   A similar development can be seen with *joan* 'go' which is used as a kind of progressive aspect. The Spanish construction is shown in (32), the Basque equivalent in (33).

(32) el   número   de   vascohablante-s   **va**
      DEF.M.SG   number   of   Basque.speaker-PL   go:PRES.3sg
      aumenta-ndo
      increase-GERUND
      The number of Basque speakers is gradually increasing

(33) euskaldun-en   kopuru-a   **gehi-tu-z**   doa
      Basque.speaker-GEN.PL number-DET increase-PARTIC-INST   go:PRES.3sg
      The number of Basque speakers is gradually increasing
      (*Dictionary Morris Student Plus* s.v. *joan*)

Another grammaticalized use of *joan* is that as a marker of prospective aspect (cf. Laffite 1944/2001: 350). This use is shown in (35) and (36). Although the grammaticalization of 'go' to an aspectual marker is common, the frequency of this construction in Spanish (as illustrated by (34)) and French once again seems to be the trigger.

(34) va   a   morir   (35) hil-tze-ra   **doa**
      go:PRES.3sg   to   die:INFIN   die-NOMZ-ALL   go:PRES.3sg
      He's about to die, he's going to die

(36) historia,   geografia   eta   biologia-ko   lan-a-k   ere
      history   geography   and   biology-MR   work-DET-PL   also
      has-te-ra   doaz
      begin-NOMZ-ALL   go:PRES.3pl
      History, geography, and biology classes are going to start, too

(Zlata/Biguri, *Zlataren egunkaria*)

2.4.4 *Derivational prefixes* An alternative to borrowing whole words is to borrow the principle of their formation. In Romance, the verb prefix *re-* is frequent and Basque found a way to express this notion without borrowing. This was complicated by the fact that Basque traditionally used word-forming prefixes only very sparingly (cf. Trask 1998: 322). The outcome is a morpheme-per-morpheme calque with the prefix *bir-* as in the examples in Table 5. Interestingly, the etymology of *bir-* is controversial. While the Morris Student Plus Dictionary gives *bihur* 'bent, twisted, i.e. redoubled' as the origin, *berri* 'new' seems more plausible, especially when considering that the prefix has the allomorph *berr-* before vowels, and that *erabili berriz* 'use again' is synonymous with *berr-erabili* 'reuse'. It may be relevant that *berr-* is also an allomorph of *bi* 'two' as in *berrehun* 'two hundred' and *berrogei* 'forty' ('two-twenty', compare with *bi mila* 'two thousand').

In Spanish or French (or English) some derivations with *re-* are more lexicalized than others, e.g. the semantic content of *recycle* cannot be derived by simply adding the contents of *re-* and *cycle*. This explains why the *cycle* component of *recycle* had to be borrowed in Basque, before *birziklatu* could be

TABLE 5. The prefix bir-/berr-

Basque	English	Basque	English
aztertu	'examine'	*berraztertu*	're-examine'
erabili	'use'	*berrerabili*	'reuse'
ikusi	'see'	*berrikusi*	'revise'
moldatu	'set up'	*birmoldatu*	'remould', 'remodel'
sortu	'create', 'found'	*birsortu*	'regenerate'
—	—	*birziklatu*	'recycle'

constructed in the usual way; *ziklatu* alone does not exist. However, the prefix can also occur with native roots, such as *erabili* 'use' or *ikusi* 'see'.

For more details on word formation patterns under the influence of Romance, see Trask (1998: 321–3).

2.5 Diffusion of pragmatic patterns and types of context

Daytime greetings follow the pattern of Spanish, as listed in Table 6. Interestingly, even in the Northern Basque Country, *arratsalde on* is used in the afternoon and *gau on* in the evening despite the lack of French equivalents.

Example (37) from telephone conversations is a typically southern expression matching the Spanish *ahora se pone*, meaning literally 'he puts himself now', and is said when answering the phone for someone else who will then take over. It is representative of patterns borrowed from the 'high language' in order to express new genres.

(37) orain-txe   jarr-i-ko   da
      now-EMPH   put-PARTIC-FUT PRES.3sg
      He's coming

3 Conclusions

Some of the contact-induced changes are to a certain extent system altering, such as postposed relatives or the neutralization of the morphosyntactic distinction between direct and indirect objects. The increased use of prefixes falls into this category as well. But others have no impact on the system, as they are only enhancements of material present in the language before: this is for example the case of the passive, or of verb semantics. There is no borrowing of material in these cases, but an imitation of foreign constructions and distinctions. The new aspectual markers derived from verbs meaning 'to carry' and 'to go' are examples of contact-induced grammaticalization. More precisely, the grammaticalization has taken place in Spanish, and the new use is only

TABLE 6. Daytime greetings

Basque	Spanish	English
egun on	buenos días	'Good morning' (before lunch)
arratsalde on	buenas tardes	'Good afternoon/evening' (between lunch and dinner/sunset)
gau on	buenas noches	'Good evening/night' (after dinner/sunset)

imitated in Basque through calquing that introduces a new grammatical construction (thereby adding a new semantic feature to the verb, cf. Zuckermann 2003: 39). A similar analysis is possible for the prefix *bir-/berr-*, although here only the internal composition [prefix-verb stem] has been calqued, while the material used for the prefix is indigenous.

Borrowing of forms is easier to avoid and more stigmatized than 'camouflaged borrowing' (Zuckermann 2003: 37). The current tendency in Basque toward purism may have the effect of reducing the huge Romance presence in the lexicon (Trask 1998: 323), but it will not stop the convergence of the grammatical systems in contact.[9] However, convergence is less prominent than one might expect after such prolonged and intense contact. Some parts of Basque grammar certainly are obsolescent, like synthetic verb morphology, and this evolution is more advanced where the status of the language is weak, i.e. where practice and transmission tend to cease. But despite generalized bilingualism, transmission and practice are not a problem in most Basque-speaking areas, and therefore the overall collapse of the grammar did not occur. Basic typological features, like the ergative system or AOV/SV order, thus remained stable. Despite the typological differences, transposition from one system to the other is quite simple in these cases.

This hints at the fundamental questions behind language contact in the Basque context: convergence occurs mainly when transposition is problematic and when adaptation in Basque grammar is gradual. The collapse of the ergative system or of constituent order would certainly be an important system-altering change; but the ergative system is fundamental for the expression of syntactic relations and reflected in both nominal and verbal morphology. And different constituent orders are used for pragmatic purposes, such as the expression of focus and anti-topic.

Most cases shown in this chapter deal with indigenous material whose functional domain or discourse frequency has been expanded. Verbs which

---

[9] Trask systematically downplays this evolution, as can also be seen in the following quotation: 'The grammatical heart of the language, its syntax and its inflectional morphology, shows hardly a trace of IE (=Indo-European) influence. Here and there we can point to the odd grammatical feature acquired by contact, such as the new relative pronoun—but these are so rare as to be inconsequential. With its SOV word order, with its preposed complex modifiers, with its lack of gender, of noun classes, and of verb classes, with its uniform inflection of noun phrases, and above all with its thoroughgoing ergative morphology, Basque remains today the most typologically distinct language in Europe west of the Caucasus' (Trask 1998: 323). But opinions opposite to that of Trask can be found: '...l'influence des langues romanes voisines...ne cesse de croître au point qu'une bonne part de la locution basque actuelle n'est largement et de plus en plus sur certains points, en phonétique et lexique mais aussi en syntaxe, que du calque ou "décalque" roman.' ('The influence of the neighbouring Romance languages keeps growing so that an important part of present Basque speech is largely and increasingly on certain points, in phonetics and in the lexicon but also in syntax, nothing but Romance calque or decalque,' Orpustan 2002: 233).

were already in the language are used in new contexts, and marginal constructions like the passive or periphrastic verb inflection could be activated to provide equivalents to Romance structures. The pronominal relative can be analysed as an expansion of the construction in use for embedded questions. In all these cases, existing material only had to be adapted to bridge important gaps between the languages, or, as Heine and Kuteva (2003: 561) put it, 'to make the categories existing in the languages that are in contact mutually compatible and more readily intertranslatable'. Basque made few concessions on its typological specificities, but gained a lot in translatability. The transposition (or even explicit translation) between different TAM systems, or between a language that has a passive[10] and one that has not, is much more difficult than between a language that has an ergative pattern and AOV/SV, and one that has an accusative pattern and AVO/SV. System bridging with the aim of intertranslatability, without too much alteration, thus seems to characterize the convergence of Basque towards Romance.

In a more general perspective, we may identify 'system bridging without alteration' as one type of convergence, one that we would expect when corpus planning is applied to non-Indo-European languages. The outcome of language contact is certainly not the same in a situation where

(a) the target language is used only in traditional domains whereas all the modern domains are expressed through the source language (i.e. 'diglossia'); and

(b) a situation where the target language takes over formal functions associated with the source language ('functional expansion', 'status planning').

The first situation is that of most sub-Saharan African countries where the colonial languages are used for formal, or modern, domains. This scenario tends towards bilingualism and, ultimately, language shift; the local language does not undergo corpus or status planning. The second situation is that of many Asian countries which adopted Western knowledge, but not Western languages; however, Western knowledge is codified in Western languages and therefore cultural and linguistic influence go together. This scenario implies only limited bilingualism, and people may be unaware of language change. Corpus planning institutions act like a mediator between languages and therefore play an important role in this scenario.

The specificity of the Basque case is that it shares similarities with both scenarios. Until recently, Basque was entirely in scenario (a); for the last

---

[10] The pragmatic salience of passive constructions may further contribute to their diffusion; cf. Chapter 1.

decades, the language has been getting closer to scenario (*b*). As a consequence of this intermediate position, the contact situation is particularly complex. Living partially in diglossia, speakers are bilingual, often even dominant in their second (Romance) language. On the other hand, they now live in an era of functional expansion, where Basque has official status, and some may want to live like monolinguals, as if they did not know, or even need, Spanish. At the same time, the contact situation is extremely old, so that certain diffused features are shared by other Iberian languages, such as Catalan or Portuguese. And to make things worse, the superstrate languages vary depending on time and place: Latin, Gascon, Spanish, French, and, increasingly, English.

References

Aurnague, M. and Roché, M. (eds.), 2002. *Hommage à Jacques Allières: Romania et Vasconia*, V.P. 1: *Domaines basque et pyrénéen*. Anglet: Atlantica.

Echenique Elizondo, M. T. 1997. *Estudios lingüísticos vasco-románicos*. Madrid: Istmo.

Haase, M. 1992. *Sprachkontakt und Sprachwandel im Baskenland. Die Einflüsse des Gaskognischen und Französischen auf das Baskische*. Hamburg: Buske.

—— 2001. 'Basque', pp. 101–22 of Stolz 2001.

Heine, B. and Kuteva, T. 2003. 'On contact-induced grammaticalization', *Studies in Language* 27.3: 529–72.

—— —— 2005. *Language contact and grammatical change*. Cambridge: Cambridge University Press.

Hualde, J. I. and Ortiz de Urbina, J. (eds.). 2003. *A grammar of Basque*. Berlin: Mouton de Gruyter.

Lafitte, P. 1944/2001. *Grammaire basque (Navarro-Labourdin littéraire)*. Donostia/ Baiona: Elkarlanean.

Orpustan, J.-B. 2002. ' "Tu" *hi* et "vous" *zu* en basque', pp. 221–33 of Aurnague and Roché 2002.

Ortiz de Urbina, J. 2003. 'Periphrastic constructions', pp. 284–300 of Hualde and Ortiz de Urbina 2003.

Stolz, T. (ed.). 2001. *Minor languages of Europe*. Bochum: Universitätsverlag Dr. N. Brockmeyer.

Trask, R. L. 1997. *The history of Basque*. London: Routledge.

—— 1998. 'The typological position of Basque: then and now', *Language Sciences* 20.3: 313–24.

Zabala, I. 2003. 'Nominal predication: copulative sentences and secondary predication', pp. 426–48 of Hualde and Ortiz de Urbina 2003.

Zuckermann, G. 2003. *Language contact and lexical enrichment in Israeli Hebrew*. Basingstoke: Palgrave Macmillan.

6

Language Contact and Convergence in East Timor

The Case of Tetun Dili

JOHN HAJEK

Tetun Dili (TD), an Austronesian language, is East Timor's main lingua franca and the first language of Dili, the nation's capital.[1] It has been heavily influenced by Portuguese (and to a lesser degree in the past by Malay). There has been since 1999 a resurgence in contact with Portuguese. Yet much remains to be understood about TD, in particular its origins, the extent to which its grammar has been influenced by other local languages, and the extent to which it has in turn influenced them. Tetun Dili is sometimes referred to as a creole (e.g. *Ethnologue* 351), or a pidgin (e.g. Hagège 2002), and for many the assumption is that it first developed as a result of contact with Portuguese. Closer inspection does not support such a position. Contact with Portuguese, albeit substantial, seems to be relatively recent, some time after the rise of Tetum as a lingua franca. Instead, comparison of TD with more conservative varieties of Tetum, as well as with neighbouring languages, in particular Mambae, shows evidence of marked areal influence.

To address the issue of the competing sources of contact and the differences in their patterns of impact on TD, the focus of this chapter is on the following comparisons:

(1) Portuguese and TD
(2) TD and Tetun Fehan (conservative variety of Tetum) and Mambae.

---

[1] Tetun Dili is also referred to in English as Dili Tetum. It is common practice in East Timor and elsewhere to refer to it (and all other varieties of Tetum) simply as Tetum, and the practice is sometimes followed here. All speakers are easily able to distinguish TD from other varieties of Tetum, with intercomprehension often difficult (see below). All Tetun Dili examples are given in currently recommended standard orthography.

Two very different patterns emerge from our results: the first involves a newer process of grammatical reinforcement and complexification (rather than the often presumed pidginization), alongside an earlier longer-term pattern of local convergence and simplification involving Mambae and other languages of the area.

1 Languages of East Timor and East Timor as a linguistic area

Some twenty languages are indigenous to East Timor. Most are Austronesian (AN) and are closely related, falling within the same subgroup (see e.g. *Ethnologue* 351). Four others (Fataluku, Makalero, Makasae, and Bunaq) are all related non-Austronesian (NAN, or Papuan) and are mostly concentrated in the far east. Both groups show marked convergence to shared patterns, with a strong tendency to isolating nature, many similar grammatical structures, lexical influence, etc. However, we note with respect to constituent order that NAN languages are strongly AOV with postpositions, while AN languages are AVO with prepositions.

There are two major varieties of Tetum, spoken in three physically separated areas: (1) TD spoken in a small enclave setting in an otherwise traditionally Mambae-speaking area on East Timor's northern coast. It has approximately 50,000–60,000 L1 speakers, and many more L2 speakers (possibly 600,000–700,000); (2) the outlying rural varieties, often referred to as Tetun Terik (TT), spoken in two large areas far from Dili. The first lies on both sides of the border between East and Indonesian West Timor (e.g. Tetun Fehan (TF) described by van Klinken 1999), and the second lies further east on the southern coast as far as Viqueque. These varieties are grammatically more conservative and show much less Portuguese influence.

A major issue remains how to determine the circumstances in which TD came to be established in Dili. There is a lack of historical and linguistic documentation, but records suggest Tetum was a lingua franca in the (otherwise Mambae-speaking) Dili area and elsewhere before the arrival of the Portuguese. This and other evidence presented below indicates that the basic morphosyntactic characteristics of TD result not from relatively recent contact with Portuguese but from longer-term contact with Mambae (and other local languages) within a wider shared linguistic area (see also Hull 2001, 2004).

2 Language Contact Situation

2.1 *Historical overview of language contact and ecology*

The Portuguese made first contact with the island of Timor in the early 1500s, and began a long and slow process of establishing control and eventual

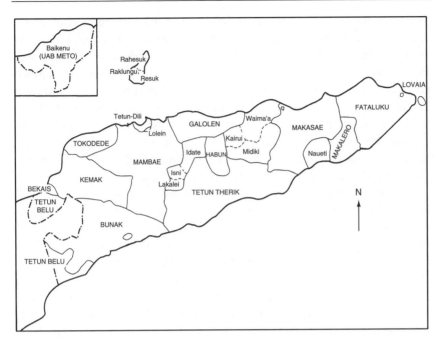

MAP 1 Location of languages in East Timor

Note: Lolein is spoken on the outskirts of Dili, as a result of resettlement in the nineteenth century (Hull 2004).

Source: Permission of J. Bowden, based on G. Hull.

colonization. However, before and after their arrival in the region, two powerful Tetum-speaking kingdoms controlled much of Timor, and dominated the ethnic groups around them, including the Mambae. Portuguese reports from the early 1600s note the use of Tetum throughout the eastern half of Timor (Thomaz 1981: 55). At the same time, both Malay and Portuguese were widely used as lingua francas throughout the wider region, with frequent creolization of Portuguese throughout Asia (Caudmont 1994). In East Timor the use of Malay, previously an important coastal trade language, declined rapidly in the nineteenth century. In the twentieth century its use persisted only in the Oé-Cusse enclave in West Timor.

Dili was founded by the Portuguese only in 1769, relatively late in the peace. Until the late nineteenth century Portuguese control outside of Dili was limited and dependent mainly on the maintenance of local alliances. Final pacification occurred only in the early 1900s but led to an intensification of Portuguese colonization. By the 1960s a major focus of this process was the active dissemination of Portuguese language and culture among the East

Timorese. Reports from the nineteenth century until the 1970s confirm the coexistence of Portuguese and TD in the colonial capital.[2] Political developments in the 1970s favoured the rapid promotion and use of TD for public expression in ways that were previously not possible. However, the Indonesian invasion in 1975 led to a process of intensive linguistic Indonesianization: Portuguese was systematically replaced by Indonesian (a variety of Malay) from the public sphere, administration, and schools. In 1981 under intense pressure from Indonesian authorities, Portuguese was also replaced by Tetum as the liturgical language used by the local Roman Catholic Church keen to avoid the adoption of Indonesian (Hajek 2000).

After the referendum in 1999 on self-determination and subsequent full independence, language policy took yet another dramatic turn: the official use of Portuguese is today fully reinstated in East Timor and shares with Tetum co-official language status. Indonesian and English (introduced by the post-1999 interim United Nations administration) are recognized as working languages until further notice, but a clear expectation remains in most quarters that the use of Indonesian will ultimately disappear from most sectors. In the meantime it still appears widely in the press, since it remains the language of literacy for the largest number of East Timorese.

Despite Indonesia's best efforts between 1975 and 1999, Indonesian influence on TD and other languages of East Timor has been decidedly superficial (as noted by Hull 2004) and is avoided, especially in written and higher registers. Recent grammatical descriptions (Williams-van Klinken, Hajek, and Nordlinger 2002; Hull and Eccles 2001) make little or no mention of Indonesian influence in contrast to frequent reference to the impact of Portuguese.[3]

Given East Timor's complex linguistic history, it is not surprising that today multilingualism is common. Most adults speak at least three languages, if not more: their own local language, TD, Indonesian, and/or Portuguese. Current estimates suggest 65–80 per cent of East Timorese speak TD, 50 per cent Indonesian, 10–20 per cent Portuguese, and only 1 per cent English. Although there is no doubt that for most East Timorese TD is the preferred means of interethnic communication, there is some local bilingualism, especially at the boundaries of ethnic groups and in some mixed areas outside of Dili.

---

[2] During this time contact between Tetum and non-standard varieties of Portuguese was also possible in Dili. These included two creoles spoken by small communities (imported Macanese Creole and local Bidau Creole which shows significant influence from TD, see Baxter 1990). Any specific impact they may have had on TD is still to be determined. See also fn. 6.

[3] Whilst direct evidence of specifically Indonesian influence on TD is difficult to find (even loans commonly used until 1999 are now usually replaced by Portuguese equivalents, e.g. Indonesian *kolusi* by *koluzaun* 'collusion' < Port. *colusão*), the possibility that a knowledge of written Indonesian has reinforced the use of Portuguese-like structures and patterns where they are similar, e.g. hypotactic syntactic style, cannot be excluded.

2.2 *Relations, roles, and contact within the community*

A clear hierarchy has long existed with colonial languages (Portuguese and Indonesian) dominating over indigenous languages (Hajek 2000). However, since 1999 TD has rapidly gained status, and the influence of Portuguese, especially on TD, is resurgent. This latter phenomenon is significantly facilitated by the need for TD to meet the challenge of co-official status since 2001. It now has to function in spheres that were once not open to it, nor previously anticipated: as a fully fledged written medium, a language of higher-level and technical registers and communication, and preferred medium of school instruction (alongside Portuguese).

In an effort to meet all these challenges, there has been a concerted effort to standardize Tetum as quickly as possible. 'Official Tetum' is the newly designated standard form under the auspices of the Instituto Nacional de Lingüística in Dili. It is overwhelmingly TD in nature but includes some (mainly lexical) elements of more conservative rural Tetum varieties more resistant to Portuguese loans (especially evident in the church register, which in turn is difficult for normal TD speakers to understand, cf. Williams-van Klinken 2001). Other normativist tendencies in Official Tetum include the regular marking of glottal stops retained in rural Tetum but completely lost in TD, and the avoidance, other than in fixed phrases, of Portuguese gender and number marking in loans (but in TD, actual practice varies considerably, see §§3.2.1 and 3.2.4).

In contrast to colonial linguistic dominance, there is evidence of a prior situation of contact of equality or balance between TD and the other East Timor languages. This is confirmed by a long-term pattern of stable bilingualism and multilingualism with no language shift to TD outside of Dili. Linguistic traits seem to have diffused in both directions—since TD and other (especially AN) languages are so similar. But there is a clearly emerging pattern of increasing TD dominance since the 1970s, and especially 1999, with an increasing use of TD loans everywhere.

Interethnic contact is high, and there are no restrictions on social relations, such as intermarriage. The use and spread of TD is also favoured by high levels of mobility, especially to Dili, and by the role of the local Roman Catholic Church in promoting Tetum.

TD is essentially an urban language, with no rural L1 base (unlike all other languages in East Timor, including other varieties of Tetum). It has as a result no traditional literature typical of all others in the region (e.g. Fox 1988; Corte-Real 1998). It is also the only local language to appear regularly in the media (especially in written and televised form), and whose use is officially promoted in schools and official fora.

2.3 *Language attitudes and awareness*

There is very high awareness of ethnolinguistic membership across the nation. Individuals' attitudes towards their own language(s) and especially to TD are generally very positive. As already noted, speakers of other languages are very receptive to the influence of TD (which has also acted as a mediator for Portuguese influence), and the only two areas (Oé-Cusse enclave, and Lospalos area) where TD was not a traditional lingua franca are moving rapidly to adopt it.

The general attitude to Portuguese is more mixed (and sometimes negative) with respect to official status and its reintroduction in schools, although at the level of officialdom and the traditional Portuguese-speaking elite, attitudes are very positive. On the other hand, the return to Portuguese influence on TD is accepted by all sides.

Attitudes to Indonesian are mixed to extremely negative, and there is an evident avoidance of using or borrowing from Indonesian since 1999, especially in the press and media, government and education (where it is being phased out). There is, however, an older and very noticeable stratum of pre-twentieth-century Malay loans that are fully accepted as native to TD, e.g. Malay *kilat* 'lightning' > 'gun'. It remains difficult however, in the absence of historical documentation, to disentangle local areo-genetic grammatical phenomena from the possible effects of pre-twentieth century contact with Malay (but see Hull 2001).

3 Grammars in Contact

3.1 *Brief typological profile of Tetun Dili*

Tetun Dili is best characterized as tending towards isolating, with very little truly productive morphology. The language is neither head- nor dependent-marking, and grammatical relations are expressed by constituent order. Constituent order in TD is typically AVO and SV, and there is no passive.

Given the combination of all of these features, the preponderance of Portuguese loans, the long period of Portuguese contact in East Timor, and until recently a lack of information about other East Timorese languages, it has been easy to presume that TD is a creolized or pidginized language arising from contact between the Portuguese and the local East Timorese population (see above). But if anything, the opposite seems more correct.

3.2 *The Impact of Portuguese on Tetun Dili*

3.2.1 *Phonology*   Of TD's twenty-two consonant phonemes, eleven (/p g v z ʃ ʒ ʎ ɳ r j/ and partly /w/) are borrowed from Portuguese (with some reinforcement by Malay). The influence of Portuguese is also clearly seen in TD phonotactics and phonological processes, such as the optional process of s-palatalization in Portuguese loans and native terms, e.g. loaned /festa/ [festa] ~ [feʃta] 'party' and native /has/ [ha:s] ~[ha:ʃ] 'mango'.

3.2.2 *Lexicon* There has been massive borrowing into TD, especially of technical terminology, from Portuguese. Given historical contact also with Malay, this has led to many doublets, triplets, and overlap: e.g. *ponte* (Portuguese), *lalete* (Tetum), and *jambatan* (< Malay *jembatan*) 'bridge'. Also common is the borrowing of phrases with full Portuguese grammatical agreement, such as *Nasoens Unidas* 'United Nations', *primeiru ministru* 'Prime Minister', *primeira klase* 'grade one', dates (*dia 30 de agostu* '30 August'), large numbers especially in prices, years, clock-times (*duazoras* 'two o'clock'), as well as greetings and most social conventions (*sentidus pézames* 'I'm sorry for your loss').[4]

Since Portuguese has long been the primary source for abstract terms and modern terminology in TD, speakers and especially writers borrow from it with renewed vigour today (cf. Williams-van Klinken 2004). As a result, the frequency of Portuguese loans (10–30 per cent of unique forms in normal spoken discourse) can rise to 60–80 per cent in complex, high-level documents such as East Timor's official constitution.

A weaker, countervailing tendency balances the use of Portuguese loanwords with that of native equivalents as well as items drawn from conservative Tetun Terik (TT).[5] TT has some status as the language of traditional oral literature and for historical reasons the influence of TT is especially evident in church register (see Williams-van Klinken 2001; Thomaz 1981). However, in practice, in non-religious contexts TT influence on TD is largely limited to the emblematic use of TT forms such as *no* (alongside TD *ho, i*) 'and' and *wainhira* (TD *bainhira*) 'when', and the variable orthographic marking of glottal stops no longer pronounced in TD, e.g. *ne'e* 'here'.

3.2.3 *Lexical borrowing and patterns of grammatical structure* Not surprisingly, the extreme levels of lexical borrowing from Portuguese also have consequences for the grammatical structure of TD. Native words are often precategorical, e.g. *moris* 'life' (N), 'to live' (V), and 'alive' (Adj). The precise function and meaning of such items can only be determined by syntactic

---

[4] In spoken TD, Indonesian-educated speakers may also use Indonesian numbers and dates. But this use is avoided in written language.

[5] The notion of balance is used here since the utility of and need to continue drawing lexical resources from Portuguese is widely recognized. At the same time native creativity is also accepted, e.g. use of loaned *independénsia* alongside *ukun rasik-an* (lit. rule self-REFL) for 'independence'.

position. However, the complex morphological structure of Portuguese ensures for that language a much clearer delineation of basic word classes, such that nouns, for instance, are immediately distinguishable from verbs. Although the morphological complexities of Portuguese are often reduced after borrowing, the distinction between categories is typically maintained in TD, e.g. *eduka* 'to educate' (V) < Port. *educa* 'educates' (3sg:PRES) vs. *edukasaun* (N) < *educação* 'education'. This difference in type leads to a major subdivision between native and loaned lexicon, each with its own morphological system.

While the borrowing of N, V, and ADJ appears to be direct and unrestricted, the borrowing of grammatical items and structures can be mediated through 'lexical pairing' where native and borrowed grammatical forms appear optionally together, as in (1):

(1)   purposive: *atu, hodi, para atu, atu para, para hodi, para* 'in order that, so that' (< Port. *para* 'for, in order to')
       relativizer: *ne'ebé* (lit. 'where'), *ne'ebé ke, ke* (< Port. *que* COMP/REL)

This process is also a mechanism for the gradual mediation of grammatical change in TD, as in (2). The native construction to express 'during' involves a complex locative-possessed body part construction. In Portuguese the equivalent construction involves the use of the preposition *durante* (similarly to English *during*). Both structures are possible in TD, as is an intermediate construction that combines them, and allows for a smooth transition from the older native structure to the newer, less complex one:

(2)   iha Agustu nia laran   'during August' (body part construction)
       LOC August 3sg inside
       durante Agustu nia laran   (< Portuguese *durante*
       durante Agustu   'during')

3.2.4 *Morphology*   TD is resistant to morphological borrowing. It avoids the complexities of Portuguese verb morphology: all verbs are borrowed 'stripped' in the 3sg form of the present tense, e.g. *eduka* seen previously.[6] There has been limited borrowing of gender and number marking in nouns and adjectives. These are system-altering changes but occur within well-defined limits.

---

[6] Baxter (1990) notes an overwhelming (although not total) preference for the 3sg form of the present in Bidau Creole Portuguese formerly spoken in Dili. It is not clear, however, which is the borrowing language, TD or Bidau Creole. In other Portuguese creoles, there is a general preference for the (typically stress-final) infinitive to be used, with a tendency to shift stress to the penult (typical of the Portuguese present tense) in connected speech (A. Baxter, p.c.).

A small set of Portuguese nouns and adjectives are obligatorily marked for gender by all speakers, e.g.:

(3)   N   *tiu* 'uncle', *tia* 'aunt', *primu* 'male cousin', *prima* 'female cousin'
          mestre 'male teacher', *mestra* 'female teacher'
     ADJ   *bonitu* 'handsome' (m), *bonita* 'pretty' (f)

With these items, gender agreement also occurs outside of NPs, e.g. *Nia bonitu* (m) 'He is good-looking' vs. *Nia bonita* (f) 'She is pretty'. Otherwise, gender agreement between nouns and adjectives is only possible within NPs. Gender agreement always occurs on Portuguese adjectives that precede a Portuguese noun, e.g. *primeira klase* 'first class' (f.sg) vs. *primeiru ministru* 'prime minister' (m.sg). Feminine gender agreement is variable—and avoided by many speakers—in postposed adjectives after Portuguese feminine nouns, in collocations which have not been borrowed as fixed phrases, e.g. *primeira faze* (f.sg agreement) vs. *faze primeiru* (no agreement) 'first phase', *desizaun kritika* ~ *kritiku* 'critical decision', *Uniaun Europea* ~ *Europeu* 'European Union'. In fixed phrases, post-nominal gender agreement always occurs, e.g. *Nasoens Unidas* (f.pl) 'United Nations'.

Portuguese loans may also be marked for number, although such marking on nouns and adjectives (involving final -*s*) is regular only in borrowed phrases, e.g. *Nasoens Unidas* (f.pl) 'United Nations'. Otherwise it is optional, and not particularly common in spoken language. It does, however, appear to be becoming more frequent in written registers. This effect seems to be reinforced by an accidental semi-overlap of grammatical forms. Portuguese plural suffix -*s* coincides with the start of the post-nominal definite plural marker *sira*. In the following examples, all taken from the same text, we see first the expected native pluralization strategy in (4). But in (5) plurality is doubly marked, with Portuguese -*s* and *s*- of TD *sira* appearing together and forming a homophonous sequence, as underlined in the first example, and then also appearing apart:

(4)   pasiente sira   'the patients' (lit. patient 3pl)
     pasiente lepra sira   'the leprosy patients' (lit. patient leprosy 3pl)

(5)   pasientes_sira   'the patients' (lit. patient:3pl 3pl)
     pasientes lepra sira   'the leprosy patients' (lit. patient:3pl leprosy 3pl)

Nouns are normally unmarked for number before postposed numerals as in (8a) with optional human classifier. However, explicit plural marking on Portuguese loans is possible, and follows the Portuguese pattern of number agreement in this context, without a classifier:

(6) (a) pasiente   (na'in) rua vs. (b) pasientes   rua
          patient   (noble)   2   patient:m:pl   2
          Two patients

The only affix that appears to have been truly nativized is the agentive -*dór* with the restricted sense in TD of 'someone who habitually does something (often pejorative)', e.g. *hemu* 'drink' > *hemudór* 'someone who likes to drink (m/f)'. Patterned on borrowed forms such as *fumadór* 'smoker', it is the only Portuguese affix that can be applied to a native root, but it never shows number or gender agreement, in contrast to -*dór* in Portuguese loans, e.g. *administradór* 'male administrator' vs. *administradora* 'female administrator'.

3.2.5 *Syntax* The syntactic patterns of TD are increasingly influenced by contact with Portuguese (the effects of which may be further reinforced by local knowledge of written Indonesian in turn long influenced by contact with Indo-European languages, such as Sanskrit, Dutch, and English). TD is showing, amongst other things, a general shift from unmarked clause juxtaposition (parataxis), through a markedly Portuguese-style use of conjunctions and coordinators (hypotaxis). This is especially evident in higher registers and it marks TD out from other East Timor languages (including conservative Tetum), which generally prefer unmarked clause chaining.

Native mechanisms to express inter-clausal relations already exist but are not obligatory and are traditionally often omitted. However, their use is clearly reinforced by the use of Portuguese conjunctions and patterns, as seen in Table 1. In all cases Portuguese loans appear in clause-initial position, which is not always the case with their native equivalents.

As in (7), native and borrowed forms and structures can also optionally coincide, appear as alternatives, or be absent, as in the following example:

(7) (se) ó   hakarak (karik),   bele bá uma
     (if) 2sg want   (perhaps), can   go house
     If you want, you can go home

TABLE 1. Native and borrowed conjunctions in Tetun Dili

	Native	Portuguese loan
Reason	*tanba*	*purké*
Purpose	*atu, hodi*	*para*
Condition	*karik* 'perhaps' (V__)	*se*
Concession	*bele* 'can' (S__, __S)	*mezmu [ké], embora*
	mós 'also' (V__)	
Sequence	*mak*	*depois*
Consequence	*ne'e duni*	*entaun*
'and'	*ho*	*i*

The frequent use of explicit complementation outside of reported speech in TD, especially in writing, is generally uncharacteristic of East Timorese languages, and appears also to be patterned after Portuguese. TD complementizers include both the fully grammaticalized native *katak* COMP (< archaic 'to say'), and the Portuguese loan *ke* (< *que* COMP/REL) which appears with this function only after Portuguese loans, as in (9).

(8) ha'u   hanoin katak   situasaun la   di'ak
    1sg   think   COMP   situation NEG   good
    I think that the situation is not good

(9) klaru   ke   situasaun la   di'ak
    clear   COMP   situation NEG   good
    It's clear that the situation is not good

Another innovation in TD, as noted by Williams-van Klinken et al. (2002: 39), is the ability of Portuguese abstract nouns to take complement clauses:

(10) iha   esperansa katak   sistema justisa sei di'ak iha 2004?
     LOC   hope   COMP   system justice still good LOC 2004
     Is there hope that the justice system will come good in 2004?

Portuguese influence also leads to verb-initial constituent order with a small set of loaned verbs (*aparese* 'appear', *akontese* 'happen', *falta* 'to be lacking'). This ordering has spread from Portuguese loans to some native verbs, such as *mosu* 'appear'.

(11) falta   ida   tan   karik
     lack   one   more   perhaps
     Perhaps there is one more missing

(Williams-van Klinken et al 2002: 56)

A comparison of serial verb constructions (SVCs) in TD and Tetun Fehan shows them to be less common in TD with contact with Portuguese identified as one of the influencing factors at play (Hajek 2006). The effect of Portuguese is seen in the appearance of single verb loans (*informa* for *fó hatene* [lit. give know] 'to inform/ advise'), and the clear separation of adjectives as a class (they remain verbal in Tetun Fehan), helping to reduce the overall range and frequency of SVCs.

3.2.6 *Conclusions*   Overall, while TD is fully open to the influence of Portuguese in phonology and lexicon, it is more resistant to borrowing from Portuguese in other areas, especially morphology. Morphological influence, although system changing, is very constrained and restricted almost exclusively to borrowed Portuguese lexicon. Syntactic influence is sometimes system altering, but mostly system reinforcing, increasing the frequency of existing structures that were less used in the past. On the other hand, there is little direct evidence, with the partial exception of SVCs, that contact specifically with Portuguese has led to grammatical simplification.

3.3 *Comparing Tetun Dili, Tetun Fehan, and Mambae*

The Mambae are the largest ethnic group in East Timor, and are located in the heart of the East Timorese linguistic area. Many languages in this area share similarities in NP structure, word order, patterns of morphological reduction, and constructions involving possessives, comparatives, focus, and pluralization, as well as verbless clauses and TAM systems (Hull 2001 provides a useful overview). Indeed, Mambae shows one of the greatest degrees of grammatical convergence and morphological simplification. Data presented here are from the northern dialect spoken in Ermera, relatively close to Dili, unless otherwise indicated.

Tetun Fehan (TF) is a rural variety of Tetum spoken in West Timor, and has had no contact with TD, and very little with Portuguese (van Klinken 1999). It is located towards the periphery of the linguistic area in question, and is accordingly more conservative, especially in its morphological structure.

Even a cursory inspection of TF, TD, and Mambae shows the last two to share many grammatical features and patterns that separate them from TF. One problem to resolve is the directionality of diffusion. The possible extent, for instance, of Mambae lexical influence on TD remains unknown while the reverse, at least in recent times, is clear. Mambae also shows significantly less evidence (mostly lexical) of Portuguese contact than TD, and remains closer to the traditional language type of the East Timorese linguistic area.

3.3.1 *Morphology*   There is no doubt that TF retains a much more productive and expansive range of morphological affixes and processes than both TD and Mambae. In TD only some of these affixes appear, but they show little or no productivity, with the limited exception of the causative *ha-* which for some speakers can be attached to borrowed roots, e.g. Port. *forte* 'strong' > *ha-forte* 'to strengthen'. Otherwise a periphrastic causative is preferred, *halo X* 'make/ do X'. In Mambae affixation is even more reduced. Fewer affixes can be identified and they occur relatively rarely. These are clearly frozen and are more typically dropped, such that the causative is now obligatorily periphrastic, as seen in the following comparison:

(12) TD: *funan* 'bloom, blossom'   Mambae: *hetu*
          hafunan 'to make blossom'   *fun hetu* (lit. make bloom)
          nakfunan 'to blossom' (INTR)   *hetu*

TF also retains a relatively wide use of reduplication, e.g. in N pluralization. By way of contrast, there is little use of reduplication as a morphological strategy in TD and Mambae, with the primary exception of temporal adverbs (TD *loron* 'day' > *loron-loron* 'daily', Mambae *lelo* > *lelo-lelo* 'daily').

3.3.2 *Morphosyntax*   Restricted subject (A/S) marking on verbs is characteristic of most of East Timor, with clear convergence towards complete loss around the Mambae area. Baikenu, spoken in the East Timor enclave of Oé-Cusse and most peripheral to the linguistic area, retains a relatively complex morphological system, including extensive marking on all verbs (cf. Table 2). In TF, only partial marking survives: there is no marking on vowel-initial verbs, subject marking for any singular forms and 3pl on verbs beginning with *h-*, and subject marking is further restricted to 1sg on other verbs with initial consonant. TD and Ermera Mambae have no marking at all, while in Southern Mambae subject marking survives only on the 3sg forms of vowel-initial verbs, e.g. *n-et* 'he finds' (3sg:-find).[7] Marking is also completely absent in neighbouring Isni, Kemak, and Tokodede, as well as Kairui-Midiki, Naueti, and Waima'a (Hull 2001). That convergence towards complete loss is still under way in the region is confirmed by the tendency to omit marking in TF (van Klinken 1999: 175), and variable patterns of marking in other varieties of Tetun Terik (cf. Hull 2001).

Many other differences separating TF from TD and Mambae also demonstrate greater convergence and simplification between the latter two. TF has a set of 'full' or tonic pronouns, alongside a reduced clitic-like set, e.g. *ha'u* (tonic) ~ *ha* (reduced) '1sg'. Both TD and Mambae have only a single unreduced set, e.g. TD

Table 2. Verb paradigms

	Baikenu *futu* 'tie'	TF, h- *há* 'eat'	TF, C- *sai* 'exit'	Mambae *et* 'find/see' (< *hetan*)	TD *hán* 'eat'
1sg	*'futu*	*ká*	*ksai*	*et*	*hán*
2sg	*mfutu*	*má*	*sai*	*et*	*hán*
3sg	*nfutu*	*ná*	*sai*	*et*	*hán*
1pl inc	*tfutu*	*há*	*sai*	*et*	*hán*
1pl exc	*mfutu*	*há*	*sai*	*et*	*hán*
2pl	*mfutu*	*há*	*sai*	*et*	*hán*
3pl	*nfutu*	*rá/ná*	*sai*	*et*	*hán*

Sources: Including van Klinken 1999; Hull 2001.

---

[7] Given a marked tendency of [h] to be deleted in Mambae, vowel-initial verbs have two historical sources: V- and h-, cf. historically related Mambae *et* 'find, see' and TF *hetan* 'find'.

ha'u, Mambae *au* '1sg'. TF has two existential verbs (*iha* or *nó*). *Nó* can be followed by the existent NP if it is a new participant, otherwise the existent always precedes the existential predicate, whether *iha* or *nó*. TD and Mambae have only one existential (*iha* and *nei* respectively) which can appear before or after the existent:

(13) TD: (la   iha)   uma   kreda   (la   iha)
     Mambae: (ba   nei)   um   kreda   (ba   nei)
              NEG   LOC   house faith   NEG   LOC
              There is no church

TF also has a copula, *nii,* optionally used to identify a unique referent. TD and Mambae have no copula, and a focus construction is preferred in this context:

(14) TF: lale, tais   ok   nii   nia
              no   cloth   2sg:POSS be   3sg
     TD: lae,   o-nia   hena mak   ida   ne'ebá
              no   2sg-3sg   cloth FOC   one   DIST
     Mambae: bai,   o-ni   ganetan pe   id   (la)ba
              No   2sg-POSS cloth   FOC   one   DIST
              No, your cloth is that one

The negator system of TF is significantly more complex than that of TD and Mambae which are identical. TF has four verbal negators: *la* 'NEG' (preverbal), *ha'i* 'NEG' (postverbal, stronger), combined *la* V *ha'i* with more emphatic force, and contrastive *lahoos* 'NEG'. NPs are negated by postnominal *ha'i* or preposed *lahoos*. TD and Mambae have two principal negators: respectively *la* 'NEG' and *ba* 'NEG' (before V) and *laós* 'NEG' and *balós* 'NEG' (always before NP and contrastively before V). They also share a more emphatic construction: TD *la* X *ida* and Mambae *ba* X *id* (lit. NEG X one).

   Relative clauses in Tetun Fehan are usually marked with relativizer *mak.* However, such clauses are marked similarly in TD and Mambae: TD *ne'ebé* (lit. where) and Mambae *bae* (lit. where), *baeid* (lit. where:one). In TD, older *mak* is today a focus marker, but it can also appear after the relativizer: *ne'ebé mak* (lit: where FOC). The same is also found in Mambae with its focus marker *pe: bae pe* (lit. where FOC).

3.3.3 *Directionality and convergence between TD and Mambae?*   Mambae is in many respects more innovative than TD: it is even more isolating than TD, and shows further reduction in other areas not examined here, e.g. the already limited use of numeral classifiers in TD (when compared to TF) is reduced much further in Mambae. If we establish a cline of increasing grammatical simplification, as at (15), we find Mambae furthest to the right, with TD close but still behind it.

(15)   ----------------------->
       Baikenu   TF   TD   M

There is no doubt of TF's greater conservatism, but there is also evidence of ongoing reduction given the tendency to omit argument marking on verbs. Baikenu, most peripheral to the East Timorese linguistic area, shares many features with all three languages, but is nevertheless the most conservative, retaining a much more complex morphological system, including full marking on verbs.

The historical origins of convergence in the East Timorese linguistic area are yet to be properly understood, but there are a number of hypotheses. Hull (2001) suggests, among other things, the influence of creolized Malay used as a local trade language. But such a hypothesis cannot explain the morphological complexity of Baikenu, spoken along the coast and the only part of East Timor where Malay has always been well established and maintained to this day, without competition from any variety of Tetum. More likely is long-term historical contact between AN and NAN languages, seen in their dispersed and partly intermingled distribution (cf. Map 1 and Hull 2004). As previously noted in §1, they have many features in common, such as a marked tendency towards largely isolating nature, and similar grammatical structures.

3.4 *Overall typology of change in Tetun Dili*

The process of TD becoming 'Europeanized' through contact with Portuguese has been under way for some time, but is clearly evident again now—as a result of the rise to co-official status of TD and language planning. Such an effect is hardly surprising given the sudden, immediate need for high-level writing and media activity in TD and the particular genres they involve. Few native structures show any simplifying effect that can be specifically associated with Portuguese contact; in the reduction of serial verb constructions for instance, Portuguese influence is one of a series of influencing factors. More common is a pattern of native structures coexisting with and reinforced by loaned forms and structures. Morphological loans in TD, however, though system altering, are in reality constrained to borrowed lexicon and are limited in scope. This resistance to morphological change reflects the largely isolating nature of the language.

Most evidence (chronological and comparative) suggests that the basic grammatical type of TD is not the result of contact with Portuguese, which is only relatively recent, but reflects longer-term linguistic convergence in the East Timor area showing a marked shift to an isolating grammatical type, especially evident in the Mambae and surrounding area. The historical direction of diffusion (Tetum > Mambae, Tetum < Mambae, Tetum < > Mambae?) is difficult to establish, although the slightly more isolating nature of Mambae suggests that the process is older and more advanced in Mambae than in TD. Moreover, Hull (2004) suggests that the sound shift in TD from [w] to [b], e.g. TT [we:] to TD [be:] 'water' and the loss of historical glottal stops may also be the result of contact with Mambae which shows the same phenomena. It is not unreasonable therefore to suggest, as Hull (2004) does, that TD is to a large extent the way it is compared to more conservative Tetun Fehan because of centuries-old contact with and diffusion from Mambae (and other languages in the linguistic area).

References

Baxter, A. 1990. 'Notes on the creole of Bidau, East Timor', *Journal of Pidgin and Creole Languages* 5: 1–38.

Caudmont, J. 1994. 'Présence de la langue portugaise dans le sud-est de l'Asie', *La Linguistique* 30: 9–28.

Corte-Real, B. 1998. *Mambae and its verbal genres: a cultural reflection of Suru-Ainaro.* Unpublished Ph.D. thesis, Macquarie University, Sydney.

Ethnologue = Gordon, R., Jr. and Grimes, B. F. (eds.). 2005. *Ethnologue*, 15th edn. Dallas: SIL International.

Fox, J. (ed.). 1988. *To speak in pairs: essays on the ritual languages of eastern Indonesia.* Cambridge: Cambridge University Press.

Hagège, C. 2002. *Morte e rinascita delle lingue*, trans. L. Cortese. Milan: Feltrinelli.

Hajek, J. 2000. 'Language planning and the sociolinguistic environment in East Timor: colonial practice and changing language ecologies', *Current Issues in Language Planning* 1: 400–14.

—— 2006. 'Serial verbs in Tetun Dili', pp. 239–53 of *Serial verb constructions*, edited by A. Y. Aikhenvald and R. M. W. Dixon. Oxford: Oxford University Press.

Hull, G. 2001. 'A morphological overview of the Timoric sprachbund', *Studies in Languages and Cultures of East Timor* 4: 98–205.

—— 2004. 'The languages of East Timor', http://laurel.ocs.mq.edu.au/~leccles/langs.html, accessed 15 Oct. 2005.

—— and Eccles, L. 2001. *Tetun reference grammar.* Dili: Sebastião Aparício da Silva Project in conjunction with Instituto Nacional de Lingüística, Universidade Nacional de Timor Lorosa'e.

Thomaz, L. F. F. R. 1981. 'The formation of Tetun Praça, vehicular language of East Timor', pp. 54–83 of *Papers on Indonesian languages and literatures*, edited by N. Phillips and A. Khaidir. Cahier d'Archipel Paris 13. Paris: Association Archipel.

van Klinken, C. L. 1999. *A grammar of the Fehan dialect of Tetun, an Austronesian language of West Timor.* Canberra: Pacific Linguistics.

Williams-van Klinken, C. L. 2001. 'High registers of Tetun Dili: Portuguese press and purist priests', *Proceedings of the 2001 conference of the Australian Linguistics Society*, http://linguistics.anu.edu.au/ALS2001/proceedings.html, accessed 24 Oct. 2005.

—— 2004. 'Developing electoral terminology for a new official language: Tetun in East Timor', *Current Issues in Language Planning* 5: 142–50.

—— Hajek, J. and Nordlinger, R. 2002. *A grammar of Tetun Dili, a language of East Timor.* Canberra: Pacific Linguistics.

7

Language Contact and Convergence in Pennsylvania German

KATE BURRIDGE

1 Sociohistorical backdrop[1]

Like any speech community, the Pennsylvania Germans do not represent a totally homogeneous group. What exists is a complex design of social, cultural, and religious diversity that must be taken into account in any appraisal of the linguistic situation. This is particularly true for patterns of contact-induced change.

The P(ennsylvania) G(erman)-speaking group examined here are the Mennonite Anabaptists of Swiss-German origin, who left Pennsylvania for Canada after the American War of Independence. The majority settled in Waterloo County, where they remain today (although the growth of the cities of Kitchener and Waterloo means some have moved into other areas). Since the 1870s, the Mennonites have been experiencing continued factionalism and the result is a complex pattern of different splinter groups. To simplify matters the community is normally divided into two major groups—the *Plain Group* and the *Non-Plain Group*. The Plain Mennonites are religiously the most conservative and are typically both rural and isolated. In Canada, this group largely comprises the Old Order Mennonites (OOMs). They have a very distinctive style of dress that has altered little over the centuries and their mode of transport is horse and buggy. This group is opposed to modern conveniences such as cars, television, telephones, and so on, although some accommodations have been made; for example, with respect to telephones and refrigeration (Burridge 2002*b*). Although a religious denomination in

[1] As always I am extremely grateful to the Mennonite community for their wonderful hospitality and their extraordinary patience in teaching me about their language.

origin, the OOMs are a distinct cultural-ethnic group with their own unique traditions, beliefs, customs, social practices, and language.

The description Non-Plain applies to two main groups. The so-called Progressive Mennonites (PMs) are least conservative. Their members are generally indistinguishable from mainstream Canadians. The Transitional Mennonites (TMs) form an intermediate group. They include, for example, the Markham Mennonites, who follow many of the same beliefs and behaviour patterns as the OOMs but have accommodated more to modern ways. Black cars now replace the horse and buggy. Their dress, like their cars, is plain and without decoration, although not in the same distinctive tradition of the OOMs—for that reason, they are sometimes referred to as the *Modern Plain.*

Competence in PG accords generally with degree of religious conservatism. The OOMs are fully bilingual E(nglish) and PG and their bilingualism has the support of stable diglossia. PG is usually only spoken and is the language of both home and community. E is read and written and only spoken when dealing with non-PG speaking outsiders. If High German (HG) is included here, then the situation is one of triglossia. This is (archaic) Luther German— the language of the Luther Bible, but with influence from PG and also E (when read aloud). It is only ever used for religious purposes and is best described as the classical variety in this model. People do not converse in it, unless to quote from the Bible. For the OOMs, language and religion are closely entwined. PG plays a crucial part in maintaining their separate existence and for this particular group, it is in no danger of disappearing. Among the Non-Plain Folk, however, language proficiency ranges from fully competent speakers to semi-speakers. The situation is an unstable one, even for the most competent speakers, with E intruding increasingly into what were originally Pennsylvania German domains.

2 English borrowings into Pennsylvania German[2]

To gain the full picture of this contact situation, I will briefly outline the phonological and lexical aspects before turning to grammar.

2.1 *Phonological considerations*

Early borrowings did not have much effect on the overall phonological structure of PG. Speakers were not bilingual PG-E and borrowings simply

---

[2] The overall patterns of influence uncovered here are similar to those recorded by Rayfield (1970) for English/Yiddish contact.

assimilated to PG phonological patterns. But borrowings have increased significantly and their impact is more obvious. Striking is the introduction of initial aspirated stops. There are also changes involving the rhotic. Until recently, the PG rhotic was pronounced as a trill before a vowel, and elsewhere as a schwa. Amongst the OOMs, however, it is now usual to find something resembling the North American retroflex before consonants and word finally after long vowels; for example, PG *Darm* 'intestine' is now frequently pronounced [dærm]. This pronunciation is on the increase, especially in the speech of younger and middle-aged OOMs.[3] Borrowings from E (such as *car*) cannot solely be responsible for introducing this pattern; otherwise the change would be affecting all groups of speakers equally. The motivation for the change does come from E, however, but indirectly; namely, via the pronunciation of the HG of their Bible and hymns. Since German is not a written language for the OOMs, they read it as they would E; in other words, they pronounce <r> wherever it is written. Moreover, they pronounce it as a retroflex, not as a trill. In the Old Order parochial schools, this is the pronunciation now taught for HG. The fact that the Non-Plain only rarely encounter HG (their church service being predominantly E) would explain why this pronunciation is less evident in this group.

2.2 *Lexical considerations*

The number of lexical borrowings into PG is enormous and growing and this is frequently commented on by the Mennonites themselves. Some are clearly *need* borrowings for new objects and concepts. PG has been in North America for nearly 400 years and cannot meet all current communicative needs. As Continental German no longer represents a viable source of borrowing, there is no alternative but to borrow from E. But by no means all borrowings arise out of need. There are many examples of everyday E words replacing original German forms, as in *remind, decide, sure, busy, really, a lot*, and so on. Prestige is often the reason for unnecessary loanwords (cf. Weinreich 1953: 59–60; Chapter 1: §4.2.3), but is not an obvious motivating force here, given the Anabaptist world-view—its emphasis on *demut* 'humility' rules out a positive evaluation of status. However, the impetus may derive from the important position of E as the written language.

---

[3] There is tremendous variety between speakers, as is typical of change in progress; e.g. in his 1977 autobiography former OOM Buehler fluctuates between spellings like *a'ahlich* versus *airlich* 'honest'; *a'ahbs* versus *airbs* 'pea'. (Note, unless I am quoting from earlier works like Buehler, I have chosen a spelling that is roughly the German-based system of pedagogical grammars such as Buffington and Barba 1965.)

2.3 *Grammatical considerations*

Grammatical interference is also strong and I discuss some of the most significant instances below.

2.3.1 *Constituent order* All Germanic languages have had at some stage in their development a feature of verb placement known as the verbal brace (*Satzrahmen*). In main clauses, this brace construction is created by the finite verb in second position and the non-finite verbal elements in final position. Together these form an imaginary bracket around all other sentence constituents. In subordinate clauses, it involves the initial subordinating conjunction and all clause-final verbal elements. A striking feature of PG constituent order, however, is the appearance of elements outside the verbal brace, bringing the discontinuous verbal constituents closer together and PG syntax, therefore, closer to E.

(1) *Mir   hen   alsemols   heemgemacht   eiscream   g'hat   do*
    we   have   before   homemade   ice cream   had   here
    We used to have homemade ice cream here

(2) *Er hot besser g'fielt wann er sich gut   hewe hot kenne aeryets*
    he has better felt   if   he self good hold has can   somewhere
    He used to feel better, if he could get a good grip somewhere

Contact here is accelerating a shift already in progress. Parallel shifts have either already occurred or are currently under way in other Germanic languages, including European Standard German (although it is usually 'heavy' elements, or genuine afterthought material that leak outside the brace).

Certain subordinating conjunctions like *weil* 'because' and *as* 'that' routinely occur with main clause constituent order. Again the exact role of English is difficult to determine here, since the same phenomenon can be found in continental dialects and is most certainly triggered by discourse factors like the assertiveness of the clause.[4]

(3) *No   verblatz ich   weil   ich bin ganz   arig   vol*
    then   burst   I   because I   am totally very   full
    Then I'll burst, because I'm completely stuffed

As this example also illustrates, PG retains the verb-second order that is so characteristically Germanic—one element only can appear in initial position in main clauses. Contact with E has done nothing to undermine this constituent order feature.

---

[4] See Burridge (1993) on main clause phenomena in medieval Dutch and German subordinate clauses.

2.3.2 *The progressive* PG has a progressive construction involving some form of the verb *sei* 'to be' followed by *am* (a fused preposition and article; literally, *an* + *em* 'on the') and an infinitival substantive. For example:

(4) *Wann du **am**   singe bischt fer mich no daerfscht graad schtobbe*
     if   you on-the sing are   for me   then may-you at once stop
     If you are singing for my benefit, then you can stop right now!

This is not an E borrowing; the same construction appears in other Germanic languages (Modern German *Er ist am Essen* 'he is eating'). Reed (1947: 9) observed of American PG: 'the proportion of progressive forms used is extremely small.' Certainly since Reed's time, the construction has increased dramatically in frequency and has spread into a number of new contexts (cf. Burridge 1992). Enninger (1980: 346–7) attributes this to E contact, but since expansion is also part and parcel of the grammaticalization process, contact with E could be simply helping the process along.

2.3.3 *Expressions of future time* PG has a new future construction derived from *geh* 'to go'. This is an immediate future, comparable to the English *gonna*.

(5) *Ich hab   geglaubt es geht ihm   happene*
     I   have thought it goes to-him happen
     I thought—it's gonna happen to him

Once again, the role of E is difficult to pin down. Contact may have triggered the grammaticalization process here. However, since this particular development is replicated in the languages around the world, E may again be accelerating a change that was independently motivated. As stated in Chapter 1, 'semantically similar verbs are likely to follow similar grammaticalization paths in languages in contact' (§4.1).

   PG has a number of E-inspired expressions that are routinely used to express future time.

(6) *Ich figger   kumme*
     I   figure   come
     I figure on coming

(7) *Ich bin   am   plaenne fer kumme*
     I   am   on-the   plan   to   come
     I plan on coming

(8) *Ich bin   supposed   fer kumme*
     I   am   supposed   to   come
     I'm supposed to come

(9) *Ich*   *zehl*   *kumme*
     I   count   come
     I am counting on coming/I will come

I have argued elsewhere that these constructions are expressing a cultural value that is central to the Anabaptist belief system; namely, subordination of individual will to the will of God. All are partial E calques and all are tentative expressions of future time—they are made to measure for a group of speakers reluctant to talk about the future. Frequency and associated 'routinization' and semantic-pragmatic loss are now seeing the grammaticalization of *zehle* 'to count' (in some dialects reduced to *zelle*) into a future auxiliary (cf. Burridge 2002a). The meaning is well on the way to shifting from 'counting on a future happening' to 'predicting a future happening'.

2.3.4 *Auxiliary-stranding ellipsis and the PG duh construction*   PG appears to have adopted the E system of auxiliary verb stranding in cases of structural gaps. Moreover, where there is no auxiliary present, PG mirrors English in having a supportive auxiliary *duh* 'do' that is added to allow the ellipsis to occur.

(10) Speaker 1 *Elam* *hoscht* *du*   *die* *sei*   *g'fiedert*
                 Elam   have   you   the   pigs   fed
                 Elam, have you fed the pigs

      Speaker 2 *Nee* *ich* *hab*   *gemeent*   *die* *Betty*   *hot*
                 No   I   have   thought   the   Betty   has
                 No, I thought Betty had

(11) *Die*   *Leit*   *dien*   *nett*   *all*   *gleich*   *gschwind* *Pneumonia*
      the   people   do   not   all   at once   quickly   pneumonia
      kriege   *e*   *deel*
      get   a   portion
      Leit   *dien*   *arrig* *gschwind* *ich* *duh*   *nau*   *nett* *awwer*
      people   do   very   quickly   I   do   now   not   but
      e   *Deel*   *dien*
      a   portion   do
      Not all people immediately get pneumonia. Some people do very quickly. I don't now, but some do

As the first (non-highlighted) *dien* 'do' in example (11) illustrates, PG also has what at first blush looks to be a *duh* support construction reminiscent of English 'dummy *do*' (although confined to the present). Buffington and Barba (1965: 26) claim that in American PG it is used for emphasis, and in question and negative formation; i.e. parallel to the English construction. However, this is not supported by the data here. Examples like (11) and (12) suggest the Canadian *duh* construction is a habitual marker that is on the way to shifting to a general present tense—a common enough change and part of the general move in PG towards greater analycity (cf. Burridge 1992). Since a similar construction occurs in colloquial varieties of Continental German, contact with E would again be having an accelerating effect here.[5]

(12) | *Speder* | *es* | *Haez* | ***dut*** | *kompensete* | *un* | ***dut*** | *noch* |
|---|---|---|---|---|---|---|---|
| Later | the | heart | does | compensate | and | does | still |
| *greser* | *waerre* | *un* | | | | | |
| larger | become | and | | | | | |
| *die* | *annre* | *Valves* | ***dien*** | *e* | *Bissel* | *mener schaffe* | |
| the | other | valves | do | a | little | more work | |

Later the heart (does) compensate and (does) become bigger and the other valves (do) work a little harder

2.3.5 *The passive* The passive construction shows a number of English influences: (1) the passive *bei* 'by' phrase always appears outside the brace (i.e. *after* the passive participle); (2) the preposition *bei* has now replaced *vun* 'of'; (3) the auxiliary *sei* 'to be' has virtually taken over from the auxiliary *warre/waerre* 'to become' in present and preterite. This means there is the same potential ambiguity in PG as in E between a verbal and adjectival reading. For example (13) has both a passive reading and a stative reading. (Note that *sei* is the only verb to maintain a preterite form; this means a preterite passive is available to speakers.)

(13) Present/Preterite:

De	*Schtrump*	***s/waar***	***geschtoppt***	*bei*	*der*	*Maem*
the	stocking	is/was	darned	by	the	mother

The stocking is/was darned by mother

The new progressive passive overcomes the ambiguity.

(14) Progressive:

Blaume	*sin*	*am*	*verkaaft*	*waerre*	*beim*	*Kael*	*am*	*Eck*
plums	are	on-the	sold	become	by-the	chap	at-the	corner

Plums are being sold by the chap on the corner

---

[5] Since present situations (i.e. situations in effect at the time of utterance) can express habitual occurrences (and also other meanings like progressive, states, and generics; cf. Bybee, Perkins, and Pagliuca 1994), we should not be surprised to find habitual generalizing to 'present tense' in this way.

2.3.6 *The 'get' construction*   In informal English, *get* has a number of auxiliary functions that have grammaticalized out of its original lexical meaning 'to receive'. It would appear that PG *kriege* 'to get, receive' is moving along strikingly similar paths—undoubtedly, once more with encouragement from E. For example, PG has a *kriege* passive that, like the E construction, typically involves situations where there is a beneficial or adverse effect on the subject referent. The following example illustrates the promotion of an indirect (dative) object to subject:

(15)   *Ich   hab   e   Buch   gewwe   griegt*
      I   have   a   book   given   got
      I got given a book

(16)   *Mir   kriege   gesaagt*
      we   get   told
      We get told

The verb *kriege* also appears in semantically similar constructions involving passive complements. Again they involve situations where something happens to the subject referent, as in the following. (Here the dative possessor is promoted to subject.)

(17)   *Er   hat   sei   Lewwe   genumme   griegt*
      he   has   his   life   taken   got
      He got his life taken/He was killed

In these constructions, the subject referent has a greater role to play in the situation (e.g. more responsibility), especially where there is an intervening reflexive pronoun. (Compare the E construction, which also attributes agent-hood to the subject.)

(18)   *Er   hat   sich   umgebracht   griegt*
      he   has   himself   killed   got
      He got himself killed

These *kriege* constructions closely resemble both the E *get* passive and the complex construction '*get* + NP + past participle'. However, it is difficult to determine the exact role of E here, since a similar construction occurs in non-standard varieties of Continental German. For example, Ruhrdeutsch:

(19)   *Sie   haben   den   Ball   weggenommen   gekriegt*
      they   have   the   ball   taken away   got
      They got the ball taken away (from them) (Werner Enninger, p.c.)

In the following examples the subject has an even more obviously agentive role. As these sentences illustrate, this complex PG *kriege* construction seems to have the same range of causative and non-causative meanings as the E '*get* + NP + past participle' construction.

(20) *Hen   dir   sel   geduh   griegt*
     have   you   that   done   got
     Did you get that done?

(21) *Sie   hen   ien   eigschteckt   griegt*
     they   have   him   put away   got
     They got him put away

(22) *Mir   hen   sie   gepsucht   griegt*
     we   have   them   visited   got
     We got them visited/We managed to visit them

Something similar also occurs in varieties of non-standard Continental German. For example, compare (21) with the colloquial German version in (23):

(23) *Sie haben ihn eingelockt gekriegt*
     They got him put away (Werner Enninger, p.c.)

2.3.7 *The case system* The original nominative and accusative cases have already merged in PG. This must have happened early in its history, since it is a general feature of south-eastern Rhine-Palatinate dialects (cf. Buffington and Barba 1965; Keller 1961). There are also signs that the dative is on the way out, although this change does not appear to be as advanced in Canada as it is in Pennsylvania (compare Huffines 1989). Some dialects of European German have also lost the dative distinction (cf. Keller 1961), but it cannot be an inherited pattern in PG, since the dative is still used freely among the Canadian OOMs—the transitional groups (TMs and PMs) show a greater degree of convergence to E here.

Case syncretism appears in other varieties of German in contact with E (cf. Eikel 1949 and Gilbert 1965 for American German and Clyne 1972 for Australian German and Dutch) and structural pressure from E is undoubtedly an issue. But since this sort of morphological levelling or 'grammatical stripping' (Markey 1987) is a general characteristic of languages in contact, once again the actual role played by E is difficult to determine.

2.3.8 *Complement clauses* In current-day PG the most usual type of complement clause construction combines a complementizer *fer* 'for' with the base form of the verb, as in:

(24) *Er   hot   sich   immer   g'faericht   fer   in   de   heh   geh*
     he   has   self   always   feared   for   in   the   high   go
     He was always frightened to go up high

This grew out of an earlier complement construction signalled with *fer-zu* 'for-to'. Ben Sauder's poetry, written in the 1930s, has examples like the following:

(25)   *Es   iss   net   dawaert,   fier   die   Schteddla   zu   saachen*
      it   is   not   worth   for   the   townfolk   to   say
      It's not worth telling those not on the land

These complement clauses superficially resemble E *for-to* clauses and have been attributed to English origins.[6] This is unlikely to be the case. For one, contact with English comes too late to provide the birthplace for the original construction. Moreover, 'for-to' purposive clauses occur in some of the Continental German dialects (west of the Rhine), including Frankish and Pfälzisch; so the makings of the PG construction would already have existed when the various dialects spoken by the Anabaptist settlers blended into one language. The spread of the construction to complement clauses, however, and the accompanying disappearance of *zu* appear to be innovations peculiar to PG (cf. Börjars and Burridge forthcoming; Burridge 2006). Clearly, if contact with E were truly a force here, we would expect a strengthening rather than loss of PG *zu* (akin to E *to*).

2.4 Summary

The grammatical changes just described for PG show the difficulty outlined in Chapter 1 with respect to determining a clear-cut distinction between 'language-internal change' and 'language-external change'. Most of the changes appear to have mongrel origins with a number of different internal and external factors playing a role. (1) We have here two genetically related languages that because of their common origin are 'drifting' (à la Sapir) in similar directions; in other words, the seeds for these changes (for example, the shift from syntheticity to analycity) would have been sown long ago in the proto-language. (2) Some of these constructions (e.g. the progressive, the 'do' construction, 'get' passive) were present in the original dialects that came into Pennsylvania from the Palatinate and surrounding areas like Bavaria,

---

[6] Louden (1988) presents an interesting proposal for PG complementation that appeals to contact with American English. While he claims the original *fer-zu* construction is native to PG, he claims there is one-to-one correspondence between PG *fer* clauses and English *to* clauses and between PG bare infinitives and English present participles (p. 212)—this correspondence he then attributes to convergence. This correspondence between PG *fer* clauses and English *to* clauses and the PG bare infinitive and English gerunds can be explained (1) by the special semantics of the different clause marking and (2) by the fact that both languages have been following the same grammaticalization paths (cf. Börjars and Burridge forthcoming; Burridge 2006).

Hessen, Swabia, and Württemberg, as well as the German-speaking areas of Switzerland. The seeds would therefore have been planted during the first wave of immigration in the seventeenth century. (3) The PG speakers may also independently have sown the seeds. Many of the developments illustrate extremely well-trodden paths of grammatical change (e.g. the 'go' future, the 'get' passive, 'for-to' complementation) and may well be a product of the universal cognitive processes driving language use. (4) In some cases E contact would have induced certain of these seeds to sprout. In other cases, it would have stimulated the growth of seedlings that had already emerged.

2.5 *Discourse/pragmatic particles, interjections, politeness formulae*

When it comes to those elements that have some kind of discourse-regulating function, PG draws heavily on E. There is a striking number of E discourse markers that have been fully integrated into the language. These include actual transfers such as *well* (example 26) and calques such as *ennichweg* < *anyway* (example 27). Such markers are complex, but a superficial investigation suggests they have been borrowed along with the E functions. PG *well* appears before surprising information, answers to questions, and self-repairs. PG *ennichweg* signals a shift of topic (often to an earlier topic). Similarly, native markers such as *juscht* 'just' and *weeschte* 'you know' have adopted functions akin to the equivalent English discourse marker—*juscht* is a classic hedge, among other things (examples 27–8) and *weeschte* emphasizes common ground between the players (examples 29–30).

(26) | *Ich* | *wees* | *nett* | *eb's* | *wise* | *is* | *as* | *de* | *Daadi* | *geht* |
I	know	not	if-it	wise	is	that	the	Dad	goes
awwer	*ich*	*hab*	*decide*	**well**	*er*	*hot*	*geluschte*	*fer*	*geh*
but	I	have	decide	well	he	has	desire	to	go

I don't know if it's wise that Dad goes. But I decided, well, he wants to go

(27) | *No* | *uff* | *eemol* | *war's* | *graad* | *wie* | *wan* | *e* | *tap* | *g'dreet* | *waer* |
so	on	once	was-it	just	as	if	a	tap	turned	would-be
un	*[...]*	*no*	*is*	*alles*		*zerrick*	*kumme*	*zu*	*ier*
and	[...]	then	is	everything	back	come	to	her
ennichweg	*ich*	*hab*	*no*	**juscht**	*g'saagt*
anyway	I	have	so	just	said
mei		*mir*	*sin*	**juscht**	*do*	*am*	*schwetze...*
my		we	are	just	here	at-the	chatting

So suddenly it was just as if a tap was turned on and [...] then everything came back to her. Anyway I just said, 'My, we are just sitting here...'

(28) *Ich   wees   net   sure   was   nutmeg   is   mir   sage   **juscht** 'nutmeg'*
      I   know   not   sure   what   nutmeg   is   we   say   just   nutmeg
      I'm not sure what nutmeg is. We just say *nutmeg*

(29) *Mir hen   arrig wenig Wadde fer Affection **weeschte**   viel   dien mir*
      we have   very few   words for affection you know many do   we
      borrowe oder dien mir mit   ener Inflection von de   Voice saage
      borrow or   do   we with an   inflection of   the voice say
      We have very few words for affection, you know. We borrow many
      or we say <them> with an inflection of the voice

(30) *Er   war   nett   **weescht**   arrig reich awwer er   war   well-to-do*
      he   was   not   you-know   very   rich   but   he   was   well-to-do
      He wasn't you know very rich but he was well-to-do

Influence of English is particularly obvious in the minimal responses listeners use to indicate they are listening and to encourage the speaker to continue. The following example ends a phone conversation between two OOM women. Note especially the E style auxiliary tag here—*hoscht du* 'have you?' The telephone, as a cultural practice borrowed from outside, would certainly encourage more E backchannel signals than regular conversations. However, these sorts of listening noises are also characteristic of PG interaction generally.

(31) ***Ok, thank you** E., no loss ich dich geh, weil du bischt likely am wesche.*
      ***Oh, I see, ja, hoscht du? Ah. Aha, I see . . . Oh. I see . . . aha. Ok,** ich loss*
      *dich wesche nau E., un no, **ok,** no seenscht du die K. aa datt. **Thanks a***
      lot, ok, bye bye.
      Ok, thank you E. Now, I'll let you go, because you are likely washing.
      Oh I see, yes, have you? Ah. Aha. I see . . . Oh I see . . . aha [. . .] Ok,
      I'll let you wash now E., and then ok then you'll also see K. there.
      Thanks a lot, ok, bye bye

Also striking here is the use of E interjections (see also *mei* 'my' in 26) and particularly E politeness formulae. Elsewhere I have commented on PG patterns of greetings, leave-takings, pleases, and thank-yous, where silence is commonplace (Burridge 2002*a*; Enninger 1991). The kind of mandatory speech used to establish social rapport during an encounter is not needed in such an integrated community, where people are deeply involved with one another and where there is no social distance. And with so many external symbols already available, like clothing, an individual's social characteristics and values are immediately obvious. There is not the same need for language to express this kind of information here as there is in the mainstream culture. However, increased dealings with the outside mean the E routines are being adopted and are now more in evidence.

3 The English of the Canadian Mennonites

The following is a brief account of the other side of the contact coin; namely PG influence on E. Much has been written on this topic and descriptions like the following are commonplace:

> When the Pennsylvanian German [goes] to speak English (which [is] for him a foreign tongue), he [is] influenced by the German syntax or sentence structure. For some such English as 'Run the steps once up' is largely unintelligible unless you know that it's really the Pennsylvania German 'Schpring mol die Schdeeg nuff'. This is the reason for many of the so-called 'quaint' or 'cute' sayings of the Pennsylvanian German *trying* [my emphasis] to speak English. 'Throw the cow over the fence some hay' is but another example of this process. (Druckenbrod 1981: 10)

More recently, April McMahon (1994) describes how 'speakers of Pennsylvania German...import the German order of modifiers into English, giving constructions like *throw the baby from the window a cookie*' (p. 206).

In reality, the only time Pennsylvania German speakers produce examples of this kind of E are when they are imitating what they have dubbed *verhoodelt* (or 'mongrel') *Englisch*. This variety is a fictional cliché that appears in jokes and anecdotes and on tourist tea towels, beer coasters, and wall plaques:

Throw Father down the stairs his hat once.
Becky lives the hill just a little up.
Yonnie stung his foot with a bee un it ouches him terrible.

Like most stereotypes, *verhoodelt Englisch* has become part of the shared cultural knowledge of the area, but has no basis in reality. There is remarkably little in the way of PG interference in the English of these speakers and studies on groups from Pennsylvania, such as Enninger et al. (1984) and Huffines (1980, 1984), suggest the same—Pennsylvanian *verhoodelt Englisch* is a modern-day fiction.

3.1 *Lexical considerations*

The least amount of interference occurs at the lexical level. The few lexical transfers from PG to E are confined to untranslatable concepts such as *Freindschaft* (which inadequately translates into English as 'family', 'relations') and words to do with buggy technology, for example.

3.2 *Grammatical considerations*

The data suggest also minimal grammatical borrowing from E. There is no evidence of the syntactic modifications that have become the clichés of PG

English. One possible influence is the frequency of the final placement of verbal particles (*I ate my dinner up* vs. *I ate up my dinner*), since it follows the expected pattern of PG separable verbs. However, since 'particle movement' is an alternative pattern for E (motivated primarily by discourse factors), it is not clear whether this particular constituent order is truly any more frequent in PG English than the standard variety of the area. Certainly, there is no evidence for the postposed prepositions of *verhoodelt Englisch*; examples like *Becky lives the hill just a little up* never occur.

3.3 *Phonological considerations*

Burridge (1998) presents an investigation into the E of 10 OOMs, 7 TMs, and 7 PMs. It is only a preliminary study, yet revealing. The most obvious interference occurred at the prosodic level, in this case a distinctive rise-rise-fall pattern for a range of sentence types, including questions and statements. The pattern spread across the whole utterance, but more often than not condensed into the last item (Figure 1).

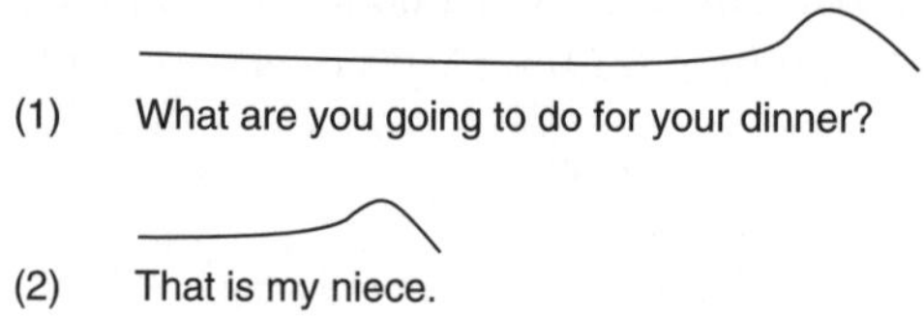

(1)   What are you going to do for your dinner?

(2)   That is my niece.

FIGURE 1 Characteristic intonation

Results for the transferral of segmental features fell basically in line with what had already been described for the Amish groups of the USA (Enninger et al. 1984; Huffines 1980, 1986, 1984). The only features that appeared uniformly for all speakers were the following:

1. dark ɫ → clear l
2. dʒ → tʃ
3. ʌ → ʋ, ɔ
4. i → ɛ, ə (in unstressed positions)

The results for the TMs also revealed obstruent devoicing word finally. Since the TMs use more E and have more contact with outsiders, this seems surprising. §4 discusses possible reasons for this distribution.

5. voiced obstruents→voiceless (word finally)

The American studies described two additional accent features:

6. v → w
7. w → v, ß

As the two most clichéd features of PG English, it is telling that these are absent from the data here. Also absent (and from the US data) is the pronunciation of dental fricatives [θ, ð] as [s, z]. So how did the stereotype arise? As any contrastive analysis of PG and E would predict, these are precisely the characteristics of the E of recent German immigrants to Canada. The reason they have come to be identified so closely with the E of the Pennsylvania Germans is historical. Up until into the twentieth century, High German played a much greater role in the lives of these speakers and there was simply not the same call to learn English. One feature of stereotypes is that they petrify. Time gives them an authenticity that seems immune to change. The horse and buggy community, being so highly visible and so 'different', is particularly vulnerable to this sort of stereotyping. In truth, their English is closer to a prescriptive ideal of 'proper' English than the English of many of their stereotypers. But it is interesting, too, that the OOMs themselves promote this stereotype. Presumably, this has to do with the importance they place on humility (*Demut*). Much like their dialect of German, their plain dress, and buggy transport, *verhoodelt Englisch* is a sign of this humility.

3.4 Discourse features

The only potentially PG discourse markers in the E of the Canadian Pennsylvania Germans are *yet* and *already*. These are sentence-final aspectual markers and literal translations of German particles. Since they are also commonplace in the E of Waterloo County people generally, including those *not* of PG heritage, they must go back to an earlier time of contact, also involving the other German-speaking groups who arrived in various waves during Ontario's history (for example, the Roman Catholic and Lutheran communities). These groups have now assimilated into the mainstream culture and have surrendered their German. Interestingly, Salmons (1990: 473) describes precisely the same discourse markers in the E of the US German-speaking communities.

4 Discussion: why these patterns of interference?

Figure 2 outlines the basic patterns of influence. Without yet taking into account the differences between the OOMs and the TMs, these can be

	Influence E —> PG	Interference PG —> E
Phonological	weak	strong
Grammatical	strong	weak
Lexical	very strong	very weak

FIGURE 2 Patterns of influence

arranged into two reverse hierarchies of increasing and decreasing strength respectively. Why is it that we find precisely these patterns of interference? Genetic or typological considerations are not much help here. Although they predict that the similarity of the linguistic systems would facilitate easy borrowing, they cannot explain why interference seems sensitive to the different levels of grammar and why, in particular, the reverse hierarchies obtain when we compare the direction of borrowing.

4.1 *The acquisition experience*

Consider, first, the different types of contact involved. PG is the language first learned at home and E is generally acquired at school (from the ages of 5 or 6). The direction PG to E, therefore, involves the type of transferral traditionally known as substratum interference—in other words, the transferral of language habits into a second language (so-called 'improper learning'). Such a situation involves potential or actual shift to E (as is currently happening among the TMs and, to a far greater extent, among the PMs). The other direction, however, E to PG, represents the more restricted sense of borrowing—the transfer of items to a group's native language (cf. Thomason 1986; Thomason and Kaufman 1988).

   The patterns of influence we find here are predictable when we take into account, first, these two different types of contacts and, secondly, the order in which each different linguistic level is acquired. Intonation and stress features are the first to be acquired and are therefore 'the most deeply anchored' features (McLaughlin 1984). These and segmental features are acquired during a child's first three years. The acquisition of grammatical features continues until much later, during the early school years, and vocabulary continues to be acquired throughout one's lifetime. It is not surprising, therefore, that the most 'deeply anchored' speech habits are the ones we find most readily transferred from PG to E (from first to second language) and—to consider the other side of the coin—are the ones which in PG show the greatest resistance to influence from E. Since the acquisition of vocabulary is ongoing, the E loans now entering PG from E are also no surprise, although the speed at which PG vocabulary is being replaced is a puzzle. But what of grammar? Language learning does not predict any specific outcome here. Both types of contact, borrowing and substratum-induced interference, can result in grammatical changes. So why then is grammatical interference much stronger from E to PG than in the other direction? The explanation for this lies in other aspects of the childhood acquisition experience.

During the early school years, children would not yet have stabilized their PG grammatical structures and they would be vulnerable to E interference at this time. Significant here is the way in which E is acquired in the formal school setting. In Canada, school is an 'E-only environment' which admits *no* PG whatsoever (even in the school playground). There is also considerable prescriptivism attached to the learning of E—a strong emphasis on 'proper English' (Enninger et al. 1984: 13 report the same for Amish parochial schools in Pennsylvania). Similarly, outside of school, the children's experience of E is within formal contexts only; i.e. in contact with outsiders and as a written language. In addition, they have no access to more colloquial varieties via television and radio, for example. Predictably, there is little in the way of style shifting; speakers confine themselves to a fairly formal register of E.

All these factors work against the transference of PG features into their E. There would be little in the way of 'imperfect learning'. This would *not* be true of E-PG interference, however. Sociohistorical studies of change have shown that linguistic innovations have a much greater chance of taking hold in a language if they attract no attention and no resistance from speakers (cf. for example, Nadkarni 1975: 681; Louden 1989, particularly pp. 34–5). There would be considerable resistance to change in E. However, since PG is not standardized and has no written form, people are quite used to variation and are tolerant of it. PG speakers constantly remark on the variation in their language, often commenting: *wie Englisch as mir sin* 'how English we are'. Despite their isolationist philosophy, these comments are never regretful, nor are they ever critical—even amongst the OOMs.

There remains the additional question of variation within the Mennonite community itself. Why do the TMs (particularly, the younger members) show more phonological interference than the OOMs? The answer lies in the different linguistic inputs these groups receive as children. For one, the early acquisition experience of the TMs involves considerably more mixing of the two languages and for many, E may well even come to dominate both linguistically and socially. Bilingual studies like McLaughlin (1984) show that both mixed input and imbalance more readily facilitate interference.

The OOM children, however, keep the languages separated from the start. They acquire the languages successively—PG is well established at home before E is later introduced in the school (although some children may acquire a little E from their elder siblings before this time). No language appears to dominate over the other and each has its own distinct functions. Also important here is the fact that the environment in which the OOM children learn E is a supportive one—something that may seem surprising in a community so intent on maintaining its separate status. All of these factors—non-mixed input, absence of dominance, and a supportive environment—have been shown to be important if linguistic structures are to remain differentiated and resist interference.

Importantly, the bilingualism of the Non-Plain groups does not have the support of diglossia. For them, PG is showing ever-shrinking domains, with English appearing more and more in contexts of use that were traditionally PG (church services, for example). Predictably, a breakdown of diglossia will result in greater general interference, as originally outlined by Fishman (1972: 105):

As role compartmentalization and value complementarity decrease under the impact of foreign models and massive change, the linguistic repertoire also becomes less compartmentalized. Language varieties formerly kept apart come to influence each other phonetically, lexically, semantically, and even grammatically, much more than before.

4.2 *Ethnic affiliation*

There are additional social and psychological factors. The TMs are in the process of shifting culturally and linguistically to mainstream Canada, but they are not yet part of the mainstream. These people keep close and continual contact with the OOMs and identify very strongly with them—the *Modern Plain* is really a more apt label for this group. However, while they share many of the same beliefs and behaviour patterns as the OOMs, they have lost the distinctiveness of this group. Gone are the features that make the OOMs so strikingly distinctive—dress, horse and buggy, and possibly now also PG. Language attitude studies show that ethnic varieties of the dominant language can be a powerful signal of ethnic group membership.

The softer the perceived linguistic and non-linguistic boundaries existing between ethnic groups, the more likely speech markers will be adopted in order to accentuate ethnic categorization. (Giles 1979: 274)

So for the TMs, PG features in their E have a value in signalling PG ethnicity. Not so, however, for the OOMs, whose linguistic and non-linguistic boundaries are still firm.[7]

---

[7] Huffines's (1980, 1984) descriptions of the Pennsylvania Amish suggest a similar situation holds there.

4.3 *Discourse features*

E discourse/pragmatic markers, interjections, politeness routines (even translated idioms like *gut fer dich* lit. 'good for you') are commonplace in PG.
However, there is no evidence of the equivalent PG features in the E of these
speakers. So why draw on E in this way? As in the case of the lexical
borrowings, need is not the answer, nor social prestige. Matras (1998) has
argued that these kinds of borrowings (dubbed 'utterance modifiers') are
highly automaticized and gesture-like and, rather than a social trigger, they
are cognitively motivated. He claims that bilingual speakers will cut down to
just one set of these items and this set will always favour those that belong to
'the pragmatically dominant language'; in other words, the linguistic system
'to which speakers show a special situative commitment'. The notion of a
pragmatically dominant contact language is an interesting one here. This is a
speech community that tries to maintain its isolation and limit its interaction
with the outside world. But the reality is it has to do business with the
E-speaking majority in order to survive. And E of course has considerable
clout as the language of literacy. This was not always the case, however, and
the presence of German modal particles in the E of the wider Waterloo
County community (i.e. not just the Pennsylvania Germans) stems from
the time when German dominated as the language of education, worship,
and writing.

5 Conclusion

There have been efforts at proposing constraints on the different ways in
which languages can influence each other. While these contribute greatly to
our understanding of the role of contact in language change, as clearly
outlined in Chapter 1, there is always a battery of counter-examples where
proposed universals simply fail. This is precisely because there are crucial
social and psychological aspects, which the constraints do not take account of.
What the PG-E contact situation demonstrates is just how complex these
aspects can be. Without precise information here, we cannot predict when
transference will take place and what the nature of it will be. Phonological,
prosodic, or grammatical features can never be considered independently of
the context in which they appear.

Linguistic factors are clearly also relevant here. In many respects, PG is
converging to E in its structure, and closeness of the linguistic systems and
structural compatibility would have assisted the changes. In virtually every
instance it was a case of E accelerating a trend imminent or already under way.

Yet there are also many instances where the language hasn't converged, the most obvious being (1) PG shows no sign of adopting verb-third order (XSV) in main clauses; (2) it hasn't used its 'do' auxiliary construction to support negation, questions, emphasis; (3) it hasn't replaced its *fer* 'for' complementizer with *zu* 'to'; (4) it hasn't chosen to revive its declining genitive 's' construction but has rather expanded its dative possessive; (5) in the case of the new auxiliary *zelle*, E has provided the verbal escape hatch for speakers in a cultural fix, but the end result is a future marker that is distinctly PG.

It would seem that PG is heading towards something akin to an E lexicon embedded within a structure still distinctively PG. Although there is no conscious language engineering involved here, speakers are definitely aware of the hybrid nature of their language. For the OOMs its 'bitser' quality has a positive, almost sacred, value. High German is the word of God and the low status of the dialect variety is, therefore, an appropriate symbol of their humility.

References

Börjars, K. and Burridge, K. Forthcoming. 'Origins and development of the Pennsylvania German "for... to" construction'.

Buffington, A. F. and Barba, P. A. 1965. *A Pennsylvania German grammar.* Allentown, Pa.: Schlechter.

Burridge, K. 1992. 'Creating grammar: examples from Pennsylvania German, Ontario', pp. 199–241 of *Diachronic studies on the languages of the Anabaptists,* edited by K. Burridge and W. Enninger. Bochum: Universitätsverlag Dr. N. Brockmeyer.

—— 1993. *Syntactic change in Germanic: with particular reference to Dutch.* Amsterdam: John Benjamins.

Burridge, K. 1998. 'Throw the baby from the window a cookie: English and Pennsylvania German in contact', pp. 71–94 of *Case, typology and grammar: essays in honor of Barry J. Blake,* edited by A. Siewierska and J. J. Song. Amsterdam: John Benjamins.

—— 2002a. 'Changes within Pennsylvania German grammar as enactments of Anabaptist world-view', pp. 207–30 of *Ethnosyntax: explorations in grammar and culture,* edited by N. Enfield. Oxford: Oxford University Press.

—— 2002b. 'Steel tyres or rubber tyres—maintenance or loss: Pennsylvania German in the 'horse and buggy' communities of Ontario', pp. 203–29 of *Language maintenance for endangered languages: an active approach,* edited by D. Bradley and M. Bradley. London: Curzon Press.

—— 2006. 'Complementation in Pennsylvania German', pp. 49–71 of *Complement clauses and complementation strategies: a typological perspective,* edited by R. M. W. Dixon and A. Y. Aikhenvald. Oxford: Oxford University Press.

Bybee, J., Perkins, R. and Pagliuca, W. 1994. *The evolution of grammar.* Chicago: University of Chicago Press.

Clyne, M. 1972. *Perspectives on language contact (based on a study of German in Australia)*. Melbourne: The Hawthorne Press.

Druckenbrod, R. 1981. *Mir lanne Deitsch*. Allentown, Pa.: Schlechter.

Eikel, F. 1949. 'The use of cases in New Braunfels (Texas) German', *American Speech* 24: 278–81.

Enninger, W. 1980. 'Syntactic convergence in a stable triglossia plus trilingualism situation in Kent County, Delaware, U.S.A.', pp. 343–50 of *Sprachkontakt und Sprachkonflikt (Zeitschrift für Dialektologie und Linguistik 32)*, edited by H. Nelde. Wiesbaden: Steiner Verlag.

—— et al. 1984. 'The English of the Old Order Amish of Delaware: phonological, morpho-syntactical and lexical variation of English in the language contact situation of a trilingual speech community', *English World-Wide* 5.1: 1–24.

—— 1991. 'Focus and silences across cultures', *Intercultural Communication Studies* 1.1: 1–38.

Fishman, J. A. 1972. *The sociology of language*. Rowley, Mass.: Newbury House.

Gilbert, G. G. 1965. 'Dative versus accusative in the German dialects of Central Texas', *Zeitschrift für Mundartforschung* 32: 288–96.

Giles, H. 1979. 'Ethnicity markers in speech', pp. 251–89 of *Social markers in speech*, edited by K. R. Scherer and H. Giles. Cambridge: Cambridge University Press.

Huffines, M. L. 1980. 'English in contact with Pennsylvania German', *German Quarterly* 54: 352–66.

—— 1984. 'The English of the Pennsylvania Germans: a reflection of ethnic affiliation', *German Quarterly* 57: 173–82.

—— 1986. 'Intonation in language contact: Pennsylvania German and English', pp. 25–36 of *Studies on the languages and the verbal behaviour of the Pennsylvania Germans 1*, edited by W. Enninger. Stuttgart: Steiner Verlag.

—— 1989. 'Case usage among the Pennsylvania German sectarians and nonsectarians', pp. 211–66 of *Investigating obsolescence: studies in language contraction and death*, edited by N. C. Dorian. Cambridge: Cambridge University Press.

Keller, R. E. 1961. *German dialects*. London: Butler and Tannen.

Louden, M. L. 1988. *Bilingualism and syntactic change in Pennsylvania German*. Unpublished doctoral thesis, Cornell University.

—— 1989. 'Syntactic variation and change in Pennsylvania German', pp. 29–40 of *Diachronic studies on the languages of the Anabaptists*, edited by K. Burridge and W. Enninger. Bochum: Universitätsverlag Dr. N. Brockmeyer.

McLaughlin, B. 1984. *Second-language acquisition in childhood: preschool children*. Hillsdale, NJ: Lawrence Erlbaum Associates.

McMahon, A. 1994. *Understanding language change*. Cambridge: Cambridge University Press.

Markey, T. L. 1987. 'Mistress of many: how Dutch was grammatically stripped', pp. 313–23 of *Third Biennial Interdisciplinary Conference on Netherlandic Studies (1986), University of Michigan, Ann Arbor*. Lanham, Md.: University Press of America.

Matras, Y. 1998. 'Utterance modifiers and universals of grammatical borrowing', *Linguistics* 36: 281–331.

Nadkarni, M. V. 1975. 'Bilingualism and syntactic change in Konkani', *Language* 51: 172–86.

Rayfield, J. R. 1970. *The language of a bilingual community.* The Hague: Mouton.

Reed, C. E. 1947. 'The question of aspect in Pennsylvania German', *Germanic Review* 20: 5–12.

Salmons, J. 1990. 'Bilingual discourse marking: code-switching, borrowing, and convergence in some German-American dialects', *Linguistics* 28: 453–80.

Sauder, B. 1955. *Der Nachbar an de Schtroas.* Toronto: Pennsylvania Folklore Society of Ontario.

Thomason, S. G. 1986. 'Contact-induced language change: possibilities and probabilities', pp. 261–84 of *Akten des 2 Essener Kolloquiums zu Kreolsprachen und Sprachkontakte,* edited by W. Enninger and T. Stolz. Bochum: Studienverlag Dr. N Brockmeyer.

—— and Kaufman, T. 1988. *Language contact, creolization, and genetic linguistics.* Berkeley and Los Angeles: University of California Press.

Weinreich, U. 1953. *Languages in contact.* New York: Linguistic Circle of New York Publication No. 2.

8

Balkanizing the Balkan Sprachbund

A Closer Look at Grammatical Permeability and Feature Distribution[1]

VICTOR A. FRIEDMAN

1 Introduction

The Balkan sprachbund[2] was the first area of contact-induced language change to be identified as such (Leake 1814: 380; Kopitar 1829: 86). Owing perhaps to this pedigree, it has been described as 'the most studied' and 'most famous' example of its kind, but, owing to the known antiquity and complexity of multilingualism in the region, it has also been described as 'notoriously messy' (Thomason and Kaufman 1988: 95). Hamp (1989) noted that one could speak of a plurality of *Sprachbünde* (for which I would now use sprachbunds) in former Yugoslavia, while Masica (2001) provides a useful summing up of the question of defining a linguistic area, an issue with which he has been occupied for many years (Masica 1976). Aikhenvald (Chapter 1) raises the fundamental question of the relationship between sociolinguistic history and typological structure to the nature and progress of contact-induced change. Moreover, many recent typological and other studies (e.g. Haspelmath 1998; van der Auwera 1998; Lindstedt 2000) treat complex Balkan

[1] Much of the research and thinking for this chapter was done while I was a Fellow at the Research Center for Linguistic Typology at La Trobe University, August–November 2005. I am grateful to Bob Dixon and Sasha Aikhenvald for the opportunity to work in such a peaceful, productive, and supportive atmosphere. Uncredited examples are from fieldwork. All English translations are my own.

[2] Among the proposed glosses for sprachbund are 'linguistic league', 'linguistic area', 'convergence area', and 'diffusion area', but here I shall treat sprachbund as a loanword into English, like French genre, so it will be neither capitalized nor italicized.

phenomena as unitary, ticking off points or drawing lines in such a way that the facts 'on the ground' disappear from view.[3] It is in this context of relative causation and typological study that I wish to examine some fundamental assumptions about the Balkan languages and argue that when viewed at close range, some apparent commonalities of the Balkan sprachbund reveal different cleavages that reflect differences in shared history, and that the relative susceptibility of contact-induced change in a given system shows language-ideological (sociolinguistic) as well as typological factors at work. At the same time, keeping these details in mind makes for better-informed typological studies that reflect more clearly existing linguistic situations.

This is not to say, with Andriotis and Kourmoulis (1968: 30), that the Balkan sprachbund is 'une fiction qui n'est perceptible que de très loin' and that the commonalities are 'tout à fait inorganiques et superficielles'. To the contrary, Balkan linguistic diversity occurs within the context of a set of structural similarities that comprise a framework of contact-induced change. Moreover, we must distinguish between 'superficial' and 'surface'. As Joseph (2001) has persuasively argued, surface realizations constitute the locus of language contact, and explanations that appeal to typological aspects of universal grammar (including so-called formalist 'explanations') tell us nothing about language contact (Aikhenvald makes a similar point in Chapter 1). Also, surface realizations are by no means 'inorganic'; they represent convergences that are evidence of the multilingualism that we know existed for centuries and even millennia. Nonetheless, while rejecting the notion that the Balkan sprachbund is a fiction, we must place the differences in the context of the similarities. In this chapter, then, I shall, as it were, Balkanize the Balkans by examining certain cleavages—particularly with respect to future marking and referentiality—and discuss the nature of their areality. In so doing, I hope not only to produce a more nuanced picture of the most famous sprachbund, but also to argue that, like all language change, degrees of convergence can take place with varying speeds. At the same time, however, based on our available documentation, processes that may have been set in motion, or at the very least begun to be reinforced during the middle ages, achieved their

---

[3] A problem with van der Auwera's (1998) methodology, for example, is the dependence on standard languages and the treatment of features as unitary. In his approach, Bulgarian comes out as 'more' Balkan than Macedonian owing to the presence of stressed schwa. Leaving to one side the inadequacy of his list (e.g. the Balkan conditional in Macedonian is more grammaticalized than in Bulgarian), there are two realities that his approach fails to capture. One is the fact that the majority of Macedonian dialects do have stressed schwa (assuming that one even wants to accept this as a Balkanism) while a minority of Bulgarian dialects (Teteven-Erkech, some Rhodopian) do not. The other is that object doubling is fully grammaticalized in (West) Macedonian, whereas it is a pragmatic feature in all of Bulgarian. What is needed is not a map of language names, but of regions, as well as distinctions for degree of grammaticalization.

current state during the *Pax Ottomanica* (and it is telling that this same period is referred to in Bulgarian as *turskoto igo* 'the Turkish yoke'). Moreover, the effects of the end of that historical period have shown a combination of mutability and resiliency, which, at this early stage, can only be hinted at.

2 The Balkans and Balkanization

A number of studies have argued that the Balkans as a concept were constructed during the late nineteenth and early twentieth centuries by West European discourse as a negative 'Other' against which it could define itself positively in much the same fashion as it constructed the Orientalist discourse identified by Edward Said (Bakić-Hayden 1995; Todorova 1997). Thus, for example, the use of the term *Balkanization* to mean 'break up into tiny entities' does not date from the nineteenth century, when the Balkan nation-states were separating from the Ottoman Empire, but rather from the end of the First World War, when the Austro-Hungarian, German, and Russian empires were resisting the national self-determination that led to the creation of Czechoslovakia, Poland, and the Baltic republics. This construing of the Balkans was part of the process by which Western Europe constituted itself as 'Europe', a process that in some ways continues to this day.

It is arguable that the linguistic construction of the Balkans as a significant contact zone, i.e. as different from the orderly genetic differentiation posited for Western Europe, was part of this same process of West European differentiation. The most extreme formulation of this was Schleicher's (1850: 143), when he described Balkan Romance, Balkan Slavic, and Albanian as forming a group of different languages 'agree[ing] only in the fact that they are the most corrupt in their families'.[4] It can be argued that a mirror image of Schleicher's view was Whorf's (1938) S[tandard]A[verage]E[uropean], which was basically a linguistic equivalent of this same West European Germano-Romance creation of Europe. Relating to this vein of occidentoeurocentrism, just as the Balkans have been deconstructed by modern historians, so, too, some Balkan linguists, e.g. Reiter (1994), and more recently the EUROTYP project, have argued that the Balkans do not constitute a special case but rather a part of SAE, albeit a periphery of the core (!) (cf. Haspelmath 1998). Nonetheless, the political separation of south-eastern Europe from the early modern upheavals that led to the creation of 'Europe' qua Europe—the so-called

---

[4] 'Es ist eine bemerkenswerte Erscheinung, dass um die untere Donau und weiter nach Südwesten sich eine Gruppe aneinandergränzender Sprachen zusammengefunden hat, die bei stammhafter Verschiedenheit nur darin übereinstimmen, dass sie die verdorbensten ihrer Familie sind'.

Pax Ottomanica—had linguistic consequences. While some of these have been erased in the ensuing century or so of 'national liberation' others remain, and this, too, is of interest to our topic. In this sense, I will be discussing the linguistic Balkanization of the Balkans, i.e. the creation of a relatively unified linguistic area owing to centuries of multilingual contact—the very opposite of political 'Balkanization'.

3 The Balkans

3.1 *The Balkan languages*

It is certainly the case that anything *can* be borrowed, but it is equally the case that not everything *is* borrowed in a contact situation in which languages maintain separate identities, i.e. when there is balanced contact. In the case of the Balkans—and differentially among the Balkan languages—these differences reflect both geography (west vs. east, south-west vs. north-east) and history. This brings us to some issues of definition. Regardless of the definition of the Balkan peninsula or of what constitutes a language versus a dialect—both issues of burning political importance in south-eastern Europe—there is a general consensus that four Indo-European groups are represented in the Balkan sprachbund: Albanic, Hellenic, Romance, and Slavic. A fifth Indo-European group, Indic (as represented by Romani), occupies a more marginal position, but precisely this marginality renders it particularly important in the examination of contact-induced change. Finally, while Turkic has long figured as a factor in the Balkans, the relevant Turkic dialects have only recently been examined in the context of mutual interaction with the other Balkan languages (see Map 1 for an overview of languages, dialects, and distribution). Of these six groups, we have documentation of forms that we can treat as representative of ancestral languages or at least much older relatives in the case of Hellenic, Indic, Romance, Slavic, and Turkic.

3.2 *The Balkans as a place*

With regard to geography, the east, south, and west sides of the Balkan peninsula are unproblematically defined by water: starting from the north-east and moving around to the north-west we have the Black Sea, the Sea of Marmara, the Aegean, the Mediterranean, the Ionian, and the Adriatic. There is no boundary—be it geographical or political—that unproblematically defines the northern limit of the Balkans. Geopolitically, the accepted definition used to be the northern borders of former Yugoslavia and Romania, but among Balkan linguists it was generally accepted that only the southernmost

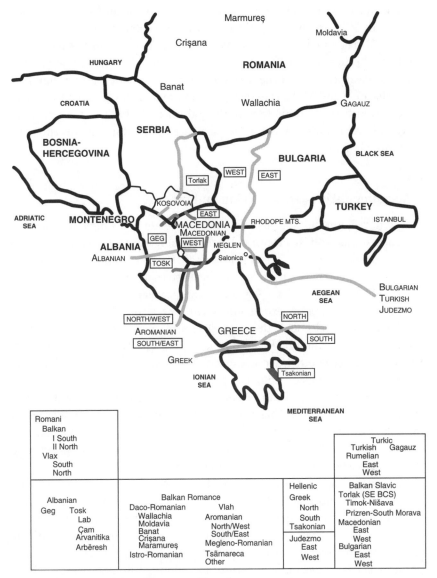

MAP 1 Languages of the Balkan sprachbund

Note: Unlike some other language contact situations, the various Balkan languages are overlapping and co-territorial. It is therefore misleading and even inaccurate to assign or limit a specific language to a specific territory, and this is even more the case if the situation of a century ago is taken into account. Thus, each of the seven groups has speakers in each of the Balkan nation-states. While the language of a given eponymous nation-state dominates most of the territory within its borders, there are local areas in all of them where other languages dominate. This is especially true near international borders. The East/West isogloss bundles for Bulgarian, Judezmo, and Turkish are close enough to be represented together. The Aromanian isogloss bundle roughly follows the Macedonian after intersecting with it.

(Torlak) dialects of former Serbo-Croatian (now Bosnian/Croatian/Serbian, henceforth BCS) are characteristically Balkan. A combination of the isoglosses defining Torlak and delimiting Albanian serves to define a northern linguistic limit on the territory of former Yugoslavia that, while not impervious, is relatively clear in terms of the spread of morphosyntactic features. Similarly, the Wallachian and Moldavian dialects of Romanian, having been the longest under Turkish rule, are more typically Balkan than those to the north (see Belyavski-Frank 2003: 235–81). As we shall see (§6.1), Romani also enters the definitional picture.

4 Sociolinguistic factors: religion and prestige

Although religion did not (and does not) correlate in a simple manner with language, it was (and is) a factor in language choice and influence. Most of the Balkan Slavic speakers, Balkan Romance speakers, and Tosk Albanian speakers of the region ended up in the Eastern (Greek) Church after the Great Schism (1054), most Geg Albanian speakers ended up as Catholics (whence the Montegrin expression *Arbanaška vjera* 'Catholicism' literally 'Albanian faith'), although the Geg villages in the Reka region of western Macedonia are Orthodox. Many Bosnian Slavs and Albanians converted to Islam, as did some other Slavs (Gorans, Torbesh, Pomaks), as well as some Greek and some Balkan Romance speakers, all at various times following the Ottoman conquest. The timing and circumstances of these conversions are still matters of historical debate and investigation. By the late middle ages in the Balkans, Turkic-speakers were Muslim except the Gagauz of the Black Sea Coast, who appear to have been descended from Turkish-speaking Byzantine mercenaries who kept their Orthodox faith (Wittek 1951/2).

In terms of social position, if we start from the situation prior to the Roman occupation of the Balkans, Greek was the only surviving language of prestige and literacy that we can decipher (Linear A remains a mystery). Even after the Roman occupation (roughly second century BCE until the Slavic invasions of the sixth and seventh centuries CE), Greek retained its position as a language of high culture, and educated Romans learned Greek, although Latin now also had prestige as the language of empire. The Slavic invasions radically altered the linguistic balance on the peninsula. The evidence of toponymy combined with survivals of Slavic linguistic islands in southernmost Greece into the sixteenth century indicate that the entire peninsula was linguistically inundated. It is presumed that Greek survived only in the coastal cities and towns, while Latin (or Romance) and Common

Albanian were pushed up into the mountains; and that, during this period, Slavic speakers and Romance/Albanian speakers occupied complementary agricultural and pastoral economic niches, respectively. It was also during this period that the other languages of the Balkans presumably disappeared, although they had been under pressure from Latin and Greek for centuries. The Slavic invasions probably also spilt Balkan Romance into Daco-Romanian and Vlah, and possibly Albanian into Geg and Tosk, although the evidence is contradictory.[5] During the late middle ages Albanian extended down into Attica and the Peloponnese, and the region still has remnants of its Albanian (Arvanitika) speaking population. The Fourth Crusade (1204) and the rise of Venice also brought in West Romance influence, but this was limited to lexicon.

During the Ottoman period (fourteenth to early twentieth centuries), Turkish became the language of urban communication and sophistication. Greek was a language of religion (for Christians) and commerce as well as literacy. Slavic was also used in these functions, generally to the north of Greek. Aromanian, Albanian, Romani (arrived tenth–twelfth centuries), and Judezmo (arrived 1492) were home languages, but their distributions varied. All these languages were spoken by settled populations in towns, and except for Judezmo, also in villages—as was also the case for Greek and Turkish. Urban Aromanians generally used Greek outside the home, Jews and Roms used Turkish (and in Salonica and Istanbul, Jews used French), although they would also know whatever contact languages were relevant. Romanian and Albanian remained predominantly rural languages until the nineteenth century, although literacy in both is attested from earlier centuries, and both these languages were spoken in towns in regions where there were significant numbers of speakers. Although language could correlate with status and thus influence marriage choices, the main determiner of eligibility for marriage was religion (except in the case of Roms, where endogamy correlated with ethnicity, i.e. Roms did not generally marry outside their ethnolinguistic group regardless of religion).

5 Balkanisms

In discussing the properties of the Balkan languages that arguably result from language contact (Balkanisms), giving a list runs the risk of oversimplification,

---

[5] Tosk rhotacism, which is consistently realized in Latin loanwords, is not consistent in Slavic ones. This may be due to non-Tosk (Balkan Romance) intermediaries, the differential spread of rhotacism on Tosk territory, or a post-Slavic date of the Geg–Tosk split.

while space limits full elaboration. For our purposes here, it will suffice to note some of the most salient. For fuller discussion see Friedman and Joseph (forthcoming) and the handbooks listed in Friedman (2000). Although the Balkan languages show convergence at every linguistic level it is the morphosyntactic convergences that first captured European attention, and these are still the most remarkable. The first observed Balkanisms (Kopitar 1829: 106) are among the simplest at first glance and more complex when viewed carefully: the postposed definite article, the replacement of the infinitive with an analytic subjunctive, and the marking of futurity with a verb or particle derived from a verb meaning 'want'. To these Miklosich (1861: 6–8) added genitive-dative merger and doubled object pronouns, while Seliščev (1925) added the use of resumptive clitic pronouns to mark dative and accusative substantival objects, datives as possessives, and the general loss of case forms (among others). (Miklosich also adduced directional/locational mergers such as 'whither/where', the use of 'on ten' to mean '-teen', repetition for quantity, intensity, and/or distributivity, and the presence of schwa as Balkan features, but these are not of interest to us here.) Sandfeld (1930), the first book-length treatment of Balkan linguistics, did not appear to have expanded significantly on Seliščev's list if one simply looks at the section headings of chapter 4 'Concordances générales en dehors de lexique' (163–216), but in fact his third chapter, 'Concordances entre differentes langues balkaniques en dehors de lexique' (100–62), while less comprehensive than later studies, contains the first observations of a number of Balkanisms that have subsequently been expanded upon: future in the past used as conditional (105); interrogatives as relatives (107); preservation of the aorist/ perfect opposition (105); zero partitives and accusatives of motion (109–11); perfect and pluperfect in 'have' (132, 149); indefinite article (130); double determination (122); intransitive perfects in 'be' (132, 149); preservation of the vocative (146–7); analytic comparison of adjectives (156, 161, 164); independent (optative) use of the analytic subjunctive (180).

6 Balkan futurity and referentiality

Two of Kopitar's 'first' Balkanisms, the 'want' future and the postposed definite article, serve as excellent starting points for illustrating the complexity hidden behind the commonly cited generalizations.

6.1 *The Balkan future*

In the case of the 'want' future, the choice of auxiliary verb is known elsewhere in Europe as is the fact that it reduced to an invariant marker (which actually is not entirely the case in the Balkans; see Kramer 1994 for details), but the fact that these developments took place in the Balkan languages at approximately the same time in a multilingual geopolitical environment, triumphed over competing models that were successful in neighbouring regions and/or related languages, and can be seen to have spread from Balkan centres of innovation, sets the Balkans apart from adjacent languages.

With regard to futurity, the attested ancestral languages had no morphological category (Slavic) or an inflected morphological one (Sanskrit, Latin, Greek). In the late middle ages in the Balkans, the verbs 'want' and 'have' competed as auxiliaries in Greek, with 'have' being predominant until the twelfth century, and only gradually giving way to 'want' during the late middle ages. The construction reduces to particle + subjunctive marker + finite verb (*the na graphō* 'I will write') in the thirteenth century and to a simple future marker (*tha graphō*) in the sixteenth, which was completely generalized by the eighteenth, except in Italo-Greek, which still has a 'have' future (Sandfeld 1930: 184).

In Latin, too, 'have' and 'want' futures competed, the former first attested in Cicero, the latter in Plautus. The 'have' construction dominated all of Romance except in the Balkans.[6] In Daco-Romanian, an invariant particle *o* plus subjunctive is characteristic of the south (Wallachia), whereas further north there is a conjugating auxiliary or a conjugating 'have' future. In Aromanian the future is marked only with the particle *va* (from 'want'), while in Megleno-Romanian the future marker merged with the subjunctive marker, except in Tsãrnareka, which has distinctive *ãs* (from *va* + *sã*).

In Old Church Slavonic, 'have' and 'want' competed with the perfective of 'be', verbs meaning 'begin', and the plain perfective. Constructions with the perfective of 'be' and plain perfectives became grammaticalized everywhere except Macedonian, Bulgarian, and the Štokavian and Čakavian dialects of BCS, but only in the Torlak dialects did 'want' reduce to an invariant particle. It is worth noting that the 'will' future was carried northward out of the Torlak area into the rest of Štokavian by migrating populations during the Ottoman period.

In Albanian, 'have' and 'want' futures still appear to be in competition in the oldest full texts (sixteenth century). Although superficial accounts generally characterize the 'want' future using invariant *do* as Tosk and a 'have' future using conjugated *kam* plus infinitive (*me* + participle) as Geg, in fact the realities are much more complex (Friedman forthcoming). On the one hand, the *do* future has completely taken over Southern Geg, the Central

---

[6] Although a 'want' future is reported for Southern Italian, the 'have' future dominates (Čelyševa 2001: 144).

Geg of Upper Reka in north-western Macedonia, the North-Western Geg of Shkrel, the left bank of the River Buna near Shkodër, and the central northern Geg of Puka. It is the predominant type in the North-Eastern Geg dialects of Has and Luma in Albania adjacent to Upper Reka, as well as in the northern Geg in Mirdita, south of Puka. In the foothills to the north-east of Shkodër and in Kelmend, Plav, and Gucî *do* competes with *kam*, and there is still a conjugated 'will' future:

(1) Jam   i   lik   e   duo   me   dek
     I.am   PC:M   ill   and   want:1sg with die:PARTIC
     I am ill and will die (Shkurtaj 1975: 55)

The Arbëresh dialects of southern Italy, which separated from the main body of Tosk in the fourteenth and fifteenth centuries, have a generalized 'have' future with invariant *ka* or *kɛt* (although *do* also occurs), while in Geg territory, the 'will' future continues to spread at the expense of 'have'.

In Romani, there are two main ways of forming the future. In northern and central dialects (outside the Balkans), the so-called 'long form' of the present tense in -*a* is used, while the short form functions as the present, e.g. *ker-a-v* (root-stem vowel-1sg)'I do'—*kerava* 'I will do'. In the Balkan dialects, the future is almost always formed by means of a particle based on the root *kam*- 'want', normally plus the short form, and the long form functions as a simple indicative present, e.g. *kerava* 'I do'—*ka kerav* 'I will do'.[7] The so-called Vlax dialects show a complex distribution. Those that are coterritorial with Torlak BCS or east of that and south of the Danube are like the Balkan dialects. Vlax dialects outside the Balkans behave like northern and central dialects, while Vlax dialects in Romania, Bosnia, and northern Serbia have the two futures in competition (Boretzky and Igla 2004: 2. 63 and 244). The extent of the future marker *ka* and its cognates in Romani is a marker of Balkan influence, and its complete absence from the northern and central dialects, its absence or attenuation in Northern Vlax dialects, and dominance in the Southern Vlax and Balkan dialects suggest the origin of the form after the diaspora of the later medieval period, which is to say the same Ottoman period when the future was grammaticalized in the rest of the Balkans. (Cf. also Boretzky 1996 on infinitive renewal outside the Balkans.)

Macedonian and Bulgarian, as well as the Romani, Turkish, and Aromanian dialects with which they are in contact, however, use a negative existential/possessive for the ordinary negated future as illustrated in Table 1, a grammaticalized remnant of competing 'have' constructions.

---

[7] Exceptions are the result of attrition of the type seen in Megleno-Romanian.

TABLE 1. Grammaticalized negative futures using possessive/existentials

Macedonian	nema		da	odime
Bulgarian	njama		da	hodime
Aromanian	noare		s'	neadzim
	not.has		*SP*	*go.1pl:PRES*
Romani	na-e	amen	te	dža[s]
	not-is	*1pl:ACC*	*SUBJ*	*go.1pl:PRES*
WRT	yok-tur		gid-elim	
	not-is		*go-OPT.1PL*	
English	we won't go			

To sum up, the 'will' future in the Balkans is an example of mutual reinforcement and feature selection that began to take shape in the late middle ages but did not reach its current situation until the early modern period, and in some areas, e.g. parts of Albania and Romani dialects, the process is still ongoing. Western Macedonia and adjacent parts of Albania emerge as a centre of innovation. In looking at the grammaticalization of future constructions, we see, on the one hand, that 'will' is still spreading at the expense of 'have', 'have' is not altogether vanquished, and reduction to invariant clitic is not altogether complete, especially in Romania, BCS, and Bulgaria (for the future in the past, where the auxiliary conjugates).

6.2 *Referentiality*

Definiteness and deixis involve reference, as does indicating topicality by means of object reduplication.[8] In the Balkans these features interact in different ways in different regions with object reduplication as the least grammaticalized but most widespread and deictic distinction being the least permeable to contact-induced change.

6.2.1 *The definite article*   In the case of the postposed article, the presence of similar phenomena in Scandinavian and in north Russian dialects and the absence of postposing in Greek and Romani (Balkan Turkish marks definiteness but not with an article) do not by themselves vitiate the Balkan contact nature of the phenomenon in Albanian, Balkan Slavic, and Balkan Romance. (See Hamp 1982 on the possible antiquity of this phenomenon in the Balkans.) For both Balkan Romance and Balkan Slavic, we know that the

---

[8] The use of resumptive clitic pronouns to mark dative and accusative nominal and pronominal objects is traditionally referred to as *reduplication* or *object reduplication* (French *redoublement de l'objet*) in Balkan linguistic literature, and this is the usage we follow here.

development took place after the arrival of speakers in the Balkans. In Balkan Slavic the Timok-Nišava dialects of north-eastern Torlakia have a three-way deictic distinction in the definite article (see §6.2.2) independent of the same phenomenon in western Macedonia, whereas the deictic distinction in Goran postposed articles represents a continuation of western Macedonian. The postposed articles are lacking in all the other Slavic dialects of Kosovo (as well as the adjacent South Morava region of Torlak in southern Serbia proper).

6.2.2 *Deictic pronouns*   The postposed definite article can be seen in the context of deixis and topicality, this latter expressed by the use of clitic pronouns to mark certain substantival direct and indirect objects (see §6.2.3). Deixis is more resistant to contact phenomena than definite referentiality, although we do have contact simplifications at the local level (see below). It also appears that certain aspects of deixis and referentiality are salient as emblems of identity (see §7).

Deictic systems in the Balkans are of two kinds: two way and three way. Moreover, Romani combines the usual proximal/distal (-*a/o*) with general/specific (*d/k-*) so that every demonstrative must express both oppositions (see Matras 2002: 103–6). In terms of attested ancestral languages, we know that Greek, Latin, Sanskrit, and Old Church Slavonic all had three-way deictic systems, as did earliest attested Turkic. In the case of Romance, the simplification to a two-term system covered the entire area. In Balkan Slavic, most of Bulgarian has a simplified two-way deictic opposition, but unlike Romance and Albanian, it is the distal rather than the proximal that is functionally marked in that the unmarked member is the one normally serving as the third person pronoun.[9] In Lower Gora, however, the two-way system parallels exactly the Albanian, which is presumed to be the source of the simplification (Mladenović 2001: 356). Typical forms are illustrated in Table 2.

6.2.3 *Object reduplication*   The use of a clitic pronoun agreeing in gender, number, and case with an accusative or dative object—usually definite—is an oft-cited Balkanism that is grammaticalized to differing degrees in different languages and dialects. Example (2) from Macedonian is typical:

(2) mu   go   davam   moliv-ot   na   momče-to
     3sg:N:DAT   3sg:M:ACC   give:1sg   pencil-DEF:M   to   boy-DEF:N
     I give the pencil to the boy

---

[9] We are referring here to functional markedness, the unmarked member being the one chosen in neutral contexts. The dialects of the central Rhodopes and the transitional dialects of the extreme west of Bulgaria have three-way deictic systems in the pronouns and the article. The former is a unique isolated development using the older Slavic proximal deictic *s-* rather than the later, originally oppositional deictic, -*v-*, while the latter is a continuation of Torlak in this respect.

TABLE 2. Balkan deictic systems

	Proximal	neutral/[3sg]	distal/[neutral]
Albanian	këtë	atë (ACC)	—
Daco-Romanian	acest (ăst)	acel	—
Megleno-Romanian	tsistu	tsăl	—
Aromanian	aist	atsel	—
Judezmo	esti	akel	—
Greek	(e)toûtos	autós	(e)keînos
Lower Gora	ovaj	taj	—
BCS	ovaj	taj	onaj
Macedonian	ovoj	toj	onoj
Bulgarian	—	tozi	onzi
Turkish	bu	[şu]	[o]
Romani	akava—adava		okova—odova[a]

[a] The original proximate/distal opposition marked by *d/k* in the root is obligatorily coupled with a non-specific/specific distinction usually marked by *d/k* in the root yielding a four-terms system in almost all Romani dialects (see Matras 2002: 103–12 for details).

Such reduplication is prescribed for all definite direct and all indirect objects in standard Macedonian, and indeed, this is generally the rule in the western dialects. In the eastern dialects, as in Bulgarian, reduplication is facultative, although there are contexts where, colloquially, it will be expected. Literary Bulgarian is at the opposite extreme, and reduplication is almost completely proscribed in formal contexts, a tendency that also influences standard Greek, Romanian, and Albanian usage, albeit to varying degrees. In Bulgarian, Greek, and Romanian, the exclusion of reduplication from formal contexts derives in part from the fact that the older prestige languages did not have it. Thus, for example, the Modern Greek and Bulgarian translations of the Gospels completely lack reduplication. (Both Albanian and Romanian require reduplication in some contexts.) In all the Balkan languages, object reduplication occurs colloquially, normally when the object is a topic, which is usually the case with definite and indirect objects. Many accounts confuse definiteness with topicality, however, claiming that indefinite objects cannot be reduplicated. As examples (3) and (4) show, however, even non-specific indefinites can trigger reduplication if they are topics. Example (3) is from a non-normalized colloquial Macedonian text and (4) is from a corpus of spoken Bulgarian, thus representing languages at the two extremes of grammaticalization of reduplication:

(3) Star čoek   da   go   pregrnuvaš vo son   [...] boles ќe
    old person SUBJ him:ACC embrace:2sg in sleep [...] illness FUT
    te   fati
    you:ACC   grab:3sg
    If you dream of embracing an old person [...] you'll get sick
    (Koneski 1967: 262)

(4) Banan   ne   običam   da   go   jam
    banana   not   like:1sg subj it:m:acc eat:1sg
    I don't like to eat banana[s] (Leafgren 2002: 176)

Except for Gora, none of the Slavic dialects of Kosovo have definite articles, but object reduplication can be used with referential topics, as seen in this example from Sretečka Župa, to the north-east of Gora:

(5) pa   de   će   vidjet dukat — zgazi   — dok   gi
    and   where FUT see:3pl ducat   step.:IMP   until them:ACC
    zbrale   sve   dukati
    gathered:3pl all   ducats
    and where[ever] they would see a ducat [they would] step on it until
    they had gathered all the ducats. (Pavlović 1939: 289)

Such examples are common in southern Kosovo but appear to be less frequent in Timok-Nišava, apparently under the influence of the standard language.

Albanian, Greek, and Macedonian illustrate the three basic types of object reduplication in the Balkans. As already indicated, in Greek, as in Bulgarian, reduplication is almost always facultative, although it will be normal in some contexts. In Macedonian, it is fully grammaticalized, while in Albanian it is less grammaticalized, being obligatory under more limited conditions than in Macedonian. Examples (6) and (7) are illustrative

(6) (a) Pap-a   Ø vizitoi madje Tiranë-n   (Albanian)
        Pope-DEF   Ø visited even   Tirana-DEF:ACC

    (b) O Papas   Ø episkeftike akoma ke   ta   Tirana (Greek)
        the Pope   Ø visited   even   and the:ACC Tirana

    (c) Papa-ta   go   poseti   duri   i   Tirana   (Macedonian)
        Pope-DEF   it   visited even   and Tirana
        The Pope visited even Tirana—Tirana is focus
        (after Kallulli 1999: 32)

(7) (a) Madje Pap-a e vizitoi Tiranë-n (Albanian)
even Pope-DEF it:ACC visited Tirana-DEF:ACC

(b) Akoma ke o Papaps [ta] episkeftike ta
even and the Pope [it:ACC] visited the:ACC
Tirana (Greek)
Tirana

(c) Duri i Papa-ta **go** poseti Tirana (Macedonian)
even and Pope-DEF it visited Tirana
Even the Pope visited Tirana—Pope is focus, Tirana is topic
(after Kallulli 1999: 34)

In (6b) Tirana is the focus and Albanian does not permit reduplication, whereas in (7b) Tirana is the topic and reduplication is required. When substantives are topicalized coming before the verb, reduplication is required in Romanian as well as Albanian. In Macedonian, Tirana has definite reference and therefore requires reduplication, whereas in Greek Tirana is not reduplicated if it is the focus and is only facultatively reduplicated when it is the topic. The northern dialects of Aromanian reduplicate as in Macedonian, whereas the southern dialects reduplicate as in Greek. Judezmo in this respect behaves like Spanish, while Romani also behaves like Greek, i.e. reduplication occurs but is never required.[10]

While object reduplication in northen Aromanian reflects the obligatoriness of this phenomenon in western Macedonian, there has been mutual reinforcement in the effect of Aromanian patterns in terms of pattern copying in local (e.g., Ohrid) Macedonian, as seen in example (8):

(8) (a) lu vidzui pi/al Marko (Aromanian)
him:ACC:M see:AOR:1sg to M.

(b) go vidov na Marko (Macedonian)
him:ACC:M see:AOR:1sg to M.
I saw Marko

The use of a directive or dative marker with an accusative object is characteristic of Balkan (and also some Western) Romance and is clearly a

---

[10] Romani does require reduplication in possessive constructions, but this is a different sort of phenomenon. Bulgarian requires reduplication with negative existentials and Greek requires it when the direct object is *ola* 'everything'.

borrowing in local western Macedonian. Moreover, it appears to be limited to animate or personal nouns, a Romance feature.

7 Conclusions

The current dialectal situation around Gora can be seen as the result of centuries of what we can characterize as *isolated contact*, i.e. a population of relatively mobile men (shepherds and migrant workers [*pečalbari*]) and sedentary women whose movements were determined by ties of kinship and marriage. Under such conditions, the dialects of Gora and neighbouring dialects in Kosovo and Macedonia illustrate an epidemiological model of feature spread (Enfield 2003: 366–9) or an ecological model of feature selection (Mufwene 2005: 106–35). The differential spread of the postposed definite article and the reduplication of non-pronominal objects indicates that they mark different allegiances as well as different types of narrative strategy. In Serbia, the definite article of Macedonian is perceived as one of its most distinctive features, and indeed the folk stereotype of Macedonian in Serbia is that it sounds like *ta-ta-ta, to-to-to* (repetitions of the feminine and neuter definite articles). This can be attributed in part, at least, to the fact that the majority of BCS dialects rely on case endings for decoding syntactic relations, and definite articles occur where most BCS speakers would expect those inflections. It is arguable, then, that the definite article has had emblematic status in Gora, given that its speakers are Muslims with ties to the Slavic-speaking Muslims to their south (cf. Storch, Chapter 3, and Enfield 2003: 267–8 on emblematic formal and structural features in a linguistic community). Reduplication, on the other hand, is more widespread but less grammaticalized, and appears to have become negatively valued in the south-east Serbian periphery during the course of the twentieth century. This same negative valuation occurs in the Albanian dialects of Kosovo, where the feature is more frequent but associated with Slavic.

Romani has been completely open to Balkan contact in future formation and the influence of Greek in using native material for a definite article, but more closed with regard to object reduplication and entirely closed in the maintenance of its deictic system. In general in the Balkans, modalities such as the future and the conditional are more subject to spread and grammaticalization, while in referentiality there is a gradation from topicalization by object reduplication through the grammaticalization of a definite article to the preservation of deictic systems. In this respect, it is worth noting that while Balkan and non-Balkan Romance followed similar paths, Balkan Romance did so in contact with Albanian, which in this respect influenced the dialects of Lower Gora. The Bulgarian development seems more consistent with what were once adjacent East Slavic dialects, while Macedonian has had the conservatism of BCS. The parallels in 'will' and 'have' future competition in the languages spoken on Balkan Slavic territory, together with the continued spread of the 'will' future in Albanian, point to central Albania and western Macedonia—areas of the most intense and complex multilingual contact and also areas of intense social contact, with speakers of the various languages being both Christian and Muslim—as a major source of both innovations and conservatisms. To be sure, influences also came up from Greek in the south and travelled east from Bulgaria as well as north from north-eastern Macedonia into Torlakia, where, however, the three-way deictic distinction points to a stronger deicitc system.

In this chapter we have seen changes that are structural, diffusional (including multidirectional), differential, and ideological (in the restriction of object reduplication as well as, perhaps, the use of definite articles). I have attempted to look at a larger picture without looking at too large a picture. On the one hand, one must be wary of the classic problem of missing the forest for the trees. On the other, however, it would be a gross oversimplification to say that the Schwarzwald and Kara Orman are merely manifestations of the same 'Black Forest'. They are both mixed, broad-leaf and coniferous, but their histories and current realities are very different.

Owing to their relatively contiguous extension over the Balkan peninsula, Slavic dialects, combined with the extent of Albanian and certain features in Romani, provide a measure of boundary definition that differs from what can be deduced from the other language groups. In this sense, Leake was not entirely mistaken in the position he assigned to Slavic in Balkan linguistic contact, for it is precisely on current South Slavic and adjacent territory that features spread and diminish.

References

Adams, D. and Mallory, J. P. 'The Greek language', pp. 240–6 in *Encyclopedia of Indo-European culture*, edited by J. P. Mallory and D. Q. Adams. London: Fitzroy Dearborn.

Andriotis, A. P. and Kourmoulis, G. 1968. 'Questions de la linguistique balkanique et l'apport de la langue grecque', pp. 21–30 of *Actes du premier congrès international des études balkaniques et sud-est européens*, Vol. 6, edited by I. Gălăbov, V. Georgiev, and J. Zaimov. Sofia: BAN.

Bakić-Hayden, M. 1995. 'Nesting orientalisms: the case of former Yugoslavia', *Slavic Review* 54: 917–31.

Belyavski-Frank, M. 2003. *The Balkan conditional in South Slavic.* Munich: Otto Sagner.

Boretzky, N. 1996. 'The "new infinitive" in Romani', *Journal of the Gypsy Lore Society,* ser. 5. 6: 1–51.

—— and Igla, B. 2004. *Komentierter Dialektatlas des Romani,* 2 vols. Wiesbaden: Harrassowitz.

Brixhe, C. and Panayotou, A. 1994. 'Le Thrace', pp. 179–204 of *Langues indo-européennes,* edited by F. Bader. Paris: CNRS Editions.

Čelyševa, I. I. 2001. 'Dialekty Italii', pp. 90–146 of *Romanskie jazyki,* edited by I. I. Čelyševa, B. P. Narumov, and O. I. Romanova. Moscow: Academia.

Enfield, N. J. 2003. *Linguistic epidemiology: semantics and grammar of language contact in Mainland Southeast Asia.* London: Routledge.

Friedman, V. A. 2000. 'After 170 years of Balkan linguistics: whither the millennium?', *Mediterranean Language Review* 12: 1–15.

—— forthcoming. 'Albanian in the Balkan linguistic league: a reconsideration of theoretical implications', in *Proceedings: ninth international congress on southeast European studies.* Tirana: Albanian Academy of Arts and Sciences.

—— and Joseph, B. J. Forthcoming. *The Balkan languages.* Cambridge: Cambridge University Press.

Hamp, E. P. 1982. 'The oldest Albanian syntagma', *Balkansko ezikoznanie* 25: 77–9.

—— 1989. 'Yugoslavia—a crossroads of Sprachbünde', *Zeitschrift für Balkanologie* 25. 1: 44–7.

Haspelmath, Martin. 1998. 'How young is Standard Average European?', *Language Sciences* 20.3: 271–87.

Joseph, B. D. 2001. 'Is Balkan comparative syntax possible?', pp. 17–43 of *Comparative syntax of Balkan languages,* edited by M. L. Rivero and A. Ralli. Oxford: Oxford University Press.

Kallulli, D. 1999. The comparative syntax of Albanian: on the contribution of syntactic types to propositional interpretation. Ph.D. dissertation, University of Durham.

Koneski, Blaže, 1969. *Gramatika na makedonskiot literaturen jazik.* Skopje: Kultura.

Kopitar, J. 1829. 'Albanische, walachische und bulgarische Sprache', *Jahrbücher der Literatur* 46: 59–106.

Kramer, C. E. 1994. 'The grammaticalization of the future auxiliary in the Balkan languages', *Indiana Slavic Studies* 7: 127–36.

Leafgren, J. 2002. *Degrees of explicitness.* Pragmatics and beyond, new series, 102. Amsterdam: Benjamins.

Leake, W. M. 1814. *Researches in Greece.* London: John Booth.

Lindstedt, J. 2000. 'Linguistic Balkanization: contact-induced change by mutual reinforcement', pp. 231–46 of *Languages in contact,* edited by D. Gilbers, J. Nerbonne, and J. Schaeken. Studies in Slavic and General Linguistics 28. Amsterdam: Rodopi Press.

Masica, C. 1976. *South Asia as a linguistic area.* Chicago: University of Chicago Press.

Masica, C. 2001. 'The definition and significance of linguistic areas', pp. 205–68 of *The yearbook of South Asian languages and linguistics*, edited by P. Bhaskararao and K. Subbarao. New Delhi: Sage.

Matras, Yaron. 2002. *Romani: a linguistic introduction*. Cambridge: Cambridge University Press.

Miklosich, F. 1861. 'Die slavischen Elemente im Rumunischen', *Denkschriften der Kaiserlichen Akademie der Wissenschaften, Philosophisch-historische Klasse* 12: 1–70.

Mladenović, Radivoje. 2001. *Govor Šarplaninske Župe Gora*. Srpski dijalektološki zbornik 48. Belgrade: SANU.

Mufwene, S. 2005. *Créoles, écologie sociale, évolution linguistique*. Paris: L'Harmattan.

Pavlović, Milivoj. 1939. *Govor Sretečke Župe*. Srpski dijalektološki zbornik 8. Belgrade: Srpska Kraljevska Akademija.

Reiter, N. 1994. *Grundzüge der Balkanologie: Ein Schritt in die Eurolinguistik*. Wiesbaden: Harrassowitz.

Sandfeld, K. 1930. *Linguistique balkanique*. Paris: Klincksieck.

Seliščev, A. 1925. 'Des traits linguistiques communs aux langues balkaniques: un balkanisme ancien en bulgare', *Révue des études slaves* 5: 38–57.

Schleicher, A. 1850. *Die Sprachen Europas in systematischer Übersicht* (*Linguistische Untersuchungen von Dr. A. Schleicher* II). Bonn: König.

Shkurtaj, Gj. 1975. 'E folmja e Kelmendit', pp. 5–129 of *Dialektologjia shqiptare III*, edited by M. Domi. Tirana: Universiteti i Tiranës.

Thomason, S. G. and Kaufman, T. 1988. *Language contact, creolization, and genetic linguistics*. Berkeley and Los Angeles: University of California Press.

Todorova, M. 1997. *Imagining the Balkans*. Oxford: Oxford University Press.

van der Auwera, J. 1998. 'Revisiting the Balkan and Meso-American linguistic areas', *Language Sciences* 20.3: 259–70.

Whorf, Benjamin Lee. 1938. 'Some verbal categories of Hopi', *Language* 14: 275–86.

Wittek, P. 1951/2. 'Les Gagaouzes = les gens de Kaykāūs', *Rocznik orientalistyczny* 17: 12–24.

9

Cantonese Grammar in Areal Perspective[1]

STEPHEN MATTHEWS

1 Historical background

This chapter focuses on the role of language contact in the development of the Yue dialect group, of which Cantonese represents the prestige and de facto standard variety as spoken in Hong Kong and the provincial capital, Guangzhou (Canton). The chapter begins with the historical background and a survey of the linguistic stocks which have been in contact with Cantonese. In §2, Cantonese is situated within the linguistic area constituted by mainland South-east Asia. §3 focuses on some features of Cantonese grammar which are shared with non-Sinitic languages rather than with Chinese as a whole, and which implicate effects of contact. In §4, mechanisms of contact-induced change are discussed in relation to these features, and conclusions are drawn regarding Cantonese as a layered language in the sense of Chapter 1.

Before the colonization of today's south China by Chinese-speaking *Han* people, it was home to aboriginal peoples known in Chinese historiography as the *bai yue* 'hundred Yue [peoples]' (Ramsey 1987). The hyperbolic qualifier *bai* 'hundred' implies that there were more ethnic groups than could be

[1] This work has been substantially supported by the Research Grants Council of the Hong Kong Special Administrative Region (project HKU 7205/99H). I thank Umberto Ansaldo, Tommi Leung Tsz-Cheung, and Michelle Li Kin-Ling for their contributions to this project, and Pan Yanqing for serving as teacher-consultant for Zhuang. Versions of this chapter were presented at the City University of Hong Kong and the University of Hong Kong, while the Research Centre for Linguistic Typology at La Trobe University provided an inspirational setting in which it was developed. For comments on earlier versions of this chapter I am grateful to the editors as well as to Felix Ameka, Mark Donohue, Randy LaPolla, Luo Yongxian, Mark Post, and Laurent Sagart.

counted; the term *yue* may be the same as that applied to the *Yue* group of Chinese dialects, although these words are conventionally written with two different Chinese characters.[2] Who were these *yue* people? While some of the groups may have been assimilated to the point where no trace of their culture or language remains, even today a great variety of ethnic and linguistic groups are present in south-west China, at least some of whom must be descendants of the 'hundred *yue*'. While Cantonese and other Yue dialects are spoken on the plain of the Pearl River Delta, non-Sinitic languages are spoken in the surrounding areas to the north and west. Based on current distribution, the most numerous are the Zhuang and other peoples speaking Tai-Kadai languages: the Zhuang alone number some 14 million people (Gordon and Grimes 2005). The Tai-speaking peoples are thought to have originated in southern China (Baker and Phongpaichit 2005); among them, the Zhuang have been recognized as a distinctive ethnic group since the Song era (960–1279, Barlow 2001). A second subset of the *bai yue* are the peoples known in Chinese as the Miao, Yao, and She, whose languages belong to the Hmong-Mien family. Today these constitute smaller minority groups than the Tai-Kadai speakers, and they mostly inhabit higher elevations left to them by the Chinese and the Tai, but their wide distribution around southern China suggests they were more numerous in the past.

Both Tai-Kadai and Miao-Yao were formerly assigned to the Sino-Tibetan family, and occasionally this affiliation is still assumed, especially in Chinese work where ideological factors may be involved. These languages are now generally regarded as having a contact relationship with Chinese. They are tentatively classified genetically as belonging to the Austric grouping (Ruhlen 1987: 148), though the evidence for this is stronger in the case of the Tai-Kadai languages, which have recently been argued to be a sub-branch of the Austronesian family (Sagart 2004), than in that of Miao-Yao.

These peoples came into intensive contact with Chinese as a result of Han settlement in south China following unification and expansion of the Chinese empire under Han Wu Di (141–87 BC). Chinese history records that *Yue* people were drafted into the Chinese army, and that intermarriage occurred between Han Chinese and *Yue* peoples (Baker 2004). The latter gradually underwent 'sinicization', adopting Chinese language and culture in a process that continues today. From basic principles of language contact, we expect language shift as part of this process to result in substrate influence. In fact, non-Sinitic vocabulary in the Cantonese lexicon allows both Tai-Kadai and

---

[2] The *yue* of *bai Yue* is 越 as used in *Yue-nan* 'Vietnam' (literally 'south of the Yue'), while that of the *Yue* dialects is 粵, used in ethnic terms such as *yue-ju* 'Cantonese opera'.

Hmong-Mien substrates to be identified. Yue-Hashimoto (1991*a*) gives examples such as the suffix *-lou²* 'guy' as in *gwai²-lou²* 'foreigner' being from Tai. Bauer (1996) identifies several other likely words of Tai origin, for example *ngong⁶* 'stupid, muddled' as in *ngong⁶-geoi³* 'foolish'; *kam²* 'cover'; and *lam⁴* 'collapse', cf. Thai *lóm* 'sink, capsize'. A Tai origin has also been suggested for the demonstrative *ni¹* 'this', a form which is typical of Tai rather than of Chinese as a whole (cf. Thai *níi*, etc.).³ It is worth asking why a grammatical word like the demonstrative 'this' should be adopted from Tai, especially given the lack of congruence: the demonstrative precedes the noun in Cantonese but generally follows it in Tai languages. As noted by Bauer (1996), some Yue dialects have two demonstratives sharing the segmental form [kɔ] and using tone to make the distal vs. proximate distinction. By adopting *ni* for the proximate demonstrative alongside *ko* for the distal demonstrative, Cantonese speakers would have made a clearer distinction that did not rely on tone. The resulting pattern also conforms to the general sound-symbolic preference for a closer vowel for the proximate demonstrative and a more open vowel for the distal one. Randy LaPolla (p.c.) suggests an additional factor: based on comparative evidence, the Cantonese third person pronoun *keoi⁵* appears to have developed from a distal demonstrative meaning 'that'. Losing the distal demonstrative in the course of this functional shift would have left a gap to be filled. There are thus several plausible motivations for adopting the Tai demonstrative.

Yue-Hashimoto (1991*a*) also identifies morphemes of Miao-Yao origin, such as the feminine suffix *-na* (> *la*) as in *zyu¹-laa²* 'sow' and *gai¹-laa²* 'hen'. An example of a more grammatical nature is the postverbal particle *saai³* 'all' as in *mou⁵ saai³* 'all gone', which lacks an equivalent in other varieties of Chinese.

Lexical examples of the kind just cited are relatively few: Bauer (1996) concluded that only seven out of twenty-nine candidate words investigated could be attributed to Tai sources. This need not diminish the case for substrate influence, however, since:

(*a*) the examples given above are from mainstream Cantonese as spoken in Hong Kong. More examples can be found in other Yue dialects,

---

³ Bauer (1996) hesitates to assign the demonstrative *ni* to the Tai substrate on the grounds that similar demonstrative forms are more widespread in South-East Asia, as in Malay *ini*. This is consistent with the general pattern whereby the Tai word corresponds to the second syllable of the Austronesian root (Malay *mata*, Thai *taa* 'eye'). The missing link is provided by Buyang, a Tai-Kadai language which preserves the initial syllable in a weakened, toneless form as in *maᵒta⁵⁴* 'eye' (Li 1999; Sagart 2004).

especially west of the Pearl River (Yue-Hashimoto 1991*a*), that is, those closer to current Zhuang-speaking territory;

(*b*) in substrate influence we expect relatively few lexical items, and more structural influence from the substrate languages (Thomason and Kaufman 1988). We shall see that the lexical influence is more than matched by structural influence.

2 Areal typology

It is now possible to speak of 'principles of areal typology' (Dahl 2001). These principles include the following:

(i) Migration and colonization are causes of language shift. Substrate influence is a normal consequence of language shift and is primarily structural, affecting at least phonology and syntax (phonology will not be discussed here).

(ii) Bilingualism can be the source of lexical borrowing (via code mixing) and also of structural influence. It is accepted that transfer in second language acquisition is a mechanism by which structural influence enters a language, while Yip and Matthews (forthcoming) suggest transfer in bilingual first language acquisition as a further mechanism.

(iii) *Grammaticalization areas* are regions characterized by recurrent patterns of grammaticalization (Heine and Kuteva 2005). To this, Dahl (2001) adds the notion of *grammaticalization cline*: there may be an 'epicentre' for grammaticalization phenomena, the extent of which declines from centre to periphery.

2.1 *Mainland South-East Asia as a linguistic area*

It is widely recognized that languages of mainland South-east Asia constitute a linguistic area, characterized by a set of features including AVO constituent order, lexical tone and monosyllabic roots, noun classifiers, and serial verb constructions (Enfield 2001: 259). Cantonese has all these general typological properties in common with neighbouring languages, and also more specific ones as described below.

2.1.1 *Double object dative constructions*   One distinctive areal feature is the dative construction with the direct object preceding the indirect, giving [V DO IO] as in (1).[4]

---

[4] Cantonese examples are represented in the *jyutping* romanization system developed by the Linguistic Society of Hong Kong, in which tones are numbered from 1 (high level) to 6 (low level). See Matthews and Yip (1994: 400) for IPA and Yale equivalences.

(1) ngo⁵   bei² cin²   keoi⁵ (Cantonese)
     1sg   give money   3sg
     I give him money

This has been called the 'Inverted Double Object Construction' in Cantonese (Tang 1998) because it contrasts with [V IO DO] order in Mandarin and most Chinese dialects. The 'inverted' construction also proves to be rather rare outside the South-east Asia/south China region (at least in languages without case): for example, many West African languages have double object dative constructions but the typical order is [V IO DO]. Even in Ewe which is unusual in having the order [V DO IO], this pattern alternates with [V IO DO] (Felix Ameka, p.c.). As the following examples show, the same order occurs in Thai, Zhuang, and Yao.

(2) phom   hai   ngən   khaw   (Thai)
     1sg   give money 3sg
     I give him money

(3) laeng   siuj fangh hawj   ngaenz gou   (Zhuang: Wang 1997)
     family   Siu   Fang   give   money   1sg
     Siu Fang's family gives me money

(4) tsi pon ti:n   lak (Yao: Mao et al. 1979)
     I   give money   he
     I give money to him

Beyond the surface similarity, additional properties suggest that a similar syntactic structure is involved. It can be argued that the dative construction is a variant of a serial verb construction of the form [V NP *give* NP] in which V happens to be 'give' and the second 'give' is omitted (Tang 1998; Xu and Peyraube 1997). Consistent with this analysis, both Thai and Zhuang as well as Cantonese allow the configuration [*give* NP *give* NP] where there is a certain distance between the two tokens of 'give'.

(5) ngo⁵ bei² hou² do¹   cin²   (bei²) keoi⁵ (Cantonese)
     I   give very much money   (give) him
     I give you a lot of money

(6) phom hai   ngən   maak maak (hai) khun   (Thai)
     I   give money much much (give) you
     I give you a lot of money

Ontogenetically, Cantonese-speaking children's earliest double object constructions often take this form [*give* DO *give* IO], suggesting that it is a precursor to the later-acquired [*give* DO IO] (Chan 2003). Historically, the 'inverted' order [V DO IO] is found in Ancient Chinese, though as a minority pattern alongside [V IO DO] and [V DO P IO] (Xu and Peyraube 1997). It is also attested in some modern dialects not connected with Cantonese. It cannot therefore be directly attributed to Tai influence, but nevertheless constitutes an areal feature.

2.1.2 *Areal patterns of grammaticalization*   The South-east Asian linguistic area is defined in part by recurrent patterns of grammaticalization (Heine and Kuteva 2005: 203). Some of these patterns are general to Chinese, while others are specific to Cantonese, or particularly extensive in Cantonese. One such recurrent pattern involves 'surpass' comparative constructions (Ansaldo 1999). The Thai comparative marker *kwaa* is derived from a Proto-Tai verb meaning 'pass, cross over' which is attested as a directional verb in Zhuang as in (7) from Diller (2001):[5]

(7) te:^{A1} yu:^{A2} kua^{B1} pay^{A1}
     3sg   swim   cross   go
     He swam across

Similarly, the Cantonese comparative marker *gwo³* also serves as a directional verb as in:

(8) keoi⁵   haang⁴   gwo³   heoi³
     3sg   walk   cross   go
     He walked across

The grammaticalized comparative constructions based on these verbs are illustrated in §3.2 below.

Another areal pattern is the 'acquire' modal, described as an 'epidemic' by Enfield (2003). In Cantonese, as in Zhuang, a verb meaning 'acquire' has become grammaticalized as a modal meaning 'can':

(9) ni¹   tou³   hei³   **dak¹-gwo³**   zoeng²   (Cantonese)
     this CL   film   get-ASP   prize
     This film has won an award

(10) ku   **day**   song   tua,   te   **day**   saam   tua   (Northern Zhuang:
                                                                    Luo 1990)

     I   get   two   CL   3sg   get   three   CL
     I got two and he got three

(11) keoi⁵   heoi³   **dak¹**   (Cantonese)
     3sg   go   can
     He can go

---

[5] Zhuang examples are transcribed as in the original sources, which use a variety of orthographies and tonal notations. Due to the extensive dialectal variation within Zhuang it is not feasible to standardize the examples, or to add tones where they are not given.

(12)   te   pay   **day**   (Northern Zhuang: Luo 1990)
      3sg   go   can
      He can go

The position of the modal here is exceptional: other auxiliaries in Cantonese precede the main verb, as expected in a VO language. How could such an unusual structure have spread the way it has? As discussed in Chapter 1, diffusion of patterns may be accompanied by some diffusion of forms. In this case, the function words themselves have undergone diffusion as well as the serial constructions: the etymon in this case is Chinese (proto-Chinese *tak* 'get, acquire', Enfield 2003). The grammaticalized functions could nevertheless have been spread by Tai speakers, in which case the influence would be bi-directional, as suggested by Sybesma (2005). The notion of grammaticalization clines, whereby patterns spread from the centre to the periphery of an area (Dahl 2001), may be relevant here: in the case of grammaticalization of 'acquire', Lao and Zhuang are at the centre of the 'epidemic', and Mandarin at the periphery. Thus the modal usage is most productive in the Tai languages, while in Mandarin it is very limited; Cantonese lies somewhere in-between, employing *dak* as a postverbal modal as in (11) but lacking several other grammaticalized usages described by Enfield (2003).

3 South-East Asian areal features in Cantonese

Cantonese occupies an important place in this linguistic area because it exhibits a number of features which are shared with non-Sinitic languages of South-East Asia, but not characteristic of Mandarin or of Chinese in general. These patterns may be due to:

(*a*) substrate influence of non-Sinitic languages on Cantonese,
(*b*) structural borrowing from Cantonese into non-Sinitic languages, or
(*c*) some combination of these processes (diffusion, convergence).

It is acknowledged that the actual mechanisms and direction of influence may not be recoverable in specific instances (Thomason 2000).

3.1 *Morphology*

A tendency towards head-initial structures where Mandarin has head-final ones can be observed in morphology, as well as in syntax (§3.2).

3.1.1 *Post-modification*   An old debate, going back at least to Chao (1968: 275), involves a small set of nouns which seem to have the head in initial position, followed by a modifying adjective. Many of these are food terms, like *je⁴-ceng¹* 'fresh coconut' in (13). The order of morphemes within the word in Cantonese corresponds to noun-adjective phrases in Tai languages.

	Cantonese	Thai		Nandan Zhuang (Kullavanijaya 2001)	
(13)	je⁴-ceng¹	khâw	sŭay	mat¹	ha:w¹
	coco-fresh	rice	beautiful	ant	white
	fresh coconut	white rice		white ant	

Such words are rare exceptions to the generalization that modifiers precede the head noun in Chinese. In general the Cantonese pattern is not productive, but Ben Au Yeung (p.c.) has pointed out what seem to be 'new' examples as in (14):

(14)　je⁵-sik⁶　je⁵-jam²
　　　 stuff-eat　stuff-drink
　　　 food　　　drink (N)

These forms may be derived by reanalysis of a serial construction as in (15):

(15)　jau⁵　hou²　do¹　je⁵　sik⁶　⟹　(jau⁵)　hou²　do¹　je⁵-sik⁶
　　　 have　very　much　stuff　eat　　　　 have　very　much　stuff-eat
　　　 There's lots of stuff to eat　　⟹　There's a lot of food

The reanalysis would be facilitated by the fact that a small number of head-initial food terms as in (13) already exist in Cantonese. At any rate, *je⁵-sik⁶* now functions as a noun, as in (16) where it serves as subject of the sentence:

(16)　[_NP_di¹　je⁵-sik⁶]　maa⁴-maa²-dei²
　　　　 CL　stuff-eat　so–so–ish
　　　　 The food was mediocre

Other new examples can be observed, such as the following item written in Chinese on the menu at a Thai restaurant in Kowloon City:

(17)　fan²　　　　dak⁶bit⁶
　　　 rice.noodle　special
　　　 special rice noodles

This is a (presumably recent) loan translation of a Thai or Vietnamese dish (where 'special' means 'containing tripe', as the waitress explained), illustrating the process by which Tai speakers shifting to Cantonese could, and still do, introduce substrate terms.

3.1.2 *'Expressive' ABB reduplication* Another head-initial pattern is 'expressive' reduplication in the 'ABB' format, where A is an adjective or

TABLE 1. ABB 'expressive' reduplicated forms

Zhuang (Qin 1995, Milliken 1998)	Kam (Gerner 2004)	Cantonese
cok-maet-maet 'strong, robust'	ton[11]-tok[31]-tok[31] round-plate-plate	jyun[4]-luk[1]-luk[1] round-wheel-wheel
lek-byaz-byaz scared-?-? 'terrified'	man[13]-phi[35]-phi[35] yellow-? 'rusty yellow'	wong[4]-kam[4]-kam[4] yellow- 'yellowed'
rang-ngau-ngau fragrant-sweet-sweet 'perfumed'	tang[45]-nong[453]-nong[45] fragrant-?-? 'perfumed'	cau[4]-bang[1]-bang[1] smelly-pong-pong 'smelly'

verb and BB a reduplicated syllable. Such forms are highly productive in Zhuang as well as in Kam, another Tai language of south-west China as described by Gerner (2004).

Such forms are productive in Cantonese too: over 100 ABB forms are given by So and Harrison (1996). They are a more marginal pattern in Mandarin, not mentioned in standard grammars (though some ABB forms such as *rehuhu* 'warm' do exist, possibly due to diffusion from southern dialects). Bodomo (2006) compares the Cantonese forms with ideophones in West African languages such as Dagaare. In many cases the reduplicated 'B' syllables lack lexical meanings, hence the gloss '?' in Table 1; many of them seem to be sound symbolic, as with many forms which use velar nasals to suggest smell. Such symbolism is also common in Austronesian, where a widespread root denoting smell contains the sequence [aŋ] (Blust 1988: 60).

In the Chinese literature these patterns are described as *houfu yinjie* or 'postposed syllables'. They are thus a further instance of postmodification (see §3.1.1) and are part of a pattern of head-initial structures shared by Cantonese and mainland South-east Asian languages. These forms are characteristic of the mainland South-east Asian linguistic area, rather than of Chinese as a whole.

3.2 Clause-level syntax

For Hashimoto (1978), who assumed the Tai languages to be genetically related to Chinese, the prevalence of head-final structures in northern Chinese dialects reflected *Altaicization*—substrate influence from Altaic languages such as Mongolian and Manchu. Given current assumptions (see §1), it could equally be that head-initial structures in southern dialects reflect *Taicization* (Bennett 1979). That is, the typology of Chinese has been moulded by diverse forms of substrate influence as it has spread north and south.

Perhaps the most well-known peculiarity of Cantonese syntax is the adverb *sin¹* 'first' which almost uniquely follows the verb as in (18). This usage is such a salient departure from standard Chinese usage that it seems to be 'emblematic' in the sense of Chapter 1 of this volume:

Cantonese			Thai			Zhuang		
(18)	ngo⁵	zau²	sin¹	phom	pai	kɔɔn	kɯn	ɣing	ko:n
	I	go	first	I	go	first	eat	lunch	first

Lucas and Xie (1994) argue that given the Zhuang counterpart in (18) the postverbal placement of *sin¹* in Cantonese is probably due to influence from Tai (the authors use the French term *emprunt* 'borrowing', presumably meaning calquing or structural borrowing). A parallel case which may have a Tai source, given a very similar usage in Thai, is *tim¹* meaning 'too' in (19):

Cantonese				Thai		
(19)	zung⁶	jau⁵	seoi²-zam⁶	tim¹	ko	naam-thuam	duay
	still	have	water-flood	too	also	water-flood	too
	There was flooding too				There was flooding too		

Postverbal adverbs also arguably occur in excessive constructions like (20). The 'surpass' comparative construction as described in §2.2 above is also head initial (whether one considers the predicate to be a verb or an adjective), and again there is a close match between the Cantonese and Thai structures (21):

	Cantonese		Thai		
(20)	jit⁶	gwo³tau⁶/dak¹-zai⁶	rɔɔn	kɯɯn	pai
	hot	overly / too-much	hot	exceed	go
	too hot		too hot		
(21)	gou¹	gwo³	keoi⁵	suung	kwaa	khaw
	tall	pass	3sg	tall	than	3sg
	taller than him			taller	than	him

This pattern has undergone some diffusion within Sinitic languages, along the lines described by Chappell (2001). For example, Chaozhou (a Min dialect in contact with Cantonese) uses the same construction as its main strategy for comparisons of inequality as in (22):

	Cantonese				Chaozhou			
(22)	lek¹	gwo³	go³	zai²	k'iang	kue	kai	kiã
	smart	pass	CL	boy	smart	pass	CL	boy
	smarter than the boy				smarter than the boy			

The grammaticalization area therefore extends from the Tai languages as far east as Chaozhou but no further, since the Min and Hakka dialects to the east and north have quite different comparative constructions which are not head initial (Ansaldo 1999).

3.3 *Syntax and semantics of classifiers*

The examples above involve distinctive features of Cantonese which suggest substrate influence from Tai languages. As discussed in relation to substrate vocabulary (§1), Miao-Yao as well as Tai elements can be found in Cantonese. It might be therefore expected that such influence also extends to the grammatical level. Evidence comes from the grammar of classifiers in Cantonese, which contrasts with Mandarin and most Chinese dialects in three respects. First, there is reduplication of classifiers to express universal quantification as in (23), in Cantonese as in Zhuang:

	Cantonese				Zhuang (Milliken 1998: 180)		
(23)	zek^3-zek^3	dou^1	hou^2	fei^4	dus-dus	cungz	biz
	CL-CL	all	very	fat	CL-CL	all	fat
	every [animal] is very fat				each and every [animal] is fat		

Note that the noun itself is typically omitted.

Secondly, Cantonese allows 'bare classifier' constructions of the form [CL N] with definite reference as in (24), whereas Mandarin does not (Matthews and Pacioni 1997):

(24)	ngo^5	wan^2	dou^2		[zek^3	maau^1]
	I	find	successfully	CL	cat	
	I found the cat					

This usage is especially characteristic of Miao-Yao languages such as Hmong. Bisang (1993: 30) describes 'the gradual discourse functions of [CL N] and [CL N DEM] constructions, where the somewhat weaker referential power of the former appears to be sufficient in a given context'. Bare classifier NPs in Hmong typically have anaphoric reference, as in (25) where the object 'the widow' has been mentioned previously:

(25)	Huab-tais	nrhiav	tau	[tus	poj nstuag]
	Emperor	find	get	CL	widow
	The Emperor found the widow...				

This anaphoric usage is also typical of Cantonese, as noted by Chao (1947: 42).

A third distinctive feature is the possessive classifier construction [POSS CL N]:

	Cantonese			Hmong (Bisang 1999)		
(26)	ngo⁵	zoeng¹	toi⁴	kuv	lub	rooj
	I	CL	table	I	CL	table
	my table			my table		

Zhuang has the bare classifier construction [CL N] but not the possessive [POSS CL N]; Hmong has both. It may therefore be suspected that substrate influence from Miao-Yao plays a role here. In fact the distribution of classifiers in Cantonese closely matches that of Hmong as described by Bisang (1993, 1999):

1. With numerals: [NUM CL N]
2. With demonstratives: [DEM CL N] in Cantonese or [CL N DEM] in Hmong
3. With noun: [CL N]
4. Between possessor and noun: [POSS CL N]

In both languages, the classifier may be omitted with inalienable possessors such as kinship terms, but not with body parts which retain the classifier:

	Cantonese		Hmong (Bisang 1993)	
(27)	lei⁵	maa⁴maa¹	kuv	niam
	you	mother	I	mother
	your mother		my mother	

The match between Cantonese and Hmong in this domain is thus very close. At issue remains the direction of influence. Bisang (1993) attributed the Hmong possessive construction to influence from Chinese where all modifiers precede the noun. However, possessive constructions with classifier are limited to Cantonese and other Yue dialects (also extending to Chaozhou which is in contact with Yue, as discussed in §3.2). The grammar of classifiers in Cantonese may reflect interaction of both Tai and Miao-Yao substrates with the head-final NP structure of Chinese. One may wonder why the Miao-Yao substrate (known to exist on lexical grounds, see §1) should play a role in this particular grammatical domain rather than in others. As discussed in Chapter 1, such interaction is determined by both typological and socio-historical factors such as numbers of speakers, and the prestige of each language must also play a role. In general, it appears that Tai has had more influence on Cantonese than Miao-Yao, at both lexical and grammatical levels. Today, Tai languages have many more speakers and Zhuang sees some use as a written language, while Miao-Yao language and culture have relatively low prestige.

4 Discussion and conclusions

Many distinctive grammatical features of Cantonese are shared with non-Sinitic, especially Tai-Kadai and Miao-Yao, languages which are known to be substrates based on history and lexical evidence. These features are more plausibly attributed to areal diffusion than to genetic inheritance: Cantonese belongs to a linguistic area constituted by the South-east Asian mainland, as well as genetically to the Sinitic branch of Sino-Tibetan. This is by no means a radical conclusion: the notions of substrate, linguistic area, and diffusion are traditional ones, though with some new twists such as grammaticalization clines.

4.1 *Cantonese as layered language*

Cantonese appears as a layered language in the sense of Chapter 1, with the pre-Han substrate constituting one layer (or two, to the extent that the contributions of Tai and Miao-Yao can be separated). The pattern of substrate influence is consistent with the view that 'to understand the southern dialects one must take into account both aspects—an archaic Han aspect and a non-Han aboriginal aspect' (Yue-Hashimoto 1991*a*: 314). It is also consistent with the notion of stratification in dialect grammar, where a substrate can constitute one layer, while other layers may be introduced from standard or prestigious varieties (Yue-Hashimoto 1991*b*). Cantonese has such a 'high' layer of grammar corresponding closely to Mandarin and written Chinese (Matthews and Yip 2001). For example, Cantonese has two possessive constructions: the classifier construction already discussed as in (26), and the linker construction with *ge³* which represents the general Sinitic pattern, corresponding to Mandarin *de* (28):

(28)   Cantonese: keoi⁵   ge³   sin¹saang¹
         Mandarin: ta   de   xiansheng
                          she   POSS husband
                          her husband

4.2 *Mechanisms of change*

We may conclude with some observations on the mechanisms by which substrate influence and diffusion take place. As noted in §2, possible scenarios include (*a*) substrate influence through language shift from non-Sinitic to

Cantonese, and (*b*) stable bilingualism. Either case implies syntactic transfer in bilingual individuals as the most basic process involved. This may be why Thomason and Kaufman (1988) invoke *interference*: interference (or *transfer*, as it is more neutrally termed) is an established feature of second language acquisition, as when adult speakers of language A adopt a dominant language B in the course of language shift. An alternative mechanism, much less widely discussed but mentioned by Thomason (2001), involves bilingual first language acquisition. Studies of bilingual first language acquisition have generally found that systematic transfer takes place, often from a dominant language to a weaker language (Yip and Matthews 2000). The effects of such transfer are similar to those in adult second language acquisition. In certain 'vulnerable' grammatical domains, however, there is also influence from the weaker language to the dominant one (Yip and Matthews forthcoming). This is less likely to occur in adult second language acquisition, and the bilingual acquisition scenario therefore makes somewhat different predictions. In principle these predictions could be tested with Zhuang-Chinese or Hmong-Chinese bilinguals, whose language development might be shown to recapitulate aspects of the history of Cantonese (one such case was observed in §3.1.1).

Finally, it may be suggested that something quite similar to the typology of language contact situations outlined in Chapter 1 also applies to bilingual acquisition. It is a truism of bilingual children and individuals that completely balanced bilingualism probably does not exist, and this no doubt also applies to language contact situations. But we can and do distinguish between more or less balanced children and imbalanced development where there is a dominant language. These types are shown in Table 2. In principle a child's dominant language need not coincide with a socially dominant or prestigious one, though some correlation between the two is to be expected.

TABLE 2. A continuum of types of bilingualism

Type	Balanced/symmetrical	Uneven/asymmetrical
Relationship	Equal	Unequal
Linguistic effects	Complexity	Transfer simplification incomplete acquisition
Results	Maintenance (of bilingualism)	Shift attrition/loss

Crucially, language dominance determines the direction of influence, or at least produces an asymmetry in this directionality. Finally, since dominance is necessarily a matter of degree, in language contact scenarios as in individual bilingualism there must be a continuum between the two 'ideal' types.

References

Aikhenvald, A. Y. and Dixon, R. M. W. (eds.), 2001. *Areal diffusion and genetic inheritance: problems in comparative linguistics.* Oxford: Oxford University Press.

Ansaldo, U. 1999. *Comparative constructions in Sinitic: areal typology and patterns of grammaticalization.* Ph.D. dissertation, Stockholm University.

Baker, C. 2004. 'From Yue to Tai'. Presented at the Centre of Asian Studies, University of Hong Kong, Sept. 2004.

—— and Phongpaichit, P. 2005. *A history of Thailand.* Cambridge: Cambridge University Press.

Barlow, J. 2001. 'The Zhuang: a longitudinal study of their history and their culture', http://mcel.pacificu.edu/as/resources/zhuang/, updated 12 Dec. 2005.

Bauer, R. S. 1996. 'Identifying the Tai substratum in Cantonese', pp. 1806–44 of *Pan-Asiatic linguistics: proceedings of the fifth international symposium on language and linguistics*, Vol. 5. Institute of Language and Culture for Rural Development, Mahidol University at Salaya, Thailand.

Bennett, P. A. 1979. 'A critique of the Altaicization hypothesis', *Cahiers de linguistique Asie orientale* 6: 91–104.

Bisang, W. 1993. 'Classifiers, quantifiers and class nouns in Hmong', *Studies in Language* 17: 1–51.

—— 1999. 'Classifiers in East and Southeast Asian languages: counting and beyond', pp. 113–85 of *Numeral types and changes worldwide*, edited by J. Gvozdanovic. Berlin: Mouton de Gruyter.

Blust, R. A. 1988. *Austronesian root theory.* Amsterdam: John Benjamins.

Bodomo, A. B. 2006. 'The structure of ideophones in African and Asian languages: the case of Dagaare and Cantonese', pp. 203–13 of *Proceedings of the 35th annual conference on African linguistics*, edited by J. Mugane, J. P. Hutchison, and D. A. Worman. Somerville, Mass.: Cascadilla Press.

Chan, A. W. S. 2003. *The development of bei2 dative constructions in early child Cantonese.* M.Phil. thesis, Chinese University of Hong Kong.

Chao, Y. R. 1947. *A Cantonese primer.* Cambridge, Mass.: Harvard University Press.

—— 1968. *A grammar of spoken Chinese.* Berkeley and Los Angeles: University of California Press.

Chappell, H. 2001. 'Language contact and areal diffusion in Sinitic languages', pp. 328–57 of Aikhenvald and Dixon, 2001.

Dahl, Ö. 2001. 'Principles of areal typology', pp. 1456–70 of *Language typology and language universals: an international handbook*, edited by M. Haspelmath, E. König, W. Österreicher, and W. Raible. Berlin: Mouton de Gruyter.

Diller, A. 2001. 'Grammaticalization and Tai syntactic change', pp. 139–75 of Tingsabadh and Abramson 2001.

Enfield, N. J. 2001. 'On genetic and areal linguistics in mainland Southeast Asia: parallel polyfunctionality of "acquire"', pp. 255–90 of Aikhenvald and Dixon 2001.

—— 2003. *Linguistic epidemiology: semantics and grammar of language contact in mainland Southeast Asia*. London: Routledge Curzon.

Gerner, M. 2004. 'Expressives in Kam (Dong): a study in sign typology (part I)', *Cahiers de linguistique Asie orientale* 33: 159–202.

Gordon, R. and Grimes, B. (eds.). 2005. *Ethnologue: Languages of the World*, 15th edn. Dallas Summer Institute of Linguistics.

Hashimoto, M. 1978. *Yuyan Dili Leixingxue* [Areal typology of language]. Beijing: Zhonghua.

Heine, B. and Kuteva, T. 2003. 'On contact-induced grammaticalization', *Studies in Language* 27: 529–72.

—— —— 2005. *Language contact and grammatical change*. Cambridge: Cambridge University Press.

Kullavanijaya, P. 2001. 'A study of lexical variation in seven Zhuang dialects', pp. 229–58 of Tingsabadh and Abramson 2001.

Li, J.-F. 1999. *Buyang yuyin yanjiu* [A study of the Buyang language]. Beijing: Zhongyang Minzu Daxue [Central University of Minorities Press].

Lucas, A. and Xie, H-H. 1994. ' "There is practically one universal Chinese grammar": à propos de xian1 en Mandarin et sin1 en cantonais', *Cahiers de linguistique Asie orientale* 23: 189–206.

Luo, Y.-X. 1990. *Tense and aspect in Zhuang*. MA thesis, Australian National University.

Mao, Z.-W. et al. 1979. *Yaozhu yuyin jianzhi* [An outline of the Yao language]. Renzhu Chubanshe.

Matthews, S. (ed.), 1998. *Studies in Cantonese linguistics*. Hong Kong: Linguistic Society of Hong Kong.

—— and Pacioni, P. 1997. 'Specificity and genericity in Cantonese and Mandarin', pp. 45–59 of *Referential properties of Chinese noun phrase*, edited by L. J. Xu. Paris: École des Hautes Études en Sciences Sociales, Centre de Recherches Linguistiques sur l'Asie Orientale.

—— and Yip, V. 1994. *Cantonese: a comprehensive grammar*. London: Routledge.

—— —— 2001. 'The structure and stratification of relative clauses in contemporary Cantonese', pp. 266–81 of *Sinitic grammar: synchronic and diachronic perspectives*, edited by H. Chappell. Oxford: Oxford University Press.

Milliken, M. 1998. 'The classifier *gij* in northern Zhuang', pp 173–97 of *Proceedings of the international conference on Tai studies*. Bangkok: Institute of Language and Culture for Rural Development, Mahidol University.

Pacioni, P. 1998. 'Possessive constructions, classifiers and specificity in Cantonese', pp. 63–80 of Matthews 1998.

Qin, X.-H. 1995. *Zhuangyu teshu yufa xianxiang yanjiu* [A study of the special grammatical features of Zhuang]. Beijing: Minzu.

Ramsey, S. R. 1987. *The languages of China.* Princeton: Princeton University Press.

Ruhlen, M. 1987. *A guide to the world's languages,* 1: *Classification.* Stanford, Calif.: Stanford University Press.

Sagart, L. 2004. 'The higher phylogeny of Austronesian and the position of Tai-Kadai', *Oceanic Linguistics* 43: 411–40.

So, L. K.-H. and. Harrison, G. J. 1996. 'A set of Cantonese trisyllabic phrases to use in learning or teaching Cantonese', *Journal of the Chinese Language Teachers' Association* 31: 41–56.

Sybesma, R. P. E. 2005. 'Zhuang as Tai with Chinese characteristics'. Paper presented at the Chinese University of Hong Kong, May.

Tang, S.-W. 1998. 'On the "inverted" double object construction', pp. 35–52 of Matthews 1998.

Thomason, S. G. 2000. 'Linguistic areas and language history', pp. 311–27 of *Languages in contact,* edited by D. G. Gilbers, J. Nerbonne, and J. Schaeken. Amsterdam: Rodopi.

—— 2001. *Language contact: an introduction.* Edinburgh: Edinburgh University Press.

—— and Kaufman, T. 1988. *Language contact, creolization and genetic linguistics.* Berkeley and Los Angeles: University of California Press.

Thurgood, G. and LaPolla, R. (eds.). 2003. *The Sino-Tibetan languages.* London: Routledge Curzon.

Tingsabadh, M. R. K. and Abramson, A. S. (eds.), 2001. *Essays in Tai linguistics.* Bangkok: Chulalongkorn University Press.

Wang, X. 1997. 'Guanyu Zhuangyu yufa ruogan wenti de shangque' [A discussion on various questions of Zhuang grammar], *Zhongyang minzu daxue xuebao* [Journal of the Central University of Minorities] 1: 97–105.

Xu, L.-J. and Peyraube, A. 1997. 'Double object and oblique constructions in Cantonese', *Studies in Language* 21: 105–27.

Yip, V. and Matthews, S. 2000. 'Syntactic transfer in a Cantonese-English bilingual child', *Bilingualism: Language and Cognition* 3: 193–208.

—— —— Forthcoming. *The bilingual child: early grammatical development and language contact.* Cambridge: Cambridge University Press.

Yue-Hashimoto, A. 1991*a*. 'The Yue dialect', pp. 294–324 of *Languages and dialects of China,* edited by W. S.-Y. Wang. *Journal of Chinese Linguistics Monograph Series 3.*

—— 1991*b*. 'Stratification in comparative dialectal grammar: a case in Southern Min', *Journal of Chinese Linguistics* 20: 172–200.

10

Semantics and Pragmatics of Grammatical Relations in the Vaupés Linguistic Area

ALEXANDRA Y. AIKHENVALD

1 Language contact and multilingualism in the linguistic area of the Vaupés River Basin

The Vaupés Basin in north-west Amazonia (spanning adjacent areas of Brazil and Colombia) is a well-established linguistic area. Its major feature is an obligatory societal multilingualism which follows the principle of linguistic exogamy: 'those who speak the same language with us are our brothers, and we do not marry our sisters.' Marrying someone who belongs to the same language group is considered akin to incest and referred to as 'this is what dogs do'.[1] Language affiliation is inherited from one's father, and is a badge of identity for each person.

Languages traditionally spoken in the area belong to three unrelated genetic groups: East Tucanoan, Arawak and Makú, or Nadahup (see Epps, Chapter 11).[2] Speakers of East Tucanoan languages (Tucano, Wanano, Desano, Tuyuca, Barasano, Piratapuya, Macuna, and a few others), and of an Arawak language, Tariana, participate in the exogamous marriage network which ensures obligatory multilingualism.

A striking feature of the Vaupés linguistic area is a strong cultural inhibition against language mixing viewed in terms of borrowing morphemes.

---

[1] The rules are not completely straightforward: see the discussion in Aikhenvald (2002: 22–3). Sorensen (1967/72) is a brief account of the Colombian part of the multilingual Vaupés area where only East Tucanoan languages are spoken. Therefore, his work is only marginally relevant here.

[2] A putative connection between Nadahup (Makú) and Arawak advocated by V. Martins (2004) is based on a misconception, poor data from Arawak languages, and lack of proper application of the comparative method.

Long-term interaction based on institutionalized multilingualism between East Tucanoan languages and Tariana has resulted in the rampant diffusion of grammatical and semantic patterns (though not so much of forms) and calquing of categories. As a result, the Vaupés area provides a unique laboratory for investigating how contact-induced changes take place, which categories are more prone to diffusion, and which are likely to remain intact.

The purpose of this chapter is to show how Tariana acquired a typologically unusual system of semantically and pragmatically determined marking of grammatical relations through areal diffusion, and reinterpretation of its own resources. An additional theoretical issue that arises here is the nature and rise of linguistic complexity resulting from language contact.

2 The Vaupés Basin as a linguistic and cultural area

2.1 *Languages of the area*

East Tucanoan languages are typologically similar; but different enough to be considered distinct languages (Barnes 1999; Aikhenvald 2002). The 'East Tucanoan type' has developed as a result of the long-term interaction of phenomena of two kinds: genetic affinity and contact. Similarities between East Tucanoan languages can be due to Sapir's parellism in drift—whereby genetically related languages tend to develop like structures—and also to the continuous contact between the groups. It is hard, if not impossible, to disentangle the impact of these factors.

West Tucanoan languages which are not in immediate contact with East Tucanoan groups, or with each other, include Koreguaje (Colombia), Siona and Secoya (Ecuador), and Orejon (north-eastern Peru). Data from these are crucial for the understanding of proto-Tucanoan patterns.

Tariana, the only representative of the Arawak family within the Vaupés area, used to be a continuum of numerous dialects (one for each of several hierarchically organized clans). The only dialect still actively spoken is that of the Wamiaɾikune, traditionally one of the lowest-ranking clans.[3] A comparison

---

[3] This chapter, like all my previous work, is based upon information obtained via original fieldwork with speakers of all existing dialects of Tariana (mostly the Wamiaɾikune of Santa Rosa and Periquitos, with about 100 speakers in all). Tariana is highly endangered. I have also worked with the dialect of the Kumandene subgroup of Tariana spoken by a couple of dozen adults in the village of Santa Terezinha on the Iauari River, and analysed all the existing materials on other dialects (see a survey in appendix to Aikhenvald 2003*a*; and a detailed analysis in Aikhenvald forthcoming). The Kumandene dialect is not mutually intelligible with the Wamiaɾikune dialect. Speakers communicate with each other in Tucano. An overview of previous work on Tariana is in Aikhenvald (2003*a*). The recently published monograph Ramirez (2001) contains numerous errors concerning Tariana and most other Arawak languages. His claim that Tariana is a dialect of Baniwa is as true as saying that Romanian is a dialect of Spanish.

between various dialects suggests that the linguistic diversity within the Tariana continuum was comparable to the differences between various dialects of Portuguese, Spanish, and Galician.

A comparison between Tariana and those Arawak languages closely related to it and spoken outside the Vaupés area enables us to distinguish between genetically inherited and contact-induced features, as well as independent innovations. Tariana is part of the 'Rio Negro' subgroup within North Arawak, which comprises Baniwa of Içana/Kurripako, Piapoco, Guarequena, Resígaro, Achagua, and Yucuna[4] (see Aikhenvald 2001, 2002). These linguistic affinities are corroborated by shared origin myths—see §2.2 below. Tariana's closest relative outside the Vaupés is the Baniwa/Kurripako dialect continuum to the north and north-east in Brazil, Colombia, and Venezuela, and Piapoco to the north-east, in Colombia. Tariana shares about 85–88 per cent lexicon with Baniwa; but their morphology and syntax are very different (see Map 1).

Speakers of the Makú, or Nadahup, languages in the Vaupés area are outside the marriage network system, and are considered traditional 'underlings' (see Epps, Chapter 11). A symbiotic relationship between the Makú and the East Tucanoan group with which it is 'associated' ensures cultural and linguistic contact between these. As a result, the Nadahup (Makú) languages in the Vaupés are influenced by East Tucanoan languages. At present, the Tariana do not have any associated 'Makú' groups of their own (mythological traditions show that such groups may have existed earlier on).

2.2 *What we know about the history of the area*

The indigenous people of the Vaupés area—spanning Colombia and Brazil—share numerous cultural and lifestyle patterns. All the groups are divided into subclans hierarchically organized by their 'seniority'. A member of a junior clan would address a member of a senior clan as an 'elder sibling', or 'elder relative'. Speakers of the same language are considered blood relatives.

The traditional settlement pattern involved multifamily longhouses each including a patrilineage. Speakers of the Arawak and East Tucanoan languages are slash-and-burn agriculturalists, with similar myths and beliefs, as well as weaponry and food-gathering techniques. Both tend to live along large rivers.

I am grateful to all my teachers of Tariana, the Britos of Santa Rosa and the Muniz of Periquitos, and to Roni Lopez from Santa Terezinha, for teaching me their remarkable language. Thanks are equally due to R. M. W. Dixon, Willem F. Adelaar, Janet Barnes, Dominique Buchillet, Pattie Epps, Terry Malone, Kris Stenzel, Clay Strom, Junia Schauer, and José Alvarez, for helpful comments and insights.

[4] The Baniwa-Kurripako form a dialect continuum; the individual dialects differ as to the degree of mutual intelligibility (see Aikhenvald 2001, 2002; and also Taylor 1991: 7–8). The materials on the Hohódene and Siuci dialects of Baniwa come mainly from my own work (Aikhenvald MS), and also Taylor (1991). Major sources on other languages are listed in the References.

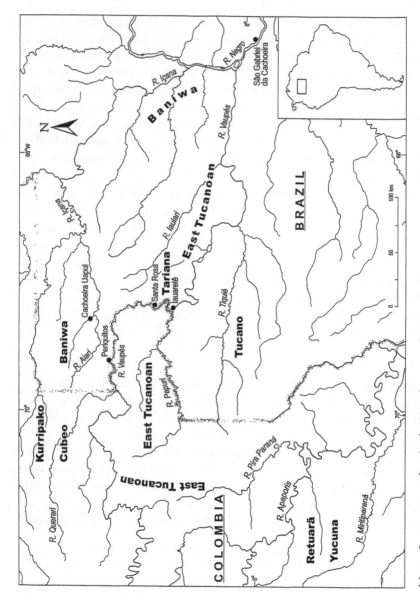

MAP 1 Languages spoken in the Vaupés area and its surrounds

A strong inhibition against the influx of borrowings—viewed in terms of lexical items and easily detectable loan morphemes—is a general feature characteristic of every group.

The Nadahup (or Makú), in contrast, lack most of these features. They are traditionally nomadic hunters and gatherers; they live mostly in the jungle, near small streams, and do not practise strictly linguistic exogamy. The Arawak and East Tucanoan peoples consider them inferior—this attitude is reflected even in early documents mentioning the 'Makú' (see Sampaio 1825: 81–2; Koch-Grünberg 1906a: 179–80, 1906b: 878; Stradelli 1890).[5]

A major problem in the ethnohistory of the peoples of the area—especially with respect to the Arawak-speaking groups—is language loss and absorption of one group by another. According to oral tradition of the Desano, Tuyuca, Cubeo, Tariana, and Baniwa peoples, a few 'Makú' groups actually lost their own languages and started using the languages of their 'conquerors'. These 'former Makú' usually have a lower status in the internal hierarchy of their tribes (see Koch-Grünberg 1906b: 878; Janet Barnes, p.c.).

The Tariana themselves often accuse rival clans of being 'ex-Makú' who had lost their language (see text 1 in Aikhenvald 1999a). We have no way of proving or disproving such statements. Their potential importance lies in a possible Nadahup, or Makú, substratum for the languages of the Vaupés, including Tariana.

The Tariana appear to be the most recent arrivals in the Vaupés. Their place of origin, the Wapui Cachoeira on the Aiary River (a tributary of the Içana River), is shared with the Baniwa/Kurripako and the Piapoco (see Brüzzi 1977; Koch-Grünberg 1911; Nimuendajú 1982; Neves 1998; Zucchi 2002). We can safely assume that language contact between the East Tucanoan languages and the Nadahup pre-dates that between the East Tucanoan languages and Tariana. Since some 'Makú'-speaking groups were likely to have been absorbed by the Tariana, the Tariana language could have acquired some features from East Tucanoan languages via a Nadahup ('Makú') substratum.

The myths and oral histories of different Tariana subgroups indicate that they may have taken different routes, and perhaps assimilated different language groups, before they arrived in the Vaupés Basin.[6] Numerous

---

[5] As shown in Martins and Martins (1999: fr. 3), the term 'Makú' is used in a number of meanings, only one of which is coextensive with 'Nadahup' as presented in Chapter 11 of the present volume. Whether the Makú mentioned by Sampaio (1825) are the same as the current members of the Nadahup family remains an open question.

[6] According to Neves (1998), the arrival of the Tariana in the Vaupés area goes back to pre-contact times (also see Brüzzi 1977, and Nimuendajú 1982). Hypotheses concerning the establishment of the Vaupés area

high-ranking Tariana groups started shifting to Tucano, whose speakers out-numbered all others, as early as the late nineteenth century (Koch-Grünberg 1911: 51). As a result, most Tariana dialects are now gone.

2.3 *Language contact and language change in the Vaupés area*

The traditional Vaupés region was a long-standing linguistic area with multi-lateral diffusion, and with no relationships of dominance between the main players—East Tucanoans and Arawak. The language changes which took place during this time (perhaps, a few hundred years) can be characterized as completed changes. These involved tangible impact of East Tucanoan lan-guages on Tariana, recognizable through comparison between Tariana and closely related Arawak languages spoken outside the area.

The impact of Tariana on East Tucanoan languages is harder to pinpoint, for the following reasons.

I. There are no East Tucanoan languages spoken outside the Vaupés area. All known East Tucanoan languages have been affected by a continu-ous multilingual interaction.

II. The Tariana—as the latest arrivals in the Vaupés area—have always been numerically the minority (see, for instance, Coudreau 1887: 161).

III. The existing descriptions of the East Tucanoan languages do not necessarily reflect the varieties in direct contact with Tariana.

Just a few features of East Tucanoan languages which seem to be atypical of Tucanoan as a whole could be attributed to an influence from Arawak languages. The development of aspirated stops in Wanano, and of pronom-inal proclitics in Wanano and in Desano could be due to Tariana influence (Stenzel 2004: 194–5; Waltz and Waltz 1997: 37; Miller 1999: ex. 662 on p. 162; cf. Aikhenvald 2002: 61 for further details). In the Wanano of Carurú (geo-graphically close to Periquitos: Stenzel 2004: 261, 267–76) stative verbs are less morphologically complex than active verbs, and less likely to occur in verbal compounds (or single word serial verbs) (p. 269). These properties are reminiscent of Tariana, and other Arawak languages of the Rio Negro area. We should, however, keep in mind that an 'Arawak-looking' feature in any

by the end of the 18th century (Hugh-Jones 1981: 42 and Chernela 1993: 24) are not corroborated by facts. Natterer's word list (1831; based on his work with the Tariana of Ipanoré/São Jerônimo) states that the Tariana originate from the Aiary River. Historical and traditional evidence suggests that neither Tucano nor Tariana are the autochthonous population of the Vaupés. That the original inhabitants of the Vaupés area were Nadahup (or Makú) groups is a statement founded on an assumption—by archaeologists and anthropologists—rather than on tangible facts (see Aikhenvald 2002).

East Tucanoan language may well have come from a now extinct Arawak language, or an extinct Tariana dialect.

At present, Tucano is rapidly gaining ground as the major language of the area, at the expense of other languages in the Brazilian Vaupés. This is a consequence of the Catholic missionaries' language and teaching policy, and a number of other, secondary factors (such as men spending more and more time away from their families working on cash crops: see Aikhenvald 2002).

As a result of this encroaching dominance of Tucano, innovative speakers of Tariana display more Tucano-like patterns in their language than do traditional speakers. These newly introduced patterns reflect ongoing changes produced as the result of gradual and imminent shift to the dominant language (see Aikhenvald 2002: 175–86, on the influence of Portuguese).

Figure 1 summarizes the types of language change and diffusion within the Vaupés area, with a focus on Tariana.

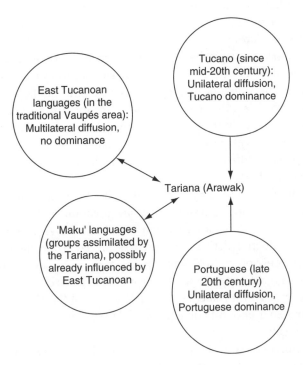

FIGURE 1 The impact of language contact on Tariana

3 Tucanoan and Arawak: a typological comparison

All East Tucanoan languages are dependent marking, with some head marking. They are almost exclusively suffixing and mildly synthetic. East Tucanoan languages are of a nominative-accusative profile, with a typologically uncommon system of semantically and pragmatically determined non-subject case marking. That is, the overt case marking of a non-subject constituent (be it a direct object, a recipient, a locative, or a temporal constituent) depends on its definiteness, specificity, and individuation. Some languages have developed pragmatically determined subject marking: contrastive subjects (A and S) acquire special marking which other subjects lack.

In contrast, Arawak languages are predominantly head marking, polysynthetic to varying extents, and mostly suffixing with only a few prefixes. The forms of prefixes are rather uniform across the family, while suffixes vary. Pronominal prefixes cross-reference the core participants—the subject of a transitive verb (A) and of an intransitive active verb (S_a). The subject of an intransitive stative verb (S_o) and the direct object (O) are either marked with suffixes, as in Baniwa and many other Arawak languages (e.g. closely related Guarequena), or not marked at all, as in Tariana and a few more languages (e.g. Resígaro, or Bare).

That is, Arawak languages display a split-S (active-stative) profile: the subject of a transitive verb and the subject of an active intransitive verb are marked in one way, and the subject of an intransitive stative verb and the direct object of a transitive verb in another (see Aikhenvald 1999b). Since the active-stative marking is obvious only for pronominal constituents, and not so much for nouns, the expression of grammatical relations can be considered asymmetrical.

The typological differences between Tucanoan and Arawak patterns are summarized in Table 1.

The Nadahup (Makú) languages spoken in the Vaupés area appear to conform to the Tucanoan mould: they are predominantly suffixing, with dependent marking, core cases, and no traces of ergativity. There are remnants of unproductive derivational prefixes in Dâw (Martins and Martins 1999); and the only prefix in Yuhup (Ospina 2002: 90) is also derivational in nature. (Cacua (Cathcart 1972: 16) has pronominal prefixes on the verb.) This is in stark contrast with Nadëb, spoken in the area of the Middle Rio Negro, which is prefixing and suffixing, exclusively head marking (with no core cases), and ergative.

Tariana combines features shared with genetically related Arawak languages and patterns acquired via areal diffusion from genetically unrelated East

TABLE 1. Proto-Tucanoan and Proto-Arawak: a comparison

Parameters	Proto-Tucanoan	Proto-Arawak
Prefixing/suffixing	suffixing	some prefixes and many suffixes: prefixes: A=S_a= possessor, relative *ka-*, negative *ma-*; suffixes: other categories
Dependent or head marking	dependent; some head marking	head marking
Core cases	yes	no
Accusative/ergative	nominative/accusative	active/stative: A=S_a; O=S_o

Tucanoan languages, in addition to independent innovations. The semantically and pragmatically based marking of non-subjects in Tariana, and in the Nadahup languages of the Vaupés (§4.8 of Chapter 11) is strongly reminiscent of the East Tucanoan pattern.

4 The East Tucanoan impact on Tariana: an illustration

Prolonged and balanced intensive language contact brings about gradual convergence resulting in structural isomorphism (see Chapter 1). A wide variety of phonological, morphological, and syntactic structures has been diffused from East Tucanoan languages into Tariana, promoting an impressive structural similarity (see further details in Aikhenvald 2002).

Consider the following examples, from a myth. (1) is from Tariana, and (2) is from Tucano. There are hardly any cognate morphemes, and yet the interlinear glosses are almost identical. Example (3) comes from Baniwa of Içana, an Arawak language closely related to Tariana, but spoken outside the Vaupés area. The Baniwa forms are cognate to those in Tariana, but the categories and the meanings expressed are very different. Baniwa and Tariana cognates are underlined.

Tariana
(1)   <u>nese</u>   pa:ma   <u>di</u>-na
       then   one+NUM.CL.ANIMATE.FEM   3sgnf-OBJ
       <u>du</u>-<u>yana</u>-<u>sita</u>-<u>pidana</u>
       3sgf-cook-ALREADY-REM.PAST.REP
       She had reportedly cooked him already

Tucano

(2) tiîta   ni'kó   kɨ̃-re
     then   one+NUM.CL.ANIMATE.FEM   he-OBJ
     do'á-toha-po'
     cook-ALREADY-REM.PAST.REP.3sg.fem
     She had reportedly cooked him already

Baniwa

(3) hnete-pida   apa:ma   ʒu-dzana-ni   ʒu-taita
     then-REP   one+CL.FEM 3sgf-cook-3sgnfO/So 3sgf-finish
     Then she had reportedly finished cooking him

Baniwa *apa-* 'one' corresponds to Tariana *pa-* 'one' (both are reflexes of Proto-Arawak form **ba* 'one'). Tariana *y* in *-yana* 'cook' corresponds to Baniwa *dz*, and Tariana *d-* in the 3sgfem prefix *du-* corresponds to Baniwa *ʒu-*. (Both go back to Proto-Arawak *ru-/lu-* 'third person feminine prefix': see Aikhenvald 2002: appendix 2). Tariana *s* regularly corresponds to Baniwa *t*. In a diphthong, *ai* in Baniwa is contracted to *i* in Tariana. Hence the correspondence of Baniwa *-taita* 'finish' to Tariana *-sita* 'perfective marker', recently grammaticalized from the verb *-sita* 'finish' (Aikhenvald 2000).

But the grammatical differences between Tariana and Baniwa are striking. First, unlike Tariana and Tucano, Baniwa has no obligatory tense and evidentiality. An optional reported clitic (with no tense distinction) attaches to the first verb in the clause in Baniwa. In both Tariana and Tucano the marker combining information on tense and evidentiality (in this case, 'remote past reported') attaches to the verb.

Secondly, the same etymon, Tariana *-sita* and Baniwa *-taita* 'finish', behaves differently: in Baniwa it is a part of serial verb construction, while in Tariana it is a bound morpheme with an aspectual meaning, 'already'—just like in Tucano, in (2).

And thirdly, Baniwa uses a bound pronoun to mark a pronominal object 'him', while Tariana employs what looks like a case form of a pronoun, 'translatable' morpheme-per-morpheme into Tucano.

Yet, despite the amazing structural similarity, it would be wrong to say that Tariana is simply 'relexified' Tucano. Most Tucano categories are replicated in Tariana, with one major difference. Subject marking in Tucano is achieved through portmanteau morphemes combining information on tense, evidentiality, and person. Tariana has subject prefixes inherited from Proto-Arawak, just like its relative Baniwa. Tariana has preserved its Arawak profile, in addition to the newly acquired East Tucanoan-like features. This brings us to the next section.

5 Grammatical relations in Tariana, in the light of the Vaupés languages

We start with a general outline of grammatical relations in Tariana (§5.1), and then discuss the semantic and pragmatic basis for the marking of non-subjects (§5.2). Oblique cases, and their development and correlation with the pragmatic marking of non-subjects, are discussed in §5.3. Pragmatically based marking of subjects is the topic of §5.4.

5.1 *Case marking in Tariana*

Just as in most Arawak languages, grammatical relations in Tariana are marked with personal prefixes, roughly on an active-stative basis. Every verbal root in Tariana is either prefixed or prefixless. Prefixed verbs can be transitive (e.g. *-wapeta* 'wait for something'), ditransitive (*-bueta* 'teach'), ambitransitive (type A = S_a, e.g. *-hima* 'hear, see, think, understand', or type O = S_a, e.g. *-thuka* 'break'), or active intransitive (S_a, e.g. *-emhani* 'walk around'). Most prefixless verbs are stative intransitive (e.g. *kasitana* 'be annoyed'); some are A = S_o ambitransitives (e.g. *nhesiri* 'enjoy (not food)') or O = S_o ambitransitives (*hui* 'enjoy (food); be tasty'). The verb 'cook' in (1) illustrates a transitive verb, with the subject (A) prefix (*du-* 'third person feminine singular').

There is no object marking on the verb. Both O and S_o acquire zero realization (whereas in Baniwa of Içana both are marked with pronominal suffixes).[7] A stative intransitive 'prefixless' verb is shown in (4).

(4) harame-pu-mahka   nhua
     be.scared(S_o)-AUG-REC.PAST.NONVIS   I
     I am/have been very scared—STATIVE INTRANSITIVE

Grammatical relations are also marked by cases, on a subject/non-subject basis. The marking of non-subjects and of subjects is determined by different semantic and pragmatic properties of the constituent, as well as its grammatical function (cf. Bossong 1985, 1991).

Table 2 summarizes the semantically and pragmatically determined marking of subjects and non-subjects on NPs in Tariana.

The non-subject case *-naku/-nuku* is used for a variety of topical constituents, including object, recipient, beneficiary, locative, manner,

---

[7] The oldest word list of Tariana, collected by Johann Natterer in 1831 at Ipanoré, contains what appears to be a bound object pronoun *nua* (reminiscent of Baniwa of Içana *-hnua* (1sgS_o/O)) attached to the verb: *tʃino li maa nuá* (dog 3sgnf bite? I) 'dog bit me'.

TABLE 2. Grammatical relations and core cases in Tariana

Grammatical function	Discourse status	Nouns	Pronouns
subject (A/S)	non-focused	subject form (noun-Ø)	subject form (pronominal prefix + emphatic formative -*ha*)
	focused	subject form + clitic -*ne/-nhe*	
non-subject (Non A/S)	non-topical	subject form (noun-Ø)	pronominal prefix + suffix -*na*
	topical	subject form + clitic -*naku/-nuku*	

instrument, and time. Its form has two variants: a more archaic -*naku* used by the representatives of the older generation (and as the main form in the Periquitos dialect; see §5.3, on its etymology). The variant -*nuku* is used by younger people: in the innovative Tariana, enclitics tend to undergo assimilation between the two final vowels.

Nouns distinguish two additional cases—locative and instrumental-comitative—while personal pronouns do not normally have a locative case (rare examples, all with inanimate referent, are discussed in Aikhenvald 2003*a*: 140, 150).

The 'topical non-subject' and oblique cases can mark the constituent with the same grammatical function, and can occur together.

Nouns and pronouns differ in their principles of case marking.

    I. Nouns in a non-subject function can be unmarked for case (as in (5b)), while pronouns are always marked.

   II. The subject form of a noun is ø-marked, as in (1). The subject form of a pronoun consists of a pronominal prefix + formative -*ha*: *di-ha* (3sgnf-EMPH) 'he', *nu-ha* (1sg-EMPH) 'I'.

TABLE 3. Oblique cases in Tariana

Grammatical function	Nouns	Pronouns
Locational	subject form + -*se*	—
Instrumental-comitative	subject form + -*ne*	pronominal prefix + -*ine*

If a noun is marked as a topical non-subject or as a focused subject, the marker is attached to the ø-marked citation form, e.g. *pa-ñha-nipe-nuku* (IMPERS-eat-NOMZ-DEF.NON.A/s) 'the food (object)' in (6b). If a pronoun is marked as a topical non-subject or as a focused subject, the marking is attached to the subject form, as in (7). If a pronoun in a non-subject function is not topical, it takes the case marker *-na* which attaches to a pronominal prefix, e.g. *di-na* 'him' in (1).

III. Both locative and instrumental-comitative case attach to a ø-marked form of a noun, e.g. *nawiki-ne* (person-INST/COMIT) 'with the man, with the help of man', *awakada-se* (jungle-LOC) 'in/to/from the jungle'. Pronouns hardly ever take the locative case. An instrumental-comitative form of a pronoun involves a pronominal prefix + *-ine*, e.g. *nu-ine* 'with me; by me'.

This is reminiscent of the two underived postpositions, the comitative *-api* 'together with' and the beneficiary *-siu* 'for the benefit of, instead', e.g. *nu-api* 'together with me', *nu-siu* 'for me'. But unlike case markers, if *-api* or *-siu* have a noun as their argument, they take a dummy prefix *i-*, e.g. *tʃiãɾi i-api* (man INDEF-with) 'with a man'. That is, the case marker *-ine* 'instrumental-comitative' (and also *-na* 'pronominal non-subject') behaves similarly to a postposition. This fully agrees with its origins: see §5.3. As expected, pronouns are more archaic than nouns.

5.2 *Semantic and pragmatic basis for marking non-subjects*

5.2.1 *General principles* Tariana and East Tucanoan languages share semantic and pragmatic motivation for marking non-subjects. An NP in a non-subject function takes the marker—East Tucanoan *-re* (Barnes 1999: 219–20) and Tariana *-naku/-nuku*—if its referent is definite. In (5), 'food' is indefinite and consequently takes no case marker. In the adjacent sentence in text, (6), 'food' is definite because it has already been introduced (Stenzel 2004: 143).

Wanano
(5) (a) hi-phiti-ro   chɯa   ~da-taʼa
          COP-COLL-PART   food   bring/take-come

Tariana
     (b) thuya pa-ñha-nipe   nheta   na-nu-na
          all   IMPERS-eat-NOMZ 3pl+bring/take 3pl-come-REM.PAST.VIS
          Everybody brings (a lot of) food

Wanano
(6) (a)   ti-~da   ~da-sa'a   chɨa-<u>re</u>
            ANAPHORIC-PL   bring/take-MOVEMENT.inside   food-DEF.NON.A/S
            chɨ   yoa-ra
            eat   do/make-VIS.IMPERFECTIVE.NON.1
Tariana
     (b)   naha   nhe-ta   na-nu-na
           they   3pl+enter-CAUS   3pl-come-REM.PAST.VIS
           pa-ñha-nipe-<u>nuku</u>
           IMPERS-eat-NOMZ-DEF.NON.A/S
           na-ñha-hyu-pena
           3pl-eat-PURPOSIVE.NVIS-FUT
           They take the food inside to eat

The presence of the marker correlates with the position of its referent on the nominal hierarchy (modified from Dixon 1994: 85), and the degree of its individuation—see Figure 2. A pronominal argument or a proper name is always case marked. A noun with an uncountable inanimate referent is less likely to be case marked than a noun with an animate or with a human referent (see Stenzel 2004: 219–25, and references there; Ramirez 1997: 224).

In agreement with this hierarchy, an animate object is likelier to acquire case marking than an inanimate object. In ditransitive constructions, the recipient or the benefactive is typically animate. Consequently, there is a strong tendency throughout the East Tucanoan family to case-mark second objects of ditransitive verbs (e.g. Tucano examples in Ramirez 1997: 226). If an inanimate 'gift' is definite, and the recipient is indefinite, the 'gift' is case marked. That is, definiteness 'overrides' animacy and individuation in choosing a case marker.

The overt case marking also correlates with the pragmatic properties of a constituent. For instance, in Desano the non-subject case -*re* appears on nouns referring to 'specific individuals already on stage in the discourse' (Miller 1999: 58–60). The case marker does not occur on nouns that have 'just been introduced to the discourse' (also see Morse and Maxwell 1999: 111

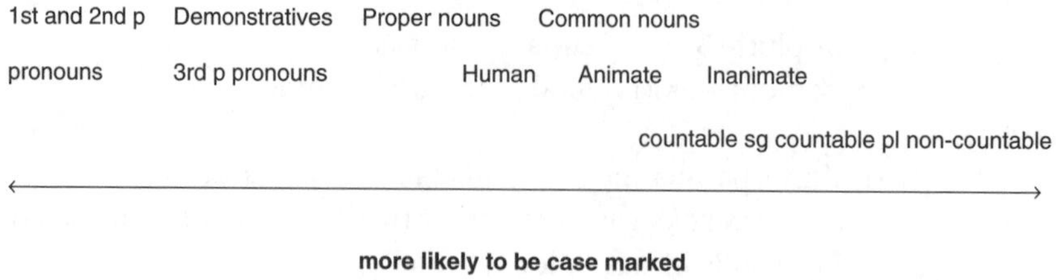

1st and 2nd p	Demonstratives	Proper nouns	Common nouns		
pronouns	3rd p pronouns		Human	Animate	Inanimate
					countable sg countable pl non-countable

←───→

more likely to be case marked

FIGURE 2 Nominal hierarchy and non-subject case marking in the Vaupés area

on Cubeo, and Kinch 1977 on Yurutí). In Tariana, the marker *-nuku/-naku* occurs on any constituent which is, or is going to be, the topic of a narrative (Aikhenvald 2003*a*: 145–6).[8]

When used on locatives and time words, the marker indicates that the constituent 'will have further significance in the discourse' (Barnes 1999: 220; also see Stenzel 2004: 177–8, 241–2). Along similar lines, the use of *-re* with locative and temporal constituents in Tucano correlates with their topicality, rather than their definiteness or specificity.

In summary: a combination of semantic properties—definiteness, specificity, and animacy—determines case marking of non-subject core constituents across the Vaupés area. In some languages topicality is an additional factor. But since topics tend to be definite this may be a corollary of the definiteness requirement. Overt non-subject case marking of locative and temporal constituents is based entirely on their pragmatics.

While the semantic and pragmatic motivation for non-subject case marking in the Nadahup languages of the area requires further investigation, the general tendency in the marking of non-subject core arguments appears to follow the 'Standard Average Vaupés pattern'. The choice of the object marker *-an* in Hupda (see §4.8 of Chapter 11) correlates with definiteness and animacy of a non-subject participant. The suffix *-dɨ* in Cacua (Cathcart 1972) occurs on pronominal and definite non-subjects (direct objects and recipients), as well as on proper names (also see Ospina 2002: 140–8, on Yuhup; and Martins 1994: 133–5; 2004: 157, 351, 667, on Dâw).

West Tucanoan languages operate on similar semantic and pragmatic principles. In Koreguaje, *-re* (Cook and Levinsohn 1985: 104–8) is used to mark a specific object, especially if it is human and individuated. An item just mentioned by the speaker takes the *-re* suffix if the speaker wishes to 'talk further about that item in particular' (p. 105). When used with inanimate and locative referents, *-re* marks them as 'being of further significance to the story' (108). Similar principles apply in Siona (Wheeler 1987: 127; 1967), Secoya (Barnes 1999), and Orejon (Gable 1975: 27; Velie and Ochoa 1977).

The semantically and pragmatically based marking of non-subjects is a feature spread from Tucanoan into all other languages of the area. Tariana adds one further complexity described in the next section.

---

[8] Case marking in East Tucanoan languages and in Tariana correlates with the position of the object argument: an unmarked argument with a generic referent is likely to occur in the preverbal position. (This may result in OV constructions interpretable as instances of noun incorporation: see Barnes 1999: 220; Morse and Maxwell 1999: 70–1.) Since the correlations between constituent order and information structure in East Tucanoan languages remain largely unexplored, we leave this question open.

5.2.2 *How Tariana differs from the 'Standard Average Vaupés' pattern*   Tariana differs from the Vaupés pattern of non-subject case choice in one important way. In East Tucanoan and in West Tucanoan languages pronominal arguments are always case marked, in the same ways as nouns. This is understandable—pronouns are high on the hierarchy in Figure 2, and inherently definite. The available data from the Nadahup languages point in a similar direction (e.g. Hup discussed in Chapter 11, and also Cacua, in Cathcart 1972: 16).

In Tariana, too, every pronominal non-subject has to be case marked, but the case marker is not the same as the one on nouns—see (1). And an additional option is available: unlike in any other Vaupés language, if the pronoun is highly topical, it can also take the non-subject case marker, as in (7). Such examples are pragmatically marked (see Aikhenvald 2003a: 147).

Tariana

(7)   nuha-naku   ma:-kade-na
       1sg.SU-DEF.NON.A/S   NEG+give-NEG-REM.PAST.VIS
       To me (that the story is about) he did not give (what he promised)

Speakers who use predominantly Tucano in their homes produce forms like *diha-nuku* (he-DEF.NON.A/S) as equivalents to the Tucano *kɨɨ-re*, in (2), and to the traditional Tariana *di-na* (1). Such usage is corrected by the few traditional speakers. The emergence of forms like *diha-nuku* is an instance of ongoing change. This indicates the loss of a difference between topical and non-topical pronominal non-subjects, as a result of 'displacive' effect of Tucano.

In summary: the pragmatically and semantically motivated non-subject case marking is a strong feature of the Vaupés area, well represented in East Tucanoan and also found in Nadahup. Its source is Tucanoan. Tariana has absorbed this feature, at the same time retaining the principle of marking pronominal and non-pronominal constituents in different ways—a feature reminiscent of a common Arawak pattern. At the same time, traditional Tariana evolved an additional formal distinction between topical and non-topical pronominal non-subjects. This distinction is on its way out in the innovative language, under pressure from the dominant Tucano.

5.3 *Oblique constituents*

In §5.3.1–2, we discuss the marking of locatives, instruments, comitatives, and benefactives in Tariana and how these have been restructured to fit in with the pan-East Tucanoan patterns. The same syntactic function can be marked twice within one NP—see §5.3.3.

5.3.1 *Locatives* Most Arawak languages of the Upper Rio Negro area have a fair number of locative markers. In contrast, East Tucanoan languages typically have just one locative case (Tucano, Wanano, Piratapuya -*pi*; Barasano -*hi*, Desano -*ge*). This case covers location 'at', direction 'to' and 'from', and also occurs on temporal constituents.

The oblique case system in Tariana follows the East Tucanoan model. Tariana has one locative case marker, -*se*, which covers all of 'to, towards, onto, out of, in/on'. In both Tariana and East Tucanoan languages, a locative constituent can be unmarked for case if the locative meaning is recoverable from the context, the referent is backgrounded (Aikhenvald 2003*a*: 155; Miller 1999: 59–60). In others Arawak languages, locative markers are obligatory.

Functional similarity between the only locative case in Tariana and in East Tucanoan (using Desano as an example language: Miller 1999: 59–60) is shown in Table 4. The last column illustrates Baniwa of Içana.

The reflexes of the Baniwa case markers in Tariana and their cognates elsewhere in the Rio Negro subgroup of the Arawak languages are shown in Table 5 (see Aikhenvald 2003*c*, for sound correspondences). Importantly, the 'surface locative' -*naku* in Baniwa corresponds to the non-subject case -*naku/ -nuku* 'topical non-subject' in Tariana.

The etymology of the pronominal non-subject marker -*na* is not included in Table 5. That the pronominal -*na* is an established feature of Tariana is corroborated by its occurrence in the Tariana sentences collected by Koch-Grünberg (1911). This marker is most likely cognate with the locative formative -*na*- attested in Piapoco in combinations with other locational morphemes, e.g. *i-rìcu-ná* (3sg-in-LOC) 'during', compare *i-rìcu* (3sg-in) 'inside', *i-rìcu-íse* (3sg-in-FROM) 'from inside (something)', *i-walí-ise*

TABLE 4. Marking location: functional parallelism of Tariana and East Tucanoan

Desano (East Tucanoan)	Tariana (North Arawak)	Baniwa	
yuki̇-ge (tree-LOC)	*haiku-se* (tree-LOC)	*haiku-naku*	on surface of a tree
		haiku-ʒiku	inside/towards (inside of) a tree
		haiku-hɾe	towards a tree
		haiku-ʒikhiţe (underlying form: *haiku-ʒiku-hiţe*)	from inside a tree

(3sg-about-FROM) 'because of', *i-wali-ná* (3sg-about-LOC) 'for desire of' (see Klumpp 1995: 40, 43; 1990: 47, 136–7).

5.3.2 *Marking instruments, accompaniment, and benefactives*   As shown in Table 6, the morpheme *-ne/-ine* in Tariana marks instrument and accompaniment, matching the East Tucanoan instrumental-comitative postposition (Tucano *me'ra*: Ramirez 1997: 249–50; Desano *bērā*: Miller 1999: 62; Wanano *-~be're*: Stenzel 2004: 172). The cognates in Baniwa and Resígaro just have a comitative meaning. The instrumental-only marker (the forms shown in Table 6) has been lost in Tariana.

In agreement with its Arawak profile, Tariana marks pronominal and nominal NPs in the instrumental-comitative function in different ways.

Two underived postpositions in Tariana, *-api* 'with (a secondary participant)', and *-siu* 'for', have no functional equivalent in East Tucanoan languages. The comitative postposition, *-api* 'together with (a secondary participant); about', in Tariana is cognate to Piapoco *-api-cha* and Baniwa *-api-dza, api-ya* 'together with, in the company of (implying equal participants)'. Note the semantic difference: Tariana *-ne/-ine* implies equal participation of the players, while Baniwa *-inai* does not. The Tariana benefactive postposition *-siu* 'for' has a cognate in Baniwa *-hriu* (other cognates are in Table 6). In languages other than Tariana this form marks all addressees and recipients (no matter whether core or oblique). Not so in Tariana: the non-subject case marks core argument addressees and recipients, and the postposition *-siu* marks a beneficiary which is an optional oblique. Its additional meaning is 'instead of, in someone's stead; on behalf of someone'. So, *pi:mi i-siu* (colibri INDEF-for) in Tariana means 'for the benefit of/instead of/ on behalf of colibri'. In Baniwa, *pi:mi i-hriu* (colibri INDEF-for) means '(give/ say) to colibri, for colibri, etc.'

The postposition *-siu* in Tariana has shifted its meaning to mark a non-core constituent. And, in one additional instance, a core relation expressed by the benefactive in Baniwa is marked by the Tariana non-subject case.

A small subclass of stative verbs referring to physical states such as 'be hungry', 'be thirsty' mark their only argument with the non-subject case (8). Their only argument has some subject properties. For instance, it obeys the same-subject requirement in serial verbs, but does not trigger same-subject switch-reference markers. There is no agreement on the verb.

Tariana

(8)   mhãisiki   kai-pidana   di-na
       be.hungry   ache-REM.PAST.REP   3sgnf-OBJ
       He was reportedly hungry (lit. hungry ache him)

TABLE 5. Locative markers in Baniwa, Tariana, and Tucano

Meanings	Baniwa	Tariana	Tucano	Cognates of Baniwa markers in Tariana	Cognate markers elsewhere in North Arawak languages
Locative and directional 'to'	*-ʒiku*	*-se*	*-pɨ*	*-riku* 'derivational suffix; the inside of', and a sequencing enclitic *-ka-riku-se* 'while'	Piapoco *-ricu* 'inside', Achagua *-ʒiku* 'inside, in full contact with', Cabiyari *riku*, Resígaro *-giko* 'in'
Locative and directional 'on or to the surface of'	*-naku*			*-naku, -nuku* 'topical non-subject'	Achagua *-naku*, Cabiyari *-naku* 'on the surface'
Directional allative 'towards'	*-hɾe*			*-se* 'locative'	Piapoco *-re/le* 'toward'
Ablative 'from'	*-(hi)te*			none (the Baniwa form occurs only in conjunction with another locative)	Piapoco *-ise* 'from'

TABLE 6. Instrumental, comitative, and benefactive

Meanings	Baniwa	Tariana	Tucano	Cognates of Baniwa markers in Tariana	Cognate markers elsewhere in North Arawak languages
Comitative (secondary)	-inai	-api	me'ra	Baniwa -inai cognate of Tariana -ne/ine	Resigaro -néé 'comitative'
Comitative (equal)	-api-dza	-ne/-ine		Baniwa -api-dza cognate to T -api	Piapoco api-cha 'comitative'
Instrumental	-iyu			No cognates in Tariana	Piapoco, Cabiyari, Achagua, Guarequena (iy)u, Yucuna a'u 'instrumental'
Benefactive	-hriu	-siu	—	-siu 'for, instead' cognate to Baniwa -hriu 'for (second argument)'	Piapoco -li, Achagua žu 'dative: to, for', Yucuna hlo 'indirect object'

The Tariana construction is similar to Baniwa of Içana:

Baniwa
(9) kaywi-pida   hrisiu   maitakay
     ache-REP   3sgnf+BEN   be.hungry
     He was reportedly hungry (lit. hungry ache for/to him)

This structure is not found in East Tucanoan languages: verbs referring to physical states mark their subjects in the same way as all other subjects:

Tucano
(10) yɨ'ɨ̂ ɨhá   me'ra   nii-sa'
      I   hunger   with   be-REC.PAST.NVIS. nonthird.person
      I am hungry (lit. I am with hunger)

Having non-canonically marked subjects for verbs of physical states is a feature of numerous Arawak languages of the area (for instance, Warekena and Bare). The non-subject case in Tariana has expanded at the expense of the benefactive postposition—which no longer marks core arguments. The Arawak non-canonical argument pattern has been preserved, but with restructuring.

5.3.3 *Marking the same grammatical function twice*   An additional contact-induced change in Tariana is the development of a system whereby the same grammatical function may be marked twice in a grammatical word. Both Tucano *yukɨ-pɨ-re* and Tariana *haiku-se-naku* (tree-LOC-DEF.NON.A/S) translate as 'in the (topical) tree'. The locative case marker (Tucano *-pɨ*, Tariana *-se*) provides locational meaning. The Tucano *-re* and the Tariana *-naku/-nuku* indicate generic 'non-subjecthood' and the topicality of the noun phrase.

Most Arawak languages combine two locative case markers to express complex locative meanings. Examples include Baniwa *haiku-naku-hre* (tree-ON.SURFACE-TOWARDS) 'towards the surface of a tree', Piapoco *capìi i-rìcu-ise* (house-3sg-INSIDE-FROM) 'up to inside the house' (Klumpp 1990: 164), and Achagua *e:ri-tui ri-ku-la* (sun-CL:ROUND LOC-INESSIVE-TOWARDS) 'towards the inside of the sun' (Meléndez 1998: 97)

Every morpheme in a Baniwa form *haiku-naku-hre* (tree-ON.SURFACE-TOWARDS) 'towards the surface of a tree' is cognate with every morpheme in Tariana *haiku-se-naku* 'on this very (topical) tree'. The differences between Baniwa and Tariana are:

(*a*) THE MEANING OF THE COMBINATION. In Baniwa the locative markers specify each other. In Tariana one marker is locative par excellence, and the other conveys pragmatic information together with the information on the non-subject status of the constituent.

(*b*) DEFINITENESS and TOPICALITY OF NOUN REFERENT is marked in Tariana, and not in Baniwa.

(*c*) MORPHEME ORDER. In Baniwa, the order of morphemes is iconic, while in Tariana it is not.

Once again, the Tariana form matches East Tucanoan structures while keeping the actual Arawak morpheme shapes.

5.4 *Pragmatic basis for subject marking*

Subjects ($A/S_a/S_o$) in Tariana are marked by the clitic, -*ne/-nhe*, if contrastive, or if they introduce a new important participant in the discourse. The distribution of the allomorphs in traditional Tariana is purely phonological: the allomorph -*ne* appears if a noun or a pronoun contains an aspirated consonant or a glottal fricative; in all other cases -*nhe* is used, e.g. *nuha-ne* (I-FOC.A/S) 'I (contrastive subject)', *nawiki-nhe* (person-FOC.A/S) 'person (contrastive subject)'. The origins of this form are not known. The subject of (11) is not focused, and remains unmarked. The subject of (12) is contrastive, and is marked.

Tariana

(11) [paita   tʃãɾi]ₐ   di-kapi-pidana_O   di-pisa
      one+CL:ANIM   man   3sgnf-hand-REM.PAST.REP   3sgnf-cut
      One man cut his hand (beginning of a story)

(12) diha   niyami-ka   di-ka   diha   waɾu-nhe
      he   3sgnf+die-SUBORD   3sgnf-see   he   parrot-FOC.A/S
      The parrot (not anyone else) saw that he (evil spirit) had died

The -*ne/-nhe* marker helps tracking referents, and disambiguating third person participants. No other Arawak language has any pragmatically based subject marking of the sort. In contrast, some East Tucanoan languages do. But, unlike the non-subject marker -*re* which is uniform throughout the family, markers of contrastive subjects vary. They include Wanano -*se'e* (Stenzel 2004: 175–6; Waltz and Waltz 1997: 45), and Tucano -'*a* (Ramirez 1997: 231–2). Desano (Miller 1999: 161–2) employs the contrastive suffix -*pɨ*, which 'most frequently occurs with the subject' but 'can be attached to any noun phrase in the sentence'.

The lack of a common morpheme for focused or contrastive subject among the East Tucanoan languages may suggest that this is a recent innovation. However, a very similar pattern is found in West Tucanoan languages, that is,

Koreguaje *-pi/-ji* 'focused subjects, instruments and locational source' (Cook and Levinsohn 1985: 92–100) and Siona *-bi/pi* with similar functions (Wheeler 1967: 61–3, 1987: 124–6). No such pattern has entered any Nadahup language.

In all likelihood the Tariana pattern of focused subject marking is a Tucanoan-based innovation. As a result of linguistic pressure from Tucano, innovative speakers lose the distinction between aspirated and non-aspirated nasals; so for many people *-ne/-nhe* is almost always *-ne*. This makes the focused subject look the same as the instrumental *-ne*. In (12), a traditional speaker said *waɾu-nhe* (parrot-FOC.A/s), and an innovative speaker repeated this as *waɾu-ne*. He then translated the sentence into Portuguese as 'The evil spirit died, he saw with parrot' (Morreu curupira, ele viu com papagaio), confirming that for him, *-ne* covers both contrastive subject and comitative.

This encroaching link between the 'focused' subject and the instrumental (see further examples in Aikhenvald 2003a: 143) partly results from language obsolescence in the situation of 'displacive' language contact with Tucano. The phonemes not found in any East Tucanoan language, such as aspirated nasals, tend to be lost; therefore, the form *-ne* becomes a general one for both contrastive subject and the instrumental-comitative. Another factor is the typological naturalness of a polysemy between the instrumental-comitative and the subject focus. This polysemy is widely attested cross-linguistically, and, as we have just seen, is also found within the Tucanoan speaking domain. That is, a new pattern of case syncretism is on its way in innovative Tariana.

6 Theoretical implications of the Vaupés language situation—what can we conclude?

The typologically unusual and synchronically complex system of marking grammatical relations in Tariana is the result of an intricate network of genetically inherited and contact-induced features, accompanied by independent innovations. Table 7 summarizes the features in the marking of grammatical relations which Tariana shares with its Arawak relatives, and those diffused from its Tucanoan neighbours. Tariana innovations which look neither really Arawak nor really Tucano are in bold and are introduced with 'but'.

The major theoretical implications of the analysis of the Vaupés linguistic area are listed below. Our particular focus is on an Arawak language, Tariana, where the area impact of Tucanoan languages is easily discernible from patterns shared with related languages.

I. DIFFUSION OF PATTERNS RATHER THAN OF FORMS. The rampant multilingualism within the Vaupés area goes together with the multilateral diffusion

TABLE 7. Grammatical relations in Tariana in the light of Arawak and Tucanoan patterns

Feature	Arawak	Tariana	Tucanoan
1 Asymmetrical marking for nouns and for pronouns	yes, but: cross-referencing	yes, but: cases and cross-referencing	no
2 Grammatical relations on active-stative basis	yes	yes	
3 Oblique subjects	yes, but: marked with benefactive adposition	yes, but: marked with non-subject case	
4 One locative case	no	yes	
5 One marker for comitative and instrumental	no	yes	
6 Two comitatives	yes	yes	no
7 Stacking of locative cases	yes	no	
8 Benefactive marker	yes, but: used for core and oblique arguments	yes, but: used for oblique arguments only	no
9 Semantically and pragmatically marked non-subjects	no		
10 Locative case and non-subject marking on same NP	no	yes	
11 Focused subject	no	yes	

of categories rather than of forms. The reason for this virtual lack of borrowed forms lies in language attitudes prominent throughout the area. 'Language mixing'—traditionally viewed in terms of lexical loans—is condemned as culturally inappropriate, and is tolerated only as a 'linguistic joke' (see Aikhenvald 2002: 189–200). This creates an impediment against any recognizable loan form, and allows us to fully concentrate on the issue of borrowability of patterns and constructions.

II. BORROWABILITY OF PATTERNS operates in terms of the following preferences (see §4.1 of Chapter 1):

(*a*) THE MORE PRAGMATICALLY MOTIVATED, THE MORE DIFFUSIBLE. We have seen that semantically and pragmatically motivated marking of non-subjects is a strong feature throughout the Vaupés area, originating in Tucanoan, and permeating both Tariana and Nadahup languages. The diffusion involved matching pragmatic motivation (topicality, definiteness, and specificity, of a non-subject argument), semantic motivation (marking non-subjects in agreement with the Nominal Hierarchy in Figure 2), and also grammatical function (whereby non-subjects include recipients, and obliques). In addition, the non-subject marking in Tariana is determined by the noun's topicality, to a larger extent, than in the Tucanoan languages.

Pragmatically determined marking of contrastive subjects, recently developed by some Tucanoan languages, readily infiltrated Tariana.

(*b*) TENDENCY TO ACHIEVE MORPHEME-FOR-MORPHEME AND WORD-FOR-WORD INTERTRANSLATABILITY. This explains the matches of instrumental-comitative and of catch-all locative in Tariana and in Tucanoan (§5.3.2).

(*c*) THE EXISTENCE OF PROSODICALLY SALIENT MARKERS ESPECIALLY IF FUSED WITH THE ROOT CREATES AN IMPEDIMENT TO THE DIFFUSION OF THE WHOLE CATEGORY. This explains:

- Tendency to retain genetically inherited patterns expressed through prefixes marking A/S$_a$ in Tariana. In all likelihood, stability of prefixes in the language is due to the fact that (*a*) they are often stressed; and (*b*) they are often fused with the root (which does not exist without them). That cross-linguistically prefixes are more resistant to diffusion than suffixes is untrue: see examples of the diffusion of both in Kruspe (2004), and Heath (1978). And a few Tucanoan languages appear to have developed bound pronominal prefixes or proclitics out of full pronouns, under the influence from Arawak (see Aikhenvald 2003*b* about the development of prefixes in Retuarã (Tucanoan), under the influence of Yucuna, Arawak; also see §2.3 above). The consequences of this tendency are:

- Retaining prefixes involves maintaining the grammatical difference between prefixed and non-prefixed verbs, and keeping alive the subtle differentiation between verbs of state with 'oblique subjects' and simple stative verbs.
- Retaining prefixes involves maintaining the difference in marking grammatical relations for nouns and for personal pronouns, that is, a typically Arawak 'case asymmetry'.

III. MECHANISMS EMPLOYED IN DEVELOPING MATCHING STRUCTURES IN CONTACT-INDUCED CHANGE. Diffusion of structural patterns—in the almost complete absence of loan forms—implies that formal marking for the new grammatical categories is developed from the language's own resources. Thus:

- Reanalysis, reinterpretation, and extension of existing categories occurred when indirect diffusion involved restructuring a pre-existing category for which there was a slot in the structure to match a pan-Tucanoan pattern—compare the reinterpretation and extension of the Proto-Baniwa-Tariana allative 'towards' as a catch-all locative matching the Tucanoan pattern; and the reinterpretation of the Proto Rio-Negro Arawak 'surface' locative case as topical non-subject marker in Tariana, mirroring the Tucanoan -*re*.
- Grammaticalization of a free morpheme, to create a completely new grammatical category with no pre-existing slots evolved via the grammaticalization of a free morpheme—compare grammaticalization of a perfective aspect in Tariana, to match a Tucanoan prototype (examples 1–2).

IV. EFFECTS OF DISPLACIVE VERSUS BALANCED LANGUAGE CONTACT. The impact of intensive multilingualism and of language contact depends on the relationships between languages. As shown in §4.2.3 of Chapter 1, 'balanced' language contact takes place in a situation of a long-standing linguistic area and stable multilingualism without any dominance relationships. A prime example of balanced contact was the traditional Vaupés area. Balanced language contact promotes typological diversity and results in increased structural complexity. The effects of balanced contact on Tariana can be seen in Table 7—the resulting structures are more complex than 'pure' Arawak or 'pure' Tucanoan. The effects of balanced contact are completed changes in Tariana.

'Displacive' language contact produces the opposite: the dominant language imposes its patterns. Its ultimate result is loss of typological diversity accompanied by language loss. The displacive effect of Tucano onto Tariana produces ongoing changes resulting in some simplification. The gradual obsolescence of asymmetrical case marking for nouns and pronouns, by replacing the pronominal non-subject case with subject pronouns marked with the nominal -*nuku*, is a prime example.

However, even in a situation of 'displacive' effect of one language onto another, we do not have to assume that the system will have to become simpler. The loss of distinction between focused subject and instrument/ comitative marking in modern-day Tariana is due to pressure from Tucano. As a result, one case is distinguished, instead of two. But the semantics of this case has become more complex.

A complex interaction of areal diffusion, genetic inheritance, and independent innovation—whose net result goes beyond mere intertranslatability—accounts for the complex system of pragmatically and semantically motivated marking of grammatical relations in Tariana.

References

Aikhenvald, A. Y. 1999*a*. *Tariana texts and cultural context*. Munich: Lincom Europa.

—— 1999*b*. 'The Arawak language family', pp. 65–105 of Dixon and Aikhenvald 1999.

—— 2000. 'Areal typology and grammaticalization: the emergence of new verbal morphology in an obsolescent language', pp. 1–37 of *Reconstructing grammar: comparative linguistics and grammaticalization*, edited by Spike Gildea. Amsterdam: John Benjamins.

—— 2001. 'Areal diffusion, genetic inheritance and problems of subgrouping: a North Arawak case study', pp. 167–94 of *Areal diffusion and genetic inheritance: problems in comparative linguistics*, edited by A. Y. Aikhenvald and R. M. W. Dixon. Oxford: Oxford University Press.

—— 2002. *Language contact in Amazonia*. Oxford: Oxford University Press.

—— 2003*a*. *A grammar of Tariana, from north-west Amazonia*. Cambridge: Cambridge University Press.

—— 2003*b*. 'Language contact and language change in Amazonia', pp. 1–20 of *Historical linguistics 2001: selected papers from the 15th international conference of historical linguistics, Melbourne, 13–17 August 2001*, edited by B. J. Blake and K. Burridge. Amsterdam: John Benjamins.

—— 2003*c*. 'Mechanisms of change in areal diffusion: new morphology and language contact', *Journal of Linguistics* 39: 1–29.

—— MS. *Baniwa texts* (*c*.300 pp.).

—— Forthcoming. 'The Tariana language: its unity and diversity'.

Barnes, J. 1999. 'Tucano', pp. 207–26 of Dixon and Aikhenvald 1999.

Bossong, G. 1985. *Empirische Universalienforschung. Differentielle Objekstmarkierung in den neuiranischen Sprachen*. Tübingen: Gunter Narr.

—— 1991. 'Differential object marking in Romance and beyond', pp. 143–70 of *New analyses in Romance linguistics*, edited by D. Wanner and D. Kibbee. Amsterdam: John Benjamins.

Brüzzi, A. A. da Silva. 1967. *Observações gramaticais da língua Daxseyé ou Tucano*. Iauarete: Centro de Pesquisas de Iauarete.

—— 1977. *A civilização indígena do Uaupés*. Rome: Las.

Cathcart, M. 1972. 'Cacua grammar. writeup stage II'. MS.

Chernela, J. 1993. *The Wanano Indians of the Brazilian Amazon: a sense of space*. Austin: University of Texas Press.

Cook, D. M. and Criswell, L. L. 1993. *El idioma Koreguaje (Tucano Occidental)*. Bogotá: Asociación Instituto Lingüístico de Verano.

—— and Levinsohn, S. 1985. 'Coreguaje: domains of focus markers', pp. 91–116 of *From phonology to discourse: studies in six Colombian languages*, edited by R. M. Brend. Dallas: SIL.

Coudreau, H. A. 1887. *La France equinoxale*, Vol. 2: *Voyage à travers les Guyanes et l'Amazonie*. Paris: Challamel Ainé.

Dixon, R. M. W. 1994. *Ergativity*. Cambridge: Cambridge University Press.

—— and Aikhenvald, A. Y. (eds.), 1999. *The Amazonian languages*. Cambridge: Cambridge University Press.

Epps, P. 2005. 'Areal diffusion and the development of evidentiality: evidence from Hup', *Studies in Language 29: 617–50*.

Gable, D. V. 1975. *Bosquejo de la fonologia y gramatica del idioma Orejon (Coto)*. Datos etno-lingüísticos 10. Lima: Instituto Lingüístico de Verano.

González-Ñánez, O. 1997. *Gramática de la lengua Warekena*. Ph.D. thesis, Universidad Central de Venezuela, Caracas.

Heath, J. 1978. *Linguistic diffusion in Arnhem land*. Canberra: Institute for Aboriginal Studies.

Hill, J. D. 1985. 'Agnatic sibling relations and rank in northern Arawakan myth and social life', *Working Papers on South American Indians 7: 25–40*.

—— 1993. *Keepers of the sacred chants: the poetics of ritual power in an Amazonian society*. Tucson: University of Arizona Press.

Hugh-Jones, S. O. 1979. *The Palm and the Pleiades: initiation and cosmology in north-west Amazon*. Cambridge: Cambridge University Press.

—— 1981. 'Historia del Vaupés', *Maguare (Revista del Departamento de Antropologia, Universidad Nacional de Colombia)* 1: 29–51.

Johnson, O. E. and Levinsohn, S. H. 1990. *Gramática secoya: cuadernos etnolingüísticos* 11. Quito: Instituto Lingüístico de Verano.

Jones, W. and Jones, P. 1991. *Barasano syntax*. Arlington: Summer Institute of Linguistics and the University of Texas at Arlington.

Kinch, R. A. 1977. 'El enfoque temático vs el enfoque no temático en yuriti', pp. 129–75 of *Estudios tucanos II*. Lomalinda, Meta: Instituto Lingüístico de Verano.

Klumpp, D. 1990. *Piapoco grammar.* Bogotá: SIL.

—— 1995. *Vocabulario piapoco-español.* Santafé de Bogotá: Asociación Instituto Lingüístico de Verano.

Koch-Grünberg, T. 1906a. 'Die Indianer-Stämme am oberen Rio Negro und Yapurá und ihre sprachliche Zugehörigkeit', *Zeitschrift für Ethnologie* 38: 167–205.

—— 1906b. 'Die Sprache der Makú-Indianer', *Anthropos* 1: 877–906.

—— 1909/10. *Zwei Jahre unter den Indianern, Reisen in Nordwest-Brasilien, 1903–1905,* 2 vols. Berlin: Ernst Wasmuth.

—— 1911. 'Aruak-Sprachen Nordwestbrasiliens und der angrenzenden Gebiete', *Mitteilungen der anthropologischen Gesellschaft Wien* 41: 33–153, 203–82.

Kruspe, N. 2004. *A grammar of Semelai.* Cambridge: Cambridge University Press.

Martins, S. A. 1994. *Análise da morfosintaxe da língua Dâw (Maku-Kamã) e sua classificação tipológica.* MA thesis, Universidade Federal de Santa Catarina, Florianópolis.

—— 2004. *Fonologia e gramática Dâw,* 2 vols. Ph.D. thesis, Vrije Universiteit Amsterdam.

—— and Martins, V. 1999. 'Makú', pp. 251–68 of Dixon and Aikhenvald 1999.

Martins, V. 2004. *Reconstrução fonológica do Proto Makú Oriental.* Ph.D. thesis, Vrije Universiteit Amsterdam.

Meléndez, M. A. 1989. 'El nominal en Achagua', *Lenguas aborígines de Colombia* 4: 3–66.

—— 1998. *La lengua Achagua: estudio gramatical. Lenguas aborígenes de Colombia. Descripciones* 11. Bogotá: Colciencias, Universidad de Los Andes.

Metzger, R. G. 1981. *Gramática popular del Carapana.* Bogotá: Instituto Lingüístico de Verano.

—— 1998. 'The morpheme *KA*-of Carapana (Tucanoan)', *SIL Electronic working papers* 1998–003.

Miller, M. 1999. *Desano grammar.* Studies in the Languages of Colombia 6. Arlington: Summer Institute of Linguistics and the University of Texas at Arlington.

Morse, N. and Maxwell, M. 1999. *Gramática del Cubeo.* Santafé de Bogotá: Editorial Alberto Lleras Camargo.

Natterer, J. 1831. 'Sprachproben (zu?) Tariana'. MS, List 28.

Neves, E. G. 1998. *Paths in dark waters: archaeology as indigenous history in the Upper Rio Negro basin, northwest Amazonia.* Ph.D. thesis, Indiana University.

Nimuendajú, C. 1982. *Textos indigenistas.* São Paulo: Edições Loyola.

Ospina Bozzi, A. M. 2002. *Les Structures élémentaires du Yuhup Makú, langue de l'Amazonie colombienne: morfologie et syntaxe* Ph.D. dissertation. Université Paris 7—Denis Diderot.

Ramirez, H. 1997. *A fala Tukano dos Yepâ-masa,* vol. 1: *Gramática.* Manaus: Inspetoria Salesiana Missionária da Amazônia, CEDEM.

—— 2001. *Línguas Arawak da Amazônia setentrional: comparação e descrição.* Manaus: Editora da Universidade do Amazonas.

Reichel-Dolmatoff, G. 1986. *Yuruparí: studies of an Amazonian foundation myth.* Cambridge, Mass.: Harvard University Press.

Sampaio, F. X. R. de. 1825. *Diário da viagem.* Lisbon: Tipografia da Academia.

Schauer, S. and Schauer, J. 1978. 'Una gramática del Yucuna', *Artigos en lingüística e campos afines* 5: 1–52.

——— ——— 2000. 'El yucuna', pp. 515–32 of *Lenguas indígenas de Colombia: una visión descriptiva*, edited by M. S. González de Pérez and M. L. Rodríguez de Montes. Santafé de Bogotá: Instituto Caro y Cuervo.

Sorensen, A. P., Jr. 1967/72. 'Multilingualism in the northwest Amazon', *American Anthropologist* 69: 670–84 (reprinted as pp. 78–93 of *Sociolinguistics*, edited by J. B. Pride and J. Holmes. Harmondsworth: Penguin Modern Linguistics readings, 1972).

Stenzel, K. S. 2004. *A reference grammar of Wanano.* Ph.D. thesis, University of Colorado.

Stradelli, E. 1890. 'Il Vaupes e gli Vaupes', *Bolletino della Società Geográfica Italiana*, 3rd ser. 3: 425–53.

Strom, C. 1992. *Retuarã syntax.* Studies in the languages of Colombia 3. Arlington: Summer Institute of Linguistics and the University of Texas at Arlington.

Taylor, G. 1991. *Introdução à língua Baniwa do Içana.* Campinas: Editora da Unicamp.

Velie, D. and Ochoa, J. R. 1977. *Textos folkloricos de los Orejon.* Datos etno-lingüísticos 54 Lima: Instituto Lingüístico de Verano.

Waltz, N. and Waltz, C. 1997. *El agua, la roca y el humo: estudios sobre la cultura wanana del Vaupés.* Santafé de Bogotá: Instituto Lingüístico del Verano.

——— ——— 2000. 'El wanano', pp. 453–68 of *Lenguas indígenas de Colombia: una visión descriptiva*, edited by M. S. González de Pérez and M. L. Rodríguez de Montes. Santafé de Bogotá: Instituto Caro y Cuervo.

Wheeler, A. 1967. 'Grammatical structures in Siona discourse', *Lingua* 19: 60–77.

——— 1987. *Gantëya Bain: el pueblo Siona del río Putumayo, Colombia.* vol. 1: *Etnología, gramática, textos.* Bogotá: Instituto Lingüístico de Verano.

Wilson, P. J. 1992. *Una descripción preliminar de la gramática del Achagua (Arawak).* Bogotá: Summer Institute of Linguistics.

Zucchi, A. 2002. 'A new model of the Northern Arawakan expansion', pp. 199–222 of *Comparative Arawakan histories: rethinking language family and culture area in Amazonia*, edited by J. D. Hill and F. Santos-Granero. Urbana: University of Illinois Press.

11

The Vaupés Melting Pot: Tucanoan Influence on Hup

PATIENCE EPPS

1 Introduction

The Vaupés region of the Brazilian and Colombian Amazon is relatively well established as a linguistic area, characterized by considerable indirect diffusion of grammatical categories and patterns, but little direct borrowing of forms (cf. Sorensen 1967; Gomez-Imbert 1996; Aikhenvald 1996, 2002: ch. 10). To date, most of the discussion regarding the Vaupés area has focused on the contact that has taken place among languages of the East Tucanoan and Arawak families (particularly Tariana). This contact has been shaped by the cultural practice of linguistic exogamy, which fosters sociolinguistic norms of multilingualism on the one hand, and strong inhibitions against overt language mixing on the other.

In addition to the Tucanoan and Arawak languages, however, the region is also home to languages of the Nadahup or Makú family, represented most centrally in the Vaupés by Hup (also known as Hupda or Jupde).[1] The approximately 1,500 speakers of Hup play an important role in the

---

[1] I prefer to use the name 'Nadahup' for two reasons: There is some confusion surrounding the name 'Makú', which occurs in the literature in reference to several unrelated language groups in Amazonia; also, 'Makú' (probably from Arawak *ma-áku* [NEG-talk] 'without speech') is widely recognized in the Vaupés region as an ethnic slur, directed against the members of this ethnic/linguistic group. 'Nadahup' combines elements of the names of all four languages (Nadëb, Dâw, Yuhup, Hup).

Information on the Hup language and its speakers was obtained via original fieldwork on the Rio Tiquié, Amazonas, Brazil, conducted in 2000–4. A comprehensive description of Hup grammar can be found in Epps (2005b). I am grateful to the Hupd'əh for teaching me their language, and to the Museu Parense Emílio Goeldi and the Instituto Socioambiental for assistance with practical issues relating to fieldwork. Thanks also to Alexandra Aikhenvald, Eve Danziger, and Orin Gensler for their helpful comments on the material in this chapter. This work was supported by a Fulbright-Hays Dissertation Research Grant, National Science Foundation Grant no. 0111550, and by the Max Planck Institute for Evolutionary Anthropology, Leipzig.

multilingual Vaupés system, but one which differs significantly from that of their neighbours. Unlike the river-dwelling, agriculturalist Tucanoan and Arawak peoples in the region, the Hupd'əh and other Nadahup peoples—who are traditionally semi-nomadic hunter-gatherers—do not practise linguistic exogamy. Nevertheless, they have long been engaged in an active socioeconomic relationship with the Vaupés river-dwellers—often characterized as a symbiotic relationship (e.g. Reid 1979)[2]—fostering close interaction and a high level of bilingualism.

This chapter seeks to establish that Hup, like the Tucanoan languages and Arawak Tariana, is fully involved in the Vaupés contact situation. Hup has undergone significant contact-induced restructuring of its grammar, probably under the influence of the East Tucanoan languages—especially Tucano, the most widely spoken member of the family—resulting in profound changes to its typological profile. The diffusion experienced by Hup closely resembles that which has taken place among other languages of the region, due to a shared regional linguistic ideology—despite the fact that Hup speakers do not practise the linguistic exogamy which fosters this ideology. This discussion demonstrates that the Vaupés linguistic area is even more complex than has been previously assumed, with three distinct language families and a variety of sociolinguistic situations implicated in the contact situation.

2 The role of the Hupd'əh in the Vaupés

In contrast to the social equality traditionally enjoyed by the various Tucanoan and Arawak language groups among themselves, the Hupd'əh[3] and other Nadahup peoples are considered by their neighbours to be socially inferior due to their forest orientation and lack of linguistic exogamy (cf. Aikhenvald 2002: 188; Jackson 1983: 158–63), and their languages are looked down on as somehow subhuman and not worth learning. In spite of these attitudes, however, the Hupd'əh are fully engaged in the Vaupés system. They participate in a 'patron–client' relationship with Tucanoan peoples, filling the role of part-time servants and labourers and engaging in trade (cf. Reid 1979).

---

[2] Ethnohistorical evidence suggests that various East Tucanoan groups were at one time associated with particular groups of Nadahup people. The Hupd'əh are classified (by their River Indians neighbours and by themselves) into two groups: 'Makú of Tucano' and 'Makú of Desano'. Whether the 'Makú of Desano' were at one time bilingual in Desano rather than (or in addition to) Tucano is an open question.

[3] The speakers of Hup use the term 'Hup' to refer to their language and ethnicity, and refer to themselves with the plural ethnonym Hup-d'əh (literally 'people').

This interaction has given rise to a situation of stable, one-sided bilingualism for nearly all Hup adults, and has also resulted in many shared aspects of ritual, music and dance, discourse, etc.

Although we currently do not know how old the Hup–Tucanoan relationship is, it is likely that it has been in place for many generations. It has been suggested that the Nadahup peoples were the original inhabitants of the region and that the Tucanoans entered sometime before 1500 (cf. Nimuendajú 1982: 169–70; Aikhenvald 1999: 390, 2002: 24), but this is highly speculative. There is nevertheless good evidence that the socioeconomic relations between Hupd'əh and Tucano have been similar to what they are now since at least the early twentieth century (e.g. Koch-Grünberg 1906).[4]

The importance of language as a badge of identity among the Tucanoan and Tariana peoples of the Vaupés has been discussed at length by Jackson (1983), Aikhenvald (e.g. 2002: 17), and others. This ideology has undoubtedly been promoted and strengthened by the practice of linguistic exogamy in the region, but linguistic exogamy is not in itself a prerequisite for a cultural connection between language and ethnic identity: the Hupd'əh do not take part in this marriage system, but have nevertheless been led to embrace the regional outlook through their cultural involvement with their neighbours. This is illustrated by the fact that Hup speakers occasionally refer to themselves as a group with the term *Pɨnɨh Pɨd-d'əh* (1pl.POSS speak-PL) 'those who speak our language'; similarly, one Hup woman characterized their Tucano bilingualism by saying, 'we don't really know their language; we're just stealing/appropriating it; it's not our language.'

In keeping with this shared regional perspective linking language and identity, Hup speakers are generally conscious of keeping their language distinct from Tucano, and react negatively toward some types of language mixing. Accordingly, Hup has resisted the direct borrowing of Tucanoan (and other non-native) forms, favouring various other strategies for coining new words. In its grammar, on the other hand—of which speakers are less consciously aware (cf. Silverstein 1981)—Hup has undergone significant diffusion, apparently with considerable innovation and restructuring of categories to fit the Tucanoan model. As one would expect given the present sociolinguistic situation, this diffusion appears to have been entirely unilateral from Tucanoan into Hup, much as has been the case for Tariana (e.g. Aikhenvald 1999: 411). In fact, an intriguing result of this region-wide Tucanoan influence

---

[4] Note that interaction between Hupd'əh and non-Indians was rare before 1970, and has been only sporadic since; accordingly, few Hupd'əh speak Portuguese. Portuguese influence on Hup is mainly restricted to loanwords for non-native items (see §5).

is that Tariana and Hup—themselves unrelated and currently not in contact—have developed numerous structural similarities, much as Tosco (2000)
describes for Ethio-Semitic languages having a shared Cushitic substratum.[5]
The Vaupés is thus distinct from many of the world's other linguistic areas in
that it has apparently been shaped largely through unilateral, rather than
multilateral, contact.

While the sociolinguistics of Hup–Tucanoan interaction has provided
fertile ground for the diffusion of grammatical features, a convincing argument for diffusion also depends on an evaluation of Hup's sister languages, in
order to demonstrate that the features Hup shares with Tucanoan were indeed
not inherited from Hup's parent language. Unfortunately, we know relatively
little about the Nadahup family. Its membership is somewhat controversial,
although the inclusion of four languages is fairly well established: Hup,
Yuhup, Dâw, and Nadëb;[6] of these, Hup and Yuhup are the most closely
related, followed by Dâw and then Nadëb. Materials on these languages are
limited, with Nadëb and Yuhup represented only by sketch grammars.

Nevertheless, as the following discussion will demonstrate, Tucanoan influence on the grammars of the Nadahup languages can be shown to correspond
rather neatly to their geographic proximity to the Vaupés region, illustrated in
Map 1. Hup—in the centre of the Vaupés—has been under the most contact
pressure; Yuhup has been under slightly less, Dâw considerably less, and
Nadëb—well removed from the Vaupés region—has apparently undergone
no Tucanoan influence at all. The fact that previous assessments of
the involvement of the Nadahup languages in the Vaupés linguistic
area were based mainly on Dâw (since data on Hup and Yuhup were not
available) explains why this involvement has tended to be underestimated
(e.g. Aikhenvald 1999).

---

[5] It is also possible that Hup has had a substratum effect on Tariana (and possibly on other Vaupés languages), given local rumours that some of these peoples may have incorporated Hupd'əh groups at some time in the past (see Aikhenvald, Chapter 10 above). However, there is at this point no conclusive evidence to support this.

[6] While some doubt has been expressed about the relationship of Nadëb to the other Nadahup languages (see Aikhenvald 2001: 191), the existence of extensive lexical cognate sets and regular sound correspondences strongly supports its membership in the family (cf. Martins 2005; Epps 2005b). On the other hand, claims for the membership of the languages Cacua and Nukak (e.g. Martins and Martins 1999; Martins 2005), for which there are very few available data, have yet to be convincingly demonstrated and appear to be highly dubious. Certain structural similarities between Cacua/Nukak and the other Vaupés languages may well be the result of areal diffusion, since the Cacua are located within the Vaupés area and are engaged in a symbiotic relationship with East Tucanoans similar to that of the Hupd'əh (see Silverwood-Cope 1972); they are even known as 'Makú of Cubeo' and 'Makú of Wanano' (Alexandra Aikhenvald, p.c.).

While diffusion from Tucanoan into Hup and some of its sister languages appears to best account for the grammatical similarities discussed in this chapter, there are possible alternative explanations. Hup could have developed these Tucanoan-like grammatical features through independent innovation, or Proto-Nadahup itself could have had features which were later *lost* from Nadëb (and in some cases also from Dâw and Yuhup), but remained in Hup. It is difficult to rule these alternatives out definitively for every individual feature; however, it is highly unlikely that they could account for the bulk of the data. There are too many striking similarities—including some that are typologically unusual—to be due to chance; likewise, a genetic relationship or early contact between the Nadahup and Tucanoan proto-families should be reflected in their relatively conservative lexicons as much as or more than in their grammatical structures, but this is not the case. Finally, many of the features shared between Hup and Tucanoan involve morphemes that appear to have grammaticalized *recently* in Hup, and clearly do not date back to Proto-Nadahup. Nevertheless, it is possible that some of the striking grammatical differences between Nadëb and the other Nadahup languages could be due not only to diffusion into Hup, Yuhup, and Dâw from Tucanoan, but also to contact undergone by Nadëb with other (now extinct) languages in the past. This question must await future research, but on the whole there is little doubt that areal diffusion has played a major role in shaping Hup's typological profile.

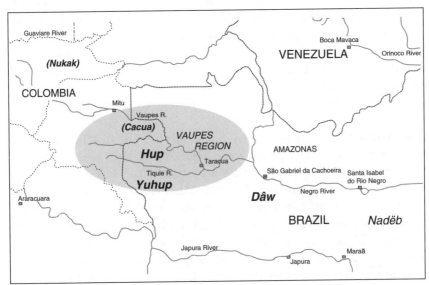

Map 1 The Nadahup (Makú) languages

The sections that follow present a broad sample of features shared between Hup and the other Vaupés languages, and provide arguments in favour of their diffusion from Tucanoan into Hup. These include aspects of phonology, nominal and verbal morphosyntax, discourse, and lexical formations and calques. Most are examples of indirect diffusion, by which categories and processes were borrowed and restructured according to the Tucanoan model, but the actual forms were created using Hup's own resources—in response to Hup speakers' resistance to direct borrowing. A significant number of these features are also shared by Tariana, and include many which Aikhenvald (e.g. 1999: 392; Chapter 1) identifies as definitive of the Vaupés linguistic area.

3 Phonology

Both of Hup's major morpheme- or word-level prosodic features, nasalization and tone, appear to have been structured via diffusion from Tucanoan. Probably because prosodic phenomena are associated with discourse-level aspects of speech (such as an accent or manner of speaking), instead of being restricted to individual lexical forms, they are known to be particularly prone to diffusion (e.g. Matisoff 2001; Urban and Sherzer 1988).

Nasal prosody exists in all East Tucanoan languages, where it occurs within the phonological word. In Hup and Yuhup (cf. Brandão Lopes and Parker 1999: 332; Ospina 2002), nasalization is likewise a morpheme-level prosody; as in Tucanoan, voiced stops and nasals are allophones. Nasal spreading is also found in Tariana, probably due to contact with Tucanoan (Aikhenvald 2002: 45). In Dâw and Nadëb (Martins 2004; Weir 1984), on the other hand, nasalization is distinctive on the level of the segment, and voiced stops and nasals are contrastive. Such cognate pairs as Hup *nǽŋ* /~dǽg/ 'honey' and Dâw *nɛ́g* /nɛ́g/ 'honey' illustrate the morpheme-level vs. segment-level nasal contrasts in these languages.

Tonal distinctions are also a pan-Vaupés feature. The East Tucanoan languages have a system of pitch-accent, realized as a high tone on stressed syllables, and a similar system of pitch-accent also occurs in Tariana (Aikhenvald 2002: 50). In Tucano, according to Ramirez (1997*a*: 21), pitch-accent on the level of the word is manifested as either a stable high tone or a rising contour. Tone in Hup is best described as a system of 'word-accent', in which stressed syllables receive either a high tone or a rising contour; since Hup morphemes tend to be of one syllable only, the resulting word-level tonal patterns resemble those of Tucano. Dâw (Martins 2004) and Yuhup (Brandão Lopes and Parker 1999: 330; Ospina 2002) also have contrastive tone, but

Nadëb lacks any tonal distinctions. Although Nadëb could conceivably have lost tone, it is likely that tone developed in Hup and its nearby sisters via diffusion, while Nadëb has preserved the family's original toneless profile.

Hup's inventory of segmental phonemes is significantly different from that of the Tucanoan languages, but there nevertheless has been some restructuring of segmental features. As noted above, Hup has apparently lost nasal and oral contrasts on the segmental level; also, /y/ in root-initial position is pronounced [ᵈy] (or [ñ] in nasal contexts) and intervocalic /d/ is typically realized as a flap [ɾ], just as they are in Tucano (Ramirez 1997*a*: 33)—and in Tariana, due to Tucanoan influence (Aikhenvald 1999: 395–6). Note that these features are not present in Dâw (Martins 2004). Finally, /g/ never begins a phonological word in either Hup or Tucano (cf. Ramirez 1997*a*: 30–3), but does so in Dâw and Nadëb (although it is quite rare in Dâw; Martins 2004: 31).

4 Morphosyntax

Previous assessments of Hup's morphosyntactic profile, such as that by Payne (1990*b*: 220), have described the language as extremely isolating. In fact, however, Hup has complex agglutinative verbal morphology involving root/ stem compounding and stacking of bound formatives, and is almost entirely suffixing and dependent marking (example 1). These features are shared by the East Tucanoan languages, as example (2) illustrates.

(1) Hup
     hayám bɨʔ-wɨd-næn-pɨ́d-mah-áh,   hib'ăh=tæ̆h=ʔíh-íh
     town   make-arrive-come-DST-REP-DEC   create=clan=MASC-DEC
     The Ancestor(s) arrived and built a town

(2) Tucano (Ramirez 1997*a*: 177)
     a'té-pa-dɨ-re   akó   waá-sãa-mu'muo-pe'o-kã'-ya!
     these-CL:PAN-PL-NON.A/S   water   pull-put-fill-completely-ASS-IMP
     Fetch water and fill these pans completely!

Hup's sisters Dâw and Yuhup also share many of these features, but Nadëb is strikingly different in that it has mostly prefixes (Weir 1984: 46–8) and is generally head marking. As the following sections will illustrate, Hup probably owes many such features of its morphosyntactic profile to areal diffusion.

4.1 *Noun classification and gender*

Noun classification is common to all of the Tucanoan languages, which categorize inanimate entities by shape (example 3) and animate entities by gender (e.g. Ramirez 1997*a*: 211 for Tucano; Miller 1999 for Desano; cf. Stenzel

2004: 145 for Wanano). The same strategy is found in Tariana, due to diffusion from Tucanoan (Aikhenvald 2002: 91–2; see also Gomez-Imbert 1996 for a discussion of changes to the classifier system of Tucanoan Cubeo under Baniwa influence).

(3)   Tucano (Ramirez 1997*a*: 211)
     ũyû-ga   (avocado-ROUND)   'avocado fruit'
     ũyû-gɨ   (avocado-SHAFT)   'avocado tree'

Hup is in the process of developing an incipient system of noun classification which conforms closely to the Tucanoan pattern of categorizing inanimates on the basis of shape, while reserving gender specifications for animate entities (particularly higher animates and humans). As discussed in detail in Epps (forthcoming), the shape-based classifiers are grammaticalizing from native words for plant parts. Compare (4) with (3) above:

(4)   Hup
     yūhúm=tat   (avocado=FRUIT)   'avocado fruit'
     yūhúm=teg   (avocado=TREE/SHAFT)   'avocado tree'

Possibly due in large part to an influx of new manufactured items requiring names, the bound plant part nouns in Hup are becoming generalized and semantically extended, and are now used to form the names of various nouns that are unrelated to plants, as in (5). A similar function is available in Tucano (example 6).

(5)   Hup
     bóda=tat   (ball=FRUIT/ROUND)   'ball' (from Portuguese *bola* 'ball')
     wayd'óʔ=teg   (fly=TREE/THING)   'aeroplane'
     b'ŏy=g'æt   (study=LEAF/BOOK)   'school book'
(6)   Tucano (Ramirez 1997*a*: 277)
     bu'e-kɨhɨ́   (study=SHAFT)   'pencil, pen' (~long thing associated
                             with study)

According to the Tucano gender system (Ramirez 1997*a*: 207–8), the nominal suffixes -*gɨ* (masculine) and -*go* (feminine) appear on nouns referring to humans and kin terms, and in anaphoric reference to animals. A similar pattern is found in Hup:

(7)   Hup
     húp=ʔĩh   (Hup=MASC)   'Hup man'
     ʔãh=cót=ʔáy   (1sg=older.sibling=FEM)   'my older sister'
     yúp=ʔĩh   (that=MASC)   'that one (animal or human)'

Unlike classifiers in Tucanoan languages, classifying nouns in Hup's system are found with only a small subset of nouns—reflecting the fact that this is an incipient system, whose development is being motivated in part by diffusion. Not only do the new classifiers in Hup reflect the other Vaupés classifier systems in their semantics, but classifiers and gender markers in Hup also occur with numerals, demonstratives, adjectives, relativized verbal forms, and on nouns as derivational markers (see Epps 2005c), as they do (somewhat more regularly) in Tucano and Tariana.

In contrast to Hup, Nadëb is reported to have only a small set of possessive classifiers, as in *subih waa maséél* 'Subih food banana' ('Subih's banana') (Weir 1984: 86). Dâw has no gender marking and only a few classifier-like forms for human referents, plant parts, and body parts; these apparently have no significant semantic extensions like those found in Hup, and are hardly ever found with numerals, demonstratives, etc. (Martins 2004: 138–9). Yuhup, on the other hand—in keeping with its position within the Vaupés region—is reported to have a system of classifier-like forms similar to Hup's (Ospina 2002: 257).

4.2 *Numerals*

Hup and the Tucanoan languages have strikingly similar numeral systems, which they also share with Tariana (apparently due to diffusion from Tucanoan, see Aikhenvald 2002: 108). These involve native roots for 1 to 3, a calqued term for 4 that translates as 'having a brother' or 'being accompanied', and a base-five system for 5 and up that relies on adding fingers and toes. (Note that the forms above 5 tend to be flexible and non-conventionalized, and have now largely been replaced by Portuguese numerals in all of these languages.) Compare Table 1.

The Hup numerals have almost certainly been shaped by Tucanoan influence.[7] In fact, comparison of the different Nadahup numeral systems provides a striking illustration of the degree to which geographic proximity to the Vaupés linguistic area (see Map 1) has structured the degree of diffusion. Only Hup and Yuhup have words for specific numeral values over 3, while Dâw falls back on an even–odd tally system and Nadëb is reported to have nothing above 3 at all (see Epps 2004) and Table 2.[8]

---

[7] A calqued term for 'four' meaning 'having a brother' or 'being accompanied' actually appears to be a much larger areal feature, occurring in several Bora-Witotoan languages outside the Vaupés (Huber and Reed 1992; Frank Seifart, p.c.).

[8] The orthographic representations of Yuhup, Dâw, and Nadëb forms have been adjusted slightly from the original sources to facilitate comparison.

TABLE 1. Numerals 'four' and 'five' in Vaupés languages

	Tucano	Tariana	Hup
'four'	*ba'pâ-ritise* (companion-NOMZ)	*kehpu-nipe* (REL+accompany-NOMZ)	*hi-bab'-ní* (FACT-sibling-be.NOMZ) *bab'-ní* (sibling-be.NOMZ) [alternative translations: 'sibling exists' and 'being accompanied']
'five'	*ni'kâ-mukāse* (one-HAND)	*pa:-kapi* (one-HAND) *pa-kapi* (IMPERS-hand)	*ʔayup-dapúh* (one-hand)

Sources: Aikhenvald (2002: 108) (Tucano, Tariana); Ramirez (1997a: 332) (Tucano).

4.3 *Number*

As Table 3 illustrates, both Hup and the East Tucanoan languages follow a system of 'split plurality' determined by animacy, marked by bound suffixes/enclitics (cf. Aikhenvald 2002: 96, Ramirez 1997a: 205 for Tucano, Miller 1999: 52 for Desano, Stenzel 2004: 130–6 for Wanano); compare Tucano *emo-â* 'howler.monkey-PL' and Hup *tŭg=d'əh* 'howler.monkey=PL'. That the Hup system was probably influenced by Tucanoan is supported by the fact that neither Dâw (whose plural focus particle *dɣh* is probably cognate with Hup's plural marker *=d'əh*) nor Nadëb adheres to this pattern. Like Hup, Tariana has also undergone a restructuring of its number-marking system under Tucanoan influence, yielding a similar animacy distinction (Aikhenvald 2002: 96).

Also like Tucano (Ramirez 1997a: 206), Hup makes use of a singulative suffix to refer to individual insects that normally occur in groups, particularly ants, wasps, bees, etc. (examples 8–9). No such singulative form is reported for any of Hup's sister languages.

(8) Hup
 yɔ̌ʔ=d'əh   'wasp=PL'   ('wasps')
 yɔ̌ʔ=ʔáw   'wasp=SING'   ('one wasp')

(9) Tucano (Ramirez 1997a: 206)
 uti-â   'wasp-PL'   ('wasps')
 uti-â-wī   'wasp-PL-SING'   ('one wasp')

TABLE 2. Numerals in the Nadahup languages

	Hup (dialectal variants)	Yuhup	Dâw	Nadëb
'one'	*Ɂayŭp, Ɂæ̆p*	*sāh, sāhyāpā*	*mæɁ*	*šæt, šæd* (lit. 'together')
'two'	*ka Ɂăp, koɁăp, kəwəg-Ɂap*	*b'ɔ̃Ɂ*	*tɨ̈ib*	*pɔwɔp* (also used for 3, 'a few')
'three'	*mɔtaɁap, mɔt-wɨg-Ɂap bab'-pã̰* (lit. 'no sibling')	*mɔdɨg-w'ap*	*mutuwap*	*tamawɔ́b*
'four'	*hi-bab'-ní* (lit. 'sibling exists; being accompanied')	*bab-ni-w'ap* 'accompany/ sibling-quantity'	*mæɁ mab* 'one (has) a brother' [Used for all even numerals 4+]	
'five'	*Ɂayup-dapŭ́h* 'one hand'	*cāh-pɔ̃h-w'ap* 'one-hand-quantity'	*mæɁ mab mæ̆h* 'one (has) no brother' [Used for all odd numerals 5+]	
'six' and up	(adding fingers and toes)	(adding fingers and toes)	Even-odd tally system (4+)	

Sources: Ospina (2002: 455–9) (Yuhup); Martins (2004: 391–2) (Dâw); Weir (1984: 103–4) (Nadëb).

Finally, Hup and the East Tucanoan languages—and Tariana, due to Tucanoan influence (Aikhenvald 2002: 98), but not Dâw or Nadëb—also have an 'associative plural' construction, involving a suffix which attaches to a referent N (typically a person's name) to mean 'those associated with N'. While the Hup, Tucano, and Tariana associative plural forms have language-specific origins, all three have a final syllable that is homophonous with the plural suffix in the respective languages.

4.4 *Evidentiality*

The East Tucanoan languages have complex systems of evidentiality, with portmanteau forms encoding person, tense, number, and distinguishing four to five different evidential specifications. Tucano, Desano, and Wanano,

TABLE 3. Plural marking in Tucano and Nadahup languages

	Inside Vaupés		Outside Vaupés	
	Nadahup **Hup**	E. Tucanoan **Tukano**	Nadahup **Dâw**	**Nadëb**
Humans	enclitic =*d'əh*	suffix -*a*	optional plural focus particle *dɣh*	suppletive forms for pronouns and a few human nouns
Animates	enclitic =*d'əh*	suffix -*a*		
Inanimates	usually unmarked	suffix -*ri* (usually + classifier)		

Sources: Martins (2004: 400–3) (Dâw); Ramirez (1997a: 205) (Tucano); Weir (1984: 58) (Nadëb).

among other languages, express the fifth evidential (an assumed or inferred value) by means of a construction involving the verb *niĩ* 'be, exist'. (Note that a shared verb form resembling *ni* is itself an areal feature in the Vaupés, appearing in various Tucanoan and Nadahup languages—but not in Nadëb— and in Tariana; this is an unusual case in which a *form* has diffused, rather than simply a grammatical function.)

As discussed in detail in Epps (2005c), Hup has developed a strikingly similar five-way evidential specification—including an inferred construction based on its own verb *ni*—through diffusion from its Tucanoan neighbors.[9] A similar development has occurred in Tariana (Aikhenvald 2002: 128). Table 4 illustrates the close resemblance between Hup's evidentiality system and that of its Vaupés neighbours, and suggests strongly that the common ancestor of Hup, Yuhup, Dâw, and Nadëb probably had only a reported specification.[10] In assimilating the evidential categories, Hup has used its own resources to create the markers themselves: the non-visual enclitic =*hɔ̃* almost certainly comes from the verb *hɔ̃h-* 'Produce sound, make noise', the inferred enclitic =*cud* probably is from the verb *cud-* 'be inside (i.e. be hidden)', and the *ni-* construction is the calqued equivalent of the corresponding Tucano inferred construction (see Epps 2005c).

[9] The inferential -*ni-* construction in Hup may be an example of grammatical accommodation, in which the Hup verb *ni-* (itself probably inherited from Tucanoan) developed a new function in accordance with the inferential construction based on the verb *niĩ* in Tucano.

[10] The evidential relating to reported information in Tariana is likewise the only inherited evidential specification in the language (Aikhenvald, p.c.). It is possible that the apparent existence of a reported evidential in the various proto-languages is indicative of an earlier linguistic area (see Epps 2005c).

Table 4. Evidentiality in Vaupés and Nadahup languages

| | Inside Vaupés | | | | | Outside Vaupés | |
| | East Tucanoan | | Arawak | Nadahup | | Nadahup | |
	Tucano	Tuyuca	Tariana	Hup	Yuhup	Dâw	Nadëb
Visual	paradigm (evid.-person-tense-number)	paradigm (evid.-person-tense-number)	paradigm (evid.-tense)				
Non-visual	paradigm (evid.-person-tense-number)	paradigm (evid.-person-tense-number)	paradigm (evid.-tense)	=hɔ̃	=hɔ̃		
Inference (assumed)	paradigm (evid.-person-tense-number)	paradigm (evid.-person-tense-number)	paradigm (evid.-tense)	=cud			
Inference2	-ni construction	paradigm (evid.-person-tense-number)	-nhina, -nihka	-ni- constr.	-ni constr.		
Reported	paradigm (evid.-person-tense-number)	paradigm (evid.-person-tense-number)	paradigm (evid.-tense)	=mah	=mah	=mah	mɨh

Sources: Ramirez 1997a: 120 (Tucano); Barnes 1990 (Tuyuca); Aikhenvald 2003: 289 (Tariana); Ospina 2002: 181 (Yuhup); Martins 2004: 487 (Dâw); Weir 1984: 254 (Nadëb).

4.5 Tense

In East Tucanoan languages, present, recent past, and distant past tense are marked obligatorily on the verb by means of portmanteau suffixes that merge tense, evidentiality, person, and number (e.g. Ramirez 1997a: 124; Aikhenvald 2002: 120; see Table 4). Several future tense specifications are also distinguished by verbal suffixes. In Hup and other Nadahup languages, explicit indication of tense tends to be relatively minimal, with most temporal information being conveyed via aspectual marking. However, Hup has developed a number of tense specifications that match those found in Tucano.

In particular, Hup has a pair of optional contrast particles that follow the verb and (in addition to indicating contrast) are specified for recent vs. distant past tense: *páh* (recent past contrast; source unclear) and *j'ấh* / *j'ám* (distant past contrast; probable source is the adverb *jám* 'yesterday'). Some speakers use these tense/contrast markers more than do other speakers, suggesting that their development represents a grammatical change in progress. Moreover, some speakers (especially of certain Hup dialects) tend to fuse these particles—particularly the 'distant past' marker—with the reported evidential in narrative (see Epps 2005c). This tendency is undoubtedly fed by the relative frequency of this combination's occurrence, since traditional narratives among the Hupd'əh and various other Vaupés peoples are typically cast in the 'distant past reported' specification (and probably involve calquing of discourse styles). This tense-evidential combination in Hup produces a form that is reminiscent of the portmanteau tense-evidential markers found in Tucanoan languages:

(10)   j'ŭg-út=**maám**   tɨh   wɔn-kot=máh-ah
       forest-OBL=REP.DST.CNTR   3sg   follow-go.in.circles=REP-DEC
       In the forest, long ago, they say, he wandered following (the tapir)

In addition, Hup has developed an obligatory verbal future suffix (the form *-teg* and its variant *-te-*) which has probably grammaticalized relatively recently from a noun (see Epps 2004a, 2005b). It is highly likely that the existence of obligatory future suffixes in Tucano was an impetus for this grammaticalization; note that the development of future tense specifications in Tariana was also structured via diffusion (Aikhenvald 2002: 126).

Further evidence that Hup's tense markers have been influenced by Tucanoan is the wide disparity among tense-marking strategies and forms across the Nadahup languages, particularly those outside the Vaupés, as Table 5 illustrates.

TABLE 5. Tense specifications in Tucano and Nadahup languages

	Inside Vaupés			Outside Vaupés	
	Tucano (East Tukanoan)	Hup	Yuhup	Dâw	Nadëb
Past	Recent Distant (obligatory portmanteau suffixes)	Recent *páh* Distant *j'ám / j'áh* (optional)	Recent *páh* Distant *ãm* (optional)	One optional past: *ʔeʔ* (cognate with Hup perfective aspect marker?)	One past: *paah* (cognate with Hup recent past marker?)
Future	Several suffixes	Suffix -*teg* / -*te-*	Tone change (temporal discontinuity in general)	Suffixes -*ʔej*, -*ë̃y* (may be largely aspectual)	Particle *dah*

Sources: Martins (2004: 281–4) (Dâw); Ospina (2002: 178) (Yuhup); Ramirez (1997a: 123, 166) (Tucano); Weir (1984: 58) (Nadëb).

4.6 *Verb compounding*

Verb compounding is an extremely productive process in East Tucanoan languages, in which multiple verb roots regularly combine according to the pattern: [Main verb—Dependent verb—Tense/mood/gender suffix] (e.g. Ramirez 1997a: 175). The dependent verb in these compounds frequently encodes aspectual or Aktionasart information, as well as information relating to causality. Hup verbs follow a strikingly similar pattern—often matching their Tucanoan counterparts so closely that they resemble calques. Such apparently calqued compounds include desideratives and directionals, as well as other combinations:

(11)   Hup:
    ʔam   **wæd-túk-uw-ăn**   **d'oʔ-nǽn-æ̆h**
    2sg   eat-want-FLR-NON.A/S   bring/take-come-DEC
    (We) brought what you wanted to eat

(12)   Wanano (Stenzel 2004: 287):
    ~bʉ'ʉ   **chʉ-dua-re**   ~**da-ta-i**
    2sg   eat-DESID-NON.A/S   bring/take-come-VIS.PERV.1
    (We) brought what you wanted to eat

Certain causative verb compounds likewise appear to be calqued equivalents in Hup and Tucano, particularly those involving the use of a dependent stem such as 'do' or 'order' (examples 13–14). Tariana has also developed a similar pattern involving a serial construction (but with a different order of components), apparently under Tucanoan influence (Aikhenvald 2002: 116; example 15). Hup's sister language Nadëb, on the other hand, uses an altogether different strategy—a prefix—to indicate causation (Weir 1984: 46).

(13) Hup

    tíh-ăn   **bi?-yǽh**

    3sg-NON.A/s   work-request.IMP

    Order her to work

(14) Tucano (Ramirez 1997a: 184)

    koô-re   **da'dá-duti**-ya

    3sgf-NON.A/s   work-request-IMP

    Order her to work

(15) Tariana (Aikhenvald 2002: 116)

    duha-nuku   **pira**   **pehpani**

    she-TOP.NON.A/s   2sg+order   2sg+work

    Order her to work

Although the verb-compounding process is found throughout the Nadahup family, the productivity and types of verb compounding found in Hup have surely been shaped by the Tucanoan model. Moreover, like verb compounding, the development of grammatical morphemes out of dependent compounded verb roots is also a shared process among the Vaupés languages. For example, evidentials in East Tucanoan languages probably grammaticalized from compounded verbs (Malone 1988), as did several evidentials in Hup (see §4.5 above) and at least one in Tariana (Aikhenvald 2002: 127 and p.c.).

4.7 *Grammatical relations and case*

In its system of grammatical alignment and case marking, Hup is largely consistent with the Vaupés regional profile (see Aikhenvald, Chapter 10). Like its sisters Dâw and Yuhup, Hup exhibits consistently nominative-accusative morphology and syntax—in marked contrast to Nadëb, which has ergative constituent order and cross-referencing pronominal forms (Weir 1984: 89–91; Martins and Martins 1999: 263).

In indicating case on nominal arguments, Hup—like Tucanoan and Tariana—does not mark subjects (although Tucanoan and Tariana have a special marker reserved for focused subjects, while Hup does not). Hup also resembles its neighbours in that it uses a single marker (the suffix -*ăn*) for a variety of non-subject arguments, including direct objects, indirect objects (recipients and beneficiaries), and other affected entities (example 16). The non-subject case suffix can also occur directly on a verb stem in both Hup and

Tucano, in order to indicate a relative clause acting as the object of the main clause; see examples (11–12) above.

(16) Hup

    núw-ǎn   ʔám-ǎn   ʔǎh   nɔʔ-té-h

    this-NON.S/A   2sg-NON.S/A   1sg   give-FUT-DEC

    I'll give you this one.

Hup follows a system of 'differential' case marking for non-subject arguments (cf. Aissen 2003), corresponding to a nominal hierarchy of animacy and definiteness. Pronouns, demonstratives, proper nouns, and human nouns are virtually always case marked; animals are optionally marked depending on their degree of individuation; and inanimates are generally not marked. This system resembles that found in Tucanoan languages and Tariana, except that these languages (unlike Hup) tend to mark definite or topical inanimate entities for non-subject case. Of the other Nadahup languages, Yuhup and Dâw exhibit systems of non-subject case marking similar to that found in Hup, although involving apparently non-cognate morphemes (cf. Ospina 2002: 139–42; Martins 2004: 157, 667); Nadëb, on the other hand, lacks a non-subject case marker altogether. These facts suggest that Hup, Yuhup, and Dâw owe their case-marking strategies to diffusion from Tucanoan, as does Tariana (Aikhenvald, Chapter 10).

In the marking of obliques, Hup also follows the regional pattern (cf. Aikhenvald, Chapter 10; Ramirez 1997a: 218–21) in that it uses a single form (the suffix -V́t) to encode location, direction to and from, and—in certain cases—temporality. Such an all-inclusive oblique form is not reported for either Dâw or Nadëb (cf. Martins 2004; Weir 1984), suggesting that Hup has indeed developed this marker via areal diffusion. Note, however, that Hup also uses the additional oblique suffix -an (probably related to non-subject -ǎn; see above) to indicate location and direction.

4.8 *Other morphosyntactic similarities*

Hup shares many other strikingly similar grammatical features with its Vaupés neighbours. Quite a few of these appear to be the product of diffusion from East Tucanoan into Hup, although in some cases more information on Hup's sister languages will be needed before these hypotheses can be confirmed.

Several of Hup's valence-adjusting strategies bear a marked structural resemblance to those found in East Tucanoan languages (and to some in Tariana), but are not shared among Hup's sister languages. These include a particular passive construction (in which a passive marker is affixed to the verb and the demoted agent is marked with the non-subject case suffix), and the use of a single form to encode a verbal reflexive, reflexive intensification or emphasis with nouns (e.g. 'I myself'), and (in limited contexts) a reciprocal. Hup also has a distinct preverbal reciprocal marker, apparently recently grammaticalized from the noun 'sibling' (see Epps 2005*a*, 2005*b*); this development was probably motivated by the Tucanoan reciprocal, which appears as the initial root in a verbal construction (compare Hup *ʔúh-j'ɔŋ-* (RECIP-punch) 'punch each other' and Tucano *a'mé doté* (act.reciprocally punch) 'punch each other'; Ramirez 1997*b*: 6).

In its syntax, Hup favours verb-final constituent order, as do East Tucanoan languages and Tariana (see Aikhenvald 2002: 167), but in all these languages constituent order is highly flexible and pragmatically based. Dâw, on the other hand, favours AVO constituent order (Martins 2004: 525). Productive noun incorporation does not in general occur in any of the Vaupés languages (Aikhenvald 1999: 386), including Hup and Yuhup, but its existence in Dâw (Martins 2004: 651) and Nadëb (Weir 1984: 1990) suggests that it may have been *lost* in Hup and Yuhup under Tucanoan influence. However, Hup does have one semi-productive process resembling noun incorporation: this involves the combination of the verb *ni-* ('be, exist'; cf. §4.5 above) with nouns as a verbalizer, resulting in a construction that typically means 'have N' (example 17). This process is strikingly similar to the use of the verbalizer *-ti* in Tucano (example 18). Hup probably developed this feature in response to areal pressure from Tucano, and may have simultaneously modelled it after its own family's process of noun incorporation, even as this was being lost.

(17) Hup
      hɔm-ní-
      wound-be-
      have sores, a wound

(18) Tucano (Ramirez 1997*a*: 353)
      kamî-ti-
      wound-VBZR-
      have sores, a wound

Hup also shares several aspects of its system of negation with the Tucanoan languages. Like Tucanoan, Hup negates predicates by means of a verbal suffix (*-nɨh*), and makes use of suppletive (and internally opaque) lexicalized expressions for 'I don't know' (*ʔam yaʔápaʔ*) and 'does not exist' (*pǎ̃*); Tariana does likewise, apparently as a result of diffusion (Aikhenvald 2002: 133). In contrast, Nadëb does not have any of these features, and no opaque negative expression for 'I don't know' is attested in Dâw (Martins 2004: 509).

Still other features that are shared between Hup and Tucanoan, but are not attested in some of Hup's sister languages, include verbal optative and apprehensive modes, an alienable possessive construction involving a possessive marker that falls between the possessor and the possessed entity, and a nominal construction meaning 'person or thing from N, inhabitant of N'. In the latter, the interrogative pronoun *ʔŭy* 'who' in Hup has grammaticalized into a suffix (example 19), closely resembling the Tucano construction (example 20). There is no report of any such grammaticalized 'inhabitant of N' expression in Hup's sister languages.

(19) Hup
      nút-ʔŭy-ʔáy
      here-WHO-FEM
      a woman from here

(20) Tucano (Ramirez 1997*a*: 352)
      a'to-kōhó
      here-being.from.FEM.SG
      a woman from here

5 Lexicon and discourse

Hup shares numerous elements of discourse with Tucano and other Vaupés languages. These include, for example, formulaic greetings phrased as questions (many of which appear to be calques, such as 'are you awake?' for 'good morning'), and certain ideophones and interjections, such as *ʔagɨ* 'ouch'. Other shared discourse features include a pattern of overlay in discourse organization (linking clauses in a text by repeating the last constituent or the predicate of the preceding clause in the new clause), which occurs in Hup, Tucano, and Tariana (cf. Aikhenvald 2002: 170).

Lexical features shared between Hup and Tucanoan are also fairly numerous, but the majority involve calqued equivalents rather than common forms. These include such expressions as 'Bone-Son' for the cultural hero or deity, 'deer' for the tripod used in manioc processing, 'star-saliva' for dew, 'day-mark' for a watch, and a single word for 'sun' and 'moon'. A number of these expressions can be considered pan-Vaupés features (cf. Aikhenvald 1996: 98).

In contrast, Hup has borrowed relatively few actual forms from Tucanoan. The majority of borrowings of Tucanoan origin are verb roots, which may be easier to 'smuggle' into the language since—unlike nouns—they are typically embedded in morphologically complex forms (as is the case in Tariana; see Aikhenvald 2002: 224). Hup has also borrowed forms (mostly nouns) from Língua Geral (a creolized form of Tupinamba spread by early missionaries as a lingua franca) and Portuguese, many of which probably entered the language via Tucano. A few shared forms are common to virtually all of the region's languages (Tucanoan, Arawak, Nadahup, and Língua Geral) such as the adverbial preposition *te* (probably from Portuguese *até* 'until').

It is difficult to judge whether Hup has borrowed more or fewer lexical items from Tucano than has Tariana, but in both cases these have clearly been kept to a minimum. While Hup speakers resist language mixing and code switching into Tucano, they do appear to have a somewhat more relaxed attitude toward these than do Tariana speakers; in particular, the use of a Tucano form in Hup discourse rarely occasions the degree of social reaction (e.g. laughter and derision of the speaker) that Aikhenvald describes (2002: 192, 214, etc.). This difference may stem not only from the difference between the two social systems—the linguistic exogamy of the Tariana vs. the linguistic endogamy of the Hupd'əh—but also from the fact that Tariana—as a dying language—is directly threatened by Tucano, whereas Hup is currently stable and fully viable.

6 Conclusion

The wide variety of features that appear to have entered Hup via diffusion provide ample evidence for a complex Vaupés linguistic area, in which all three language families represented in the region are fully involved. Just as is true for Tariana (Aikhenvald 2002, etc.), direct borrowing of forms from East Tucanoan into Hup is minimal due to cultural inhibitions against language mixing, but indirect diffusion of grammatical categories and patterns is rampant.

Diffusion into Hup has followed a number of general patterns. Some features relate to discourse expectations, pragmatic salience, and information packaging within the clause, such as the development of evidentiality, tense specifications, and case marking; others apparently derive from cultural practices, such as the expansion of the numeral system (probably motivated by economic relations and trade with River Indian neighbours). Many changes to Hup's grammar have been system preserving, such as the expansion of an existing evidential system from one term to four terms, while others appear to have been system altering, such as the development of case marking. In almost all cases, Hup has relied on its own resources in developing the actual forms with which to fill in the new categories, deriving new functions for native forms via grammaticalization and reanalysis.

While the linguistic aspects of the essentially unilateral diffusion of Tucanoan features into Hup are largely consistent with the general profile of the Vaupés linguistic area (and with that of Tucanoan–Tariana contact), the sociolinguistic situation behind this diffusion reveals some striking differences. The Hup situation is noteworthy in that it involves stable, long-term language contact with Tucanoan peoples, resulting in enrichment of the Hup language rather than language loss, but within a context of social inequality. Most importantly, Hup speakers embrace the regional equation of language and identity without taking part in the social system of linguistic exogamy that fosters it. This suggests that the crucial factor driving this kind of language contact situation—in which grammatical patterns diffuse freely but borrowing of forms is actively resisted—is the link between identity and language, and that the social practice of linguistic exogamy is only one of the ways by which this link can be made. The Hup situation serves as an illustration of the remarkably complex range of social factors that may work together to create a linguistic area such as that of the Vaupés.

References

Aikhenvald, A. 1996. 'Areal diffusion in northwest Amazonia: the case of Tariana', *Anthropological Linguistics* 38.1: 73–116.

—— 1999. 'Areal diffusion and language contact in the Içana-Vaupés basin, northwest Amazonia', pp. 385–416 of *The Amazonian languages*, edited by R. M. W. Dixon and A. Aikhenvald. Cambridge: Cambridge University Press.

—— 2001. 'Areal diffusion, genetic inheritance, and problems of subgrouping: a North Arawak case study', pp. 167–94 of Aikhenvald and Dixon 2001.

—— 2002. *Language contact in Amazonia*. Oxford: Oxford University Press.

—— 2003. *A grammar of Tariana*. Cambridge: Cambridge University Press.

—— and Dixon, R. M. W. (eds.). 2001. *Areal diffusion and genetic inheritance*. Oxford: Oxford University Press.

Aissen, J. 2003. 'Differential object marking: iconicity vs. economy', *Natural Language and Linguistic Theory* 21.3: 435–83.

Barnes, J. 1990. 'Classifiers in Tuyuca', pp. 273–92 of Payne 1990*a*.

Brandão Lopes, A. and Parker, S. 1999. 'Aspects of Yuhup phonology', *International Journal of American Linguistics*, 65. 3: 324–42.

Epps, P. 2004. 'Tracing the development of numerals in the Vaupés-Japura (Makú) family'. Paper presented at the Workshop on numerals in the world's languages, Leipzig, 29–30 Mar.

Epps, P. 2005a. 'The tale of a promiscuous morpheme: grammaticalization in Hup'. Paper presented at the winter meeting of SSILA (Society for the Study of Indigenous Languages of the Americas), 6 Jan.

—— 2005b. *A grammar of Hup.* Ph.D. thesis, University of Virginia.

—— 2005c. 'Areal diffusion and the development of evidentiality: evidence from Hup', *Studies in Language* 29: 617–50.

—— 2006. 'From "wood" to future tense: nominal origins of the future construction in Hup'. MS.

—— Forthcoming. 'Birth of a noun classification system: the case of Hup', in *Language endangerment and endangered languages: linguistic and anthropological studies with special emphasis on the languages and cultures of the Andean-Amazonian border area*, Indigenous Languages of Latin America series (ILLA), edited by L. Wetzels. Leiden: Publications of the Research School of Asian, African, and Amerindian Studies (CNWS).

Gomez-Imbert, E. 1996. 'When animals become "rounded" and "feminine": conceptual categories and linguistic classification in a multilingual setting', pp. 438–69 of *Rethinking linguistic relativity*, edited by J. Gumperz and S. Levinson. Cambridge: Cambridge University Press.

Huber, R. and Reed, R. 1992. *Vocabulario comparativo: palabras selectas de lenguas indígenas de Colombia.* Bogotá: Asociación Lingüístico de Verano.

Jackson, J. 1983. *The fish people: linguistic exogamy and Tukanoan identity in north-west Amazonia.* Cambridge: Cambridge University Press.

Koch-Grünberg, T. 1906b. 'Die Makú', *Anthropos* 1: 877–906.

Malone, T. 1988. 'The origin and development of Tuyuca evidentials', *International Journal of American Linguistics* 54: 119–40.

Martins, S. 2004. *Fonologia e gramática Dâw.* Ph.D. thesis, Vrije Universiteit, Amsterdam.

—— and Martins, V. 1999. 'Makú', pp. 251–68 of *The Amazonian languages*, edited by R. M. W. Dixon and A. Aikhenvald. Cambridge: Cambridge University Press.

Martins, V. 2005. *Reconstrução fonológica do Protomaku Oriental.* Ph.D. thesis, Vrije Universiteit, Amsterdam.

Matisoff, J. 2001. 'Genetic vs. contact relationship: prosodic diffusibility in South-East Asian languages', pp. 291–327 of Aikhenvald and Dixon 2001.

Miller, M. 1999. *Desano grammar.* Studiesssss in the languages of Colombia 6. Arlington: SIL and the University of Texas at Arlington.

Nimuendajú, C. 1982. *Textos indigenistas.* São Paulo: Edições Loyola.

Ospina Bozzi, A. 2002. *Les structures élémentaires du Yuhup Makú, langue de l'Amazonie Colombienne: morphologie et syntaxe.* Ph.D. thesis, Université Paris 7—Denis Diderot.

Payne, D. (ed.). 1990a. *Amazonian Linguistics.* Austin: University of Texas Press.

—— 1990b. 'Morphological characteristics of lowland South American languages', pp. 213–42 of Payne 1990a.

Ramirez, H. 1997*a*. *A fala Tukano dos Ye'pa-Masa*, Vol. 1: *Gramática*. Manaus: Inspetoria Salesiana Missionária da Amazônia, CEDEM.

—— 1997*b*. *A fala Tukano dos Ye'pa-Masa*, Vol. 2: *Dicionário*. Manaus: Inspetoria Salesiana Missionária da Amazônia, CEDEM.

Reid, H. 1979. *Some aspects of movement, growth and change among the Hupdu Maku Indians of Brazil*. Ph.D thesis, Unversity of Cambridge.

Silverstein, M. 1981. 'The limits of awareness'. *Working Papers in Sociolinguistics* no. 84. Austin, Tex.: Southwest Educational Development Laboratory.

Silverwood-Cope, P. 1972. *A contribution to the ethnography of the Columbian Maku*. Ph.D. dissertation, University of Cambridge.

Sorensen, A. 1967. 'Multilingualism in the Northwest Amazon', *American Anthropologist* 69: 670–84.

Stenzel, K. 2004. *A reference grammar of Wanano*. Ph.D. thesis, University of Colorado.

Tosco, M. 2000. 'Is there an "Ethiopian language area"?', *Anthropological Linguistics* 42: 329–65.

Urban, G. and Sherzer, J. 1988. 'The linguistic anthropology of native South America', *Annual Review of Anthropology*, 17: 283–307.

Weir, E. M. H. 1984. *A negação e outros tópicos da gramática Nadëb*. MA thesis, UNICAMP, Campinas.

12

The Quechua Impact in Amuesha, an Arawak Language of the Peruvian Amazon

WILLEM F. H. ADELAAR

This chapter addresses the issue of language contact between Quechua and Amuesha, an Arawak language spoken in the Andean foothills of central Peru. The presence of lexical borrowings from Quechua in Amuesha has been discussed in a pioneering article by Mary Ruth Wise (1976). Wise considers it possible that Quechua loans may have contributed to the phonological characteristics of the Amuesha language, which are highly divergent and unusual from the viewpoint of the remainder of the Arawak language family. Here we will try and supply a further specification, both geographical and temporal, of the sources of borrowing from a Quechua perspective. It will be argued that the diffusion of Quechua lexicon in Amuesha is very different in nature from the incidental borrowings that affected other Andean and Amazonian languages. In accordance with the theme of the present volume, we will then focus our attention on the possibility of a Quechua impact on Amuesha grammar. It will be shown that, although such influence probably did occur, it was very limited when compared with the rather spectacular lexical influx. The discussion of the linguistic facts will permit us to reflect on the social and historical context of the contact situation in this particular case. Our discussion will begin with a characterization of the geographical setting of the Amuesha people and language in relation to Quechua-speaking areas.[1]

---

[1] I am grateful to Mary Ruth Wise and to Alexandra Aikhenvald for many valuable suggestions during the preparation of this paper.

1 Geographical and historical setting

The Amuesha, now preferably known as *Yanesha'* [ya:neša$^{\gamma}$], are located in the eastern, Amazonian parts of the Peruvian departments of Huánuco, Junín, and Pasco. Pozzi-Escot (1998: 73) reports that the Amuesha language is used by some 8,000 speakers (among an ethnic group of *c*.10,000). Most Amuesha speakers are bilingual and also know Spanish. Nowadays, the greatest concentration of speakers is found along the upper courses of the Palcazú and Perené rivers and, to a lesser extent, on the lower Palcazú as well. These relatively remote forest areas do not coincide with the historical homeland of the Amuesha people, which was situated further to the west and closer to the Andean highlands. According to Chase Smith (1974), it included a river axis that ran approximately from Pozuzo in the department of Huánuco to San Ramón in the department of Junín, including the locations of modern towns such as Oxapampa, Villa Rica, and San Luis de Shuaro. Some parts of the Amuesha homeland, especially near Oxapampa, reached an altitude of 1,800 metres and offered an easy gateway for communication with the Quechua-speaking highland people further to the west. During several centuries the Amuesha people were the keepers of the *Cerro de la Sal* (Salt Mountain)[2], situated on the Paucartambo River between San Luis de Shuaro and Villa Rica. This place was frequently visited by native traders from all directions (cf. Varese 1968). The salt commerce must also have attracted inhabitants of the Quechua-speaking highlands, with whom the Amuesha may have been in close contact.

It is likely that such commercial connections were severed when after the conquest of the Inca empire Peru was occupied by the Spaniards. Highland people were forced into villages ('reducciones'), whereas the eastern lowlands, including the semi-mountainous Amuesha homeland, remained largely independent (cf. Taylor 1999). After a period of uneasy relations between Spaniards and local Amazonian natives, the rebellion of Juan Santos Atahuallpa in 1742 turned the areas inhabited by the Amuesha and their Arawak neighbours, the Campa, into a no-go area for all Europeans, including missionaries. This situation lasted until the second half of the nineteenth century, when the Amuesha suffered aggressive colonization efforts. Many Amuesha moved eastward to their present forest strongholds seeking to avoid bondage and forced labour (cf. Chase Smith 1974). After having suffered heavy losses in population, the Amuesha are increasing in number again

---

[2] It is called *Posopen* in Amuesha (Wise forthcoming).

(see Map 1). Although the languages of the Amuesha and the Campa differ substantially, colonial historical sources do not normally make a sharp distinction between the two ethnic groups and tend to treat all tribes in the Andean foothills of central Peru as Campa subgroups.

2 Linguistic affiliation of Amuesha

The classification of Amuesha as a Preandine Arawak language is generally attributed to Tello (1913). However, from a lexical and phonological point of view, Amuesha is strikingly different from other Arawak languages, including its closest neighbours. As a result, Amuesha for some time continued to be considered a language of uncertain classification, either a linguistic isolate or a possible remote member of the Arawak family. A first convincing treatment of lexical cognates connecting Amuesha and other Preandine Arawak languages (in particular, Campa Asháninka and Campa Nomatsiguenga) is given in the above-mentioned article by Wise (1976). In a reconstruction of 200 Proto-Arawak lexical items, Payne (1991) identified about ninety items of Arawak origin in Amuesha (Aikhenvald, p.c.). As a result, the Arawak affiliation of Amuesha is no longer in doubt, a conclusion which is also unambiguously supported by the grammatical structure of the language. At the same time, Amuesha contains a substantial amount of non-Arawak lexicon, much of which is assignable to Quechua borrowing influence. It would go too far, however, to treat Amuesha exclusively as the product of a clash between Quechua and Arawak. Many lexical roots and bound elements in Amuesha cannot be traced to either one of the two language groups and must have been derived from some other source.[3] There are in Amuesha at least two well-established loans from Panoan, namely *non^yt^y* 'canoe' and the reciprocal verbal post-base suffix -*ann*- (Wise 1976). A matter that deserves close attention is the relationship between Amuesha and Chamicuro, another divergent Arawak language of the eastern Peruvian forest. The hypothesis of a special genealogical link between Amuesha and Chamicuro is elaborated in Parker (1991). Our main source for Amuesha is Duff-Tripp, who provides a detailed grammatical description (DT 1997) and a dictionary (DT 1998) of the language. More information on Amuesha can be found in Taylor (1954), Duff (1957), Fast (1953), Wise (1963, 1986, 2002), and Aikhenvald (1999).

---

[3] Mary Ruth Wise is currently carrying out a comparison of Amuesha and Machiguenga lexicon. This will hopefully provide more information about the provenance of lexical items in Amuesha.

3 Quechua as a source language

Quechua lexical influence is widely attested in the native languages of Andean and western Amazonian South America. However, the denomination Quechua does not refer to a monolithic language, but rather to an internally differentiated language group with a history that harks back to the beginning of our era. Most Quechua loans in Amazonian languages are relatively recent and have their origin in lingua franca type varieties of Quechua associated with a short period of Inca expansion (roughly from 1470 to 1532) or with Spanish colonial and missionary policies (roughly from 1532 to 1770). Amuesha is special in that the Quechua loans it contains were mainly taken from an adjacent Quechua dialect that, as far as we know, was never used as a lingua franca or as a missionary language.

Quechua or, more correctly, the Quechua language family is divided into two main dialect groups which accommodate most (though not all) known Quechua languages. The contours of these two main groups were outlined in Parker (1963) and in Torero (1964). In accordance with Torero's initial terminology they will be referred to here as Quechua I and Quechua II, respectively. The former is also known as Central Quechua (Mannheim 1991) or Quechua B (Parker 1963), whereas the latter is roughly equivalent to Parker's Quechua A. Both the Quechua I and Quechua II dialect divisions are internally diversified from a phonological, morphological, and lexical point of view. However, in spite of local loan traffic and dialect mixing at the boundaries, each group shares a number of fundamental characteristics supporting its genealogical cohesion. After forty years of Quechua language research the bipartition of the Quechua family is still widely accepted (see, for instance, Cerrón-Palomino 2003).

All Quechua languages associated with Inca or Spanish expansion belong to the Quechua II group. They include the official language of the Inca empire in its final decades, the *lengua general* ('general language') of the Spanish colonial administration, the prestigious dialect of Cuzco, as well as all varieties of Quechua spoken outside the borders of what is today Peru. Quechua II dialects are furthermore found in the Amazonian regions of Ecuador and northern Peru. By contrast, the Quechua I dialects are geographically more or less restricted to the highland areas of the departments of Ancash, Huánuco, Lima, Pasco, and Junín (all in central and central-northern Peru). Most Quechua I dialects are seriously endangered. As a matter of fact, the southern Quechua I dialects spoken in Pasco and Junín are nearing extinction, although they were still widely used until the middle of the twentieth century.

Quechua I accounts for far fewer than a million of the total number of Quechua speakers, which probably amounts to between 7 and 8 million.

A further division of the Quechua I dialects is presented in Torero (1974). It includes the subgroups *Huaylas-Conchucos, Alto Pativilca-Alto Marañón-Alto Huallaga, Yaru, Jauja-Huanca,* and *Huangascar-Topará* (see also Adelaar 2004: 184–5). The first two subgroups constitute the northern division of Quechua I, whereas the last three subgroups make up a southern division. Alto Huallaga (in its Panao-Pachitea variety) and Yaru are both adjacent to the original Amuesha homeland.

4 The Quechua I layer in Amuesha

Two layers of Quechua borrowing can be distinguished in Amuesha: a Quechua I layer mainly represented by the Yaru dialect complex and a Quechua II layer associated with the cultural and political domination of the Incas (see §5). There is little or no evidence of Quechua influence in Amuesha traceable to the colonial period.[4]

The Yaru dialect complex can be shown to account for most of the lexical loans from Quechua in Amuesha. Quechua loans liable to originate from the Yaru dialect are (*a*) items found in both Quechua I and Quechua II dialects, (*b*) items which are exclusive for Quechua I, and (*c*) items which are characteristic of Yaru.

From a point of view of geographical distribution, the Yaru dialect complex bestrides the Andean highlands from the oceanic side to the Amazonian versant. Today, the most vital Yaru-speaking communities can be found in the department of Lima, on the oceanic versant of the Andes (Chirinos Rivera 2001). The originally Yaru-speaking areas that are adjacent to the Amazonian foothills coincide with parts of the province of Pasco (department of Pasco) and the provinces of Junín and Tarma (department of Junín). These areas also share a boundary with the Amuesha homeland as defined in Chase Smith (1974; see above).

In linguistic literature the Yaru dialect complex has been known under different names depending on the subarea where the data underlying the studies at hand were recorded: Northern Junín Quechua, (South-Eastern) Pasco Quechua, Tarma Quechua, etc. There is a certain amount of phonological, morphological, and lexical variation within the Yaru-speaking

---

[4] Wise (forthcoming) observes that the loan *e:ša* 'sheep' from Spanish *oveja* may have entered Amuesha by the intermediary of Quechua. It could also have been a direct loan considering the fact that the Amuesha form does not contain the back vowel of the Quechua form *uyša* or *u:ša*.

territory, but it does not go beyond mutual intelligibility. Lexical data concerning the Yaru dialect complex can be found in Adelaar (1977) and Black, Bolli, and Ticsi Zárate (1990). For lexical data of the Alto Huallaga dialect complex see Weber *et al.* (1998); for Jauja-Huanca Cerrón-Palomino (1976). Note that the Panao-Pachitea dialect, which has been classified as Alto Huallaga, is nevertheless close to Yaru.

An example of a Yaru loan not traceable to other Quechua dialects, as far as we know, is *kon^{y}č-* 'to suffer' (Yaru *kunču-*). (Theoretically, this could be an Amuesha loan to Yaru, if such an event would not contradict the registered trend.) The item *konkorp-* 'to kneel down' was derived from Quechua *qunqurpa-*, a form which appears to be restricted to Yaru and Alto Huallaga. Both ingredients of this item (*qunqur* 'knee' and the affix *-pa-* with several functions) are used throughout Quechua, but the combination is proper to the two dialect groups in question. The monoconsonantal verb root *č-* 'to arrive' in Amuesha could be derived from the Quechua verb root *ča(:)-* 'to arrive', which is used in Yaru and Jauja-Huanca (if indeed this is a borrowed form). For all these cases taken together, Yaru is the dialect complex that combines the necessary conditions to be the donor language.

Quechua I loans (not restricted to Yaru, Alto Huallaga, or Jauja-Huanca) are more numerous, e.g. *akr-* 'to choose' (Quechua I *akra-*, but Quechua II *akl^{y}a-*), *ča:č-* 'to stretch oneself' (Quechua I *čača-* 'to lie down on one's back'), *pel^{y}et* 'braid' (Quechua I *pilta*) and *yerp-* 'to remember' (Quechua I *yarpa-*). Examples of lexical items found in a wider selection of Quechua dialects (not restricted to Quechua I) are *e:č* 'meat' (Quechua *ayča*), *on-* 'to last' (Quechua *una-*), *ran^{y}t^y-* 'to buy' (Quechua *ranti-*), and *yenp-* 'to help' (Quechua *yanapa-*).[5]

Some Quechua words which were borrowed into Amuesha have apparently fallen out of use in most Quechua dialects or were overlooked by lexicographers. For instance, *yoko^{h}r* 'shrimp' from Quechua *yukra* was recorded in the seventeenth century (González Holguín 1608) and in the modern dialect of Lamas (San Martín) in the Peruvian Amazonian region (Park, Weber, and Cenepo Sangama 1976). It seems safe to assume that it had a wider distribution originally.

---

[5] The root-final bilabial in *konkorp-*, *mosp-*, *yenp-*, and *yerp-* is labialized before front vowels: *konkorp^w-*, *mosp^w-*, *yenp^w-*, and *yerp^w-*.

5 The Inca layer in Amuesha

A few borrowed words in Amuesha are indicative of the impact of Inca rule. These words were probably taken from a variety of Quechua II, although their use may have been quite generalized at the time of borrowing. Typical cases of Inca influence are *enk* 'Inca' and *enka:ne^hša?* 'man (woman speaking)' from Quechua *inka* 'Inca'; *koya:neša?* 'woman (man speaking)' from Quechua *quya* 'the Inca's wife and sister'; *šopše^hša?* or *šepše^hša?* 'young lady' from Quechua *sipas* (< *šipaš*) 'girl'.[6] The ending *-(V:n)eša?* ~ *-(V:n)e^hša?* is used to designate a group of people or one of its representatives (Duff-Tripp 1997). Other cases are *pal^ya* 'princess' (Duff 1957) from Quechua *pal^ya* 'noble woman'; and *womenk* ~ *γomenk* (bound forms *-wamenk, -wmenk*) 'strong', 'brave' from Quechua *waminka* 'experienced warrior or captain'. We found one item that could be interpreted as a non-cultural loan from Quechua II (it does not occur in Quechua I), namely *kow-* 'to look at' (Quechua *qawa-* or *q^hawa-*). However, Wise (forthcoming) proposes that this may be a cognate of Nomatsiguenga Campa *kog-* 'to want', 'to look for'. If her interpretation is correct, the similarity with Quechua *qawa-* (~*q^hawa-*) would be fortuitous.

6 Impact and nature of Quechua loans in Amuesha

The amount of lexical borrowing is one of the most striking features of the Quechua impact in Amuesha. With the possible exception of the Aymaran languages, which have been involved in age-old processes of convergence with Quechua (cf. Adelaar 1986), probably no other languages were influenced by Quechua to the extent of Amuesha. McQuown (1955: 563) suggests that Amuesha is being replaced by Quechua, but Wise (1976: 358) points out that this is a case of completed contact in that there is hardly any diffusion from Quechua going on at present. The process of borrowing, which must have been unusually intense at a certain stage, has come to a standstill.

Quechua loans in Amuesha cover all word classes, including nouns, adjectives, numerals, verbs, and particles; they can be both cultural and non-cultural (core vocabulary), for instance, *pe^hrek~pe^hrok* 'reservoir' from Quechua *pirqa* 'wall'; *rakït* 'thick' from Quechua *rakta*; *l^yek-* 'to be sad' from Quechua *l^yaki-*; *eskon(t)* 'nine' from Quechua *isqun*; and *ama* 'not' from Quechua *ama* 'do not'.

---

[6] The Yaru and Alto Huallaga dialects show an irregular development of this root to *hipaš*, which makes them an unlikely source for this loan.

Most remarkable is the high number of borrowed verb roots. In a brief examination of Duff-Tripp's dictionary we found about sixty Amuesha verb roots that are likely to be borrowed from Quechua and several others that were borrowed from Spanish. The highly modified phonological shape of the Amuesha verbs sometimes makes it difficult to decide whether we are dealing with a loan or with a coincidental similarity. This applies to all loans, not only from Quechua, but also from Spanish. Loans in Amuesha tend to become so different from their models that they end up almost unrecognizable from the viewpoint of the lending language. However, in all but a few cases the borrowed status of the verbs in question is not open to discussion.

Most borrowed verbs in Amuesha refer to basic concepts for which the Arawak language family can be expected to have its own expressions. Lexical deficiency of the proto-language cannot be adduced as a motive for borrowing because the Amuesha lexicon is extremely rich and varied. Verbs that have two different meanings in Quechua may turn up in Amuesha with the same semantic duality; an example is *yeč̣-* 'to learn'; 'to live (inhabit)' from Quechua *yača-* 'to learn', 'to know'; 'to live (inhabit)'. (Note, however, that Amuesha has a different verb for 'to know' *en^{y}o^{h}t-*.)

Interestingly, verb borrowing in Amuesha does not seem to be hindered by morphological opacity. Quechua verb roots never occur in isolation in the source language, and they end up as bound verb roots in the target language as well. When borrowed from Quechua into Amuesha, all verb roots and many noun roots undergo the same type of phonological adaptation namely, the loss of their final vowel, even though their morphological valency is different: noun roots can occur as free forms in both languages, whereas verb roots never do.[7]

7 Phonological considerations

From a phonological point of view, Amuesha is strikingly different from the neighbouring Arawak languages. A superficial feature that is easily identified when comparing Amuesha with other languages is a tendency to eliminate root-final vowels. The resulting clusters can then be broken by a new internal vowel which does not necessarily reflect the eliminated vowel. See, for instance, Quechua *waqra* 'horn', which appears as *wokor* in Amuesha, and the cases of *pe^{h}rek* ~*pe^{h}rok* 'reservoir' and *yoko^{h}r* 'shrimp' (in §6 and §4, respectively). The choice of inserted vowels depends on considerations of vowel

---

[7] Only Quechua verb roots in *-ti-* retain a possible reflex of a root-final vowel in Amuesha: *kot^y-* 'to follow' (from Quechua *qati-*) and *ran^{y}t^y-* 'to buy' (from Quechua *ranti-*).

harmony and the features of adjacent consonants. This phenomenon of apparent metathesis determines the shape of most post-base affixes in Amuesha, which are -VC rather than -CV. Wise (1976: 361) cites the non-possessive suffix -*e:c* in Amuesha *orm-e:c* (bracelet-NPOSS) versus Nomatsiguenga Campa *mari-ci* (bracelet-NPOSS) as an example (cf. Shaver 1996).[8] Another important characteristic of Amuesha is internal vowel suppression in roots, which can eliminate all but the consonants of a borrowed root, as in *ne-ľk-a* (1sgS-grieve-REFL) 'I became sad' from Amuesha *ľek-* (<Quechua *ľaki-* 'to grieve') and *po-mn-a:r* (3POSS-want-POSSN) 'his loved one' from Amuesha *mon-* ~ *mʷen-* (<Quechua *muna-* 'to want', 'to love'). Similar root-internal vowel suppression is found in Cholón, an unrelated language formerly situated in an area north of the Amuesha homeland, but not in Quechua (cf. Alexander 2005).

Notwithstanding the radical changes that affect borrowed forms in Amuesha, it is not easy to establish a chronology of these changes. Much of the variation consists of morphological processes which apply to all items in a similar way, regardless of the antiquity of their presence in the language. For instance, the verbs *mon-* ~ *mʷen-* 'to want' (from Quechua *muna-*) and *monʸ-* ~ *mʷenʸ-* 'to send' (not from Quechua) show an entirely parallel behaviour. Borrowed lexical items are drawn into a morphological blender that must have been in place for a long time. Note that recent loanwords from Spanish are treated in more or less the same way as the earlier Quechua loans.

Wise (1976) attributes some of the changes that characterize Amuesha vis-à-vis the phonologically more conservative Campa languages to Quechua influence. It would have resulted in (*a*) the existence of a three-vowel system /a, e, o/;[9] (*b*) the absence of vowel sequences; (*c*) the introduction of a retroflex affricate /č̣/. Three-vowel systems are rare in the Americas, and the fact that such a system is shared by Quechua, the Aymaran languages, Amuesha, and two Campa dialects (Wise forthcoming) may have some significance. It is not clear, however, how Amuesha could have adopted such a system solely through the borrowing of Quechua vocabulary. The Quechua vowels /a, i, u/ are not always maintained in loans to Amuesha, where their presumed reflexes are largely dependent on phonological and morphological rules internal to the language. There is no indication that the Amuesha were

---

[8] We thank Ghil'ad Zuckermann (p.c.) for the observation that this is a case of loss of a final consonant followed by vowel insertion, rather than metathesis. (It does not mean that metathesis does not occur at all in Amuesha.)

[9] A fourth vowel [ɨ] is found after velar stops and is either an allophone of /a/ or /e/, or a dialectal variant.

Arawakanized Quechua speakers, which would make the three-vowel system a possible inherited system. As for the retroflex affricate /č̣/, it is found in Amuesha and in southern Quechua I (originally in all Quechua). Admittedly, the /č̣/ of Quechua loanwords is preserved in Amuesha, but the language has many lexical items with /č̣/ that are not of Quechua origin. At least one of these items, -č̣en-op^y 'neck' (-č̣n- as a nominal classifier), appears to have a cognate č̣ano in the Chamicuro language, which also has the retroflex affricate in its inventory (Parker, Orbe, and Patow 1987).[10] So there seems to be no reason to attribute the existence of /č̣/ in Amuesha to the presence of Quechua loans, although the genesis of this sound within the Arawak family is certainly a matter of interest.

Another curious coincidence with Quechua that cannot remain unmentioned is the absence of non-palatal [l]. Amuesha has plain and palatalized realizations for most consonant types and positions, and palatalized consonants occur almost unrestrictedly. Quechua has only a few consonant pairs distinguished by palatality (mainly nasals and liquids). However, both Amuesha and conservative varieties of Quechua share a peculiar gap in the system due to the fact that there is no plain [l], whereas palatal /l^y/ is abundant. Incidentally, it does not hold for the Yaru dialect complex, which went through a process of depalatalization, in which */l^y/ was replaced by [l] (e.g. Early Quechua I *l^{y}aki-, Yaru laki-, Amuesha l^{y}ek- 'to grieve'). The fact that Yaru depalatalization is not reflected in Amuesha loans from Quechua is an indication of the antiquity of the loans at issue, which must have pre-dated that change. Little is known about the chronology of Quechua depalatalization, but it may have occurred rather recently.[11] It must be added that palatal /l^y/ in Amuesha is by no means restricted to loanwords.

Amuesha vowels can be plain, long, aspirated, or glottalized. These distinctions must be the result of internal developments or be due to the influence of some non-Arawak language other than Quechua. Lexical items in Amuesha that lack both an evident Arawak and Quechua etymology are often monosyllabic and contain a long vowel; e.g. ma:m 'manioc', č̣o:p 'maize', yo:m 'sweet potato'. The source of such words remains unidentified so far.[12]

---

[10] The element -(V)p^y is a nominalizer for long objects, which reflects the Proto-Arawak root *ap^{h}i for 'snake', reconstructed by Payne (1991: 419).

[11] Depalatalization in Yaru may be connected with the rise of sound-symbolic distinctions in the Yaru dialect complex, in which palatality has become associated with 'diminutive' (Adelaar 1977: 290–2).

[12] The word ma:m may be related to Aguaruna mama 'manioc' (Simon Overall, p.c.).

8 Structural diffusion

One might expect the high incidence of Quechua lexical borrowings in Amuesha to be matched by a substantial amount of structural diffusion. This supposition does not come true, however. The influence of Quechua upon Amuesha grammar is limited. Amuesha has hardly yielded to structural pressures from outside and essentially retains its Arawak structure. When structural diffusion may be suspected, it usually remains a matter of speculation. In order to separate inherited and innovative elements in Amuesha it will be necessary to thoroughly investigate its relations with other Arawak languages, not only the neighbouring ones. It is necessary to know whether elements that might be attributed to indirect diffusion from Quechua may not be due to influence from other sources. The present study, which focuses on the Quechua perspective, cannot answer all these questions. Some of the cases of structural influence that we suspect to exist may just have a different source.

The structural differences between Quechua and Amuesha are considerable, and the language type represented by Amuesha is not found in any other Andean language. By contrast, there are clear parallels between Amuesha grammar and that of other Arawak languages, some of which are situated at a considerable distance (compare, for instance, the formation of relative clauses in Amuesha and Guajiro). In Table 1 we compare some of the grammatical features of Quechua and Amuesha. It can be seen that there are only a few areas similar enough to act as interface areas in which diffusion is particularly likely to occur. These are post-base verbal morphology and, to a lesser extent, the discourse markers and case.

8.1 *Direct grammatical diffusion*

We will first address cases of direct diffusion, which involve borrowing of form.

8.1.1 *Distributive -kama*   There is only one suffix in Amuesha whose Quechua origin is not open to debate, namely the nominal suffix *-(V:)kma*, from Quechua *-kama*. This suffix has an etymological basis in Quechua because it is derived from a verb stem *kama-* meaning 'to fit', 'to create', or 'to animate'. In many Quechua dialects, including Yaru, but also Quechua II Ayacucho, *-kama* has two related meanings:

(*a*) as a case marker: 'until', 'as long as'
(*b*) as a distributive marker: 'each time', 'always', 'without exception', 'plural of adjectives'

TABLE 1. Structural differences and similarities between Amuesha and Quechua

Quechua	Amuesha
AOV and SV constituent order	VAO and VS constituent order
Many suffixes	Many suffixes
No prefixes	Quite a few prefixes
	Affix frames (consisting of a prefix and a suffix)
Post-base verbal morphology well developed	Post-base verbal morphology well developed
All suffixes convey a distinct meaning or have a distinct function	Meaningless 'buffer' suffixes separate members of distinct suffix classes or follow suffixes that cannot occur in word-final position
Fusion of verbal personal reference markers	Personal reference markers consisting of a prefix (A/S) and a suffix (O/VCS) set (hence no fusion)
Copula 'to be' is a verb	Copula 'to be' is morphological
No formal distinction between transitive and intransitive verbs	Transitive and intransitive verbs behave differently in relative clauses
Nominal case well developed	Nominal case weakly developed
Genitive construction: head and dependent marking	Genitive construction: head marking
Inclusive/exclusive distinction based on a four-person system (inclusive is 4th person)	No inclusive/exclusive distinction (three persons plus plural)
Strictly organized subordinate clauses based on: (*a*) adverbial verbal paradigms with switch reference (*b*) combinations of nominalized verbs and case	Loosely organized subordinate clauses combining finite verbs with sentential markers
Relative clauses based on nominalization or correlative constructions	Relative clauses with specialized verbal paradigms sensitive to transitive-intransitive distinction leaving person of antecedent unmarked
Topic-comment construction with specialized discourse markers	Cleft constructions based on same principle as relative clauses
Many discourse markers or sentential suffixes	Some discourse markers or sentential suffixes

The Amuesha suffix -*(V:)kma* is similar in meaning to the Quechua distributive. It covers related meanings such as 'always', 'precisely', 'totally', 'of same sex', and it is used with demonstratives, possessive pronouns and adverbial expressions. Note that CV reversal (see §7) has applied to the first syllable of the suffix, not to the second.

(1) na:-kma
     1sg-DISTR
     Always me; Of same sex as me
     (DT 1997: 62)

(2) na:-nm-a:kma
     1sg-first-DISTR
     Always me first
     (DT 1997: 62)

(3) no:-kma
     1sgPOSS-DISTR
     (Several) of mine, all mine
     (DT 1997: 64)

(4) a:lʸ-oʰtʸ-e:kma
     there-ABL-DISTR
     Always from there
     (DT 1997: 126)

This suffix can occur twice with slightly different meanings.

(5) ya:-kma-:kma
     1plPOSS-DISTR¹-DISTR²
     All of them people of same sex as ours
     (DT 1998: 382)

The same element is contained in the ending -*(V:)kmanʸen* 'with all one's . . .'

(6) po-kš-e:nʸ-eʰš-o-:kmanʸen
     3sgPOSS-rejoice-NOMZ-COLL-INST-DISTR:INTENS
     With all his joy
     (DT 1998: 147)

8.1.2 *Case marker -paq*   The Amuesha case marker -*(V:)kop*, analysed as a 'referential case' in Duff-Tripp (1997), is similar in use and meaning to the Quechua benefactive case marker -*paq*. The suffix -*paq* has a well-defined place in the internal history of the Quechua language family. The shape of the suffix -*(V:)kop*, which contains two stops, is somewhat unusual for Amuesha, and, allowing for non-adjacent metathesis, one may hypothesize a formal connection with *-paq*. Given the limited, predominantly spatial character of the Amuesha case system, diffusion would not come as a surprise in the area of case marking.

(7) a:č-e:kop
     mother-BEN
     For mother
     (DT 1997: 36)
(8) no-:kop-pa'   ama   ne-mn-o
     1sgPOSS-BEN-TOP   NEG[1] 1sgA-want-NEG[2]
     As for me, I don't want it.
     (DT 1997: 175)

8.1.3 *Discourse marker -n^{y}a*   There is one sentential suffix in Amuesha that may have been borrowed from Quechua, namely *-n^{y}a*. In Duff-Tripp (1997) *-n^{y}a* is analysed as (*a*) an 'emphatic' or 'intensifier' and (*b*) as a 'marker of chronological and logical sequence' (see especially Duff-Tripp 1997: 232–8; Wise 1986: 626–31). An example of the second use is (9).

(9) al^y-empo-n^{y}a-pa$^?$ a:w-o$^?$ ot-a:n-e^{h}t-n^{y}a   korne$^h{}^y$sa$^?$
     there-time-SEQ-TOP AUX-REP   say-3plO-3plA-SEQ   chief
     Then the chief said to them: ...
     (DT 1997: 236)

In most Quechua dialects *-n^{y}a* indicates completion (compare English 'already'). It is often used in sequential contexts, where it resembles the second interpretation (*b*) of its homophonous counterpart in Amuesha. A problem is that *-n^{y}a* has not been found in the Yaru dialect complex, which has a free form *na:* instead. However, the use of *-n^{y}a* (and its reflex *-na*) is widely spread throughout Quechua, suggesting that it may have fallen out of use in Yaru at a relatively recent stage. A connection between the sequential uses of *-n^{y}a* in both languages seems likely (see also Wise forthcoming). It is difficult to decide whether emphatic *-n^{y}a* (*a*) is the result of a secondary development in Amuesha or whether it already existed before sequential *-n^{y}a* (*b*) was introduced.

8.1.4 *Post-base verbal morphology*   Quechua and Amuesha resemble each other in the richness of their post-base verbal morphology. Many categories are similar in meaning, but formal similarities are few. They may be due to diffusion or simply to coincidence. The semantic similarities may be significant at the level of Amerindian languages with complex derivational morphology in general, but not necessarily as a product of the Quechua–Amuesha contact situation in particular. Two suffixes that show formal similarity (allowing CV to VC reversal in Amuesha) are: (*a*) -*Vn^y*-'desiderative' (Duff-Tripp 1997: 107), -*na(:)*- in Quechua I but -*naya*- in Quechua II; and (*b*) -*V:r*- 'stative' (Duff-Tripp 1997: 104–5), -*ra(:)*- in Quechua I.

Duff-Tripp gives only two examples of a desiderative derivation (which evidently is not to be confounded with the homophonous frustrative marker of Amuesha). These examples illustrate a use which is strikingly similar to the Quechua desiderative.

(10)   Ø-m-oñ-eʔt-eːn
       3sgS-sleep-DESID-BUFFER[13]-DUR
       He is sleepy
       (DT 1997: 107)

Compare Yaru Quechua (11):

(11)   punu-na-ya-n
       sleep-DESID-DUR-3A:3O
       He is sleepy, He feels the need to sleep

In Quechua, desiderative expressions have an impersonal agent, whereas the affected person is encoded as an object. Unfortunately, the available examples do not allow us to determine whether this is also the case in Amuesha.

As in Quechua I, the Amuesha stative suffix refers to a state resulting from a previous or ongoing action. There is an interesting coincidence in the way this suffix combines and interacts with aspect in both languages. The Yaru dialect complex has separate markers for perfective, -*ru*-, and durative, -*ya(:)*-. Amuesha has only durative, -*eːn*, but the unmarked form can act as a perfective. This is illustrated with Quechua 'to sleep' in (12) and Amuesha 'to get drunk' in (13), from Duff-Tripp (1997: 90, 104).

(12)	punu-ru-n	sleep-PERV-3S	He (has) slept
	punu-ya-n	sleep-DUR-3S	He is asleep
	punu-ra-ru-n	sleep-STAT-PERV-3S	He got into a state of continuous sleep
	punu-ra-ya-n	sleep-STAT-DUR-3S	He is in a state of continuous sleep

[13] The term 'buffer' refers to suffixes that are used to separate members of distinct suffix classes or that follow suffixes which cannot occur in word-final position. These suffixes can be meaningful in other environments, but not in the combinations illustrated here.

(13)   Ø-po:saʔt   3S-get drunk   He (has) got drunk
        Ø-po:saʔt-e:n   3S-get drunk-DUR   He is drunk
        Ø-po:saʔt-a:r-eʔt   3S-get drunk-STAT-BUFFER   He got into a state
                                                        of drunkenness

        Ø-po:saʔt-a:r-e:n   3S-get drunk-STAT-DUR   He continues to be
                                                        in a drunken state

Wise (forthcoming) proposes a different etymology for the stative suffix in Amuesha, associating it with the ending -*V:r* of possessed nouns (e.g. *po-mn-a:rʔ* 'his loved one' in §7).

8.2 *Indirect grammatical diffusion*

The Arawak structural heritage of Amuesha has remained nearly intact, but some incipient cases of diffusion can tentatively be attributed to Quechua influence. It has been suggested (for instance, in Wise forthcoming) that the lack of grammatical gender in Amuesha (as opposed to the Campa and most other Arawak languages) may be due to the influence of Quechua, which also lacks grammatical gender. This may very well be true, but it should be observed that contact with another non-Arawak language (e.g. Panoan) could have produced the same effect. Furthermore, the loss of a distinction may also occur independently from any external pressure.

A comparable case is the existence of a reportative evidential marker (affix -*oʔ* or adverbial particle *a:w-oʔ*) in Amuesha. The important place of reportative evidentials in Quechua and Aymara is well known. However, a different source, such as Panoan, could also have triggered the introduction of the reportative, assuming that it is not the result of an internal development altogether. Reportative evidentials are widely found in Amazonian languages (Aikhenvald 2004). Wise (forthcoming) also mentions the possibility that the use of the topic markers -*qa* in Quechua and -*paʔ* in Amuesha in discourse strategies may represent an example of structural convergence. This would seem to be possible, under the reservation that topic markers are quite general in the world's languages.

The following cases are instances of positive structural coincidence between Amuesha and (Yaru) Quechua.

8.2.1 *Negation in two parts (an adverb and a suffix)*   The negation of main clauses in Amuesha is obtained by means of a frame consisting of the adverbial particle *ama* (*a:ma* according to Duff-Tripp 1998) in combination with an affix -*o*. The element *ama* 'not' (cf. §6) is clearly a Quechua loan. (Interestingly, a different negation marker *a:nʸ-* is used to carry the reportative suffix -*oʔ*.) In Quechua, *ama* is used in imperative and jussive sentences with

meanings such as 'don't' or 'hopefully not'. Both *ama* and *mana*, the declarative negation particle in Quechua, are used in a frame with a suffix (*-ču* in most dialects). Similar frames are used in the Aymaran languages.

(14) Quechua mana-m   muna-n-ču
                NEG[1]-WIT   want-3A-NEG[2]
                He/she does not want (it).

(15) Amuesha ama   Ø-m^{w}en-o
                NEG[1]   3sgA-want-NEG[2]
                He/she does/did not want (it)
                (DT 1997: 128, 1998: 243)

8.2.2 *Negative recommendation in affirmative form (apprehensive construction)*
This concerns the use of verbs in an affirmative optative or potential mood as a warning for events that should be prevented from happening.

(16) Quechua rata-ru-nki-man-taq
                fall-PERV-2S-OPT-SEQ
                Take care lest you may fall; Watch out not to fall!

(17) Amuesha pe-šo:r-a$^?$n-m^w-e:pa$^?$
                2sgS-fall-INCH-COMPL-OPT
                Take care lest you may fall; Watch out not to fall!
                (Wise 1986: 602)

8.2.3 *Reversal of affecter and affected in applicative constructions* Both Yaru Quechua and Amuesha have constructions in which the grammatical subject or actor of a verb can take the role of an affected entity by means of an applicative derivation on the verb. In Quechua this derivation is marked by *-pa-ku-*, a fixed suffix combination consisting of *-pa(:)-* 'applicative' and *-ku-* 'reflexive'; a transitive object then refers to the affecter. The Amuesha derivation (see also Wise 2002: 334–5) is marked by the applicative marker *-am^{y}p^y-* (*-am^{y}p-* before a front vowel); no cases with an affecter-object were found in Amuesha. It was not possible to find fully matching examples between the two languages for the constructions at issue, which are relatively infrequent. The main functions of *-pa-ku-* and *-am^{y}p^y-* are applicative (with the involvement of the actor as a beneficiary in the first case but retention of the actor role for A/S in both cases). As far as we know, the reversal construction has not been recorded in other Quechua dialects than Yaru. It shows that we are dealing with a rather special phenomenon, which may have had a place in the interaction between the two languages. There is no certainty about the direction of the diffusion in this case.

(18) Quechua qišpi-ru-:
       escape-PERV-1^S
       I (have) escaped

(19) Quechua suwa-ta-m   qišpi-paku-ru-:[14]
       thief-ACC-WIT   escape-APPL-REFL-PERV-1S
       I was affected by the thief's escape

(20) Amuesha Ø-čekmet-e:n   ca:p-o[15]
       3sgS-get dark-DUR   night-LOC
       It is getting dark at night
       (DT 1998: 152)

(21) Amuesha ye-čekmet-am^{y}p-es   t^{y}o:n^y-o
       1plS-get dark-APPLIC-BUFFER road-LOC
       We were overtaken by darkness on the road
       (DT 1997: 100)

8.2.4 *Incipient switch reference* The structure of complex sentences is one of the areas in which Quechua and Amuesha differ most. Whereas Amuesha favours a rather loose connection between subordinate clause and main clause, Quechua has a well-developed system of adverbial verbal paradigms with an explicit switch-reference distinction. These paradigms include obligatory encoding of the grammatical person of the subject of a subordinate clause, whenever it is not identical to the subject of the main clause. Duff-Tripp (1997: 193) discusses a construction in Amuesha that may be tentatively interpreted as some sort of incipient development towards an explicit switch-reference paradigm. The meaning of the construction is to indicate coincidence in point of time. It is unusual in several respects. It consists in a combination of a verb form containing the marker -*(a)c*, whose regular function is to indicate that the subject of the verb remains unspecified, with a suffix that normally encodes the grammatical person of an object (O) or a verbless clause subject (VCS). However, in this case the encoded person refers to the subject (S) of the (intransitive) verb, rather than to an object or a verbless clause subject. According to Duff-Tripp, such forms have to be treated as nominalizations in which the pronominal element indicates a possessor. However, person of possessor in Amuesha is normally indicated by prefixes, not by suffixes. The fact that an unspecified (privative) subject

[14] This example has been adapted from the Tarma subdialect, where its pronunciation is slightly different (*suwatam ... xišbibakuru*: Adelaar 1977: 147).

[15] The verb *čekmet-* 'to become dark' is curiously reminiscent of Quechua I *čaka-*, which has the same meaning. However, due to the presence of the unique element -*met*- we cannot be sure of its status as a loan. Note that the stem-final element -*et*- is analysed as an epenthetic suffix in Wise (2002).

marker and an object or verbless clause subject marker both appear to be used 'for the wrong purpose' in this construction strikes us as an attempt to express a category not previously existent in the language. With due caution we may venture the hypothesis that this is a case of grammatical diffusion triggered by the Quechua switch-reference practice.

(22) e$^{\textrm{?}}$n$^{\textrm{y}}$-e:pa$^{\textrm{?}}$t-ča$^{\textrm{?}}$ č-e:ž-c-ay-pa$^{\textrm{?}}$
      recently-SURPRIDE-FUT   arrive-ITER-PRIV-1pl-TOP
      ot-en
      3A-say-1sgO
      n-o$^{\textrm{h}}$č̣
      1sgPOSS-sister
      As soon as we came back, my sister said to me:...
      (DT 1997: 193)

8.2.5 *Accumulation of possessive markers*   In most Quechua dialects nouns can be marked for the person of a possessor by means of a set of personal reference suffixes. Speakers of Yaru Quechua occasionally use double possessor marking (that is, two different person markers). In that case the external marker refers to the 'owner' of the person indicated by the internal marker. A similar phenomenon has been recorded for Amuesha, where possessive prefixes can be cumulated (Duff-Tripp 1997: 35). Example (24) shows that not only the personal reference prefixes are cumulated, but also the possessed noun suffix *-(V)r* that goes with each of them.

(23) Quechua   pača-n-la-yki   nana-ya-n
                stomach-3POSS-DIM-2POSS   hurt-DUR-3S
                Your X's (baby's) stomach hurts
(24) Amuesha   no-p$^{\textrm{w}}$e$^{\textrm{?}}$-l$^{\textrm{y}}$o:m$^{\textrm{y}}$-r-er
                1sgPOSS-3POSS-seed-POSSN[1]-POSSN[2]
                Seed of X (=fruit) that belongs to me
                (DT 1998: 313)

The existence of possessive marker accumulation in both Amuesha and Yaru Quechua is a remarkable coincidence. In view of the rarity of this phenomenon in general it may not be entirely fortuitous.

9 Final considerations

Although the genealogical origin of Amuesha is unquestionably Arawak, it is also a layered language (see §2.1 and §2.4 of Chapter 1) containing several stages of borrowing, first from Quechua and then from Spanish, but possibly from other languages as well. Language contact between Quechua and Amuesha took place in a period preceding or during the Inca domination (probably about the fifteenth century). The contact situation was one of balanced contact (see §4.2.3 of Chapter 1). The social characteristics of this contact situation cannot be reconstructed beyond the level of speculation, but the introduction of Inca religion may have contributed to it, possibly in combination with local cults from the Yaru region and by way of religious specialists. The salt trade or possible early relations based on interchange between ecological levels may also have played a role. The Amuesha may have occupied a key position in the trade relations between the central Peruvian highlands and the Ucayali basin. The contact situation, which resulted in a huge quantity of lexical borrowing, both cultural and non-cultural, has long been completed (cf. §3.2 of Chapter 1). There are probably no recent loans from Quechua.

In spite of abundant borrowing and possible phonological remodelling due to Quechua influence, the observable effects of language contact on Amuesha structure are meagre. They appear to be limited to very specialized constructions of a non-essential character. Any assessment of the amount of indirect diffusion from Quechua to Amuesha will have to take into account the position of Amuesha within the Arawak family and its relations with the neighbouring Campa languages. There seems to be a contradiction between close structural parallelisms (e.g. non-possessed forms, the formation of relative clauses, the behaviour of the reflexive suffix, etc.) uniting these languages and the striking differences noticeable in the lexicon. Are the similarities due to common inheritance or to intra-Arawak language contact? How much borrowing has been going on between Amuesha and its neighbour languages on the Amazonian side? Does Amuesha form a genealogical subgroup with Chamicuro? Is there more Panoan influence than has been detected so far? How come Amuesha has changed so much? What other influences, apart from Quechua, may have been responsible for this? All these questions will have to be answered before we can fully appreciate the modifying force generated by the Quechua impact.

For the moment one of the most intriguing questions about Amuesha is the provenance of a substantial amount of linguistic form that cannot be easily explained by assuming an Arawak, Panoan, or Quechua origin. Superficial similarities seem to point in different directions and open the road to speculation. What are we to think, for instance, of lexical coincidences with outlying languages such as Aguaruna (*mama* 'manioc' vs. Amuesha *ma:m*) or Mosetén (*pʰen* 'woman' vs. Amuesha *peno* 'female', cf. Sakel 2004), etc.? The existence of incorporated nominal elements (nominal classifiers) in Amuesha is at the basis of scores of double forms in the nominal lexicon, including one

Arawak and one non-Arawak form in many cases. Quechua influence plays no role in this. Root-internal vowel suppression is reminiscent of Cholón, and monosyllabic roots with palatalizations are suggestive of the lost language of the Chachapoyas culture further north (cf. Taylor 1990). What all these languages have in common is that they are or were spoken by Preandine groups of undetermined linguistic affiliation, which may have been present in the area before the arrival of the Arawak peoples. It would not be surprising if the Amuesha were Arawakanized descendants of one of these groups. This may help to bring the role of Quechua diffusion in Amuesha into a proper perspective.

References

Adelaar, W. F. H. 1977. *Tarma Quechua: grammar, texts, dictionary.* Lisse: Peter de Ridder Press.

—— 1986. 'La relación quechua-aru: perspectivas para la separación del léxico', *Revista Andina* 4. 2: 379–426.

—— 2004. 'The Quechua language family', pp. 179–259 of *The languages of the Andes*, by W. F. H. Adelaar with P. C. Muysken. Cambridge: Cambridge University Press.

Aikhenvald, A. Y. 1999. 'Arawak', pp. 65–106 of *The Amazonian languages*, by R. M. W. Dixon and A. Y. Aikhenvald. Cambridge: Cambridge University Press.

—— 2004. *Evidentiality.* Oxford: Oxford University Press.

Alexander, A. 2005. *Eighteenth century Cholón.* Utrecht: Netherlands Graduate School of Linguistics (LOT) and Leiden University Centre for Linguistics.

Black, N., with Bolli, V. and Ticsi Zárate, E. 1990. *Lecciones para el aprendizaje del quechua del sureste de Pasco y el norte de Junín.* Yarinacocha: Dirección Departamental de Educación-Pasco and Instituto Lingüístico de Verano.

Cerrón-Palomino, R. M. 1976. *Diccionario quechua Junín-Huanca.* Lima: Ministerio de Educación and Instituto de Estudios Peruanos.

—— 2003. *Lingüística quechua,* 2nd edn. Cuzco: Centro Bartolomé de Las Casas.

Chase Smith, R. 1974. *The Amuesha people of central Peru: their struggle to survive.* IWGIA Documents 16. Copenhagen: International Workgroup of Indigenous Affairs.

Chirinos Rivera, A. 2001. *Atlas lingüístico del Perú.* Cuzco: Centro Bartolomé de Las Casas.

Duff, M. 1957. 'A syntactical analysis of an Amuesha (Arawak) text', *International Journal of American Linguistics* 23: 171–8.

Duff-Tripp, M. 1997. *Gramática del idioma Yanesha' (Amuesha).* Serie Lingüística Peruana 43. Lima: Ministerio de Educación and Instituto Lingüístico de Verano.

—— 1998. *Diccionario del idioma Yanesha' (Amuesha).* Serie Lingüística Peruana 47. Lima: Ministerio de Educación and Instituto Lingüístico de Verano.

Fast, P. W. 1953. 'Amuesha (Arawak) phonemes', *International Journal of American Linguistics* 19: 191–4.

González Holguín, D. 1608. *Vocabulario de la lengua general de todo el Peru llamada lengua qquichua o del Inca.* Lima: Francisco del Canto (reprinted Lima: Universidad Nacional Mayor de San Marcos, 1989).

McQuown, N. A. 1955. 'The indigenous languages of Latin America', *American Anthropologist* 57: 501–70.

Mannheim, B. 1991. *The language of the Inka since the European invasion.* Austin: University of Texas Press.

Park, M., Weber, N. and Cenepo Sangama, V. 1976. *Diccionario quechua San-Martín.* Lima: Ministerio de Educación and Instituto de Estudios Peruanos.

Parker, G. J. 1963. 'La clasificación genética de los dialectos quechuas', *Revista del Museo Nacional* 32: 241–52.

Parker, S. G. 1991. *Estudios sobre la fonología del chamicuro.* Serie Lingüística Peruana 30. Yarinacocha: Ministerio de Educación and Instituto Lingüístico de Verano.

—— with Orbe, G. and Patow A. 1987. *Vocabulario y textos chamicuro.* Yarinacocha: Instituto Lingüístico de Verano.

Payne, D. L. 1991. 'Maipuran (Arawakan)', pp. 355–499 of *Handbook of Amazonian languages*, Vol. 3, edited by D. C. Derbyshire and G. K. Pullum. Berlin: Mouton de Gruyter.

Pozzi-Escot, I. 1998. *El multilingüismo en el Perú.* Cuzco: Centro Bartolomé de Las Casas.

Sakel, J. 2004. *A grammar of Mosetén.* Berlin: Mouton de Gruyter.

Shaver, H. 1996. *Diccionario nomatsiguenga-castellano castellano-nomatsiguenga.* Serie Lingüística Peruana 41. Yarinacocha: Ministerio de Educación and Instituto Lingüístico de Verano.

Taylor, A. C. 1999. 'The western margins of Amazonia from the early sixteenth century to the early nineteenth century', pp. 188–256 of *The Cambridge history of the native peoples of the Americas*, Vol. 3: *South America*, Part 2, edited by F. Salomon and S. Schwartz. Cambridge: Cambridge University Press.

Taylor, D. M. 1954. 'A note on the status of Amuesha', *International Journal of American Linguistics* 20: 240–1.

Taylor, G. 1990. 'La lengua de los antiguos chachapuyas', pp. 121–39 of *Temas de lingüística amerindia: Actas del Primer congreso nacional de investigaciones lingüístico filológicas, Lima 1987*, edited by R. M. Cerrón-Palomino and G. Solís Fonseca. Lima: Consejo Nacional de Ciencia y Tecnología.

Tello, J. C. 1913. 'Algunas conexiones gramaticales de las lenguas campa, ipurina, moxa, baure, amuesha, goajira, del grupo o familia arawak o maipure', *Revista Universitaria* 8. 1: 506–32. Lima: Universidad Nacional Mayor de San Marcos.

Torero Fernández de Córdova, A. A. 1964. 'Los dialectos quechuas', *Anales científicos de la Universidad Agraria* 2. 4: 446–78.

—— 1974. *El quechua y la historia social andina.* Lima: Universidad Ricardo Palma.

Varese, S. 1968. *La sal de los cerros.* Lima: Universidad Peruana de Ciencias y Tecnología.

Weber, D. J., Cayco Zambrano, F., Cayco Villar, T. and Ballena Dávila, M. 1998. *Rimaycuna. Quechua de Huánuco: diccionario del quechua del Huallaga con índices castellano e inglés.* Serie Lingüística Peruana 48. Lima: Instituto Lingüístico de Verano.

Wise, M. R. 1963. 'Six levels of structure in Amuesha (Arawak) verbs', *International Journal of American Linguistics* 29: 132–52.

—— 1976. 'Apuntes sobre la influencia inca entre los amuesha: factor que oscurece la clasificación de su idioma', *Revista del Museo Nacional* 42: 355–66.

—— 1986. 'Preandine Arawakan', pp. 567–642 of *Handbook of Amazonian languages*, Vol. 1, edited by D. C. Derbyshire and G. K. Pullum. Berlin: Mouton de Gruyter.

—— 2002. 'Applicative affixes in Peruvian Amazonian languages', pp. 329–44 of *Current studies on South American languages: selected papers from the 50th international congress of Americanists in Warsaw and the Spinoza workshop on Amerindian languages in Leiden, 2000,* edited by M. Crevels, S. van de Kerke, S. Meira, and H. van der Voort. ILLA Series 3. Leiden: Research School of Asian, African and Amerindian Studies (CNWS).

—— Forthcoming. 'Loans in Yanesha': a glimpse of language contacts in the Andean foothills'.

MAP 1 The original territory of the Amuesha people and the Yaru Quechua dialect area

Source: www.expedia.com, Chase Smith (1974).

χ = approximate locations of present-day Amuesha communities.

13

Feeling the Need
The Borrowing of Cariban Functional Categories into Mawayana (Arawak)[1]

EITHNE B. CARLIN

1 Introduction

This chapter deals with a situation of language contact over a period of some 150 years in the southern Guianas that has resulted *inter alia* in the borrowing, across language families, of a pronoun to express first person plural exclusive, and some functional categories pertaining to nominal past tense marking, affective and frustrative marking, and the marking of a noun to express change of state. All of these borrowed categories into Mawayana are obligatory in the Cariban languages. Lexical borrowing in either direction between Mawayana and the Cariban languages is minimal.

§2 gives an overview of what we know about the Mawayana people and their history of contact up to the present. §3 gives a typological linguistic profile of Mawayana based on data collected in Suriname. §4 shows the instances of contact-induced change in Mawayana, looking at the borrowing of a pronominal form *amna* to express first person plural exclusive (§4.1); nominal past marking (§4.2); the affective marker *_kwe* (§4.3); the use of the frustrative marker *_muku* (§4.4), and the borrowing of the similative, a category that is essential in the Cariban languages (§4.5).[2] Conclusions are given in §5.

---

[1] I would like to thank Maarten Mous and the editors of the volume for their invaluable suggestions and comments on this chapter. All remaining errors are my own.
[2] In this chapter, enclitics are indicated by a preceding underscore.

2 The Mawayana, past and present

The Mawayana (literally: 'Frog People') are a small Arawak group who live in the southern Guianas, in the frontier corner of Brazil, Guyana, and Suriname, and whose language is closely related to Wapishana. Since the Mawayana are generally subsumed under the term Waiwai it is not known how many ethnic Mawayana there are, except for the community in Suriname where almost 100 people claim Mawayana ethnicity. We know very little of the early history of the Mawayana, their first possible mentioning as Mapoyena being from Fray Francisco de San Marcos in 1725 (see Rivière 1963: 153). Since the first definite reference to the Mawayana in the literature in 1841, however, the history of the Mawayana has been intertwined with and has run parallel to that of consecutively the Taruma group on the one hand, and, on the other hand, the Waiwai groups within which Mawayana is now included. It was the naturalist Robert Schomburgk who reported Mawayana presence in the area to the east of the Parukoto (Cariban) people and not far from the Taruma people (Schomburgk 1841:170). When Schomburgk actually met some Mawayana in 1843, he gave their number as about thirty-nine individuals in one settlement living close to and in constant contact with a group of Taruma who, as requested by the Mawayana, had moved in order to be close to them (Schomburgk 1845: 55). Since the Taruma chief was also acting as chief over the Mawayana we can conclude that relations were indeed friendly and close. Population numbers of most Amerindian groups in the area were declining drastically at Schomburgk's time, mainly due to outbreaks of smallpox and other illnesses, and intermarriage between the smallest groups was prevalent. Thirty years later, in the 1870s, the explorer Barrington Brown mentions meeting up with a group of Mawayana and Taruma together and established that they maintained trading relations with the Wapishana and the Waiwai (Brown 1876: 247–51). Indeed throughout the nineteenth century, the southern Guyana region was a hub of trading activity that spanned most of the Amerindian groups as well as the Maroons on the Surinamese side of the Corentyne River, with the Taruma a major link in all trade relations.[3] At that time, and indeed since the migration of the Taruma from the Rio Negro some time after 1732 until the end of the nineteenth century, we find

---

[3] The term Maroons refers to runaway slaves from plantations during the early colonial period in Suriname, who now form distinct ethnic groups in the interior of Suriname, namely the Ndyuka, Saramaccans, Paramaccans, Kwinti, and Matawai. It was predominantly with the Ndyuka that trade relations were upheld with the Amerindian populations.

several references to the trading acumen of the Taruma who had become quite an influential group before, presumably, disease reduced their numbers dramatically. This influence is also corroborated by the many place names of Taruma origin found in the south of Guyana. From the mid-nineteenth century onwards, the Taruma are hardly mentioned without reference to the Mawayana with whom they had intermarried in spite of a reported aversion to marrying outside their own group (see Schomburgk 1845). In the early twentieth century the numbers of Mawayana had surpassed those of the Taruma: Farabee (1918: 172) estimated the number of Mawayana as around 100, and the Taruma as about 50. In the early 1920s, the anthropologist/archaeologist Walter Roth claimed that the Taruma had all but become extinct as a separate group, which is corroborated by the missionary Father Cary-Elwes's statements that in mid-1922 he had advised the Taruma to intermarry with the Waiwai: 'Last time I was here [1919, EBC], I told the Tarumas that they were a sickly lot and clearly dying out, due probably to their in-marriage, and their only chance of survival was for them to take unto themselves Waiwai wives' (Butt-Colson and Morton 1982: 240; see also Rivière 1963: 164). In spite of their incessant precarious situation over the last two centuries, there are still three Taruma speakers in Guyana, living among the Wapishana. The Mawayana in the meantime are mentioned sporadically in the literature, in the Mapuera region which is still the home of a large Waiwai-speaking group today, and by the late 1950s they were already being absorbed by the Waiwai.

In view of the complex history of shuffling and reshuffling identities and ethnicities which was characteristic of the southern Guianas regions, the ethnic term Waiwai is now used to refer to a conglomeration of ethnic groups, namely the Parukoto, Shereo, Tunayana, Katuena, Karafawyana, Mawayana,

TABLE 1. The Waiwai groups

Group	Linguistic affiliation
Parukoto	Cariban
Shereo	Cariban
Tunayana	Cariban
Katuena	Cariban
Karafawyana	Cariban
Mawayana	Arawak
Taruma	Unclassified

and Taruma.[4] As shown in Table 1, all of these groups are of the Cariban linguistic stock, specifically the Guyana branch of the family, with the exception of the latter two. Mawayana belongs to the Arawak language family and Taruma is an as yet unclassified language. What is known as the Waiwai language is actually a lingua franca which has at least two main dialects, Tunayana, and Karafawyana, the latter of which, according to the Tunayana and Katuena speakers in Suriname, is the 'nicer' and more elaborated dialect. The original language before amalgamation of the groups was apparently Parukoto, also the name of the group who had most input into the formation of the lingua franca. At some time in the early twentieth century the Parukoto ceased calling themselves by that name and were subsumed under the name Waiwai. Thus the remaining language Waiwai is itself a hybrid based on several Cariban dialects that were closely related to Parukoto (see also Hawkins 1998). The input of Mawayana and Taruma to the Waiwai language seems to have been minimal if present at all; rather there are clear indications that the Waiwai lingua franca, and later Trio, likewise a Cariban language, have had quite some impact on the structure of Mawayana.

2.1 *The Mawayana speech community, language attitudes, and patterns of language use*

From the 1950s onwards it looked as though the Mawayana would remain for outsiders an inconspicuous group absorbed by the Waiwai, which is already the case in Brazil and Guyana, where only a few old people still remember some of their former language. However, a strange turn of fate saw the preservation of the language in a Mawayana group in diaspora in the south of Suriname. In the early 1960s, an American missionary who had been active among the Waiwai in Guyana and Brazil set off on an evangelizing mission to the Trio (Cariban), in Suriname, taking with him some 'Waiwai', who were actually ethnic Mawayana, Tunayana, and Katuena. At present these groups reside in the predominantly Trio village Kwamalasamutu, in the Sipaliwini Basin. The originally Waiwai-speaking groups in this village in Suriname together number some 200–300 people who are increasingly becoming monolingual Trio speakers. The ethnic Mawayana community in Kwamalasamutu numbers some 100–150 people, but the number of speakers of Mawayana has

---

[4] Both Hawkins (1998) and Howard (2001) who carried out research among the Waiwai in Guyana and Brazil include Sikïiyana (Chikyana) among the Waiwai groups: in general, although the Sikïiyana do speak Waiwai, they are not perceived, either linguistically, or socially, as constituting part of the present-day Waiwai groups. For this reason I have excluded the Sikïiyana here. However, given that they reside in the Surinamese village Kwamalasamutu, where the remaining Mawayana speakers live, they are mentioned below in the description of the social structure of that village.

declined to the last three of the oldest generation, that is, those first native missionaries. These are the community leader and his wife, and his wife's half-sister. The Kwamalasamutu Mawayana are thus the only Mawayana-speaking community of importance left. The linguistic competences of the ethnic Mawayana in Suriname vary considerably according to generations. In Table 2, I give an overview of the language use patterns that are found among the ethnic Mawayana in Suriname.

As can be seen in Table 2, the older generations of Mawayana are trilingual, younger generations are bilingual, and the youngest generation is monolingual in Trio which is the dominant language of the village. In contrast to the Waiwai groups, the Trio are highly monolingual although some few may have a passive knowledge of Waiwai. As shown above, even the oldest generation of Mawayana speak Trio, and the ethnic Mawayana in Kwamalasamutu now all speak Trio as their only or primary language respectively; however, this is not to say that the older generations who learned Trio as their third or even second language ever learned to master Trio fully or with the competence of a native

TABLE 2. Speech patterns of the ethnic Mawayana in Suriname

Generation of ethnic Mawayana	Languages spoken with whom
oldest (+/−75 years)	Mawayana among each other (3 people); Waiwai with their own children and with other Waiwai groups; Trio with their grandchildren, great-grandchildren, and all other villagers
second generation (+/−60 years)	Waiwai with their parents and their own children, and with other Waiwai groups; Waiwai and increasingly Trio with their grandchildren; Trio with all other villagers
third generation (+/−40 years	Waiwai with Waiwai speakers of older and peer groups; decreasingly Waiwai and increasingly Trio with their own children; Trio with all other villagers
fourth generation (+/−22 years)	Trio with everyone although they may have a passive knowledge of Waiwai
fifth generation (<20 years)	Trio only

originally Trio speaker. In fact, many of the more complex grammatical aspects of Trio were never fully mastered by the non-Trio groups. Indeed, the fact that the non-Trio groups were numerically so large in the village of Kwamalasamutu rapidly led to some changes in Trio, namely simplification and sometimes reanalysis (see Carlin 2004: 9–11). The ethnic Mawayana belong to the village elite, and hold high positions in the Western-style polyclinic. Of the other Waiwai-speaking groups, the Tunayana are well represented and dominant in the church elders' council and the Sikiiyana, who are considered to be experts in medicinal plants, run the traditional polyclinic. Thus in all, the Waiwai-speaking group in Kwamalasamutu, taken as a whole, is politically and socially quite dominant. Normally, however, this dominance does not immediately translate into a linguistic dominance: Trio remains the dominant language of the village. There is, however, a good deal of linguistic chauvinism as evidenced by the prevailing language attitude in the village in as far as Waiwai is regarded as being more or less on a par with Trio, but Mawayana, and also Sikiiyana, are regarded as lesser languages, just the old people's jokes. At least that was the general feeling before language documentation of Mawayana started, after which Mawayana became a very real language in the eyes of all the villagers, and in the eyes of the speakers themselves it has become an important and valuable language, one which offers an excuse for their not being able to speak perfect Trio.

There has been no borrowing whatsoever from Mawayana into Trio, either grammatically or lexically. Given the sociolinguistic situation sketched above and the negative language attitude towards the minority obsolescent languages, and taking into account the fact that all the groups involved are relatively homogeneous culturally so that the borrowing of new words along with new concepts was not neccssary, this is hardly surprising. The question remains, however, as to whether or not Mawayana has had any influence on Waiwai. It would seem not, although more in-depth research on Waiwai may in the future require this statement to be revised somewhat. There has been a negligible number of lexical borrowings, the most notable one being *kamu* 'sun' in Waiwai, which is a loan from an Arawak language, possibly Mawayana. In addition, other lexical cognates in Waiwai, Wapishana, Trio, Mawayana, and Taruma are found in the specific semantic domains of flora and fauna where we find lexical items that are common to the entire larger Guyana area but it is not possible to determine the direction of borrowing.

What is evident, however, is that certain functional and pragmatic pan-Cariban features have been borrowed into Mawayana, presumably from Waiwai, which were then reinforced under influence from Trio. The features of contact-induced change in Mawayana are dealt with below in §4 after a short linguistic profile of the language.

3 Linguistic profile of Mawayana

At the current stage of research, it would appear that the closest genetic relative of Mawayana is Wapishana. The two languages share a large portion of the basic vocabulary. Both exhibit grammatical patterns that are common to many Arawak languages, for example, the pronominal system, the reflexes of the attributive prefix *ka-*, the negation marker *ma-*, and the like. Mawayana exhibits many Arawak features, that is, it is polysynthetic, has head marking, it is mainly suffixal but also has prefixes for the person markers on the main word classes noun (1), verb, and postposition (2). Mawayana has an attributive (3) and a privative prefix (4). The suffixes are mostly derivational; gender is also marked by means of suffixes but is not productive.

(1) n-kïnï   'my spirit song'
(2) n-siima   'with me'
     ï-buuka   'towards you'
(3) k-etinu-re-sï   jimaada
     ATTRIB-kin-POSS-3   jaguar
     Jaguar had family (i.e. he wasn't alone)
(4) mï-ūsū   'without a wife'

Transitive verbs take prefixes to mark the A argument and suffixes to mark the O (5). Intransitive verbs generally, but not always, mark the S by means of a suffix (6). In addition, the S/O markers are cliticized to the verbal negation and conditional markers *ma-* and *a-* respectively (7) and (8).

(5) (a) rï-kataba-na   (b) n-kataba-sï
          3A-catch.PAST-1O   1A-catch.PAST-3O
          He grabbed me   I grabbed him

(6) (b) tõwã-nã̱_kwe   (b) tõwã-sï
          sleep.PAST-1S_AFF   sleep.PAST-3S
          Unfortunately   He fell asleep.
          I fell asleep

(7) na   kaa-tïna   ma-sï   tõwẽ_kwe
     DISC   INTER-who   NEG-3S   sleep.PRES_AFF
     Well, who doesn't sleep then?

(8) nnu   a-na   mauda   chika-dza   Mawayana
     1PN   when-1S   die   NEG.PART-COMPL   Mawayana
     When *I* die there will be no Mawayana left at all

Phonologically Mawayana has a four-way vowel system, as does Wapishana, namely a high front unrounded vowel realized as *i/e*; a high back rounded vowel realized as *o/u*; low (back) *a*; and a high central *ɨ*. The Cariban languages, on the other hand, have six or seven vowels, the vowels of Waiwai being *i, e, ɨ, u, o, a*. Both Waiwai and Mawayana are lacking the mid-central vowel *ë* that Trio has. In addition, Waiwai, Mawayana, Taruma, and Wapishana have nasal vowels and unlike Trio they all have two implosive consonants, *ɗ* and *ɓ*. Mawayana and Wapishana have a retroflex fricativized rhotic *řž* in common that none of the other languages has, which may be indicative of a shared innovation.

4 Contact-induced change in Mawayana

The instances of contact-induced change to the structure of Mawayana that are dealt with in the following sections are: the borrowing of a pronominal form to express person 1+3 'we (exc)'; and the borrowing of functional categories of nominal tense marking, marking of affective, on nouns or verbs, to express the speaker's attitude of 'pity' or 'recognition of unfortunate circumstance'; marking a similative 'as if' on nominals; and the marking of frustrative on verbs. All of these features, with the exception of affective marking, are obligatory in the Cariban languages.

4.1 *The borrowing of a pronominal form*

Originally Mawayana had three exponents of the category of person, 1, 2, and 3. The relevant Cariban languages, Waiwai and Trio, have four exponents of the category of person, that is, 1, 2, 1+2, and 3, with an additional semantic 1+3 person, which is morphologically a combination of first and third person, first for evidential value (on verbs) and third for person agreement (all relevant word classes). In their daily speech, when speaking Waiwai and Trio, the Mawayana are required to use the distinction between first person plural inclusive and exclusive. When speaking Mawayana, a language only spoken in the home, the speakers apparently felt there to be a gap in their pronominal system left by having only one marker (*wa-*) in their own language for the first person plural without an inclusive/exclusive distinction. The Mawayana filled this gap by borrowing the Waiwai pronoun *amna* to express the concept of first person plural exclusive. The Trio counterpart of *amna*, namely *ainja*, exhibits different surface morphosyntactic behaviour from *amna* and although Mawayana uses the pronoun from Waiwai, it oscillates between the behavioural pattern of the Trio and the Waiwai first person exclusive. In both Cariban languages the pronoun is obligatory and as such acts like an independent noun. In Trio the pronoun is used in combination with the third person prefix *i-* (Ø before vowels) on a noun in possessive constructions, as shown in (9a), and as an argument on a postposition (9b). In Waiwai, the possessed noun preceded by *amna* has a zero third person prefix before a consonant-initial element and a prefix *y-* before a vowel-initial element as exemplified by the possessed noun in (9c) and by the inflected postposition in (9d). As these examples show, the Waiwai construction is identical to the Trio but the surface allomorphy is reversed, that is, *y-* before vowel-initial nouns or postpositions, and zero before consonant-initial elements[5].

(9) (a) ainja i-pakoro   'our (exc) house'   (Trio)
     (b) ainja Ø-akërë   'with us (exc)'   (Trio)
     (c) amna krapa-n[6]   'our (exc) bow'   (Waiwai)
     (d) amna y-akro   'with us (exc)'   (Waiwai)

In Mawayana, when nominal possessive constructions are formed with *amna*, the third person prefix is never used, rather the noun is left unmarked as shown in (10a). The original Mawayana equivalent is given in (10b). As these examples show, Mawayana now distinguishes between a first person plural inclusive and exclusive by using the original first person plural possessive prefix *wa-* to express inclusivity and the borrowed pronoun *amna* and the possessive construction from Waiwai, which is identical to the Trio construction, to express exclusivity. Mawayana simplifies the form of the possessed noun, leaving it zero marked, which is an option in both Trio (with vowel-initial elements) and Waiwai (with consonant-intial elements), reconciling thus partly with both languages by choosing the simplest form.

(10) (a) amna saruuka   (b) wa-saruuka
          1+3PN fishtrap   1pl.POSS-fishtrap
          Our (exc) fishtrap   Our (inc) fishtrap

With verbs in both Waiwai and Trio, person 1+3 is expressed by means of the pronoun (*amna* and *ainja*) in combination with the prefix of the third person marked on the verb: the form of the prefix is *n-* in both languages. In Trio the third person prefix on the verb is always marked but in Waiwai some high-frequency verbs, such as 'say', 'come', and 'go', drop the third person prefix.[7]

---

[5] This is actually a simplified version of reality: in Trio a reflex of the relational prefix which is encoded in the glide in Waiwai is found in vowel-initial elements (see Carlin 2004: 74 ff.). However, this does not affect the argumentation presented here.

[6] The final *-n* in this example is a possessive suffix.

[7] In Trio the third person personal prefix is only dropped whenever the verb is immediately preceded by an overt lexical object. This is not the case in Waiwai.

Mawayana, on the other hand, when using the pronoun *amna* with the high-frequency verb *me* 'say' consistently marks the verb with the third person prefix *rï-* thus following the Trio but not the Waiwai pattern, as shown in (11a). Example (11b) shows the original Mawayana first person plural prefix *wa-* in use.

(11) (a) amna   rï-me   ALSO: rï-me amna
           1+3PN   3A-say.PRES
           We (exc) say

      (b) wa-me
           1pl-say.PRES
           We (inc) say

As in Waiwai and Trio, when *amna* is the subject it can occur either before or after the verb in Mawayana; see (11a). However, in most of the occurrences of *amna* as the subject of a verb, with the exception of the verb 'say' as stated above, Mawayana does not mark the verb with the third person prefix, leaving the verb unmarked: examples are given in (12a–b).

(12) (a) amna   chake
           1+3PN   go.PRES
           We're going back

      (b) atïmara   amna   karara-ɗe
           fish sp.   1+3PN   catch.with.rod-IT.PRES
           We're going to catch *anjumara* (Hoplias Aimara) with a rod

Thus Mawayana has in common with Waiwai that it treats a high-frequency verb differently but while Waiwai uses no marking for these verbs, Mawayana does use a third person prefix *rï-* for the verb 'say' as both Waiwai and Trio do for other verbs for which Mawayana uses no third person marking.

To sum up, Mawayana has introduced the grammatical marking of a first person exclusive by the obligatory use of a pronoun borrowed from Waiwai, and also by copying the Waiwai pattern of usage. Mawayana also copies the Waiwai pattern in that the high-frequency verb *me* 'say' is treated differently from other verbs; namely for this verb it copies the Trio practice of using a prefix, rather than no marker at all. The marker itself, namely *rï-*, is the regular third person of Mawayana, and thus not a plural marker, and in this respect Mawayana follows the pattern of both Waiwai and Trio.

4.2 *Nominal past*

Nominal past marking is widespread and obligatory in the Cariban languages and is used to express former possession, a deceased possessor, a dead entity, or a referent that is useless or no longer usable. There is no doubt that nominal past as a category in Mawayana has emerged due to contact with the Cariban languages, in particular Waiwai. Mawayana's closest relative Wapishana does not have nominal past marking. The form of the nominal past marker in Mawayana is -*ba* which is suffixed to a nominal element; when the nominal ends in a vowel, that vowel changes to *e* before past marking. The forms and meanings expressed by the nominal past in Waiwai are given in Table 3. Apart from the two nominal past tense markers -*tho/-thïrï* and -*nhïrï/-nho*, Waiwai has what Hawkins (1998: 129) calls a modifying particle *pen* that is used to express that the referent which precedes it is 'dead' or 'gone' or in some way deserving of 'pity'. This function of marking a referent as 'past', 'dead', or 'gone' is collapsed in other Cariban languages (e.g. Trio and Wayana) and is expressed by the suffixal past tense markers. In Mawayana, the functions are also collapsed and marked by the marker -*ba*, but exclude the expression of 'pity', which is present in the semantics of Waiwai *pen*, rather expressing this meaning by means of an affective marker _*kwe* which is dealt with in §4.3 below.

The meanings expressed by the nominal past -*ba* in Mawayana are the following, exemplified in (13a–e):

- former: possessed (13a) and non-possessed (13b) nouns;
- past possession: possessed nouns and nominals (13d–e);
- dead: nouns (13b);
- gone: nouns (13c).

These examples show nominal past marking exactly where it would be required in the Cariban languages, with the exception of 'dead' in (13b) which is not found in Trio. Similar equivalents exist in Trio for all of these examples in (13). In (14a–b) I give only the Trio equivalents of the nominal-ized forms in (13d–e) respectively; as can be seen, the forms are structurally identical (notwithstanding some verbal marking required in Trio to mark verb types).

TABLE 3. Forms and meanings expressed by nominal past in Waiwai

Form	Meaning (marked on)
-tho/-thïrï	former; past possession (possessed nouns)
-nhïrï/-nho	former; past possession (nominalized verbs; non-possessed nouns)
pen	dead, gone, pity

(13) (a) r-ūsūre-ba_koso   chacha
           3POSS-wife-PAST_REP   cry.PAST
           His wife cried

      (b) ɗu   tõ   mauɗa_koso jimaaɗe-b a_kwe
           ideo.hit. ground ideo.die   die.PAST_REP jaguar-PAST⁻AFF
           Poor jaguar fell down and died

      (c) adze   n-mĩĩse-ba   rï-ma_ku-sï
           where.PAST 1POSS-husband-PAST   3A-say.PAST_PERSIST-3O
           'Where has my husband got to?' she kept saying

      (d) a'u-riki   ï-chaka   n-chĩĩyā-se-ba-riki
           DEM.DIST-DIR 2-go   1POSS-be-NOMZ-PAST-DIR
           Go over there to where I was! (to my former place of being)

      (e) ⁿjee   katabi-ke-ba   jimaaɗa
           human.being   catch-AG.NOMZ-PAST   jaguar
           Jaguar used to catch people (jaguar was a catcher of people)

(14) (a) irë-pona   të-kë   ji-w-eh-topo-npë-pona
           DEM.INAN.ANA-DIR   go-IMP.SG   1POSS-1TR-be-TMP.NOMZ-PAST-DIR
           Go over there to where I was!

      (b) wïtoto   apëi-ne-npë   teese   kaikui
           human.being catch-AG.NOMZ-PAST   he.was   jaguar
           Jaguar used to catch people

The Waiwai element *-pen* differs slightly in meaning from the suffixal past markers since besides the function of marking a human referent as 'past', that is, 'dead', it can also express the notion of 'gone' and 'deserving of pity', as shown in (15a–b) from Hawkins (1998: 129).

(15) (a) [ahtao na] n-Ø-a-y   Raatu   pen
           wherever   3s-be-SF-UNP   Rod   gone
           Who knows where Rod (a friend) is?

      (b) tuuna   ɲ-ekama   oy-akno   pen
           rain   3s-receive.s/thing.undesirable+TP   1POSS-brother pity
           My poor brother caught a lot of rain

Thus the scheme for Mawayana relative to Waiwai and Trio as regards nominal past marking with the suffixes and the so-called particle *pen* is given in Table 4.

Thus Mawayana has introduced the category of 'former' marking on nominals which is an obligatorily marked category in Waiwai and Trio. The marker itself, *-ba*, is different from the markers in Waiwai and Trio and its

TABLE 4. Nominal past marking

Meaning	Mawayana	Waiwai	Trio
former, past possession	*-ba*	*-tho/-thïrï; -nhïrï/-nho*	*-npë, -hpë*
dead	*-ba*	*pen*	*-npë, -hpë*
gone	(*-ba*) or *_kwe* (affective enclitic)	*pen*	—
pity	*_kwe*	*pen*	—

origin is as yet unknown. The semantic range of the Mawayana past marker shows the Waiwai pattern in that the marker is also used for the meaning 'dead'. At the same time it also shows Trio influence in that one form is used for all meanings where Waiwai uses two different markers. It also shows Trio influence in its exclusion of the semantic aspect of 'pity' for this 'former' marker. This latter aspect is expressed in Mawayana by a different marker, namely, by the affective enclitic *_kwe* which is dealt with in the following section.

4.3 *The affective marker _kwe*

Affectivity, that is, the notion that someone is deserving of pity, or is (has been or will be) adversely affected by an action or state, can be expressed by means of an interjection in Mawayana, Waiwai, Wapishana; the forms, which are clearly related, are as follows:

Affective interjections
>   Mawayana: okwe
>   Wapishana: kowas
>   Waiwai: okwe

Trio only knows one interjection, *pë*, to express the general notion of 'oh dear!' or 'how terrible!' and thus is not further included here. Besides having the interjection *okwe* at its disposal, which is used to modify the entire clause, Mawayana has developed the enclitic *_kwe* to mark the affectedness of the constituents. As such, this clitic's meaning and the translation of the sentence depend on the constituent to which it is cliticized. The meanings expressed by the affective enclitic in Mawayana include the notions 'gone', 'pity', 'embarrassment', 'pain', 'dismay', and 'suspicion': some examples in Mawayana are given in (16a–c), where the translations are highly context dependent.

(16) (a) tõwã-sï   kodo'kodorï_kwe
           sleep.PAST-3S   frog.sp_AFF
           Poor frog couldn't help it, he fell asleep

      (b) nko-sï   tõwã-nã_kwe   rï-ma_koso   kodokodorï
           3PN-3   sleep.PAST-1S_AFF   3A-say.PAST_REP   frog
           'That's it, I fell asleep', frog said, embarrassed

      (c) r-aucha-na_kwe
           3A-bite.PAST-1O_AFF
           Ouch, he bit me!

While the affective interjection *okwe* in Waiwai seems to occur either sentence
initially or sentence finally, its equivalent in Wapishana, *kowas*, can occur
following a particular constituent as shown in examples (17a–c) below. The
meaning of *kowas* is given as 'too bad, poor thing, life's like that' (WWA 2000:
53) and as such both in meaning and in position in the clause is more similar
to the clitic in Mawayana.

(17) (a) Taraiporo   zuna   tuma   kowas maonapatan   kootaro ati
           prop.name   woman   COMIT   AFF   approach.PAST Kutari DIR
           Taraiporo with the lady came closer to the Kutaro creek
           (where something terrible was about to happen to them)

      (b) u-nawuzu   dobata naa   kowas   pa-ba'orantin
           3POSS-brother pass   ASP   AFF   3S-be.alone
           Unfortunately his brother passed alone in front

      (c) u-ikodan   barara na'akan kibaro, kowas
           3A-find.PAST   crab   carry   frog   AFF
           He (the man) found a crab carrying a frog, poor thing.
           (Wapishana Primer n.d.: 29)

Given that the affective-marking elements are similar in form and meaning in
all three languages, we can assume that they are related, and considering that
the usage of the interjection in Wapishana is more closely aligned with the
enclitic in Mawayana than with the more restricted pattern in Waiwai, we may
conclude that Waiwai probably borrowed the affective interjection from
Mawayana rather than the other way around.

All the meanings expressed by the Mawayana enclitic *_kwe* are expressed in
Waiwai by the particle *pen* as shown above, and it is only with the meaning
'dead' that there is some discrepancy since it can only be expressed by the

nominal past marker *-ba* in Mawayana and not by the affective enclitic. Mawayana may have been influenced by Waiwai in that it has developed a clitic in addition to the interjection for the same functions as the Waiwai particle *pen*.

4.4 *The Mawayana frustrative _muku*

Frustrative marking is an obligatory feature of Cariban languages, the form of which is the clitic *_re(pe)* in both Waiwai and Trio, as well as in many other Cariban languages. The form of the frustrative enclitic in Mawayana is *_muku*. This enclitic has, for the most part, exactly the same morphosyntactic properties as the Cariban frustrative, that is, it can be marked on the major word classes, and it carries the same meaning. When marked on nouns it implies that at least one semantic feature of that noun is not fulfilled, see (18a), which is followed by the equivalent in Trio in (18b); on verbs it has the meaning 'to carry out an action in vain', that is, the action was unsuccessful, incomplete, or it did not have the required effect, as in (19). On postpositions it has the meaning 'almost', as in (19b), cf. also the Trio equivalent in (19c). Identical examples are found in Waiwai.

(18) (a) kïwï-ɗi_koso_muku   ku-re   (Mawayana)
         head-cover_REP_FRUST   like-NOMZ
         It was something like a sort of hat (but not quite)

     (b) kïrïwenpë-re   apo-n   (Trio)
         hat-FRUST   like-NOMZ
         It was something like a sort of hat (but not quite)

(19) (a) ï-cha_ku-sï?   a'u'a   n-cha_muku_ku-sï   (Mawayana)
         2A-do.PAST_PERSIST-3O yes   1A-do.PAST_FRUST_PERSIST-3O
         Did you fix it? yes I fixed it (in vain)

     (b) kïwï-ɗi-kura_koso_muku (Mawayana)
         head-cover-like_REP_FRUST
         It was almost like a hat (but it wasn't really one)

     (c) kïrïwenpë   apo-repe   (Trio)
         hat   like-FRUST
         It was almost like a hat (but it wasn't really one)

A few structural instances have been found where the Mawayana usage of the frustrative differs slightly from that in the Cariban languages in that the frustrative is marked on the first element in the clause, see example (20a), rather than on the verb as it would be in the Cariban languages, see the Trio equivalent in (20b).

(20) (a) kusara_muku naaka-na   riichïka ma-ï   yaadʲa   (Mawayana)
         deer_FRUST   take.PAST-1O fast   NEG-2S come.PAST
         The deer took me (would have taken me) if you hadn't come soon

(20) (b) j-apëi_re   wïkapau tëe-se-wa-nkëre   ëmë
         1O-take.PAST_FRUST deer   come-NFIN-NEG_PERSIST 2PN
         ahtao   (Trio)
         when
         The deer took me (would have taken me) if you hadn't come soon

Synchronically Wapishana does not seem to have a frustrative marker, nor is it known whether the language ever had a frustrative marker. The etymology of the form of the Mawayana frustrative _muku is unknown, since similar forms do not occur in any of the relevant languages; whether or not the source could be Taruma cannot be answered until more data on Taruma are forthcoming. However, we can see from the comparison of structures given above that Mawayana in general follows the Cariban pattern of marking frustrative either on the verb to refer to the action, or on the relevant constituent.

4.5 The Mawayana similative -ni

A further obligatory category in the Cariban languages is the similative which expresses the notion of 'being for all intents and purposes X but not in essence so' which has the form -me (or -pe) in all the Cariban languages. For example, the Trio wïtoto 'human being', when marked with the similative -me, wïtoto-me 'a human being' has the meaning 'manifestly but not inherently a human being', as for example when a spirit manifests itself as a human being. In earlier work I have referred to this marker by the gloss facsimile (FACS) to indicate that its basic meaning is 'manifestly but not inherently X', see Carlin (2002, 2004). In the Cariban languages the similative -me can be analysed structurally as an adverbial or a depictive, and a marker of secondary predication, and it also has a grammaticalized aspectual meaning. The functional category similative that has been transferred into Mawayana is found in its basic meaning (21a–b) and as a marker of secondary predication (21c–d), and with grammaticalized aspectual meaning as in (21e). In the first instance, the Mawayana similative -ni, as illustrated by the examples (21a–b), is found mostly, but not only, in the context of physical or spiritual transformations from one state to another which is typically where it is also found in Trio and Waiwai. For purposes of structural comparison, some Trio examples are given in (22a–c), and a Waiwai example in (23).

(21) (a) waata-ni   r-ayãdĩyã   (Mawayana)
          opossum-SIMIL 3s-transform.PAST
          He changed into an opossum

     (b) na rï-kura n-ayãdĩyã   rïnaru-ni   kuira (Mawayana)
          disc 3PN-like 3pl.s-transform.PAST woman-SIMIL INTERJ
          So like that they transformed into women

     (c) ukuɗa-sï wa-wïnï-ni   (Mawayana)
          shoot-3O 1pl.POSS-meat-SIMIL
          Shoot it as our meat!

     (d) uwiya_koso   kïmïnïka rïnaru   kataba   a-ïža-ni   (Mawayana)
          anaconda_REP long.ago woman catch.PST 3COREF-pet-SIMIL
          A woman caught an anaconda as her pet long ago

     (e) wiyōkārï-ni_koso   xahñe[8]   (Mawayana)
          young.man-SIMIL_REP   he.was (Waiwai)
          he was a young man

(22) (a) kaikui-me   tëmetae   (Trio)
          jaguar-SIMIL   he.transformed
          he transformed into a jaguar

     (b) k-ootï-me   tïwë-kë!   (Trio)
          1+2POSS-meat-SIMIL   shoot-IMP.sg
          shoot it as our meat!

     (c) kïrïmuku-me   teese   (Trio)
          young.man-SIMIL   he.was
          he was a young man

Waiwai: -*me*

(23)   noro   ɲi-ir-a-tkeɲe   kayaritomo me
        3PN   3A-make-SF-UP   chief   ADVZR
        they made him to be the chief
                                          (Hawkins 1998: 128)

The source of the similative -*ni* in Mawayana is unknown but it could be related to a morpheme *nii* in Wapishana which is described in the WWA (2000: 172) as expressing a non-current event, as shown in example (24a).[9]

---

[8] The verb form *xahñe* 'he was' is an interference from Waiwai. In Mawayana there would not have been a verb form 'to be' here.

[9] WWA stands for *Wapichan Wadauniinao Ati'o* 'Wapishana for our Descendants', which is the name of a language project initiated by the Wapishana community in Maroronao in Guyana.

However, there are occurrences of *nii* as a marker of secondary predication in Wapishana as shown in (24b).

Wapishana: *-ni*

(24) (a) n-ikiyan ni pïgar ɓaïrɗukur kiyan (non-current event)
        1A-eat   *ni* 2PN jaguar   say
        I'm going to eat you, the jaguar said

   (b) u-'aipiyan   pa-žamatan   pa-wanyïkïnï-ni   (similative function?)
        3A-want   3A-grab   3COREF.POSS-food-*ni*
        He wanted to grab him as his meat

These examples show that it is quite possible that secondary predications were marked as such by the morpheme *nii* in Wapishana and thus that this category is native also to Mawayana but that its functions were expanded under influence from Waiwai and Trio where it was used to mark those instances where transformations took place between the spirit world and the human world. Synchronically in Wapishana such transformations are formed by means of a noun plus a verbalizer.

5 Conclusions

It has been shown in this chapter that Mawayana has undergone grammatical expansion in that it has borrowed those categories that are obligatory in the Cariban languages. Some agreement categories that do not exist in the Cariban languages, such as gender marking, or a classifier system which possibly existed in Mawayana, became irrelevant and were lost, in contrast to Wapishana which retained gender. Some, if not all, obligatory categories in the Cariban languages, which do not express agreement but which nevertheless are obligatorily expressed, were transferred first and foremost from Waiwai and were then reinforced and modified by subsequent Trio influence.

Mawayana shows clear resistance to the transfer of actual morphological forms but not to the transfer of structural categories, that is, the actual grammatical material used for these structural innovations is not taken over with the category marker with the exception of the free-standing forms. In the lexicon there is only a negligible number of borrowings. In fact, as shown here there are only two markers that in form Mawayana has in common with its closest relative Wapishana, namely *-ni* with a different meaning synchronically, and *_kwe* which is clearly related in form to the Wapishana *kowas* and

Waiwai *okwe*.[10] The actual direction of transfer of the latter category cannot be determined. However, while *kowas* in Wapishana and *okwe* in Waiwai are free forms, Mawayana has developed it into a grammatical form, namely the enclitic *_kwe*. Thus, once transferred, these markers are restructured according to Cariban patterns, whereby the affective enclitic *_kwe* clearly patterns along with the Waiwai particle *pen*.

The sources of the other new categories that have been introduced, namely the nominal past *-ba* and the frustrative *_muku*, cannot be traced, leading us to the conclusion that language-internal sources were pressed into service for the purposes required by the Cariban categories. Alternatively, given the history of the Mawayana and their intermingling with the Taruma, the Taruma language may ultimately be shown to be this unknown source. It is clear, however, that Mawayana has fully incorporated the past marking as shown also with the *-ba* on the nominalized forms which are identical to the Cariban structures; the examples given above look like calqued forms. Thus, in this situation of language shift that is leading to language death, the structural properties of obligatory inherent inflection are taken over from the dominant second language Waiwai and are transferred into the maintained first language Mawayana.

In spite of the fact that Mawayana is a moribund language, and has been for the better part of 150 years, the language did not lose any major categories; on the contrary, it has actually gained from the contact situation: the features given above are additions or at least expansions on functions that were already present. Thus there has been no grammatical breakdown of Mawayana as one might expect in such a language death situation. The fact that the southern Guianas can be seen as a cultural area only worked in favour of this acceptance of the new or expanded forms and functions. I think it has been the case that Mawayana chose to overlay the functions on its existing resources. In fact, this expansion by means of new functions is quite spectacular in a situation of language shift followed by language death, where the usual pattern of influence of language A (original language) on language B (target language being shifted to) is reversed. We can deduce from the resultant structural changes in Mawayana that although the Mawayana speakers were not originally bilinguals, their dominant language had become Waiwai and that it was for

---

[10] We cannot of course rule out the possibility that Wapishana did have a marker *-ni* with similative meaning comparable to the Cariban *-me*. The Wapishana were Christianized much earlier than the Mawayana and Waiwai and it is quite possible that if this marker belonged to the realm of the spirit world and transformations, it may have been thrown out with the spirits required for its use. If this is the case, then it could be that Mawayana has simply retained what Wapishana lost, and its usage became reinforced under Cariban influence.

reasons of 'feeling the need' to express the same obligatory categories that they transferred these into their original language.

References

Brown, C. B. 1876. *Canoe and camp life in British Guiana.* London: Edward Stanford.

Butt-Colson, A. and Morton, J. 1982. 'Early missionary work among the Taruma and Waiwai of Southern Guiana: the visits of Fr. Cuthbert Cary-Elwes, S.J. in 1919, 1922, and 1923', *Folk* 24: 203–61.

Carlin, E.B. 2002. 'Patterns of language, patterns of thought: the Cariban languages', pp. 47–81 of Carlin and Arends 2002.

—— 2004. *A grammar of Trio, a Cariban language of Suriname.* Duisburger Arbeiten zur Sprach- und Kulturwissenschaften 55. Frankfurt: Peter Lang.

—— and Arends, J. (eds.), 2002. *Atlas of the languages of Suriname.* Leiden: KITLV Press.

Derbyshire, D. C. and Pullum, G. K. (eds.). 1998. *Handbook of Amazonian languages,* Vol. 4. Berlin: Mouton de Gruyter.

Farabee, W. C. 1918. *The central Arawaks.* Philadelphia: University of Pennsylvania Press.

Hawkins, R. E. 1998. 'Wai Wai', pp. 25–224 of Derbyshire and Pullum 1998.

Howard, C. V. 2001. *Wrought identities: the Waiwai expeditions in search of 'unseen tribes' of Northern Amazonia.* Ph.D. thesis, University of Chicago.

Rivière, P. G. 1963. *An ethnographic survey of the Indians on the divide of the Guianese and Amazonian river systems.* B.Litt. thesis, Oxford University.

Schomburgk, R. H. 1841. 'Report of the third expedition into the interior of Guayana, comprising the journey to the sources of the Essequibo, to the Carumá Mountains, and to Fort San Joaquim, on the Rio Branco, in 1837–8', *Journal of the Royal Geographical Society* 10: 159–90.

—— 1845. 'Journal of an expedition from Pirara to the Upper Corentyne, and from thence to Demerara', *Journal of the Royal Geographical Society* 15: 1–104.

WWA. 2000. *Scholar's dictionary and grammar of the Wapishana language.* Lethem: Wapishana Language Project.

Glossary of Terms

This glossary summarizes the terminological conventions adopted through-out this volume. This is done in order to avoid terminological and conceptual confusion. When appropriate, we provide the number of a section of Chapter 1 where a particular point is discussed in detail, or a major reference on the subject. References are at the end of Chapter 1.

balanced language contact occurs in a long-standing linguistic area with no significant dominance relationships (or with stable, traditional hierarchical rela-tions) among languages. There is no pressure to shift languages, and the net result is increase of linguistic complexity and typological diversity (§4.2.3 of Chapter 1).

borrowing implies transfer of linguistic features of any kind from one lan-guage to another as the result of contact. (Borrowing of forms is known as direct diffusion, and borrowing of patterns as indirect diffusion: Heath 1978; Aikhenvald 2002.)

code mixing and **code switching** refer to the alternative use of two languages either within a sentence or across sentence boundaries. We distinguish between

- code switching which follows established conventions and practices and has certain functions (e.g. used to quote someone; to indicate one's authority, or allegiance: see Clyne 1987: 740) and
- spontaneous code mixing which does not obey such pragmatic rules (see Hill and Hill 1986: 348).

Borrowings and **code switches** are extremes on a continuum potentially distinguished by

- frequency of occurrence (code switches are often one-off occurrences);
- phonological integration;
- morpho-syntactic integration; and
- lexical criteria:

  (*a*) does an equivalent exist in the other language?
  (*b*) if so, is it in use in the community?
  (*c*) is the equivalent known to the speaker?
  (*d*) to which language does the individual regard the word as belonging?
  (*e*) is it in use by monolingual speakers?

See Bernsten and Myers-Scotton (1993: 145), on the absence of a watertight difference between borrowing and code switching; and a summary in Heath (1989: 40–1).

convergence is a process whereby languages in contact gradually become more like each other in terms of grammatical categories and constructions (§4.3 of Chapter 1).

diffusion is the spread of a linguistic feature within a geographical area or between languages. Diffusion can be **unilateral** (where A affects B) or **multilateral** (where A affects B in some ways and B affects A in others).

displacive language contact occurs when one group aggressively imposes its language on another group. It promotes language displacement, loss of the language's own features, and, ultimately, language shift (§4.2.3 of Chapter 1).

grammatical accommodation involves a change in meaning of a morphological marker or a syntactic construction based on superficial segmental similarity with a marker or a construction in a different language. (§3.3 of Chapter 1; Haugen 1969 uses the term 'homophonous extensions', while Campbell (1987) calls these 'shifts due to phonetic similarity'.

grammaticalization is the process whereby an item with lexical status changes into an item with grammatical status (§3.3 of Chapter 1, Heine and Kuteva 2005). A typical example of grammaticalization is the verb 'finish' becoming a marker for 'completed' aspect. Grammaticalization necessarily involves reanalysis (see Harris and Campbell 1995: 92).

language engineering refers to conscious human effort to effectuate language change (§4.2.2 of Chapter 1).

layered languages are languages with a significant proportion of forms and patterns recognizable as resulting from diffusion from other language(s) which makes them atypical representatives of language families or subgroups they belong to. The core lexicon and morphology allow us to unequivocally trace a layered language to one proto-language (§§2.1, 2.4 of Chapter 1).

lexical accommodation refers to change or extension of meaning of a lexical item resulting from superficial segmental similarities with a lexical item in a different language (§3.3 of Chapter 1).

linguistic area (or sprachbund) is a geographically delimited region including languages from two or more language families, or different subgroups of the same family, sharing significant traits, or combinations of traits (most of which are not found in languages from these families or subgroups spoken outside the area) (§2.5 of Chapter 1).

An alternative use of the term 'linguistic area' just for bilateral interaction between languages, reserving the term 'sprachbund' for multilateral areas, was proposed by Thomason and Kaufman (1988); this, however, goes against the mainstream terminological consensus. The difference between contact involving two, or more than two, languages is captured by the notion of unilateral and multilateral diffusion, and uni-, bi- and multidirectional diffusion.

The term 'linguistic area' or 'sprachbund' is sometimes used to refer to the spread of one type of linguistic feature or an isogloss over a geographic area (which is not necessarily a linguistic area involving bi- and multilingualism, or even contact between languages). One of the most salient features of all the South-East Asian languages is their 'monosyllabicity' and 'tone-proneness'— as a result they have been called *Tonbund*, or 'tonal area' (Matisoff 2001). The fact that numerous Eurasian languages share phonological features (e.g. palatalization) prompted Jakobson (1938) to describe this as a 'phonological' sprachbund. Since most languages of India are spoken in a comparable sociolinguistic situation, India came to be called a 'sociolinguistic area' (papers in Abbi 1991). Heine and Kuteva (2005) distinguish 'grammaticalization areas' which share similar mechanisms of transforming more lexical morphemes into more grammatical ones. And also see Haarmann (1970) for evidentiality-type meanings as an 'areal' feature (in this sense) characteristic of the whole Eurasian continent.

mixed, or **intertwined, languages** are products of semi-conscious language engineering under specific social circumstances with many lexical and grammatical forms taken from two linguistically different sources. The genetic affiliation of mixed languages in terms of its core lexicon and morphology is therefore mixed (Bakker 1997, 2003; §2.4 of Chapter 1).

reanalysis is a historical process by which a morphosyntactic device comes to be assigned a different structure from that which it had, without necessarily changing its surface form and with little change to its semantics. For instance, in Udi a number of verbs—which originally contained noun class agreement markers—were reanalysed as simple stems, as part of the process of losing the noun class system (Harris and Campbell 1995: 66–7; §3.3 of Chapter 1).

reinterpretation (or **extension**) is a change in the surface manifestation of a pattern 'which does not involve immediate or intrinsic modification of underlying structure' (Harris and Campbell 1995: 97). Reanalysis most often occurs together with reinterpretation. Examples of reinterpretation without reanalysis involve 'a shift in the categorial status of a linguistic form resulting from its occurrence in ambiguous positions'. For instance, the English noun *fun* has been reinterpreted as an adjective, leading to its use in contexts like *This is a fun game* (Trask 2000: 274, 280; §3.3 of Chapter 1).

substratum, or **substrate,** refers to the impact of a language previously spoken in an area onto a new arrival in terms of vocabulary (hence substrate vocabulary), phonological, morphological, and syntactic features. **Superstratum,** or **superstrate,** refers to the influence exercised by a language spoken by a dominant group over that of a subordinate group. **Adstratum,** or **adstrate,** refers to one language influencing another, without dominating it. This term is occasionally employed as superordinate for substratum, adstratum, and superstratum. The dangers of overusing the idea of substratum in explaining language change are outlined by Trask (2000: 328–9) and Thurston (1987).

Author Index

Index of languages, language families, and linguistic areas

Subject Index

DATE DUE